Business Economics

Business Economics

Andrew Gillespie

OXFORD

UNIVERSITY PRESS

Great Clarendon Street, Oxford OX2 6DP

Oxford University Press is a department of the University of Oxford.
It furthers the University's objective of excellence in research, scholarship,
and education by publishing worldwide in

Oxford New York

Auckland Cape Town Dar es Salaam Hong Kong Karachi
Kuala Lumpur Madrid Melbourne Mexico City Nairobi
New Delhi Shanghai Taipei Toronto

With offices in

Argentina Austria Brazil Chile Czech Republic France Greece
Guatemala Hungary Italy Japan Poland Portugal Singapore
South Korea Switzerland Thailand Turkey Ukraine Vietnam

Oxford is a registered trademark of Oxford University Press
in the UK and in certain other countries

Published in the United States
by Oxford University Press Inc., New York

British Library Cataloguing in Publication Data

Data available

Library of Congress Cataloging in Publication Data

Data available

Typeset by MPS Limited, A Macmillan Company
Printed in Italy
on acid-free paper by
LEGO SpA – Lavis TN

ISBN 978–0–19–956518–4

1 3 5 7 9 10 8 6 4 2

To Tor and John for their support from day one. To Ali, Clemmie, Roms, and Seth for bringing sunshine.

Outline contents

Detailed contents

7 Market failures and imperfections   201

How to use this book

Chapter-opening features

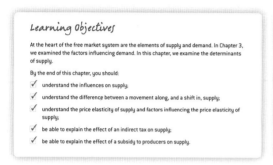

Learning Objectives

Each chapter contains a bulleted list of the key economic concepts and tools.

Opening Case Study

A topical business case study at the beginning of each chapter provides you with an introduction to the subject and helps to set the scene. As you progress through the chapter you will find the answers to the case study questions.

In-text features

Each chapter includes four different features, each designed to test your knowledge and aid your understanding. Comprehensive solutions and guidance for each of these features can be found online at **www.oxfordtextbooks.co.uk/orc/gillespiebusiness/**

Think about it

Short reflective questions help you to consider the significance of the theory you have covered and apply your learning to a new problem.

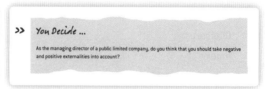

You Decide

This feature asks you to think like a manager and decide on the best course of action when faced with a business economics dilemma. It highlights how you can use your understanding of economics in practice to make decisions.

Business Analysis
Real life business examples highlight how economics works in action. Economics is based on essential theory, but as a business student or practitioner you need to know how this applies to the real world and what is happening around you.

Data Analysis
Provides you with economic data to analyse and interpret.

End-of-chapter features

Summary
Chapters conclude with a brief summary of the key concepts and points made within the chapter.

Short Answer Questions
Questions at the end of each chapter test your grasp of the key concepts

One Step Further
At the end of chapters you'll find a link pointing you to the Online Resource Centre where you will find more challenging material to expand your knowledge.

Case Study Review
You can review the opening case throughout the chapter as you gain the skills and knowledge to answer the questions.

Checklist
A checklist at the end of each chapter helps you review the work you have covered.

Essay Questions
The essay questions are an opportunity for you to practice essay writing and to explore wider business economics issues.

The Online Resource Centre

The Online Resource Centre (ORC) comprises resources for both lecturers and students

Free and open-access material available to students

Solutions for Chapter 1

£ *Business Analysis* 1.1

In 2008 and 2009, the global business environment changed dramatically and unexpectedly with the decline of many major economies, yet the response of many managing directors seemed to be to continue as if it were 'business as usual'. According to management consultants, KPMG, 45 per cent of business directors appeared to be adopting a 'head in the sand' approach, failing to make strategic changes to their decision making and continuing to pursue the same options for their organization as they had twelve months before. After twenty years of planning for growth, many directors had no plans for a downturn. Reacting to falling sales was the main challenge in most sectors, requiring difficult decisions involving cost cutting, improving cashflow, mothballing plants, and even plant closure. Each of these decisions has its own follow-on decisions, such as whom to make redundant, which asset to sell, or which costs to cut. According to KPMG:

Solutions
After you've answered the questions raised in the textbook, you'll be able to check your answers online.

Audio animated PowerPoint® slides
More complex graphs and figures are clearly explained through audio animated Power-Point® slides.

Chapter summary podcasts
Author podcasts summarize the key concepts of each chapter. These can be downloaded straight to your mp3 player.

Instructions

Choose your answer by clicking the radio button next to your choice and then pre

Question 1

Which of the following is likely to increase the equilibrium price and quantity?

- ○ a) An increase in demand.
- ○ b) An increase in supply.
- ○ c) A decrease in demand.
- ○ d) A decrease in supply.

Self test questions
These provide a quick and easy way to test your understanding, with instant feedback.

Additional case study: Government intervention

In Germany in 2009 there was considerable debate about the extent to which the government should be intervening in the economy. For example, its citizens were worried about the future of Opel, a German car brand that was part of the ailing General Motors. Some wanted the government to make sure jobs were saved not matter what. Others, however, were more hesitant and worried about becoming the government becoming too interventionist. Traditionally since the Second World War the German government has seen itself as a referee in market issues and has avoided trying to control parts of the economy. It would regulate anti-competitive behaviour, for example, but not try to run many industries. However in the recession of 2009 when the economy was shrinking the government was forced to spend more to stimulate demand and had to intervene heavily to save the banking sector from collapse. The government also had to offer aid to businesses to keep them alive.

Questions
1.   What are the possible benefits of a government intervening in an economy?

Additional short case studies
Extra case studies help to highlight how business economics can be applied in real business situations.

Oxford NewsNow
Each time you visit this page you will receive the most up-to-date news through articles specially filtered to be relevant to business economics.

Library of video and podcast links
A comprehensive library of links to topical lectures by key economics and business academics and practitioners.

Sample essays
Essay questions and suggested answers provide you with guidance on how to tackle essays.

One Step Further
This material covers more complex economic theories and concepts and is designed to stretch and challenge you.

For registered adopters of the book

PowerPoint® lecture slides
A suite of customizable PowerPoint® slides has been provided to use in your lecture presentations.

Case study teaching notes
Notes and guide answers are provided for each chapter's opening case.

Group exercises
Ideas for group activities based on the 'You Decide' feature in the book are provided.

Test bank
A ready-made electronic testing resource that is fully customizable and contains feedback for students will help you to save time creating assessments. There are over 200 questions, each with feedback.

Artwork from the book
Figures and tables form the text have been provided for you to download for lecture presentations, or to include in handouts.

All of the material on the Online Resource Centre can be incorporated into your institution's Virtual Learning Environment.

Acknowledgements

Many thanks to everyone at OUP for all their help and guidance, especially Sarah Lodge, Kirsty Read, Gareth Malna, and Marionne Cronin.

Introduction

There are many economics textbooks on the market that provide an introduction to the subject. These generally provide the theory without highlighting the value of the subject to people studying business. The aim of this book is to introduce you to key economic concepts and theories, and to demonstrate how these can be useful to business managers. What determines the demand for your product? What influences your costs? What affects your ability to compete abroad? What effect will a change in interest rates have on your business? These are the types of economic issue that we consider in this book and which are vital for managers to understand so that they can make effective decisions. We hope that reading this book will enable you to analyse economic changes, such as movements in the exchange rate and prices, and understand the impact of such changes on business decisions. By the end of the book, we hope that you will appreciate the value of studying economics to anyone wanting to manage in a business.

Economics focuses on the causes and effects of economic change; this covers both changes in your immediate environment, such as new firms entering your market, and global changes, such as greater trade between countries or the effect of political instability among a country's trading partners. If, as managers, we can understand these issues, we can forecast and plan more effectively. If we know what influences demand for our product, for example, and from this can predict future sales, then this is extremely important when it comes to planning for marketing, human resources, finance, and production.

Overall we hope this book will give a good insight into economic issues, introduce you to the language of the subject and help you to analyse the cause and effects of economic change. We hope it will demonstrate the importance to managers of studying economics and give you the tools you need as a student to analyse a business situation more effectively.

Introduction

1

/e also introduce some o*
i your analysis of a v
rious points in

Learning Objectives

In this chapter, we provide an overview of the book. We also introduce some of the key tools that are used by economists. These will help you with your analysis of a wide range of topics and you are likely to want to come back to them at various points in your studies.

By the end of this chapter, you should:

☑ appreciate the importance for managers of studying economics;

☑ understand what is meant by PESTEL analysis;

☑ appreciate the difference between microeconomics and macroeconomics;

☑ understand the meaning of index numbers;

☑ understand the difference between nominal and real values;

☑ be able to explain the reasons why economists produce models;

☑ understand the value of index numbers and of weighted indices.

Case Study

Alison Mitchell joined The Look three months ago. The Look is a high street clothes retailer mainly based in the UK, but has some stores in continental Europe. Alison is a management trainee who recently finished a history degree at university. She has just come back from a management presentation in which the annual results of the company were announced. She left feeling slightly worried and a little confused:

'I know the economy has been poor and this has hit customer spending. Customers are worried about their jobs, which is not surprising given the high unemployment figures, and have had their wealth hit hard by falling house prices. The economic climate is making everyone a little more cautious. This year's profits for the company this year were nearly £6 million, which is better than our competitors'. But the board of directors is apparently unhappy with this return, given the investment that has been made into the business. It wants a significant improvement in the coming year and stressed our role in bringing this about. Six million is hardly a small number, but it's not enough. Apparently, we're looking at cost-cutting measures including switching more to suppliers based in China and Vietnam. There are also plans for growing faster by opening up stores in emerging markets, such as Russia and India. The growth rates of these economies are much faster than the UK and the board thinks that this opens up opportunities, although the weak value of the pound won't help the expansion plans. In the UK, we've been told to prepare for a difficult future and need to work closely with our **stakeholders** to push up our profit margins.

What I don't understand is why none of the economists seemed to predict this downturn: what's the point of studying economics if you can't do anything with it? What I do know is that I'm going to get a pay increase of only 1 per cent this year and that, as a result, I'm going to be a lot worse off.'

Questions

1. What economic factors that affect business success are highlighted in the above text?

2. All businesses are involved in the transformation process. Outline the transformation process that The Look undertakes and explain how it can add value doing this.

3. Can you think of other economic factors that might affect a clothes retailer?

4. What about other external, non-economic, factors?

5. Who are the stakeholders of The Look? How might working with them help the business?

6. Why might the board of directors be unhappy with a profit of £6 million?

7. What is the difference between the profit margin and the profit of a business?

8. If the growth rates of the economies in India and Russia are much higher than that in the UK, does this mean that their citizens are better off? Explain your answer.

9. Why do you think the Russian and Indian economies might be growing relatively quickly?

10. Which other types of business do you think are likely to want to target economies such as India and Russia? Why?

11. How can Alison receive a pay increase of 1 per cent and yet be worse off?

12. If economists failed to predict the global downturn of 2008, is Alison right to say that there is no point studying economics?

Why all business managers should want to be economists

In recent years, there have been massive changes in global economies, leading to economies shrinking, banks closing, governments spending billions of pounds to try to save particular industries, and share prices collapsing. The result has been dramatic, frightening change in the business environment for many managers. Nothing highlights better that managers should not only want to be economists, but that, in fact, they cannot afford not to be. Wherever managers look, they see economics in action, and an understanding of the fundamentals will give them the tools they need to analyse their environment and make better decisions. In a world of rapid and what, at times, seems like chaotic, business-threatening change, managers need to know what to focus on, how to make sense of the events happening around them, and, ideally, how to work out in which direction to move the business in the future. How badly would your sales be affected if you were to increase your price? Can you afford to accept your employees' pay claim of 5 per cent? Is the government's decision to increase income tax for high-income earners going to have an impact on your sales? What effect would a lower interest rate have on your business? These are all important economic issues and, not surprisingly, managers should and will want to know the answers to such questions.

Economics studies the way in which choices are made within an economy: for example, what products are made, what **resources** are used, and who gets what in an economy. By understanding economic theory, managers are able to make more sense of the environment around them and make better decisions for their businesses. A failure to understand the economic environment leaves managers without a clear view of what is, or has been, happening in their markets and what is likely to happen in the future.

Managers need to understand how changes in economic conditions can affect the demand for their products and their costs. They need to understand economic theory to appreciate why changes have occurred, what the possible impact of changes might be, and how they should prepare for, or respond to, them. Gaining an understanding of economics provides managers with more insight into their environment, enabling them to develop more effective strategies to exploit the opportunities and protect themselves from the threats.

Business Analysis   1.1

In 2008 and 2009, the global business environment changed dramatically and unexpectedly with the decline of many major economies; yet the response of many managing directors seemed to be to continue as if it were 'business as usual'. According to management consultants, KPMG, 45 per cent of business directors appeared to be adopting a 'head in the sand' approach, failing to make strategic changes to their decision making and continuing to pursue the same options for their organization as they had twelve months before. After twenty years of planning for growth, many directors had no plans for a downturn. Reacting to falling sales was the main challenge in most sectors, requiring difficult decisions involving cost cutting, improving cashflow, mothballing plants, and even plant closure. Each of these decisions has its own follow-on decisions, such as whom to make redundant, which asset to sell, or which costs to cut. According to KPMG:

> 'Accurate and relevant forecasting has been a victim of the credit crisis, as the usual variables that previously went into a forecast are shrouded in uncertainty. Sales volumes, prices and availability of finance can all change dramatically in a short time. Businesses can't even be confident that their main suppliers and customers will be around for very long. This has a dramatic impact on a manager's ability to develop strategy, after all, it's pretty hard to look six months or a year ahead, when you're not even sure what the next day is going to bring. As a result, some managers may be tempted to believe that forecasting is a waste of time. In fact, it's more important than ever to understand the short and long-term business impacts of critical business decisions.'

1. How do you think understanding the severity of the global crisis might have helped managers to plan more effectively?
2. If forecasting is so difficult, does this mean that managers should not try to predict economic change?

Business as a transformation process

All businesses are involved in a transformation process (see Figure 1.1). They take resources, such as people, ideas, equipment, and land, and turn them into goods and services. The aim of doing this will be to add value so that the outputs are worth more than the inputs used up in producing them. All around the world, millions of businesses are transforming resources in different ways to meet the needs of their customers:

- Fedex moves products around the world safely and quickly;
- Sony produces DVD players;
- Disneyland provides an entertainment experience;

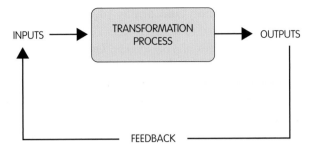

Figure 1.1 The transformation process

- Fox produces films;
- EMI makes music;
- management consultants McKinsey provide advice; and
- Toni and Guy cuts hair.

The transformation process therefore happens in many different ways, and results in many different types of goods and services. The process will be constantly reviewed as feedback suggests whether or not it is effective; a failure to sell or to make a profit may make managers review the inputs used or the nature of the process itself. Increases in the charges at Manchester airport, for example, led Ryanair to close its operations there and open up at Leeds instead.

The resources in an economy relate to the following factors.

- *The land available* This refers to the physical resources in an economy and includes the minerals, climate, and natural resources in the area. Some countries have much more physical space than others (compare China to the UK, for example); some have more of some natural resources than others (think of oil in Saudi Arabia and diamonds in South Africa); some have warmer climates (think of Brazil compared to Norway). The resources of different economies therefore vary considerably at any moment and this will affect what can be produced in each region.

- *The population* This refers to factors such as the number, health, age, skills, and training of the population of a region. The effect of the population on the amount that a country can produce will depend on the quantity of people, but also their 'quality', in terms of contributing to the transformation process. This will be affected by trends such as health care, the general standard of living, and cultural issues, all of which will influence the birth and death rates in a region. Immigration may also be significant. In 2004, eight Eastern European countries (including Latvia, Lithuania, and Poland, as well as Malta and Cyprus) acceded to (that is, joined) the **European Union** (EU), which made the movement of people to the UK easier. Between May 2004 and December 2006, it led to over half a million people from these accession countries coming into the UK. This provided a source of cheap labour in the UK, particularly in factories, bars, cafes, restaurants and hotels, and construction.

- *Capital* This refers to the quantity and quality of capital goods in an economy. A 'capital good' is one that is used to produce other goods in the future: for example, factories, office premises, machines, and equipment. The value of this resource depends on the amount and quality of the capital goods, which, in turn, depends on the level of technology. Investment is essential to the growth of an economy; it can lead to more efficient processes, innovation, and greater **productivity**. Imagine trying to turn a screw using only your hands; now imagine using a screwdriver; now imagine using an electric screwdriver: you will see the benefits of investment.

- *Ideas and enterprise* Economies benefit from entrepreneurs—that is, people who have ideas and think of new business opportunities—who are willing to take risks and who make things happen. Entrepreneurs set up new businesses, which create jobs, and provide more goods and services for customers. Entrepreneurs identify new possibilities for products and processes that move an economy forward. This is why governments are often interested in creating an environment in their economies that encourage start-ups.

These can be transformed in an enormous variety of ways, such as refining, manufacturing, transporting, and mixing. Look at all of the businesses in your area and you will see the many different ways in which resources are combined to provide an incredible array of products designed to meet customer needs.

The aim of these transformation processes is to create products that are worth more than the cost of the resources used up in the process of providing the products. The worth of a product and the costs of providing it are usually (not always) measured in monetary terms—that is, the aim is to produce a product for which customers are willing to pay more than it costs to provide; this generates a profit for the business.

Investors and managers are constantly making decisions about which projects to invest in and which business ideas to pursue. They are faced with a variety of choices at any moment. To decide on the best option, they need to measure the likely returns on a project in relation to the investment. If, for example, a particular project would cost more than it is likely to earn, then it should not be pursued; the resources should be used elsewhere.

This highlights the concept of **opportunity cost**. Opportunity cost measures the benefits given up in relation to the next best alternative. A decision to put more money into advertising a product, for example, means that this money cannot be used to modify the product or to put into employee training. These alternatives have been sacrificed. The alternatives to any action need to be considered before choosing which ideas or project to pursue. Investing in a new marketing campaign, for example, might make a £2 million profit, but it might be that, with the same investment, you could develop a new product and make £3 million profit. Opportunity cost is a fundamentally important concept in business and economics: whenever a decision is made, another option has been given up; just because one choice offers a reward does not make it the right choice, because of what is being sacrificed. Holding stocks may be useful to meet demand, but means that money is tied up in stocks rather than earning a return in a bank. Existing products may earn a 5 per cent return, but given the resources that they use up, this may not be enough.

Questioning the use of resources is a key management skill: are the resources being used **adding value** for the business and helping to generate a high return? Are they generating a high enough return to justify their use in this activity? Understanding how resources should be allocated efficiently (that is, how they are used without wastage) and effectively (that is, ensuring that they are used for the right purpose) is at the heart of business management and economics.

>> You Decide ...

The board of directors of Apple is thinking of investing heavily into new product development over the next five years rather than paying the profits out to investors.

1. Do you think that this is a good use of its funds?

2. What would you think if it were to increase its rewards to its staff?

3. How should the managers decide on the best way of allocating profit?

? Think about it ... 1.1

1. Can you think of two industries in which the transformation process has been changed significantly by technology in recent years? Explain your choices.

2. What is the opportunity cost of going to university?

The most common measure of how effectively resources are being used in business is profit. This shows that the value of the output sold is greater than the costs of providing it. But when measuring the performance of other, less financially driven organizations, such as a hospital, a school, a community centre, or a political party, other measures of performance are required.

? Think about it ... 1.2

1. What is the best way of deciding how well a university is performing?

2. What about a hospital?

3. In what ways, apart from profit, might a business such as BP, the multinational energy company, measure its success?

>> **You Decide ...**

1. Do you think it is enough to look at the amount of profit made by a company to judge its performance?

2. Nowadays, what else might an investor want to measure apart from profit to decide whether the business is successful or not?

As economic conditions change, the inputs you use, the way in which you transform your resources or even what you actually produce may need to change as well.

■ Higher wages or rents in the UK may encourage businesses to relocate aspects of production abroad.

■ Lower costs of borrowing may encourage investment in new technology.

■ Changes in the levels of demand in the economy may affect your sales and your expansion plans.

■ Falling incomes might lead you to introduce a budget line of products.

■ New entrants may force you to modify and improve your product.

Managers must therefore prepare for, and react to, economic change. This change can be at a local, national, or international level: for example, the community Council Tax in the UK is set by local authorities, the income tax rate paid by employees is set by the national government, and taxes on foreign products are set by the EU.

? **Think about it ...**   1.3

Can you think of economic changes at a local, national, and international level that might affect a road haulage business?

Can you now answer question 2 from the opening case study?

Classifying production

Businesses produce many different types of product. These can be classified in different ways, as follows.

■ *Goods versus services*   Goods are physical items, such as iPhones and guitars; they are tangible. Goods can be stored by businesses in anticipation of future demand.

The customer can touch them and inspect them before buying. Services are intangible items, such as a karate class or medical advice. These cannot be stockpiled and customers cannot physically see what they are buying; they consequently rely on other indicators, such as word of recommendation or inspections by regulating bodies, that provide a stamp of approval.

The distinction between a good and service is not always clear. When you visit a restaurant, you are buying the food (a good) and the environment of the restaurant (a service). When you choose where to shop, you are influenced by the items that are stocked, but also the quality of the service. When you study for a degree, the lectures are a service, but elements, such as the lecture handouts and the degree certificate, are physical products. When you visit a theme park, the physical goods are the tickets and food that you buy; the service is the experience that you get on the rides.

? **Think about it ...** 1.4

Music acts, such as Coldplay and Iron Maiden, have contributed to huge sales around the world for the UK music industry. The most lucrative market for British artists was the USA, where revenues rose to £21.7 million last year. The second biggest royalty generator was Germany, with £15 million, followed by France, with £11.6 million.

Do you think that music acts, such as Coldplay and Iron Maiden, are producing a good or a service?

■ *Economic versus* **free goods** To produce the vast majority of products, resources have to be used up; these resources could be used elsewhere. To have more cars, for example, it is necessary to sacrifice something else, such as the production of furniture, because resources will have been diverted into one sector rather than another. When sacrifices have to be made to increase production of a particular product, that item is known as an 'economic good'. By comparison, in some cases, a product is provided 'free of charge'; no sacrifices have to be made, so there is no opportunity cost. Air, for example, simply exists and no sacrifice is needed to provide it. This type of product is known as a 'free good'.

? **Think about it ...** 1.5

Air is a free good. Do you think that 'clean air' is a free good as well?

■ *Capital versus* **consumption** *products*   Capital items are products that are bought to help in the production process and produce more products in the long term. They represent an investment for the future: for example, a company may invest in new technology. They are not bought to consume themselves, but because of their contribution to the transformation process. Consumption items, by comparison, are products that are for immediate consumption, such as food and holidays. If all spending in an economy were to be on consumption products, there would be no investment for the future.

>> You Decide ...

Microsoft, the computing business that began trading on the stock exchange in 1986, paid its first dividends to investors in 2003. Up until then, it invested all of its profits into the business.

1. Is retaining profits rather than paying a dividend a good strategy for Microsoft?
2. What factors should determine the proportion of profits invested in the business for the future and the proportion paid out for immediate consumption?

Sectors of the economy

There are many ways in which businesses can transform resources. To assess how different businesses are performing and to monitor changes in their performance over time (perhaps in response to government policies), it is useful to categorize businesses in some way.

For example, we can distinguish between the following.

■ *Primary, secondary, and tertiary businesses* The primary sector comprises businesses involved in the extraction of, and production using, natural resources: for example, farming, oil extraction, and forestry. The secondary sector refers to manufacturing and construction; the tertiary sector refers to services such as finance and tourism. Economies can differ significantly in the composition of their business. For example, the UK is dominated by the tertiary sector, whereas many developing economies are dependent on the primary sector.

■ *The size of businesses* The size of a business can be measured in several ways. For example, you could measure the value of sales, the number of employees, or the number of outlets. In most economies, smaller enterprises are much greater in number than large-sized ones. In the European Union, small and medium-sized enterprises (SMEs) comprise approximately 99 per cent of all businesses and employ between them about 65 million people. Globally, SMEs account for 99 per cent of business numbers and 40–50 per cent of the output generated.

■ *Private and* **public sector** *businesses* Businesses that are owned by private individuals and organizations are part of the private sector: for example, BT, Ford, and IBM are private-sector organizations. Businesses that are owned by the government are part of the public sector. Some organizations are part-owned by the government and private owners: for example, the UK government bought a controlling interest in the Royal Bank of Scotland in 2008 when this bank was in difficulty. In the UK, there are also a number of public–private partnerships (PPPs), in which both sectors work together to provide a service. Private-sector businesses tend to pursue profit to reward their investors and owners. Public-sector organizations are overseen by government ministers and committees, but are ultimately owned by everyone in the country. These organizations are more likely to have social objectives, such as improving the welfare of the country's citizens, even if this does not maximize profits.

? Think about it ...   1.6

1. Think of three large private-sector organizations in your economy. What do you think their objectives are?

2. How might these objectives differ from those of much smaller organizations?

3. Can you think of organizations in your economy that are owned by the government. What do you think their objectives are?

Business Analysis   1.2

Table 1.1

Rank	Company	Country	Industry	Sales (US$bn)	Profits (US$bn)	Market value (US$bn)
1	General Electric (GE)	USA	Conglomerates	182.52	17.41	89.87
2	Royal Dutch Shell	Netherlands	Oil and gas operations	458.36	26.28	135.10
3	Toyota Motor	Japan	Consumer durables	263.42	17.21	102.35
4	ExxonMobil	USA	Oil and gas operations	425.70	45.22	335.54
5	BP	UK	Oil and gas operations	361.14	21.16	119.70

Source: Forbes 2009
Reproduced with the kind permission of Forbes

1. Why do you think so many of the biggest businesses in the world are involved in oil and gas operations?
2. Can you think of other industries that tend to have large companies?

>> You Decide ...

1. Which sectors of your economy do you think are most likely to grow in the future?
2. How might this affect your business planning?

Business as an open system

A business can be regarded as a system. This is because it comprises a number of different elements that need to work together for success. Within an organization, there are, for example:

■ *marketing activities*, which focus on understanding the market and customer, developing a marketing strategy, and developing a set of marketing plans (such as developing the product, setting the price, developing the promotional mix, and developing the distribution channels);

■ *operations activities*, which focus on decisions such as new product development, developing the method of production, managing stock levels, and deciding on the best way of delivering the products;

■ *financial activities*, which are involved in raising finance, budgeting, managing cash flow, and producing financial statements;

■ *human resource (HR) activities*, which involve decisions relating to the recruitment and selection of staff, developing remuneration systems, training, and career development.

All of these activities must combine to contribute towards the overall corporate strategy. For example, a decision to expand the business may require an increased marketing effort to boost demand, while also increasing the capacity to be able to provide necessary products; this, in turn, may need investment provided by the finance function and the recruitment of staff to produce the products required.

Businesses are open systems, because they interact with their environment. Business activities will be affected by changes in legislation or the population, for example. At the same time, business behaviour will influence the external environment, such as the wealth of the local community or levels of pollution.

Analysing the external environment and understanding their place within in it is therefore important for managers. This can be undertaken using **PESTEL analysis** (see Figure 1.2).

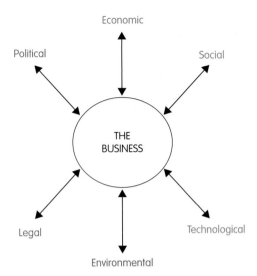

Figure 1.2 PESTEL analysis examines the relationship between a business and political, economic, social, technological, environmental and legal factors

PESTEL analysis

PESTEL analysis provides a framework for managers when examining the external environment. It helps managers to categorize the relevant issues in their environment, so that they can assess their relative importance and develop an appropriate strategy (see Figure 1.3).

The letters in the acronym stand for the following factors.

- *Political* For example, a government may sign a treaty with another country that makes trade easier or more difficult. Over the last fifty years, the EU has expanded considerably, making it easier for British firms to export within Europe. It started with six member countries in 1951 and now has twenty-seven members, with other countries wanting to join.

- *Economic* These refer to local, national, or international economic conditions, which can affect a business in terms of its supply and demand conditions. For example, a change in the cost of borrowing money may affect the ability of a business to expand and influence the amount that customers are willing to spend.

- *Social* These include factors such as the population size and the age of the population. In the UK, for example, the average age of the population is increasing, which will affect the demand for different goods and services (for example, blood pressure tablets and care homes).

- *Technological* This refers to changes, such as developments in the speed of accessing the Internet, which can create business opportunities, such as online banking and video streaming.

- *Environmental* This refers to changes, such as global warming, which influence what is produced, as well as the production methods that a business will use as it tries to be more environmentally friendly in its approach.

- *Legal* This refers to factors such as national or local government legislation. For example, changes in the national minimum wage may affect the costs of a business.

You Decide ...

What do you think are the key issues in the external environment facing managers in your economy?

£ **Business Analysis**   1.3

In 2009, there were fears of a worldwide flu pandemic (known as 'swine flu'). Global investors quickly identified potential businesses that could win and lose. Shares in airlines and hotel firms suffered, as shareholders decided that the outbreak of swine flu would lead to a fall in global travel. US soy and corn prices also suffered, because there were fears that a swine flu outbreak in North America would reduce global meat consumption and hit demand for grain to feed animals.

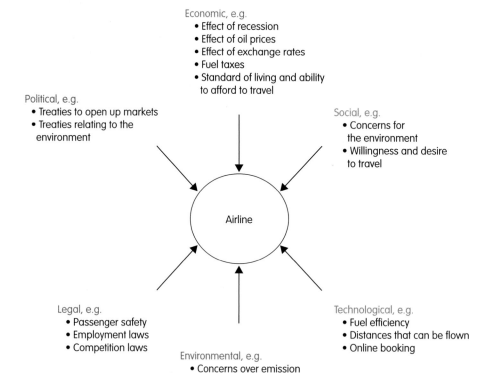

Economic, e.g.
- Effect of recession
- Effect of oil prices
- Effect of exchange rates
- Fuel taxes
- Standard of living and ability to afford to travel

Political, e.g.
- Treaties to open up markets
- Treaties relating to the environment

Social, e.g.
- Concerns for the environment
- Willingness and desire to travel

Airline

Legal, e.g.
- Passenger safety
- Employment laws
- Competition laws

Technological, e.g.
- Fuel efficiency
- Distances that can be flown
- Online booking

Environmental, e.g.
- Concerns over emission
- Concerns over take-off / landing

Figure 1.3 PESTEL analysis for an airline

By comparison, shares in pharmaceutical companies—such as Roche, the maker of Tamiflu®—have increased given expectations that demand for antiviral drugs would rise. In Mexico, where the flu originated, bars, shopping centres, cinemas, and even churches were closed to avoid spreading the virus. Fears about the flu leading to people cancelling their visits hit Mexico hard because foreign tourism was the third largest source of outside money in the economy.

This all highlights how external change can create opportunities and threats for businesses. Can you think of other businesses that might suffer or gain due to fears of a pandemic?

 ## Business Analysis 1.4

The European Commission suggests that the continued increase in how long people are living will ensure that the old-age dependency ratio, which measures the number of elderly people as a proportion of those of working age, will increase significantly in most countries over the next forty years.

The biggest absolute increase will be in Japan, where the ratio of 35.1 per cent in 2010—already the world's highest—will more than double, to 73.8 per cent, by 2050. At that point, the number of pensioners in China will be equivalent to 38.8 per cent of its labour force, up from 11.6 per cent in 2010. The EU, which had 84.6 million elderly people in 2008, will have 148.4 million in 2050 and the ratio for the world as a whole will reach 25.4 per cent, up from 11.7 per cent in 2010.

Sources: ONS, *The Economist*, 7 May 2009, www.europa.eu.com

1. What do you think are the likely effects on businesses in the countries mentioned above of the increasing old-age dependency ratio?
2. Can you think of businesses that will see this as an opportunity?
3. Which ones are likely to see it as a threat?

Monitoring the external environment is an important part of a manager's job. Managers should be looking for future changes in the environment that create opportunities and threats. Using your own sales team and analysing your own data can help you to do this, as well as studying other sources, such as government publications and information provided by industry associations.

An 'opportunity' is a change that is potentially beneficial for a business. A 'threat' is a change that is potentially damaging to a business. Whether a change is an opportunity or a threat depends on the nature of the change, and on the strengths and weaknesses of the business. The development of e-books may be an opportunity for companies, such as Sony and Technics, which already have the appropriate skills and resources in electronic markets. It could be a threat to traditional publishers, such as Penguin, which do not have the same experience in producing electronic products. The growth of mobile phone usage might be a threat to the calculator industry because they had calculators as one of their features, but may be an opportunity to the network operators.

Understanding, predicting, and preparing for external change is very important for managers, so that they can exploit opportunities as they arise and protect themselves against potential threats. The **exchange rate**, for example, is vitally important for any business involved in trading with customers or other companies abroad, because it influences the price of products sold to, or bought from, other countries. If the exchange rate is US$1.5:£1, then a £100 product costs US$150; if the exchange rate changes to US$1.8:£1, the same product will now cost US$180 simply because of the exchange rate movement. Over 50 per cent of the Minis produced in Oxford by BMW are sold in the USA: imagine how important changes in the value of the pound relative to the dollar is to the company and its success. If you were to fail to understand the implications of a change in the exchange rate, this would most likely mean that you would miss opportunities to target particular countries or fail to plan properly for price increases. An understanding of economics should, therefore, help managers to understand the relevant issues in their environment and plan more effectively to help the business to succeed.

>> *You Decide ...*

1. What is the best way for the manager of a producer of a range of soft drinks to monitor the external environment?
2. What external changes might be affecting that business?

Stakeholders

All business activities affect, and are affected by, other individuals and organizations. These individuals and groups are called **stakeholders**, and they include the community, suppliers, employees, investors, the government, and distributors. These groups may try to change a firm's behaviour: for example, suppliers may request faster payment to improve their cash flow and employees may ask for better working conditions. Managers' decisions will also have a direct effect on them. Expansion of a business may put pressure on local amenities, such as the road system; a decision to relocate may cost local jobs.

When considering whether a decision is fair (not necessarily whether it is economically efficient), managers may want to consider the impact on the different stakeholder groups. Some managers adopt what is called a 'stakeholder approach'—that is, they believe that a partnership approach with these groups will enable all of them to benefit. Better relationships with staff may cost more in the **short run**, but can lead to greater productivity and better performance in the **long run**. Similarly, working closely with suppliers may mean higher and faster payment for them, but can also help to ensure the quality and continuity of supply. Other managers adopt a stakeholder approach that focuses only on the rewards to investors;

this type of manager believes that the views and interests of other stakeholders should not be considered. The only thing to focus on is profit; everything else is a distraction.

? Think about it ...   1.7

How do you think good relationships with the local community improve the performance of a business?

>> You Decide ...

1. Should your business pay attention to the interests and demands of the local community or not?
2. Some clothing businesses have been criticized for using very cheap labour abroad to produce their clothes. Would it be right to switch your production from the UK to a low-wage area in Vietnam?

Can you now answer question 5 from the opening case study?

The economic environment

As we have seen, the economic environment is an element of the external environment. Economic change can affect businesses on both the demand and supply side:

■ on the *demand* side, economic change can affect the income and confidence of customers, which, in turn, affects their spending and levels of demand;

■ on the *supply* side, economic changes can affect factors such as the price of resources and therefore costs, which, in turn, will affect profits.

Changes in factors such as the income of the country, the value of a currency, the prices of resources, the degree of competition in a market, levels of unemployment, and the cost of borrowing are all examples of economic factors that can play a very important role in the success or failure of a business.

Economic changes can be very dramatic. The sudden collapse of many banks across the world in 2008 and 2009 was unexpected by most people. In such situations, managers often have to make important decisions on the basis of imperfect information. In other cases, the change may happen over a much longer period of time. The decline of the mining sector in the UK has happened over many years, for example, as it became uncompetitive relative to other countries. In this situation, managers have more time to understand the issues and plan ahead; in theory, this should make managing change easier.

?   Think about it ...   1.8

What significant changes can you identify in your economy over the last five years?

£   Business Analysis   1.5

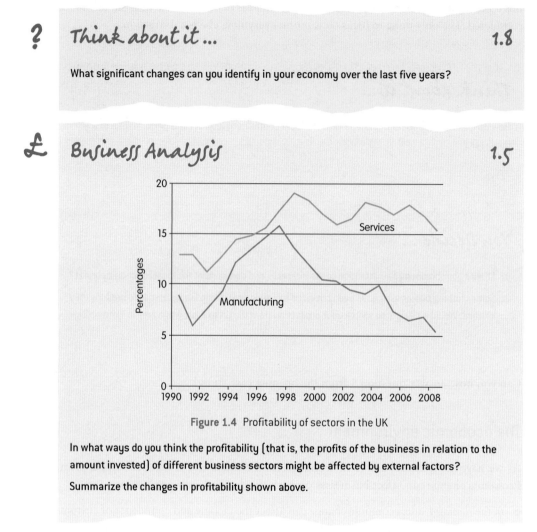

Figure 1.4 Profitability of sectors in the UK

In what ways do you think the profitability (that is, the profits of the business in relation to the amount invested) of different business sectors might be affected by external factors?

Summarize the changes in profitability shown above.

Can you now answer questions 1, 3, and 4 from the opening case study?

Microeconomics and macroeconomics

The study of economics can be divided into two sections, although these are interrelated.

■ *Microeconomics* ('micro' meaning small) focuses on the study of particular markets: for example, the markets for oil, for clothes, or computer games. Managers may be interested in how much competition there is in their markets, how much power their suppliers have, how easy it is for other firms to enter, and the projected growth of the market. By analysing conditions in a given market, this can help to explain changes such as the price, output, quality, degree of innovation, and likely profits in a market.

■ *Macroeconomics* ('macro' meaning large) analyses the whole economy—that is, all of the different markets combined. Whereas microeconomics focuses on the price of one product, macroeconomics focuses on the general price level in the economy. Whereas microeconomics examines the output in one market, macroeconomics examines the total output of the economy.

Managers will be interested both in what happens in their own market (microeconomics) and what happens to the economy as a whole (macroeconomics). An understanding of microeconomics analysis may help them to predict what will happen to their costs or the prices in the markets in which they compete. An understanding of macroeconomics might help them to understand what is happening to broader factors in the economy, such as the average income level, the general level of prices, and the rate of growth in the economy.

? *Think about it ...*   1.9

Which of the following do you think are microeconomic matters and which are macroeconomic?

A The causes of unemployment.

B The value of the pound sterling compared to other currencies.

C The salaries of employees in the advertising industry.

D The output of the chemical industry.

E The growth of the Malaysian economy.

» *You Decide ...*

The microeconomic environment for a business consists of organizations such as its rivals, its suppliers, and its distributors. The macroeconomic environment refers to general economic factors, such as the interest rate and exchange rate.

Do you think that it is more important for managers to pay attention to the microeconomic environment than the macroeconomic environment?

Thinking like an economist

In this first chapter, so far, we have examined the role of business and its interrelationship with the economic environment. In the next section, we consider how an economist thinks and what tools he or she has at his or her disposal to examine a given situation to understand the causes and consequences of change. These tools enable economists and managers to understand a problem more fully, and thereby to understand the potential effects and how best to react to, or prepare for, change. This section provides a background to the rest of the book and you may well want to refer back to it at various points later on. Looking at any toolkit may not immediately inspire you, but, when you want to get a job done, having the right tools available enables you to get things done more effectively.

While it is important for managers to understand economic issues, they also need to think like an economist to analyse and make judgements. Economics involves the study of choices; so does management. Economics looks at how resources are allocated and the returns generated in different market conditions. The key tools used by economists are therefore also vital for managers and include the following.

Interpreting data

One important skill for economists is the ability to analyse data. This means looking at data and to be able to explain what might have caused changes in it, and what the effects of such changes might be, as well as being able to make a judgement on the relative importance of a given change. For example, when considering the effects of a change in the overall income of an economy, you might want to know why it has occurred and how sensitive demand for your product is to changes in the income of this one region.

When analysing data, you may want to consider the following.

Absolute versus relative numbers

Some business and economics data may be presented in absolute terms. For example, the profits of a business may be £250,000 this year—that is, an absolute number. But to know whether this is a 'good' level of profit or not, you might want to compare it with something else—that is, you might want to think about the scale of it *relative* to another figure.

For example, you may want to compare the profit figure with the level of sales that generated it: if sales were £5 million and profits were £250,000, this means profits were 5 per cent of sales. This is known as the 'profit margin' and is calculated as:

$$\frac{\text{Profit}}{\text{Sales turnover}} \times 100$$

You might also want to know how your profits relate to the number of people whom you employ. For example, if you have ten employees and your profits were £250,000, your profits per employee were £25,000. Profits per employee are calculated as:

$$\frac{\text{Profit}}{\text{Number of employees}}$$

You might also want to know about your profits in relation to the investment that has been made in the project or the business. For example, if the investment was £2.5 million and profits were £250,000, this means that the return on investment (ROI) is 10 per cent. ROI is calcuated as:

$$\frac{\text{Profit}}{\text{Capital invested}} \times 100$$

Can you now answer question 6 from the opening case study?

Data Analysis   1.1

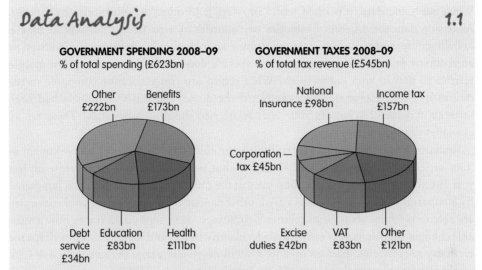

GOVERNMENT SPENDING 2008–09
% of total spending (£623bn)

Other £222bn
Benefits £173bn

Debt service £34bn
Education £83bn
Health £111bn

GOVERNMENT TAXES 2008–09
% of total tax revenue (£545bn)

National Insurance £98bn
Income tax £157bn

Corporation tax £45bn

Excise duties £42bn
VAT £83bn
Other £121bn

Figure 1.5 Government spending and government taxes

Source: HM Treasury

The data in Figure 1.5 shows UK government spending. The spending on education was £83,000 million in this financial year.

1. Why is it useful to see spending on other items?

2. Why is it useful to see the revenue?

3. What else do you think you would want to know to decide whether the government was spending enough on education in this year?

Data Analysis   1.2

Marks and Spencer plc (M&S) is a major retailer in the UK.
For the financial year ending March 2009 it had:

- profit before tax of £706 million;
- a sales turnover of £9,000 million;
- 77,864 employees;
- £2,000 million capital invested in the business.

To assess the profits of the business, you may want to compare it to other data such as the level of sales or investment.

1. Calculate its profit margin (that is, the profit per sale). This shows the profit that M&S makes for every pound spent in its stores.

2. Calculate the profit per employee.

3. Calculate the company's ROI.

Trends and comparisons (time series and cross-section data)

When analysing data, it is often useful to relate it to other organizations or countries. Analysing data for different businesses or countries at a particular moment in time is known as 'cross-section data': you are gaining an insight into a business, an industry, or an economy in comparison to others at a specific date. How high is your profit margin relative to that of your competitors? What return are you generating compared to the returns available elsewhere, for example, if the money used in the business had been invested in a bank? What are your sales relative to those of your rivals? These are all examples of cross-section data.

Similarly, it is important to look at how a variable has changed over time—known as 'time series data'. Sales may be £200 million, but is this an increase or decrease on last year and what proportion of the total sales in the market as a whole does this represent? By comparing data with the past or with other similar organizations (or countries), you are able to get some sense of its relative significance. Time series data tracks how a variable changes over time. This enables you to identify trends and identify links: perhaps the economy goes through periods of slow growth every few years; perhaps your sales are seasonal; perhaps your share price is linked to the returns available on other investments. These patterns would not be spotted by simply looking at cross-section data; rather, they need a context over time to be able to identify them effectively.

 ## Data Analysis   1.3

The profit margin for M&S in 2009 was 7.8 per cent, meaning that the profit before tax for every £1 spent in its stores was 7.8 pence. Without any other information, it is difficult to know whether this is good or bad. We might, therefore, want to use cross-section data to compare with its competitors. We might also want to compare this figure with previous years.

In this case:

- in 2009, the profit margin was 7.8 per cent;
- in 2008, 12.5 per cent;
- in 2007, 10.9 per cent;
- in 2006, 9.6 per cent; and
- in 2005, the profit margin was 7.4 per cent.

This time series data highlights that, after four years of improving profit margins, they fell in 2009. This suggests that the performance of M&S has worsened.

But before making any final judgements it is important to consider the context of this performance: for example, was this part of an overall strategy to cut prices and boost sales?

How could a business have a lower profit margin but a higher overall level of profit?

? *Think about it ...*   1.10

In 2009, Tesco plc earned a profit of nearly £3,000 million. What other data would you want in order to be able to decide whether or not this was a 'good' level of profit?

Nominal and real data

Another factor to consider when looking at data is the effect that price increases can have. When there is a sustained increase in the general price level, this is called **inflation**. If annual inflation is 3 per cent, for example, this means that prices, in general, have increased by 3 per cent over the last twelve months. This is important when considering other changes, such as wage increases. Imagine that employees receive a pay increase of 2 per cent. In **nominal** terms (that is, the amount received at the given time), employees have 2 per cent more money. But in terms of what this can actually buy, given that prices are generally going up by 3 per cent, this means that employees are worse off. This means that, in **real** terms, they cannot buy as much as they could last year and their earnings have actually fallen in terms of their purchasing power.

Similarly, if you receive interest at 1 per cent on your savings in the bank, but when you go shopping, you find that prices are 3 per cent higher, then, in real terms, the interest rate that you have received is negative. Real figures are, therefore, numbers that have been adjusted to take account of inflation.

Can you now answer question 11 from the opening case study?

 Data Analysis   1.4

In Zimbabwe, in July 2008, inflation was estimated to be 231 million per cent. In January 2009, it was estimated to be 5 sextillion per cent (that is, 5,000 million million million). Prices were more than doubling in a single day and this made banknotes useless very quickly. As a result, local banknotes were hardly used and people preferred to use overseas currencies if they had them. In January 2009, a new series of banknotes was issued, including a Z$100 trillion (that is, 100 million million) note.

What must happen to the pay of employees to maintain their real earnings in this type of economy?

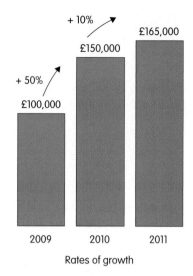

Figure 1.6 Rates of growth

Absolute figures and growth rates

A growth rate shows the percentage increase (or, if the growth rate is negative, the percentage decrease) in a given number. It is important for managers to understand the importance of growth: when analysing a given number, you might want to know whether it has increased or not, and, if so, by how much (see Figure 1.6). A manager who has increased the size of the business by 20 per cent in a year may be more impressive than a manager who has increased the size by 5 per cent. But you also need to think about the absolute size of figures: a 20 per cent increase on sales of £2,000 may be a lot easier to achieve than a increase of 2 per cent on sales of £2,000 million (and would be smaller in absolute terms).

It is also important to consider the rate of growth. If your sales are growing by 10 per cent, this means that they are 10 per cent higher by the end of the period than they were at the start. If the growth rate is then 5 per cent, this means that sales have continued to grow, but by 5 per cent, not 10 per cent. The rate of growth has fallen, but sales are still rising.

Similarly, if inflation falls from 3 per cent to 2 per cent, this means that prices are still growing, but at a slower rate. It does not mean that prices have fallen; a price would only fall in value if the growth rate were negative.

Can you now answer question 8 from the opening case study?

Averages and totals

The difference between average numbers and totals is another important distinction to consider when analysing data. When considering costs, for example, it is important to distinguish between the **total cost** of producing a product and the **average cost** (the cost per unit). When mass producing bottled water, for example, the total costs will be high,

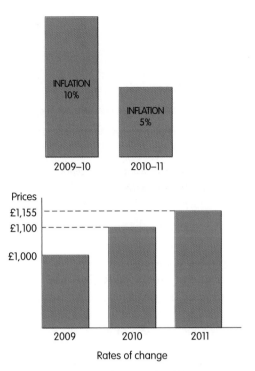

Figure 1.7 Rates of change. If prices generally increase by 10 per cent one year and 5 per cent the next year, the rate of growth of prices (called inflation) has decreased but prices are still going up. For example, they would have increased from £1,000 to £1,100 to £1,155 over the two years.

Data Analysis   1.5

To calculate a percentage change, use the formula:

$$\frac{\text{Change in value}}{\text{Original value}} \times 100$$

For example, if profits increase from £10 million to £12 million, then the percentage change can be calculated as:

$$\frac{(\text{£12 million} - \text{£10 million})}{\text{£10 million}} \times 100 = 20\%$$

1. If sales increase from £250 million to £300 million, what is the percentage increase in sales?

2. If sales fall from £300 million to £250 million, what is the percentage fall in sales?

To calculate the percentage of a number, use the formula:

$$\frac{X \times Y}{100}$$

For example, 5 per cent of 250:

$$\frac{5}{100} \times 250 = 12.5\%$$

3. What is a 10 per cent change in sales of twenty units?

4. If the growth rate for your sales was –2 per cent last year, what does this mean?

5. If the growth rate for your sales next year is predicted to be 5 per cent and, the year after, 2 per cent, what is happening to your sales?

6. If the sales of a business have increased across three years from £200,000, to £220,000, to £230,000, calculate the growth rates over the three years.

but if enough bottles are produced, the cost per bottle (that is, the average cost) may be relatively low. The cost per unit of producing Rolls Royce cars may be more than that of producing Toyotas, but the total cost of producing Toyotas is much higher, because they are produced on a much larger scale. On average, a business might not make a high profit per item, but if it sells a high volume of items, the total profit may be high.

When looking at economies, it may not be enough to consider the total income of the country; you may also want to consider the population size to calculate the income per person. According to the International Monetary Fund (IMF), the top five countries in terms of total income of the country were: the USA; Japan; China; Germany; and France. The top five in terms of income per person were: Qatar; Luxemburg; Norway; Singapore; and Brunei.

 ## Data Analysis   1.6

According to the IMF, Qatar had the highest gross domestic product (GDP) per person in 2008—but its total income ranked it 56th in the world.

How this can be?

Index numbers

As we have seen, it is often important, when making business and economic decisions, to analyse relative changes in data—that is, to calculate the percentage change in a given variable. If someone receives a pay increase of £50 a week, is this a big increase or not? The answer is that it depends on the amount that the person was receiving before—that is, how much the increase is as a percentage of the original pay. Similarly, if a business increases the price of its products by £10, is this significant or not? This depends on whether it is 0.0001 per cent or 10 per cent of the original price. Again, calculating the percentage change can be helpful to gain some sense of the significance of any change.

To help them to analyse data, economists often use **index numbers**. Index numbers make it easier to identify a percentage change quickly. Index numbers are, therefore, designed to help decision makers analyse data more easily.

When calculating percentage changes, you need to choose a starting point—that is, you need to compare whether something has increased or decreased relative to a given point. This point is called the 'base'. It is usually given a value of 100 (sometimes 1,000). Any change in the variable is then calculated in percentages and converted into an index number. If the index number is 105, then this represents 5 per cent more than the base (because it is five points more than the 100); if the index number is 125, this is 25 per cent more than the base. If the index is 95, this is 5 per cent less than the base.

% Worked Example

Imagine that you are trying to convert a country's national income figures into index numbers and want to compare these figures over four years.

Table 1.2

	National income (£mn)	Index number
2007	5,000	100
2008	5,100	102
2009	5,200	104
2010	5,500	110

If we were given only the first two columns, we could, of course, work out the percentage changes between 2008 and 2007, 2009 and 2007, and 2010 and 2007. But if the index has been calculated already, the percentage changes are easier to identify: for example, we can see there is a 2 per cent increase in GDP from 2008 to 2007, a 4 per cent increase from 2009 to 2007, and a 10 per cent increase from 2010 to 2007. Using the index numbers, percentage changes can quickly be seen without needing to calculate anything.

In some instances, you may only be given the index numbers and not the underlying data.

Table 1.3

	Index of unit costs
2008	100
2009	99
2010	97
2011	94

What we can see from this is that unit costs have fallen over the period relative to 2008. In 2009, they are 1 per cent lower than 2008; in 2010, they are 3 per cent lower; in 2011, they are 6 per cent lower. Note that, in this instance, we do not know what the unit costs actually are, but we do know how much they have changed.

Weighted indices

A weighted index takes account of the relative importance of the variables being considered. For example, when working out inflation, economists are interested in how much prices have increased in a typical basket of goods. But not all goods in your shopping basket are equal in terms of their relative importance because you spend much more each week on some items than others and so this needs to be reflected in the calculation. The weight given to an item reflects its relative importance. In this case, a 'weight' is given to each item, which depends on how much is spent on each item.

Table 1.4

Item	Index	Weight	Weighted index
A	120	60	7,200
B	110	30	3,300
C	110	10	1,100
			$\dfrac{11,600}{100} = 116$

In the example above, there are three products. A has increased in price by 20 per cent, while B and C have increased by 10 per cent; this is shown by the index number. The relative importance of these items in terms of the individual's expenditure is given by the relative weights. A accounts for 60 per cent of his or her spending, B accounts for 30 per cent, and C accounts for 10 per cent. This means that the change in price of A is relatively more important than the change in price of B and C. This is seen when the weighted index is calculated.

The following formula is used to calculate a weighted index:

$$\frac{\text{Index} \times \text{Weights}}{\text{Total weights}}$$

The weighted index in this instance is 16 per cent—this means that prices, taking account of the relevant importance of the different items have increased by 16 per cent, on average.

Data Analysis   1.7

Calculate the weighted index for the increases in prices shown below.

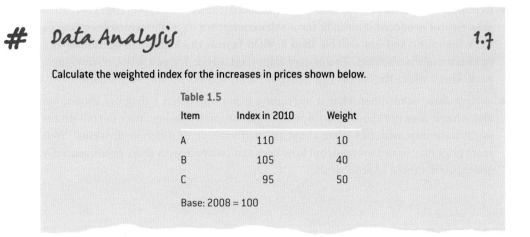

Table 1.5

Item	Index in 2010	Weight
A	110	10
B	105	40
C	95	50

Base: 2008 = 100

Analysing diagrams

Quite a lot of economics data is presented in the form of diagrams. The data relating to two variables may be plotted to see if there is any relationship: do sales of your products appear to be linked to the average income in the economy? What about your spending on marketing? Diagrams provide a visual representation of data and can be a useful way in which to help economists to analyse trends and relationships.

When examining a chart, be sure to look carefully at:

■ its *title*—what exactly is it showing? Is it the sales of the industry as a whole or only for your specific business? Is it past data or a projection? Is it showing the absolute figure for sales or the growth rate?

■ its *scale*—a change in the scale of a chart can create a very different impression (see Figure 1.8 below);

SALES

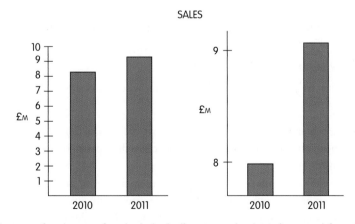

Figure 1.8 Impact of a change of scale. In both diagrams sales have increased from £8m to £9m between 2010 and 2011; however by changing the scale the increase looks much greater in the diagram on the right.

- its *source*—how reliable is the data? Who produced it and for what purpose? Forecasted sales figures produced internally for a sales conference to inspire employees may be more optimistic and less reliable than audited figures checked by an outside agency to present to shareholders. This is very important advice for you when researching a topic: check where the data is from, because some sources are not very reliable;

- *missing data*—sometimes what is interesting is not only what a diagram shows, but also what it does *not* show—that is, what information is missing. Your overall profits might have increased, but what about the performance of different divisions? Your share price may have increased, but how does this compare with share prices generally and especially those of your rivals?

Economic models

To analyse the effects of changes in the economy, economists have to build models to explain how the economy works. A model is a simplified framework to help to organize the way in which we think about a problem. These models make assumptions, for example, about what motivates the various groups in society, such as employees, businesses, and consumers. The aim of a model is to explain changes that have occurred and to predict future changes in key variables. A model involves a set of assumptions: for example, if we were trying to estimate future customer spending, we might make assumptions about the factors that influence this expenditure.

When trying to analyse a situation, the model that is constructed may not necessarily predict the behaviour of one individual household, firm, or employee, but the aim is to be able to predict the behaviour of these groups in general; one individual may not act in the way predicted, but if the majority do, then the model will still be valid.

Economic theory generally assumes that the various groups involved in decision making act in a rational way and aim to maximize their own welfare—that is, that:

- businesses aim to maximize profit when deciding what to produce and how to produce it;

- customers aim to maximize their **utility** (satisfaction) when deciding how to spend their money and what to buy;

- employees aim to maximize their satisfaction when choosing between work and leisure.

When analysing a market, economists will look for the results that would maximize the outcomes for those involved; the value of the model will depend, in part, on how appropriate this assumption is.

Of course, models may prove accurate for a given situation, but, over time, turn out to be ineffective when it comes to explaining or predicting what is happening in an economy. This may be because conditions have changed. Consider the present-day labour market compared to that of your grandparents: employees are generally better educated; the workforce is more diverse, in terms of gender and ethnic origin; there is more information available on job opportunities; and employees are more likely to move area and jobs during the course of their careers. This means that any model of labour markets would need to be modified over time to reflect a changing world.

The marginal condition

When trying to identify the output that maximizes the returns to any particular group, economists often consider the 'marginal benefit' and '**marginal cost**'. The marginal benefit refers to the extra rewards from selling or consuming another unit; the marginal cost refers to the extra cost involved in providing another unit. If the marginal benefit from producing a unit is greater than the marginal cost, then the firm or household will benefit from it and it should be provided or consumed; total welfare will increase. If, however, the marginal benefit is less than the marginal cost, then this unit should not be made; total welfare will fall (see Figure 1.9). To maximize the returns (when the extra benefit exceeds the extra costs), all units should be made up to the point at which the extra

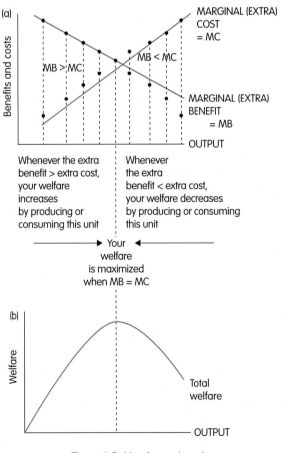

Figure 1.9 Margins and totals

benefit equals the extra cost—that is, the point at which there are no additional rewards to be gained. This is known as 'equating at the margin'.

The concept of 'equating at the margin' is an important one in many areas of economics (and, indeed, life). Many people complain about levels of pollution, for example, and want it removed completely—but this would be economically inefficient. Pollution is generated by production, which brings benefits to people (such as more products to consume); production needs to be continued up to the point at which the marginal benefit is equal to the marginal costs (including the pollution), which does not mean that all pollution will disappear.

 # **Data Analysis**   **1.8**

Table 1.6

Units	Extra benefit (MB)	Extra cost (MC)	Impact on total welfare (MB − MC)	Total welfare
0	0	0		0
1	20	9		
2	18	11		18
3	16	13		21
4	14	14		
5	12	17		

1. Complete the above table.

2. At what level of output is welfare maximized and why?

3. What is the relationship between the extra increase in welfare by consuming a unit and the total welfare?

>> **You Decide ...**

1. Do you think that profit is the most important objective for managers?

2. What other objectives do you think that they might have?

Rational decision making

Economics also assumes that employees, consumers, and managers act rationally—that is, that they make logical decisions to maximize their benefits. This is why the marginal condition applies. If the extra benefit of an activity is greater than the extra cost, then the individual will undertake that activity to increase his or her welfare. While some individuals may act irrationally, a model will still have value if the majority act rationally; a problem arises if the majority act irrationally.

? Think about it ... 1.11

1. When you are deciding where to go on holiday, how logical is your decision-making process? Do you do lots of research to choose the location and resort?

2. What about when you chose the university at which you are studying: did you do a high level of research to ensure that a logical decision was made?

Normative and positive economics

When analysing economic issues, managers need to distinguish between decisions based on assumptions that can be tested and decisions based on what they think is right. For example, it is possible to test whether a cut in price leads to a significant rise in sales: managers can cut the price and see what happens. This is an example of **positive economics**, because it can be tested to see if the assumptions or theories are right or not.

If, however, managers believe that they should invest more in the local community rather than pay out profits to shareholders, this is an opinion—that is, their view of what they think is right—and is therefore an example of **normative economics**.

A decision to reward employees more because you think that they deserve it is an example of normative economics; a decision to do so because you think that it improves the business performance can be researched and is an example of positive economics. Similarly, a government's decision to make reducing inflation a priority is an example of normative economics; the view that lower inflation improves the competitiveness of a country is an example of positive economics.

? Think about it ... 1.12

1. What do you think is the biggest economic issue with which your government should deal?

2. Is your choice an example of normative or positive economics? Why?

Distinguishing fairness and efficiency

Positive economics focuses on evidence-based and testable analysis. It examines issues to identify the most efficient solution; this does not necessarily mean that this is the decision that a manager would want to make in terms of what he or she feels is fair. For example, it may be efficient to pay an employee £100 a week, because this is for what he or she is prepared to work, and this might be the profit-maximizing decision. But if the employee has worked for you for many years, you may feel that it is only fair to pay him or her more. Similarly, it may be efficient to make redundancies, but managers may feel, out of a sense of responsibility, that they should not do this if it can be avoided. There will be times therefore when the economist's desire to be efficient may clash with a manager's desire to be fair: what may seem right may not be efficient.

Distinguishing cause and effect

Economists are often looking for links between different variables: for example, what causes prices of property to increase? What affects how much households spend? What determines how fast an economy grows? There is a correlation when there is an apparent link between different variables: if the two variables move in the same direction, this is a 'positive correlation'; if they move in different directions, this is known as a 'negative correlation'. For example, there may be a positive correlation between the amount of income that people have and the amount that they spend. There might be a negative correlation between the price of an item and the quantity demanded.

Economists are constantly analysing data to understand how the economy works; the economy is, after all, like a complex machine with trillions of interconnected parts. Even when a relationship appears to be understood, it is capable of change, because there are so many different factors, and the mix is always changing and developing.

It is also important to be careful not to assume that a correlation shows that there is a direct effect between two variables or that one factor leads to another. Correlation is not the same as 'causation'. When income in the economy is falling, governments often lower interest rates to make borrowing cheaper—but a simple observation of numerous instances of falling income and low interest rates may make you think that low interest rates cause falling income, whereas, in fact, it is a reaction to it.

If, however, a correlation can be identified, this can obviously be of value to managers. For example, if the sales of their products are linked to the income in the economy and a growth in the economy is predicted, then they should prepare for higher sales by recruiting staff and making sure that they have the capacity that they need.

? *Think about it ...*   1.13

1. There are more shark attacks on people when the weather is hot. Does this mean that the hot weather causes more sharks to attack people?

2. There are often more people employed at the government's Treasury (that is, the department that controls its finances) when the economic situation is poor. Does this mean that these economists cause the poor economic situation?

Are economists scientists?

Economists look to build models and quantify factors to make the optimal decisions. They seek out the maximizing solution in a given situation: for example, what would maximize consumers' satisfaction or business profits. They seek to explain what has happened in the past and to predict what might happen in the future, to help policymakers make better decisions. To do this, they analyse data so that they can base decisions on evidence. In this sense, they are like scientists: analysing data to find relationships and, hopefully, fundamental truths.

There are, however, some problems with treating economics as if it were a science, as follows.

- It deals with highly complex relationships between millions of groups of producers, consumers, and employees; it can be difficult to build a model that illustrates how all of these relationships interact.

- It deals with people who are not always as rational as the models predict; predicting behaviour is always difficult. For example, people's decisions will be influenced by many factors, such as their expectations, which are not necessarily easy to incorporate in models.

- Data can be difficult to gather quickly and accurately, given the scale of economies and the number of organizations that belong to it. Making the right decisions can be difficult even if the model is right if the data is not.

- It is not possible to undertake large-scale experiments on economies to test relationships, so the learning often comes after an event has happened and the findings can be incorporated into the models, which may already be out of date.

This does not mean that studying economics is useless for managers; rather, that its findings and models need to be reviewed as new issues develop and new thinking emerges. This makes it all the more interesting to study as our understanding evolves and, hopefully, improves over time.

Can you now answer question 12 from the opening case study?

 Business Analysis   1.6

Accurate economic data in China has, historically, been extremely difficult to find. One reason why they are not always trusted is simply the speed with which they are produced. China is always one of the first countries to report its national income figures, usually only two weeks after the end of each quarter. Most developed economies take between four and six weeks to produce them. Most economists reckon that China has understated its growth in recent years. The country's National Bureau of Statistics (NBS) has recently revised China's GDP growth up by half a percentage point for both 2006 and 2007—to 11.6 per cent and 11.9 per cent, respectively—thanks to stronger growth in services, which government statisticians find harder to count than industry. Yet even these revised numbers may be conservative.

Stephen Green, an economist at Standard Chartered, calculates that, in 2007, the combined output of the Chinese provinces was 10 per cent more than that reported by the national government.

Some of the least reliable figures are those relating to the labour market. The urban unemployment rate is meaningless, for example, because it excludes workers laid off by state-owned firms, as well as large numbers of migrant workers, who are normally not registered.

Sources: Central Intelligence Agency, National Bureau of Statistics of China,
The Economist, 1 May 2008

Why do you think that problems with data might limit the effectiveness of a government's decision making?

Why do economists disagree?

Building models to try to explain the complexities of trillions of interrelationships between households, governments, businesses, and employees is understandably difficult. Not surprisingly, economists will sometimes build different models that make different predictions. Furthermore, the data that they use to build their models will sometimes differ simply because it can be difficult to gather information on this scale accurately and because identifying causation is not always straightforward.

Even if their models were the same, there would still be plenty of room for debate because of normative economics: we might all agree how the economy works, but still have completely different views of what the priorities should be in terms of economic policy. Is lower unemployment more important than stable prices? Should the government be aiming for a more equal income distribution? These views of what we should be aiming to achieve provide plenty of opportunities for disagreement.

Summary

Businesses undertake a transformation process, taking resources and adding value to these, to produce goods and services worth more than the inputs used up in the process. Businesses are an open system in which managers are affected by the external environment. This environment can be analysed using PESTEL analysis, which examines political, economic, social, technological, environmental, and legal factors.

Economists build models to understand how markets and economies work. They aim to understand how choices are made and how resources are allocated. To build these models, they make assumptions about the objectives of individuals, employees, and managers. To construct and use these models, economists must be able to interpret data, which requires an understanding of concepts such as marginals, averages, totals, index numbers, and weighted indices.

Checklist

Having read this chapter, you should now understand:

- ☐ the importance of economics to managers;
- ☐ the difference between a nominal value and real value;
- ☐ the value of index numbers;
- ☐ the meaning of a weighted index;
- ☐ the meaning of correlation;
- ☐ the difference between normative and positive economics;
- ☐ the difference between fairness and efficiency;
- ☐ the value of time series and cross-section data.

Case Study Review

Having read this chapter, you should now be able to answer the following questions.

1. What economic factors that affect business success are highlighted in the above text?

2. All businesses are involved in the transformation process. Outline the transformation process that The Look undertakes and explain how it can add value doing this.

3. Can you think of other economic factors that might affect a clothes retailer?

4. What about other external, non-economic, factors?

5. Who are the stakeholders of The Look? How might working with them help the business?

6. Why might the board of directors be unhappy with a profit of £6 million?

7. What is the difference between the profit margin and the profit of a business?

8. If the growth rates of the economies in India and Russia are much higher than that in the UK, does this mean that their citizens are better off? Explain your answer.

9. Why do you think the Russian and Indian economies might be growing relatively quickly?

10. Which other types of business do you think are likely to want to target economies such as India and Russia? Why?

11. How can Alison receive a pay increase of 1 per cent and yet be worse off?

12. If economists failed to predict the global downturn of 2008, is Alison right to say that there is no point studying economics?

Short Answer Questions

1. If you receive a 10 per cent bonus, what determines whether you are better off in real terms?

2. If sales of your product increase from 200,000 units to 220,000 units a year, what is the percentage increase in sales? If sales fall from 220,000 units to 200,000 units, what is the percentage decrease in sales?

3. 'Lower interest rates lead to more spending.' Is this an example of positive or normative economics?

4. If the base value of your share prices was 100 in 2009 and the index is now 86, what does this mean has happened to the share price?

5. Sales of your product two years ago were 300,000 units. The growth rate last year was 8 per cent and has been 5 per cent this year. How many units did you sell this year?

6. Your profits two years ago were £2 million; they then increased to £2.4 million the following year and to £2.6 million the year after that. What were the growth rates for each of the two years?

7. If the extra revenue from selling a unit is £8 and the extra cost is £5, would profit increase or decrease if the unit were sold?

8. If the extra revenue from selling an additional unit equals the extra cost of producing it, does this mean that no profit is being made? Explain your answer.

9. What is a model and why do economists create them?

10. Your business made a profit of £300,000 last year. Is this a good level of profit or not? Explain your answer.

Essay Questions

1. To what extent is the economy likely to be the key external factor determining the success of businesses?

2. Discuss the possible value to managers of undertaking PESTEL analysis.

3. What two changes in your economy in recent years do you think are likely to be most important for businesses? Justify your choices.

 # One Step Further

Visit our Online Resource Centre at **www.oxfordtextbooks.co.uk/orc/gillespiebusiness/** for test questions, podcasts, and further information on topics covered in this chapter.

The fundamental
economic problems

2

Learning Objectives

In this chapter, we consider the fundamental economic problems facing every economy, and the different ways in which decisions about what to produce, how to produce, and for whom to produce the products are answered.

By the end of this chapter, you should:

- ☑ understand the meaning of scarcity and choice;

- ☑ understand the key economic problems in society;

- ☑ be able to explain the difference between a free market, a planned economy, and a mixed economy;

- ☑ be able to outline the key advantages and disadvantages of each type of economy;

- ☑ understand the meaning of the production possibility frontier and productive efficiency.

© **Case Study**

In 2009, the French government invested over €26,000 million to stimulate its economy. The spending was on over 1,000 projects across the country, including motorway upgrades, ports, and the Train à Grande Vitesse (TGV, meaning 'high-speed train').

The policies of the French government have typically been interventionist, including relatively high taxes, protection against foreign competition, and a high level of regulation.

In 2007, France's government spending accounted for 52 per cent of national income, compared to 45 per cent in the UK and 37 per cent in the USA. In France, 5.2 million workers, or 21 per cent of those with jobs, are employed by the public sector. Until recently, the French approach was criticized for failing to generate enough economic growth and for the costs of intervention.

But while its growth may have been relatively slow, the French economy seemed to have been less affected by the global **recession** of 2008—perhaps because it was less dependent on exports than economies such as Germany and benefited from not having been involved in high-risk lending. Furthermore, life expectancy is high, and the gap between the incomes of the top 10 per cent and the bottom 10 per cent is far smaller than in the UK and the USA.

In the UK, the Prime Minister declared—like the French President—that 'laissez-faire has had its day'. 'We have something to learn from continental practice,' said Peter Mandelson, the UK's Secretary of State for Business, Innovation and Skills, identifying French long-term strategic planning in such sectors as energy and transport. To provide the infrastructure it needs, the French state has either created companies (such as EDF and Areva) or bailed out troubled private ones (including Alstom, the manufacturer of the TGV train), in order to keep the supply side going. Its long-term planning also extends to education. France has a world-class layer of engineering, business, and public administration schools, known as *grandes écoles*, which produce a technically skilled elite to run such firms.

The French are also champions when it comes to making rules. There are rules about how many pharmacies any one pharmacist can own (one) and how many taxis there are on the Paris streets (15,300). There are rules about when lorries can use motorways (not on Sundays), or when shops can hold sales (twice a year, on dates set by officials). Tighter regulation extended to the financial markets and French banks were more wary of lending than were banks in other countries. In 2007, French mortgage debt represented only 35 per cent of national income: less than in Germany (48 per cent), the UK (86 per cent), Ireland (75 per cent), and Spain (62 per cent).

But the downside of such intervention is that the government taxes employers and employees with such heavy social security contributions to pay for all of the health and welfare that it ends up deterring firms from creating jobs in the first place. One reason why French workers are more productive per hour than Americans is that firms employ so few of them. Many make widespread use of students working for them in the holidays and other temporary staff. Also, French governments have seemed to be better at devising and managing big planned projects than at dealing with bottom-up ideas and uncertain markets. France lacks start-ups and its small firms have difficulty growing. Hardly any of the biggest companies listed on the Paris Bourse were founded during the last fifty years. Moreover, the old-style policy of picking national champions has had, at best, a mixed record. Transport and utility firms may be one thing; in other sectors, including computers or banking, it has been a disaster—as shown by the failure of companies such as Groupe Bull and Crédit Lyonnais. Even the French have been unwinding public stakes in private enterprise over the past fifteen years. There has been no widespread nationalization for more than a quarter of a century.

Source: Adapted from *The Economist*, 7 May 2009

Questions

1. According to the above case study, the growth rate of the French economy has been slow. What factors do you think might determine the growth rate of an economy?

2. What do you think is meant by a 'laissez-faire' approach to managing the economy?

3. The French government has decided to invest heavily in transport. Why might other governments not have invested so much in this sector?

4. Apart from transport, what services might you expect a government to provide? Explain your choice.

5. Why do you think the French government's attempts to intervene in computing and banking might have been unsuccessful?

6. Discuss the case for and against government intervention in an economy. Do you think that it would be better to leave an economy to run itself?

7. What do we learn from the case study about external factors that might influence the success of a business?

Introduction

In this chapter, we examine the fundamental economic questions that face every economy and compare these with the issues facing business managers. We then consider the range of approaches to solving these questions found in different economies, and compare their advantages and disadvantages.

Economic resources

We have seen how a business takes resources and transforms them. Think of a construction project and you can imagine all of these resources combining as part of a transformation process.

- A manager has the idea to develop a piece of land and then acquires this. The money used to do this could have been used on another project, so this highlights the concept of opportunity cost.

- The manager then employs an architect to design the building, making use of his or her creativity, imagination, and technical skills and experience.

- The next stage is to build the building, which involves employing staff and using capital equipment. This stage will involve many other businesses providing the construction materials used and, in some cases, undertaking some of the specialist work, such as the gas supply and electrics. This highlights how businesses in an economy are interrelated and how the success or failure of one will affect others.

- Once constructed, the building has to be sold, which requires the skills and ability of the marketing function.

The project therefore involves the careful coordination of many factors of production to produce a saleable building that generates a profit for the business. Decisions must be made throughout the process on what factors of production to use to produce the building; resources must be used efficiently to avoid waste and the objective is to generate a final product that is worth more than the costs of providing it. This profit must justify the use of the resources in this way; after all, they could have been used for a completely different project.

An economy is made up of millions of different businesses like the construction project, all of which are transforming resources and producing outputs. An economy involves different resources being combined to produce billions of goods and services every day. Given that the quantity and quality of resources available in an economy is fixed at any moment in time, managers are competing for these to use in their production processes. Given the limited resources, this constrains the maximum amount that an economy can produce and so decisions about using resources for one project means that something else will not be produced. Having said this, not every economy has the same resources: some economies have more or better quality resources, either because of natural endowment or due to investment in the past, and this enables them to produce more than other economies.

?   *Think about it ...*   2.1

1. For what resources is your economy well known?
2. Which products does it sell worldwide?

Data Analysis   2.1

Global innovation of selected countries, 2004–08

Rank		Index*
1	Japan	10.000
2	Switzerland	9.711
3	Finland	9.503
4	United States	9.497
5	Sweden	9.444
6	Germany	9.404
7	Taiwan	9.369
8	Netherlands	9.165
9	Israel	9.126
10	Denmark	9.077
11	South Korea	8.940
12	Austria	8.934
13	France	8.885
14	Canada	8.868
15	Belgium	8.788

*On a scale of 1–10

Figure 2.1 Global innovation

Source: Economist Intelligence Unit. Reproduced with kind permission

A **patent** provides legal protection for a new invention (see Chapter 9). *The Economist* Innovation Index measures innovation performance in eighty-two countries, and is based on the number of patents granted to people from different countries by patent offices in the USA, European Union (EU), and Japan. It also takes into account factors that help and hinder the ability to innovate, such as the amount of research and development undertaken, and the technical skills of the country's workforce.

1. What do you think might influence how innovative some countries are compared to others?

2. How might greater innovation affect the transformation processes that occur in an economy and the growth of an economy?

Scarcity and choice

The fact that the quantity and quality of resources in an economy are limited at any moment restricts the amount that can be produced. But the wants of customers are not limited; rather, they are unlimited: whatever we have at the moment, we want more. This means that there is a scarcity of products relative to what we would like to have—that is, unfortunately, we cannot have everything. As a result, choices have to be made in terms of how the resources of an economy are allocated. Just as an individual manager must decide how to allocate the people, equipment, and funds that he or she has within the business, decisions must be made within an economy in terms of where the country's resources are used. Should the available land be used for a health club or should we build flats on it? Should equipment be used to produce microwaves or high-definition televisions? Should employees be used to work in hotels or insurance? Decisions need to be made to determine how resources are used. The concepts of 'scarcity' and 'choice' lie at the heart of economics: because of scarce resources all the different parties in an economy must make choices.

Businesses, for example, have limited resources and have to decide on how to use these efficiently and effectively to maximize their returns. Households have limited income and have to decide how to allocate their spending to maximize their utility. Employees have limited time, and have to decide how to allocate this time between leisure and work to maximize their welfare. All of the different groups in society therefore face constraints and have to make choices to try to maximize their returns.

? Think about it ...   2.2

1. What might change the resources that an economy has available over time?

2. How do you think a government might increase the resources available in its economy?

3. Which products in your economy do you think have experienced a significant increase in demand in recent years and which have experienced a fall? Why do you think this is?

The production possibility frontier (PPF)

The limited availability of resources in an economy at any moment in time determines its capacity—that is, the maximum output that it can produce. The maximum combination of products that can be produced given the existing resources in the economy are illustrated by a **production possibility frontier (PPF)**.

? Think about it ...   2.3

1. Can you think of businesses in which the labour resource is particularly important?

2. Can you think of one in which capital is the key resource?

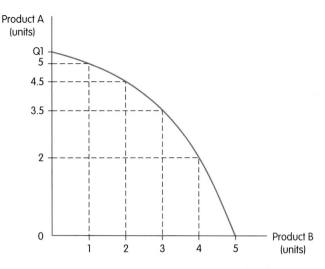

Figure 2.2 A production possibility frontier (PPF)

The PPF in Figure 2.2 highlights an economy that is choosing between only two products (this makes it easier to illustrate the key issues on a diagram). If all of the resources in the economy were dedicated to the production of product A, then Q1 can be produced. If resources are transferred out of the production of A and into the production of B, then less of A is produced, but more of B is produced. The extra output of B comes at the expense of some of the A, which again highlights the concept of opportunity cost. The opportunity cost of the extra units of B is the amount of A that has to be given up. For example, to produce the second unit of B, resources are transferred out of product

 Data Analysis 2.2

The following table shows combinations of products on an economy's production possibility frontier.

Complete the column showing the opportunity cost of each extra unit of B in terms of the number of units of A sacrificed.

Table 2.1

A	B	Opportunity cost of extra B
100	0	
90	1	
75	2	
55	3	
32	4	
0	5	

Business economics

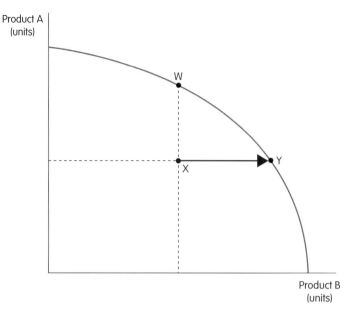

Figure 2.3 Productive inefficiency

A and the amount of A produced falls from 5 to 4.5; this means that the opportunity cost of the second B is 0.5 units of A. Similarly, the opportunity cost of the third B is one unit of A; of the fourth B, it is 1.5 units of A.

Any combination of products on the PPF displays **productive efficiency** (see Figure 2.3). This is because the resources of the economy are fully employed and more of one product can only be produced if less of another product is made. The only way to increase production in one sector is to transfer resources out of another, thereby making a sacrifice and generating an opportunity cost.

Any combination of products produced inside the frontier, such as 'X', is productively inefficient. More of one product could be made without less of another if resources were to be used more efficiently. For example, an economy could have the same amount of product A as it has at X, but have more units of B if resources were used more efficiently and production occurred at Y. Similarly, W has more of A than X and so, if resources were used more efficiently, the economy could produce more.

An economy producing at X is the equivalent of a business producing less than its maximum capacity. A business that is producing less than it can, given its current resources, is underutilizing its capacity; it is being inefficient, because people or machines are sitting idle. A business solution to this would be to try to boost demand to increase sales. Similarly, if an economy is at 'X', a government may want to try to increase demand in the economy for goods and services, and thereby reduce the levels of unemployment.

The shape of the production possibility frontier

The shape of the PPF (see Figure 2.4) will depend on the effect of transferring resources from one industry to another. If the transfer has constant returns—that is, if, every time

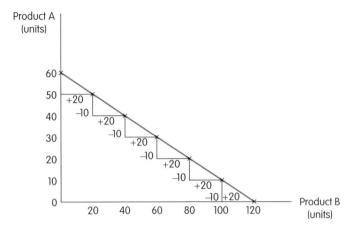

Figure 2.4 Straight-line production possibility frontier

a resource is transferred from industry A to B, the same amount of output is sacrificed in A and the same amount is gained in B—then the PPF would be a straight line.

If, however, increasingly fewer units of B were produced each time a given amount of resources were switched out of industry A and into B, this would lead to a PPF that was concave to the origin (Figure 2.5). This could occur due to the **law of diminishing returns**.

The law of diminishing returns focuses on the short run, which, in economics, is defined as the time period when there is at least one fixed factor. The law of diminishing returns states that, in the short run, the extra output produced from adding a variable factor (such as labour) to the fixed factor (such as machinery) will eventually diminish. This law occurs because, at some point, the variable factors of production will get in each other's way. Imagine recruiting more staff to your insurance office or your travel agency, but not increasing the number of

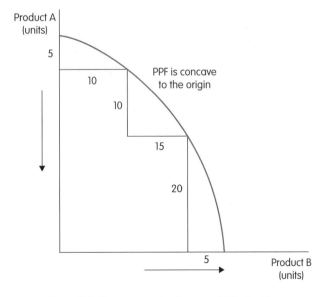

Figure 2.5 Concave production possibility frontier

computer systems or desks: the extra people would struggle to be as productive as the first few, only because they do not have the resources that they need to work. The extra employees are not any less efficient in themselves, but the conditions and the lack of additional equipment restricts the contribution that they are able to make to production. This means that the extra output (also called the 'marginal product') of additional employees will fall.

As a result of the law of diminishing returns, when resources as transferred from one industry to another, the extra output will diminish, causing the PPF to be concave to the origin. In fact, if the law of diminishing returns is assumed to apply in both industries, as factors of production are transferred from one to the other, successively more units of one product are given up for successively fewer units of the other product, which makes the PPF even more concave to the origin.

 ## Data Analysis   2.3

Table 2.2

Number of employees in A	Units produced		Number of employees in B
	Product A	Product B	
5	100	0	0
4	90	50	1
3	75	90	2
2	55	125	3
1	30	150	4
0	0	170	5

1. Plot the PPF for the data shown above.

2. Calculate the number of units sacrificed as each employee is transferred from industry A to industry B.

3. Calculate the number of units gained as each employee is transferred from industry A to industry B.

4. Is the law of diminishing returns operating in both of these industries? Explain your answer.

? ## Think about it ...   2.4

If technology improves in industry B so that any resources there are more productive, but does not improve in industry A, what would happen to the PPF? Illustrate your answer.

Economic growth

Over time, as an economy grows, this will increase the amount of products of A and B that can be produced. This is shown by an outward shift of the PPF (see Figure 2.6). The economy can now produce more of product A and product B.

Economic growth may be caused by an increase in the quantity and/or quality of resources, such as:

- an increase in technology enabling capital equipment to be more productive;
- a better educated or better trained workforce, or a better approach to managing people;
- an increase in the land available—perhaps because new technology allows more land to be reclaimed or to be used more productively.

This economic growth is similar to a business increasing its capacity over time through investment, training, or the acquisition of more land.

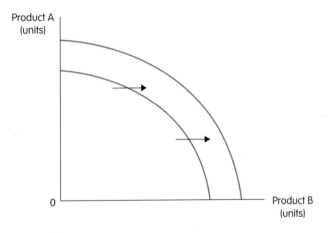

Figure 2.6 Outward shift in the production possibility frontier

>> *You Decide ...*

For the last few weeks, your bottling plant has been operating at, or close to, full capacity.

1. Should you increase the capacity of your business?

2. What factors would influence your decision?

Can you now answer question 1 from the opening case study?

Looking at the growth of an economy will be important to managers who are examining potential markets in which they might compete. Managers will be interested in the following factors.

- *The maximum output of a country now and in the future* Is it a large potential market or not? If so, it may be worth targeting. The emerging markets, such as Brazil, Russia, India, and China (BRIC), have been growing very rapidly in recent years and many multinationals, such as Unilever, are targeting these regions for future expansion, because they offer the potential of much faster growth than more developed and mature economies such as the UK.

- *The combination of goods and services produced in the economy, and the opportunities and threats that this creates* Is an economy mainly producing consumption goods? If so, this might provide sales opportunities for producers of consumer electronics. Or is it more focused on capital goods? If so, this might create opportunities for producers of machinery.

? Think about it ...   2.5

1. Why do you think the aim of most governments is to achieve economic growth?
2. The PPF illustrates how much an economy can produce. What factors do you think might affect the general well-being of a population other than how many goods and services are available?

>> You Decide ...

1. If you were in charge of a business, what could you do to improve the quality of your workforce?
2. When deciding which markets to target, what do you think are the most important factors that the managers of a consumer electronics business should consider?

The output gap

The **output gap** measures the difference between the amount that an economy is able to produce if its resources are fully employed and the level of demand at present.

If the demand in an economy is too low, the output being produced will be below the potential output (that is, the economy is producing within the PPF): this is called a 'negative output gap'. This happened in the UK in the 1980s, the early 1990s, and in 2008–10, when demand in the economy was very low.

If, however, the actual output in the economy is above the level that could be sustained in the long term (for example, demand is only being met by employees working overtime, firms working extra shifts, and machines being used far more than is usually recommended), this will put pressure on prices to increase. This is because, if there are very high levels of demand and businesses are struggling to meet all of the orders that they have, managers may feel that they can, and have to, increase their prices to ration the demand. This is known as a 'positive output gap'.

Figure 2.7 illustrates the economy output gap in the UK.

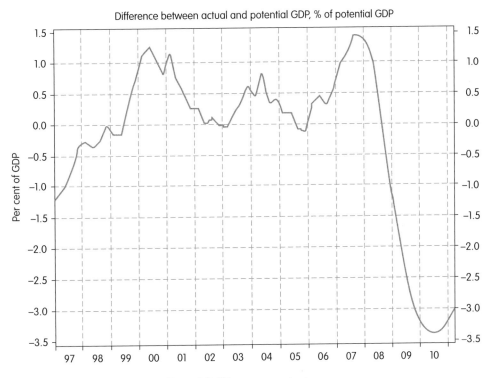

Figure 2.7 UK economy output gap

Source: OECD Economic outlook. Reproduced with kind permission of OECD

? **Think about it ...** 2.6

How might a negative output gap in an economy affect the operations and human resource (HR) functions of a business?

The three fundamental economic questions

The PPF highlights that it is not possible to produce more of all products: more of one can only be produced if fewer are produced of another because of the limited resources. What to produce is therefore a fundamental question (see Figure 2.8). But decisions also have to be made regarding how these products are made. Given the constraint of limited resources, how should these be used most efficiently? And who should benefit from the products produced?

These fundamental economic problems (that is, what to produce, how to produce, and for whom to produce) can be solved in different ways, depending on the type of economy (see Figure 2.9). The solutions include the following.

■ *The market mechanism* In what is known as a 'free market economy', the decisions about what and how to produce are determined by supply and demand. If there is a high level of demand for a particular item, this will attract businesses to produce it, because of the profits that can be made. How to produce will depend on the resource markets, such as the demand and supply of labour, which will affect its price. If labour is scarce, there will be more incentive to switch to capital, for example. In terms of who gets the products, this will depend on who can afford them: if you have money in the **free market**, you can buy the products that you want.

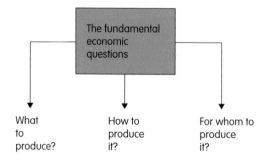

Figure 2.8 The fundamental economic questions

- *The government* An alternative to the free market would be for the government to intervene and determine what is produced, how it is produced, and who receives the rewards of production. This is known as a **planned (or command) economy**. In this scenario, the state decides what products need to be made and also how resources are allocated. People are directed to work in particular industries. The government also determines who gets what by determining how individuals are rewarded and how the products are distributed.

- *A mixed economy* A '**mixed economy**' occurs when resources are allocated by a combination of the market system and the government. In reality, all economies are mixed; where they differ is the extent to which the government intervenes. North Korea and Cuba, for example, have a high level of government involvement in the provision of goods and services, whereas in Hong Kong and the USA, the free market dominates.

? *Think about it ...* 2.8

Look at your economy.

1. What goods and services are provided by your government?

2. Has the provision changed in recent years?

3. If so, why do you think this is?

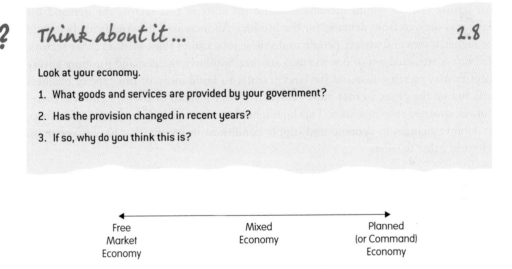

Figure 2.9 Range of economies

The free market

In a free market economy, decisions about what to produce depend on market forces. In any market, there is supply (which shows what producers are willing and able to produce at different prices) and demand (which shows what customers are willing and able to purchase at different prices). These forces interact, and a price is found at which the quantity supplied and demanded are equal. This is known as 'equilibrium' in the product market. Millions of producers and customers are making decisions to maximize their own returns (profits, in the case of producers, and utility, in the case of consumers) in many different markets; the price mechanism adjusts to bring their decisions into line. Market forces operating in all of these different markets determine what an economy produces overall. For example, if demand for Blu-ray DVDs is high, this will increase demand in this sector. This will tend to increase the price that customers are willing to pay, which will encourage suppliers to produce more (or more producers to enter this industry). The result will be that more resources are shifted into this industry and pulled out of another one in which demand is lower, such as CDs.

Similarly, if demand falls for a product, such as fax machines, this will mean that there are fewer rewards available for producers in this industry and so some will move out, looking for higher rewards elsewhere. The free market is made up of all of the different markets for goods, ideas, and services, interacting with the price, which adjusts to equate demand and supply in each one, and thereby determine what an economy produces.

Changes in the demand for a product will not only influence what is produced, but will also affect how items are made. This is because the markets for factors of production are linked to the markets for products. For example, an increase in the demand for leisure centres would increase demand for staff in this sector; the demand for labour is derived from demand for the product. An increased demand is likely to lead to higher wages and attract people to do these jobs rather than work in other sectors. Labour is attracted out of one use into another. Similarly, the demand for more leisure centres may increase demand for land in order to build more of this type of business and bid up the price, so that more centres are built instead of shops. Land will therefore be diverted into new uses. This highlights how interrelated markets are within an economy: changes in demand and supply conditions in one market have a knock-on effect in other markets.

? Think about it ...   2.9

1. What markets would be affected by a decrease in demand for cars?
2. Do you think it is fair to let the free market determine who gets what in the economy?

The allocation of resources will also depend on their supply within their factor markets. For example, an improvement in technology reducing the costs of using machinery would encourage the use of this resource relative to labour. An increase in supply of labour, perhaps because of immigration, may lead to more of this resource being used as it becomes relatively cheaper.

In the free market, it is assumed that decisions are driven by individual desires to maximize personal welfare and acting in a rational manner. Businesses want to maximize profits: for example, they move resources into the markets in which the demand is relatively high to earn more. Individuals want to maximize their own satisfaction and returns, and will move to work in markets in which the demand is high and their rewards can be higher.

The beauty of the free market system is that it is the result of millions of independent decisions by managers, employees, landowners, banks, and other organizations, all serving their own interests and looking for the highest rewards that they can get. If you have a business idea and want to pursue it, you can set up a business and, if it meets customer needs and generates enough income, you can make a profit. If you are a household, you can choose to spend your money on whatever maximizes your utility. As market conditions change, either in the markets for goods and services, or the markets for resources, the allocation of factors of production and the output of different products change; these changes are all driven by market forces. This approach is also known as 'laissez-faire' because individuals and businesses are left to make their own decisions.

Managers may welcome the free market because it allows them to make decisions without any intervention. There are no government regulations and therefore no controls on their behaviour. They are therefore able to do exactly what they want without needing government permission or meeting set regulations. But this means that other businesses are also able to do the same. As a result, some businesses may sell unsafe products, may mislead other organizations in terms of the ingredients or specifications of a product, or may force its customers to pay extremely high prices because of a lack of choice. To protect themselves against behaviour such as this, managers may prefer to have some government intervention rather than a totally free market.

 Business Analysis   2.1

In 2008, Bernard Madoff was accused of running a fraudulent investment scheme that lost up to US$50,000 million of his clients' money. These clients included HSBC, a British bank, Santander of Spain, and BNP Paribas of France. Investors thought that they were receiving superb returns because of Madoff's skill at investing. In fact, he was allegedly paying these returns out using the money of new investors into his fund.

As long as he kept attracting more investment into his scheme, Madoff could continue the impression of being an investment guru. But when the money coming in slowed up, he could not pay out and what seems to have been a huge fraud was eventually discovered. Even so, he seemed to have fooled investors and regulators for many years.

Do you think that fraud is inevitable when managers try to maximize profits?

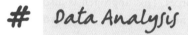

You Decide ...

Imagine that you are the manager of a major pharmaceutical business.

1. Can you think of ways in which a government might intervene that you would not want?
    Justify your choice.

Data Analysis   2.4

Table 2.3

Price (£)	Quantity demanded (units)	Quantity supplied (units)
10	100	270
9	120	220
8	150	170
7	170	130
6	200	90
5	250	50

The above table shows the quantity that consumers want to buy at different prices all other things unchanged. It also shows what producers are willing and able to sell at different prices all other things unchanged.

1. At which price do the decisions of producers and consumers match each other?

2. How much is supplied and demanded at a price of £10? What does the price need to do for the market to reach equilibrium?

3. How much is supplied and demanded at a price of £5? What does the price need to do for the market to reach equilibrium?

The planned (or command) economy

In a completely planned economy, all resources would be allocated by government directives. The government would determine exactly what is produced in what quantities each year, how the products are produced, and how much people are rewarded.

In a planned economy, the government decides the key economic questions—that is:

- what to produce;

- how the available resources are allocated to produce the goods and services that it has decided need producing; and

- who benefits from the economy by allocating the rewards (for example, by setting income levels for differing jobs).

There are advantages to this approach, in that it can avoid some things being produced that may be profitable, but which society as a whole may regard as undesirable (such as drugs and prostitution). It can also prevent unethical or unfair behaviour, such as mis-selling the products, by imposing regulations in these areas.

In a planned economy, the government can focus on the production of socially desirable goods and services even if they are not necessarily the most profitable. Late-night bus services, school buses, opera performances, hosting the Olympics, and health education programmes may not be particularly profitable, but a government may decide that they are in the interests of their society and ensure that these are provided rather than violent films, reality television, disposable fashion items, and fuel-guzzling sports cars.

There are, however, disadvantages of a planned economy—not least that what is being produced may not match with what customers actually want. Customers may want to buy the latest computer software only to find shops' shelves full of economics textbooks that the government wants them to read. And people may end up working in industries in which they do not want to work, resulting in low job satisfaction.

The planned economy relies on a government making the major decisions in the economy and allocating all of the resources available. This is a huge amount of planning for one organization (as opposed to the free market, which is decentralized and so does not rely on one body overseeing everything that happens). As a result, it may lead to slow decision making and an overload of work, leading to inefficient decisions being made. For example, if the production of products does not match what customers want, there may be stockpiles of items that are not wanted and **shortages** of ones that are in demand, but not produced. Poor decision making may also mean that employees and equipment may be used inefficiently, wasting resources. In particular, the lack of the profit motive may lead to inefficiency and a lack of innovation. In the free market, businesses keep the profits that they make, and this means that there is a desire to keep costs down and produce what is wanted; this may also encourage innovation to stay competitive. In the planned economy, all rewards belong to the state, so there may be less incentive to look for better, cheaper ways of doing things; indeed, this may encourage inefficiency because, if the government has decided that a certain amount of an item has to be produced, then it does not necessarily matter to managers how efficiently this is done and they will not personally gain from any savings made to the resources used. The role of the central government in an economy may, therefore, take away the ability of individual managers to respond quickly to market opportunities and the desire to be efficient or provide a better customer service.

? Think about it ... 2.10

1. What goods and services are provided by the government in your economy at the moment?
2. What do you think would be the key differences between working as a manager for the government and managing in a private-sector business?
3. If a government provides products that benefit society, is it acceptable for people to be told where to work?

Table 2.4 Summary of the free market and the planned economy

The free market	The planned economy
Resources allocated by supply and demand	Resources allocated by government intervention
No control over what is produced, but responds to demand, so produces what is wanted	Government determines what is produced, so can plan for the economy as a whole and plan long term; can produce socially desirable products
Decisions taken by individual households, firms, and employees	Government can take an overview of the economy and its priorities, and can cross-subsidize production to provide some products cheaply or for free
No need for central planning; lower administration costs	Central planning is expensive and can be bureaucratic
Incentive to be efficient and innovative, because individuals and businesses directly gain	Individuals and businesses may lack incentive, because profits go to the state

Can you now answer questions 3, 5, and 6 from the opening case study?

? Think about it ... 2.11

Do you think that it is fair if a government determines what products are produced and what you earn?

The mixed economy

The free market model and the planned economy model outlined above are extremes to highlight what can happen as you move nearer to one or other of these, and to help decision makers to determine how much they want the government to intervene in an economy. In reality, all economies are mixed to some degree. That means that there are some aspects of the economy in which market forces operate and the price mechanism determines what is produced, how it is produced, and who gets it; there are also some parts of the economy in which the government intervenes. For example, laws might cover the way in which products are produced and sold. There may also be areas of the economy in which the government directly provides goods and services, such as education, health, or the military. The government may provide these products because it wants to keep control of key services—perhaps because of security reasons or because the government wants to make sure that these products are more affordable for people than they would be in the free market. A government that regulates business activity heavily, and provides many goods and services itself, is said to be 'interventionist'; a government that leaves the market more to itself is said to be 'laissez-faire'.

While all countries are mixed economies, they vary in the relative size of the free market compared to the government sector. This depends on the extent to which society wants the government to regulate business behaviour and be responsible for the direct provision of products. All managers will want some intervention—not least to protect themselves against other businesses and unfair competition—but they may want to restrict the extent of regulation, because of the costs of meeting its rules and because it may limit their actions.

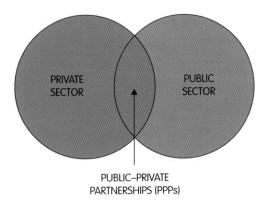

PUBLIC–PRIVATE
PARTNERSHIPS (PPPs)

Figure 2.10 The private and public sectors

Can you now answer questions 2 and 6 from the opening case study?

? **Think about it ...** 2.12

Think about your own economy.

1. To what extent are goods and services provided by the government rather than the free market?

2. Has this balance changed at all over recent years? If so, why do you think this is?

Summary

All economies have limited resources, but their population has unlimited wants. This means that all economies face the problems of scarcity and choice: resources are scarce and so choices have to be made to determine what is made, how it is made, and who gets the product. Choices will involve an opportunity cost. The solution to the fundamental economic questions could, in theory, be via a free market economy, a planned economy, or a mixed economy. In reality, all economies are mixed to some extent.

Checklist

Having read this chapter, you should now understand:

- [ ] what is meant by scarcity and choice;
- [ ] what is shown by the production possibility frontier (PPF);
- [ ] the effect of growth on a PPF;
- [ ] the determinants of the shape of the PPF;
- [ ] the meaning of productive efficiency;
- [ ] the meaning of the law of diminishing returns;
- [ ] the three fundamental economic problems;
- [ ] the differences between the free market, the planned economy, and the mixed economy;
- [ ] the meaning of opportunity cost;
- [ ] the meaning of the output gap.

Case Study Review

Having read this chapter, you should now be able to answer the following questions.

1. According to the above case study, the growth rate of the French economy has been slow. What factors do you think might determine the growth rate of an economy?

2. What do you think is meant by a 'laissez-faire' approach to managing the economy?

3. The French government has decided to invest heavily in transport. Why might other governments not have invested so much in this sector?

4. Apart from transport, what services might you expect a government to provide? Explain your choice.

5. Why do you think the French government's attempts to intervene in computing and banking might have been unsuccessful?

6. Discuss the case for and against government intervention in an economy. Do you think that it would be better to leave an economy to run itself?

7. What do we learn from the case study about external factors that might influence the success of a business?

Short Answer Questions

1. What is meant by scarcity and choice in economics?

2. What are the three fundamental economic questions?

3. What is shown by a production possibility frontier (PPF)?

4. What might cause an outward shift of the PPF?

5. What is meant by opportunity cost?

6. What is meant by productive efficiency?

7. How are resources allocated in the free market?

8. What is the output gap?

9. What is meant by a mixed economy?

10. What problems might occur in a planned economy?

Essay Questions

1. Is 'what to produce' the fundamental economic problem?

2. Discuss the importance of opportunity cost in economics.

3. Is the free market the best solution to the fundamental economic questions?

 One Step Further

Visit our Online Resource Centre at **www.oxfordtextbooks.co.uk/orc/gillespiebusiness/** for test questions, podcasts, and further information on topics covered in this chapter.

Demand

3

Learning Objectives

By the end of this chapter, you should:

- ✓ understand what influences the demand for products;

- ✓ understand why you should be interested in the demand for products;

- ✓ understand how an understanding of the concept of elasticity of demand can help you in your business decision making;

- ✓ understand what actions you might have to take if demand changes.

Case Study—Fountains Fall

Alan Ceranti, the managing director of Fountains Construction plc, is looking at the company's latest sales figures. The business has been growing rapidly over the last few years. It has found good locations in the north-west to build houses and apartments, and it has acquired a reputation in the region for high-quality premium properties. Market conditions in the last few years have been favourable and the properties have sold quickly. Money has been reinvested in the business to finance further growth and this has been supported by extensive borrowing.

But Alan is seriously worried by the company's latest sales figures. Sales are down 30 per cent and the business is sitting on a large number of unsold finished properties, as well as many others under construction. Worse still, UK property prices are down 8 per cent on average on last year and the number of mortgages being taken out is at its lowest for ten years. The company's share price has fallen 40 per cent in the last three months and investors are demanding that action is taken.

Questions

1. Why do you think the demand for houses and apartments might have fallen so significantly?

2. How sensitive do you think demand for houses and apartments is likely to be in relation to changes in price?

3. How sensitive do you think demand for houses and apartments is likely to be in relation to changes in income?

4. What do you think the possible effects of the 30 per cent fall in sales might be on Fountains Construction plc?

5. What do you think determines the share price of a company such as Fountains Construction plc?

6. What actions do you think Alan should take in this situation?

Introduction

A great deal of economic analysis focuses on how markets work. If resources are limited relative to individuals' wants, markets develop to determine who gets what for what price. Whether these are individuals offering to barter different products and services to exchange goods, buyers and sellers haggling in a street market, customers and sellers meeting online, prisoners trading items in jail for cigarettes, or consumers shopping on the high street, economies are made up of millions of markets. And every one of us is operating in many of these markets throughout our lives either as a buyer or a seller. For example, you will have chosen one university and course from among thousands of other options in higher education, and you will have chosen this rather than full-time work. You are a buyer in this market and the university is a seller. In a few years' time, you will enter the job market, where you will want to supply labour and will want to find someone to employ you; you will then be trading in the labour market. Once employed, the organization for which you work will be selling its services in a marketplace competing against other providers for customers—another market. Outside of work, you will choose how to spend your income and be a buyer in many different markets, such as the housing market, the transport market, the food market, and the clothes market. All around us there are buyers and sellers exchanging goods, services, and even ideas, and you are part of many of these yourself.

In this chapter, we focus on the factors influencing demand. We then examine supply in Chapter 4 and bring the two sides of the market together in Chapter 5.

Understanding demand

The success of any business depends on its ability to the meet the needs of its customers. According to Drucker (1954), 'there is only one valid definition of business purpose: to create a customer'. A film company must produce movies that people want to watch; an airline must offer the right combinations of routes, times, and fares to attract passengers; a car manufacturer must produce an engine, a design, and an image that will appeal to potential buyers; and a band needs to make a sound that gets people to download. Whatever you do, whether you manage an insurance business, university, or leisure centre, you need customers to choose your products if you are to survive. To make sure that you win and keep customers, you need to understand what they are willing and able to buy. It is not enough for customers to want a product (after all, there are many things that we want, but cannot have); they also need to have the purchasing power to buy it. This is known as 'effective demand'.

Finding out what people want and how much they can afford to buy is the role of market research. Research gathers and analyses data that is relevant to the marketing function, and helps a business to understand the drivers of demand for its product. One of the key roles of the marketing function in a business is to provide information on existing and potential customers to help to ensure that the business provides what customers want, while also meeting the needs of the organization (not forgetting that it will probably want to make a profit). Marketing therefore acts as the link between the customer and the operations of the business.

As a manager, you will want to understand what influences the demand for your product, so that you can plan how best to control it and anticipate changes in it, so that you can be ready to take appropriate actions. If you know that demand is going to fall, for example, you may want to consider issues such as your staffing levels and how much stock to reorder; you may also want to delay any expansion plans.

Without demand, there are no customers; this means no revenue and no profit. Every year, thousands of businesses have to shut down because they are not meeting their customers' needs. In July 2007, for example, Kwik Save, a UK supermarket, was forced to close down due to a lack of demand; since 1993, its market share had fallen from 7.5 per cent to less than 1 per cent of supermarket spending. As Kotler (1983) says: 'Companies produce what the consumers want and in this way they maximize their customer satisfaction and earn their profits.' If they fail to do this, they fail.

? Think about it ... 3.1

1. Why is it not enough to consider what customers *want* to buy when trying to measure the demand for a product?

2. Managers are not always aiming to increase demand; sometimes they might want to decrease it. When might this be the case?

Marketing and demand

Your potential customers will have a given income at any moment in time and will have to decide how to allocate this between a variety of goods and services available. Imagine a student, who has a weekly allowance or grant of £200: he or she will have to make decisions on how best to spend this. This involves thinking about what types of product to buy, such as books, food, rent, films, and clothes. It also involves decisions about which specific products to buy: which newspaper title should he or she buy? Where should he or she eat? Which DVDs should he or she watch? Your aim as a manager is to get customers to choose your product rather than that of a competitor; the aim of the customer, we assume, is to maximize his or her welfare (or utility).

A customer's choice of whether or not to buy your product (as opposed to that of your rival) will depend on many factors, some of which are under your control and some of which are not.

The factors that you can directly influence include your marketing activities. These can be summarized using what is known as the '4Ps' of the marketing mix (McCarthy, 1960).

- *Price* Obviously, given a limited income, the price will influence what is affordable and how much money is left for other items. How much did you pay for this book, for example? Would you have bought it if it were twice as expensive? Companies will have to think of pricing points in a market that they are targeting relative to the benefits that the product provides, and the products and prices of competitors.

- *Product* This will include the tangible factors relating to the product, including its specifications, quality, and design. You might choose a particular television because of the size or depth of its screen, for example. The product also includes intangible factors, such as the brand image, the after-sales service, and the guarantees provided. Presumably, you bought this book because you think that it covers the material that you need for your studies: was your decision affected by the design? The layout? The number of pages? The support material? The reputation of the publisher? The online material?

- *Promotion* This refers to the messages that the producer gives out about its product and the way in which the business communicates these messages (for example, via advertising, public relations, or a sales force). What made you buy this book? Was it recommended to you? Did you see an advert? What message about the book appealed to you most?

- *Place* This refers to the distribution of the products. How accessible is it to the customers? One of the strengths of Coca Cola, for example, is that it is so widely distributed, that you can easily find it whenever you are thirsty. One of Coca Cola's aims is to be within 'an arm's length of desire'. Where did you buy this book? How far would you travel to find a bookstore that stocked it? If it was not available in your nearest bookstore or online, would you have bought it?

The combination of factors such as the price, promotion, product, and place all influence how much customers are likely to want to buy your product and whether they can afford it. By changing these elements of the marketing mix, managers hope to shape, influence, and control demand.

Of course, this model can be extended to include other factors that can influence customers' buying decisions, such as:

- the physical environment—customers may choose a restaurant or cafe because of the nature of the store;

- the people—customers may choose some stores because of the expertise or helpfulness of the assistants;

- the process—customers may choose a drive-through because of the ease of service.

? *Think about it ...*   3.2

1. The demand for *Harry Potter* products has been very high around the world in recent years. Discuss the ways in which the marketing mix has been used to sustain this demand.

2. Do you think that marketing can create demand?

>> *You Decide ...*

Imagine that you are the managing director of the Burger Paradise, a UK chain of fast food outlets. Sales have been falling in recent years due, in part, to greater concerns about health and diet.

1. What marketing actions do you think that you might take to boost demand?

2. What do you think will determine the effectiveness of such actions?

Price and demand

Price is an important element of the marketing mix (just think how often you look at the price tag of an item); a decision facing many managers is, firstly, what price to set, and then, when and whether to change it up or down at a later stage. The importance of price in relation to customers' buying decisions can be analysed using a **demand curve**.

A demand curve shows how much customers are willing and able to buy at each and every price, assuming that all other factors are unchanged. For most products, the demand curve is downward sloping. This is because as the price falls, the quantity demanded by customers increases, and vice versa (see Figure 3.1). Every unit that we consume generates a certain value (utility) for the customer. The drink that you buy when you are thirsty, the meal that you buy when you are hungry, the film that you go to see when you want something to do in the evening, and the club to which you go with friends all generate extra value for which you are willing to pay. According to the law of diminishing marginal utility, each extra unit of consumption generates less additional (marginal) benefit: the second cup of tea consumed in a given period is not as satisfying as the first;

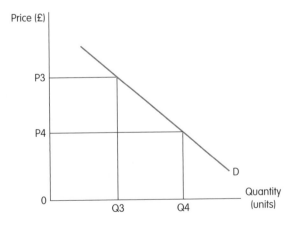

Figure 3.1 Price and quantity combinations

the third sandwich is not as good as the second; and the fifth Mars bar may add little to your well-being. If you are rational and trying to maximize your utility, you will want to consume every unit that you can that generates more value than the price charged, given your budget. With a lower price, there are now more additional units that create value that you think provides benefits that are worth more, or at least the same, as the price that is being charged—that is, the quantity demanded increases.

? Think about it ...   3.3

1. Can you think of anything in relation to which your extra consumption does not fall as you consume more? What would it imply if your extra utility were always to increase with more consumption?

2. If the extra (marginal) utility of consuming a product is falling, but positive, what is happening to your total utility? Could the marginal utility be negative when you consume a unit? If so, what would happen to your total utility?

A change in price is shown as a movement along the demand curve (see Figure 3.2). A lower price usually leads to an increase in the quantity demanded because customers can afford to buy more with a given income and because more units of the product represent value for money at this price relative to alternative products. This is known as an extension of demand. The movement along the curve can be analysed by dividing it into:

- The income effect – which occurs because you have more purchasing power and so can buy more of something if it is cheaper and you have the same income (in real terms your income has increased).

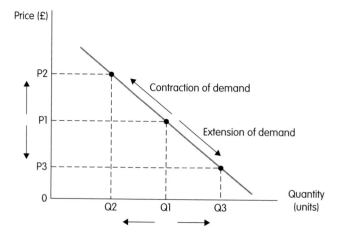

Figure 3.2 Effects of a price change on the demand curve

- The substitution effect – which occurs because with a lower price the product is now relatively cheap compared to other products.

An increase in price will usually lead to a contraction in demand (a fall in quantity demanded); this is because less can be afforded and less units are worth the higher price in the customers' mind.

? Think about it ... **3.4**

Explain the fall in quantity demanded following a price increase using the income and substitution effects.

In some cases, a demand curve may be upward sloping (see Figure 3.3). This could be because the product is perceived to be of a better quality if the price is higher (when faced with an unfamiliar selection of wines, you might decide that the higher priced ones must be better). These products are known as 'ostentatious' goods: customers buy more because they want to be seen buying them, because they are more expensive—a practice known as 'conspicuous consumption' (Veblen, 1949)—and/or because they feel confident that the more expensive products must be better quality.

Another type of an upward-sloping demand curve is known as a 'Giffen good'. Imagine a very low-income family in a poor country, which spends nearly all of its money on rice and, very occasionally, can afford some meat. The rice is essential to live; the meat is a luxury. If the price of rice increases, this will use up even more of the family's limited budget; it may be that the family can no longer afford the meat and so what money is left

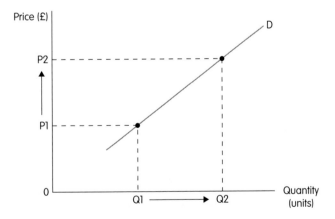

Figure 3.3 Upward-sloping demand curve

?   Think about it ...   3·5

1. A demand curve shows the quantity demanded at different prices, assuming that other factors, such as customers' incomes, advertising, and competitors' actions, stay constant. Why do you think it is important that these factors are held constant when constructing a demand curve? What do you think would happen if they were to change?

2. How important do you think price is when it comes to each of the following?

   A Determining what you eat for lunch.
   B Determining what shoes you buy.
   C Choosing a university.
   D Buying a car.
   E Buying a wedding ring.
   F Buying a birthday present.

3. How might the importance of price affect the way in which each of the above products is marketed?

4. Can you think of times when price has been extremely important to your decision to buy a product and other times when it has not seemed so important? What were you buying and what influenced the importance of price in your decision?

5. Why do you think the relative importance of price might vary from one type of product to another?

6. If a demand curve is downward-sloping, what do you think stops managers from simply cutting price to increase sales?

over, having been spent on the essential quantity of rice, is only enough to buy more rice. The higher price of rice has actually increased the quantity demanded.

Consumer surplus

Consumer surplus shows the difference between what consumers are willing to pay for a unit (which depends on the marginal utility of an extra unit) and the price actually paid.

In Figure 3.4, a consumer is willing to pay P1 for Q1, as shown by the demand curve. For the next unit, it is assumed that there is diminishing marginal utility and therefore the customer is willing to pay only P2. If he or she pays P2 for both units, the customer gains consumer surplus on the first unit, because he or she is willing to pay more for it. As more units are demanded, the price that the consumer is willing to pay continues to fall; if all units are acquired at the same price, there is consumer surplus on all of the units before. At Q3, for example, the shaded area represents the consumer surplus.

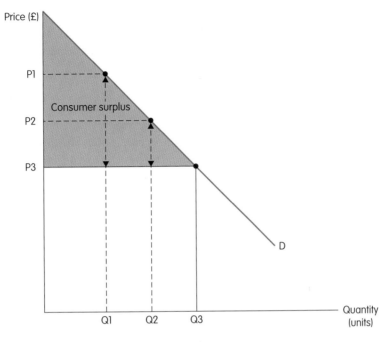

Figure 3.4 Consumer surplus

A consumer will be eager to benefit from consumer surplus because this represents utility for which he or she does not pay. But the ideal for a producer would be to get consumers to pay what they are willing to pay for each unit and thereby remove the consumer surplus. Ways in which this can be done are examined when we consider **price discrimination** in Chapter 9.

To what extent is a change in price likely to affect demand for products?

A demand curve highlights that the amount that customers want, and are able, to buy depends on the price and that a change in price changes the quantity demanded, all other things unchanged. Of course, the sensitivity of demand to price changes varies from product to product; this sensitivity is measured by the **price elasticity of demand**.

The price elasticity of demand measures the extent to which the quantity demanded of a product changes following a change in price, all other things unchanged.

It is calculated using the equation:

$$\frac{\text{Percentage change in the quantity demanded of the product}}{\text{Percentage change in price}}$$

If the change in quantity demanded is greater than the change in price, then demand is said to be 'price elastic'. Imagine that a 10 per cent increase in price leads to a 20 per cent fall in quantity demanded. This means that the price elasticity of demand is:

$$\frac{-20}{+10} = -2$$

The price change has had twice as much impact on the quantity demanded, meaning that demand is sensitive to price. When you see business promotions stressing special offers, winter and summer sales, and discounted products, this clearly suggests that managers think that these products are sensitive to prices.

If the change in quantity demanded is less than the change in price, then demand is said to be 'price inelastic'. Imagine that a 10 per cent increase in price leads to a 5 per cent fall in quantity demanded. This means that the price elasticity of demand is:

$$\frac{-5}{+10} = -0.5$$

The price change has had half as much impact on quantity demanded, meaning that demand is not sensitive to price.

Table 3.1 Price elasticity and demand

Value of price	Elasticity	Effect on demand
0	Totally price inelastic	A change in price has no effect on quantity demanded
<1	Price inelastic	A change in price has a less than proportional effect on quantity demanded
1	Unit elasticity	A change in price has the same proportional effect on the quantity demanded
>1	Price elasticity	A change in price has a more than proportional effect on the quantity demanded
Infinity	Total price elasticity	A change in price leads to an infinite change in quantity demanded

When the price elasticity of demand is zero, it means that demand is totally price inelastic—that is, a change in price has no impact on the quantity demanded. When the value of the price elasticity is <1, demand is price inelastic. (By value we mean the size of the number ignoring the negative sign e.g. –0.5 is less then 1 but –2 is more than 1.) When the price elasticity is 1, demand is unit elastic (that is, a change in price has the same percentage effect on the quantity demanded). When the price elasticity is >1,

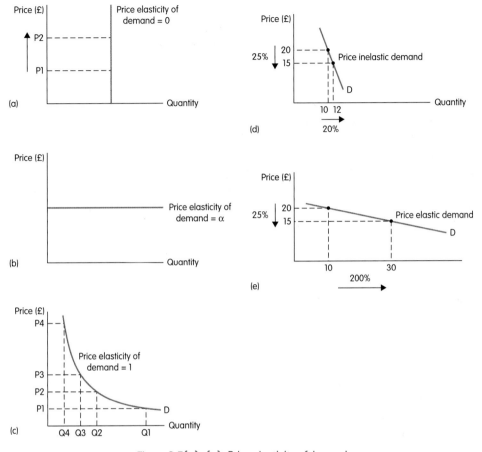

Figure 3.5(a)–(e) Price elasticity of demand

demand is price elastic (e.g. –3 has a value that is greater than 1 because we ignore the negative sign). When the price elasticity is infinity, a change in price has an infinite effect on the quantity demanded.

The concept of the price elasticity of demand is very important to managers who might be considering whether to change the price of their products. For example, they will want to know the likely effect of a short-term promotional price cut on sales, because this will affect the amount of stock that needs to be held, the likelihood of queues or shortages occurring, and whether extra staff may be required to help with sales. The effect of price changes therefore affects all of the different functions of a business, as Figure 3.6 illustrates.

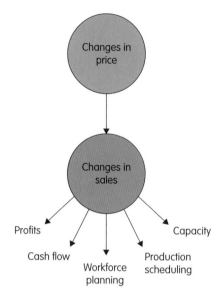

Figure 3.6 The effect of price on other functions

Data Analysis 3.1

1. If the change in quantity demanded is an increase of 8 per cent following a decrease of price of 2 per cent, what is the price elasticity of demand? Is demand price elastic or inelastic? Explain your answer.

2. If the change in quantity demanded is an increase of 8 per cent following a decrease of price of 20 per cent, what is the price elasticity of demand? Is demand price elastic or inelastic? Explain your answer.

Think about it ... 3.6

1. What impact do you think a 1 per cent increase in the price would have on your demand for the following items? Think about why differences might occur.

   A A daily newspaper.
   B A health club membership fee.
   C The television licence fee.
   D The bus fare into town.
   E The price of a sandwich.
   F Car insurance.

2. Do you think that demand for the following is price elastic or inelastic?

   A Emergency plumbers.
   B Children's school clothes.
   C Tickets to music concerts.

Business Analysis 3.1

In 2006, TalkTalk became the first company to offer 'free' broadband (in reality, it was only a low-price offer). It signed up 340,000 customers in the first eight weeks following a big publicity campaign. But things started to go wrong when it could not cope with demand. At one point, up to 200,000 people were waiting for their broadband connection. Thousands were left without a service for months as TalkTalk struggled to get them online and, even when they were connected, many suffered frustrating problems.

1. How might the concept of the price elasticity of demand have helped the managers of TalkTalk when making the decision about whether to lower the price of its services and, if so, how much by?

2. Why might the managers of TalkTalk have had difficulty estimating the price elasticity of demand?

3. What might be the long-term effects for TalkTalk of the problems that it had in 2006?

Data Analysis 3.2

A price reduction from 40 pence to 38 pence increases sales of an energy bar from 200,000 units a week to 210,000 units. Calculate the price elasticity of demand for these bars.

Price and revenue

The **total revenue** that a business receives is called its 'income', 'revenue', 'sales', or 'turn-over'. Out of this income, a business will pay costs; what it is then left with is profit. The total revenue that you earn will depend on the number of products sold and the price of each one. For example, twenty products sold at £10 each generates a revenue of £200.

If demand is price elastic (see Figure 3.7a), a decrease in price will increase the total revenue earned by the business. This is because the fall in the price per unit leads to a bigger proportional increase in the quantity demanded; the increase in sales more than compensates for the lower unit price.

If demand is price inelastic (see Figure 3.7b), a decrease in price will lead to a fall in total revenue. This is because the increase in sales is less than the fall in price (in percentages). If demand is price inelastic, managers can actually increase the price to boost turnover. Although sales will fall to some extent, this is more than offset by the increased price per unit and overall income will increase.

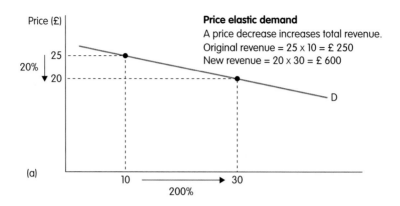

Price elastic demand
A price decrease increases total revenue.
Original revenue = 25 x 10 = £ 250
New revenue = 20 x 30 = £ 600

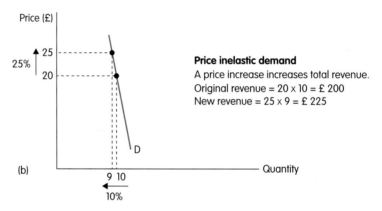

Price inelastic demand
A price increase increases total revenue.
Original revenue = 20 x 10 = £ 200
New revenue = 25 x 9 = £ 225

Figure 3.7(a) & (b) Prices, sales, and revenue

% Worked Example

Last year, you were selling membership to your health club at £400 a year. You had 500 members. This year, you wanted to boost sales revenue and so you decided to reduce your membership fee to £360. The number of members has risen to 525.

1. Calculate the price elasticity of demand.

   The percentage change in quantity demanded is:

   $$\frac{+25}{500} \times 100 = +5\%$$

   The percentage change in price is:

   $$\frac{-40}{400} \times 100 = -10\%$$

The price elasticity of demand is:

$$\frac{+5}{-10} = -0.5$$

This is price inelastic (because the value is <1).

2. Calculate the change in total revenue.

The total revenue last year was:

$$£400 \times 500 = £200,000$$

The total revenue this year is:

$$£360 \times 525 = £189,000$$

The change in total revenue is:

$$£200,000 - £189,000 = £11,000$$

3. Explain the link between price elasticity of demand and total revenue.

A fall in price has led to a fall in total revenue, because the demand is price inelastic; the increase in membership does not compensate for the lower membership fee.

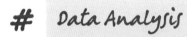 Data Analysis   3.3

1. What would the price elasticity of demand have been in the worked example if membership numbers were to have risen to 800?

2. What would have happened to total revenue?

3. What does this show about price changes, price elasticity, and revenue?

>> You Decide ...

Meg Adams is the marketing manager of Newsfocus plc, a chain of regional newspapers. Sales of the newspapers have been falling and Meg is concerned that she will not hit this year's sales targets. She is considering whether to cut the price or increase the spending on promotion and has asked your opinion.

Which do you recommend? Justify your answer.

How does the price elasticity of demand vary along a demand curve?

The price elasticity of demand will vary at different price points on a demand curve (see Figure 3.8). A customer's sensitivity to a 10 per cent increase in the price of a £1 newspaper may be very different from his or her sensitivity to a 10 per cent increase in a £500 suit. Generally, demand will not be sensitive to price changes at low prices; but at some price points, customers will become more sensitive. This is reflected on a demand curve: demand is more price elastic at higher prices than lower prices.

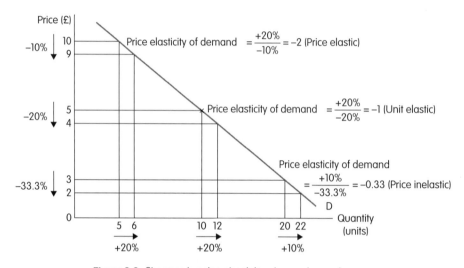

Figure 3.8 Changes in price elasticity along a demand curve

The price elasticity of demand for a product can therefore change and this highlights that managers need to be careful if they keep increasing the price. Demand may originally be price inelastic, in which case, a price increase will lead to an increase in revenue. At some point in a product's life cycle, however, with successive increases in price, demand will become price elastic and revenue will fall.

? *Think about it ...*   3.7

Before making pricing decisions, managers will want to know whether demand is price elastic or price inelastic. How do you think managers could find out whether demand for their product is going to be price elastic or price inelastic?

Business Analysis   3.2

For many years, it seemed as if demand for fuel and coffee were price inelastic. But US$4 seems to be the price at which demand becomes price elastic for coffee. On 1 July 2008, Starbucks announced that it was closing another 500 stores in the USA in addition to the 100 already announced; it was also reducing its workforce by 172,000 (around 7 per cent). Customers are moving away from the high prices at Starbucks for its premium coffee.

The share price at Starbucks in 2008 was one third of its peak two years before. As well as closures, the company is reacting by retraining, greater emphasis on cleanliness and comfort, and new products, such as smoothies. The company is also looking at improving its food and introducing a loyalty card.

1. What effect do you think it would have on Starbuck's marketing if demand for coffee were to have become more price elastic?

2. What factors do you think will determine the long-term success of Starbucks?

Table 3.2 Summary of price elasticity of demand

	Value	Effect on revenue of a price increase	Effect on revenue of a price decrease
Price inelastic	<1	Rises	Falls
Price elastic	>1	Falls	Rises

Determinants of the price elasticity of demand

Ultimately, the sensitivity of demand to a price change depends on how much the product is needed and how easily customers can switch away to something else. The more that customers think you are offering something that provides them with a real benefit that cannot be provided easily in another way, the more price inelastic demand will be. San Pellegrino is not only bottled water: it is bottled water chosen by the very best restauranteurs. Jack Daniels is not only bourbon: it is bourbon that has been distilled for at least twelve years. If, however, you offer something that customers think they can easily get somewhere else, then demand will be sensitive to price. An increase in your price will lead to a relatively large fall in quantity demanded as they switch to competitors. This is why companies work so hard to convince you of their unique selling proposition (USP) to lock you in and make you less sensitive to price, because, in your mind, 'there is no alternative'.

The price elasticity of demand therefore depends a great deal on the marketing activities of a business and the way in which a product is perceived. If a Sony product is seen as reliable and innovative, demand may be price inelastic. If you trust Hilton hotels, admire the Body Shop, feel warm about Google, respect Mont Blanc pens, respect Harvard University, and admire Nike trainers, then these products are likely to be price inelastic. The greater the perceived uniqueness and the greater the brand loyalty, the more price inelastic is demand. Apple users often claim that their products are significantly different from other brands in terms of design, user-friendliness, and 'cool'; this makes demand price inelastic. If, by comparison, there are lots of alternative products that you rate as highly, demand is likely to be price elastic.

The value of the price elasticity of demand therefore depends on factors such as the following.

- *The product itself* Does it offer something that people want and is it perceived to be unique in some ways? Newly developed drugs are often expensive, because they are protected in law by a **patent** and so, if hospitals want it, they have to pay quite a lot; demand will be price inelastic if the product is effectively patented.

- *The availability of* **substitutes** The more of these there are, the more price elastic is demand. A substitute may be a rival product that performs the same function (for example, a Toshiba laptop versus an HP laptop) or a product that is chosen instead of yours (for example, a Playstation rather than a bicycle as a Christmas present for your child). Managers may try to make it difficult to compare products to make demand price inelastic: try to work out the best mobile deal and you can see the problems of comparing **tariffs**, due to an enormous variety of offers, deals, and different features. But if a business thinks that it can win by offering a lower price, it will try to make comparisons easier to encourage customers to change to it. The food retailer, Tesco, for example, highlights which of its prices are cheaper than those of its rival, Aldi.

 Business Analysis   3.3

Speedo's LZR swimsuit was introduced in February 2008. Thirty-eight of the forty-two world swimming records that have been broken since then have gone to swimmers wearing LZRs. The product is very innovative. The new suit is cut from a densely woven nylon-elastane material that compresses the wearer's body into a hydrodynamic shape, but which is extremely light. There are no sewn seams, because the suit is bonded by ultrasonic welding. Seams act as speed bumps in the water. Ultrasonic welding removes 6 per cent of the drag that would otherwise occur.

The suit also has what Speedo calls an 'internal core stabiliser'—that is, something like a corset that holds the swimmer's form. As a swimmer tires, his or her hips hang lower in the water, creating drag. The LZR not only lets the swimmer go faster, because it maintains a tubular shape, but also allows him or her to swim for longer with less effort.

Drag is further reduced by polyurethane panels that have been placed in spots on the suit. The LZR was designed using a three-dimensional pattern rather than a two-dimensional one. It hugs a swimmer's body like a second skin; when it is not being worn, it does not lie flat, but has a shape to it.

The results are a suit that costs US$600 and takes 20 minutes to squeeze into. Some analysts believe that the LZR improves performance by as much as 2 per cent—a huge leap considering that tenths of a second may mark the difference between first and fourth place.

Concern over the effect of the suit on swimmers' performance has, however, led to it recently being banned from some competitions.

Sources: *The Economist*, 12 June 2008, *Telegraph*, April 2008, www.speedo.com

1. Do you think that demand for the LZR is likely to be price elastic or price inelastic? Justify your answer.

2. How might this value for the price elasticity of demand change over time? Why?

3. How might an understanding of the price elasticity of demand affect the decisions made by the managers of Speedo?

4. Do you think that it is fair for a swimmer to compete wearing a LZR suit?

- *Switching costs* Changing from one product to another may involve switching costs (for example, a fee to change mortgage providers, the time taken to organize a new Internet provider, the costs of transferring your videos onto DVD, the time and effort needed to learn the features of a Mac compared to a PC, and the time needed to find out about and compare alternatives). The greater these costs are perceived to be, the greater the incentive is to stay put and continue with your existing products, making demand price inelastic.

- *Time* Over time, you have more opportunities to find substitutes, to research and test them, and to be sure that they will do the job properly. You also have time to organize a switch from one to the other, which makes demand more price elastic.

- *Who actually pays for the product* The demand for business travel on trains and planes is very price inelastic, because the businesses, rather than the individuals, tend to pay. This means that the individual is not particularly concerned about the price and so the providers can increase it. That is why business class or first-class tickets cost so much more than the standard fare.

- *The percentage of income spent on a product* If customers do not spend much on your product, they may be less sensitive to price, because it will have less effect on their overall spending power: a doubling in the price of chewing gum, for example, would not increase our overall spending considerably. How much would you be affected by a 5 per cent increase in the price of milk or sugar? What about your rent or your tuition fees?

?   *Think about it ...*   3.8

1. What is likely to be the difference between the price elasticity of demand for a category of product (such as chocolate) and a particular brand of chocolate (such as Mars)? Explain your answer. (Note: Think about how easy it is to find a substitute for a brand compared to the product as a whole.)

2. What effect do you think the following actions are likely to have on the value of the price elasticity of demand for your product?

   A Heavy investment in branding.
   B The launch of a rival product by a competitor.
   C A very favourable rating in a magazine.

3. Imagine that you are given £1,000: for what three things might you use the money? (Note: These alternatives are substitutes for each other even if they are very different products.)

Can you now answer question 2 from the opening case study?

What is the 'ideal' price elasticity of demand for a product?

The 'ideal' price elasticity of demand depends on what you are trying to achieve and how you want to market your product. In many cases, managers may want the demand for their products to become less sensitive to price. If you can make customers perceive that your product is different from that of the competition—that is, if you can make them think that there is something special about what you offer—the price becomes less significant and demand becomes more price inelastic. By promoting the particular features of your product, by highlighting how different it is from competitors, or by developing something that meets the customers' needs more precisely than anything else, you can make customers less sensitive to the price. They are buying the brand and the experience.

This type of strategy is known as a 'differentiation strategy' (Porter, 1985): 'we deliver pizzas more quickly'; 'we use only organic products'; or 'we use only local suppliers'. In this situation, managers want demand to be price inelastic, enabling them to increase the price of their products: a Starbucks is not only a coffee, an iPhone is more than a mobile phone, and Chanel No. 5 is not only a nice smell.

An alternative approach to marketing is to focus on a low-cost approach. Companies such as Primark and Ryanair have gained market share by offering products at a low price relative to competitors. In this case, managers would want demand to be price elastic—that is, they would want any cut in price to lead to a bigger increase in price (in percentages). Companies such as Poundstretcher, TK Maxx, Superdrug, and Ikea all compete using a relatively low price as a factor, and therefore would want demand to be sensitive to price.

Business Analysis 3.4

A gourmet coffee blended from animal droppings is being sold at a London department store for £50 per cup. Jamaican Blue Mountain and the Kopi Luwak bean are used to create Caffe Raro, which is thought to be the most expensive cup of coffee in the world. Kopi Luwak beans are eaten, then passed, by the cat-like Asian palm civet and sell for £324 a kilogram.

1. What do you think the value of the price elasticity of demand might be for Caffe Raro? Justify your answer.

2. How do you think this compares with the price elasticity of demand for other coffees? Why?

The ideal pricing strategy for a business therefore depends on the overall marketing strategy. This strategy may well change as market conditions alter. When a product is first launched, for example, it may have a unique feature, such as its design (think of the first Dyson, the Blackberry, the Honda Prius, or the iPhone); this enables the business to charge a high price because demand is price inelastic. The first buyers are known as 'early adopters' in marketing terms and the product may be a 'must have' item for buyers at this stage; in this case, demand is price inelastic and is likely to be set high. Over time, other firms may imitate the product, the original technology may no longer be cutting edge, and demand may become more price elastic. In marketing terms, the product may be entering the 'maturity phase' of its life cycle (see Figure 3.9).

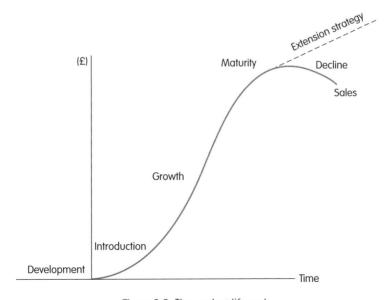

Figure 3.9 The product life cycle

Managers may want to cut the price at the maturity stage of the product life cycle to boost demand; this is known as an 'extension strategy'. When cutting price, the managers will want demand to be price elastic.

>> **You Decide ...**

Imagine that you are the brand manager of Barbie for Mattel. In the last few years, you have been losing market share to Bratz dolls.

Should you cut the price of Barbie dolls?

?   Think about it ...   3.9

Which of the following statements about the price elasticity of demand are true and which are false?

A If demand is price inelastic, a change in price does not change the quantity demanded.

B If demand is price inelastic, a fall in price increases revenue.

C A heavily branded product is likely to be price elastic.

D If the price elasticity of demand is −2, an 8 per cent fall in price will lead to a 4 per cent rise in quantity demanded.

E The price elasticity of demand along a demand curve is constant.

Apart from the price, what else can affect the demand for products?

Changes in the price will lead to a movement along the demand curve and a change in quantity demanded. But this is only one of many factors that might influence the demand for a product. There is, for example, the rest of the marketing mix to consider. Advertising plays an important role in generating many products, such as bottled water and cars, for example. Similarly, improvements in distribution can stimulate demand by making the product more visible. In 2008, Levi Roots won investment, through the *Dragon's Den* television show in his 'Reggae Reggae Sauce'. Sales shot up once he won a contract with Sainsbury's to distribute the sauce, because he was able to access the mass market. The product itself is another key influence on demand: just look at the success of the Apple iPod, the BMW Mini, Lego bricks, Wagamama noodles, or the TetraPak carton.

Business Analysis   3.5

In 2006, Magners cider almost single-handedly brought cider back into the mainstream as a drink in the UK. Sales of cider in the UK grew 23 per cent in 2006 to 965 million pints. The success has been dubbed the 'Magners Effect'—a reference to the brand's Irish owner, C&C Group, promoting its drink as being served poured from a pint bottle, over ice, into a glass. According to the National Association of Cider Makers:

> 'There has been a step change in consumer attitudes ...''Cider is no longer something that you just buy in a two litre plastic bottle ... It's something that you wouldn't be embarrassed to put on the dinner table, offer to guests or take round to the boss's house if he was having a barbeque.

> The target group is the "mature alcopop generation"—people in their 20s who have grown up with sweeter drinks, as being a key new audience for cider makers ... They're attracted by the brands, the adverts with orchards and depicting lazy summers and also by the proposition, especially the cider served over ice. And it's not red or green or blue. They know it's natural.'

Sales of Magners grew 225 per cent in 2006—the first time that it had been sold in England outside of London (having been in Scotland since 2003 and with an established heritage in Ireland). The hot UK summer and the football World Cup helped, along with a promotional campaign costing over £25 million. And because of the way in which it is served (having the ice means that all of the cider does not fit into the glass at once), the bottle generally sits on the table next to the drinker, making the brand highly visible.

'The cider market is not as seasonal as you might think,' said a company spokesman. 'But spring and summer is a very important time in recruiting new drinkers into the brand.'

Sources: BBC News, 'Cider firms look to build on boom', available online at http://news. bbc.co.uk/go/pr/fr/-/1/hi/business/6522855.stm, and www.thismoney.co.uk

1. **Explain how Magners' managers used the marketing mix to increase demand for their product.**

2. **Do you think that demand for Magners is price elastic or inelastic? Explain your answer.**

3. **What do you think will determine the long-term demand for the cider market?**

The demand for a product is also influenced by external factors that a manager cannot control, including the following.

■ *The income levels of the target market*   The ability of the customer to buy a product at any given price depends on his or her income. With more income, he or she has more purchasing power and is able to buy more of a product if he or she wishes. But the impact of higher incomes on the demand for any given product can vary depending on its perceived nature. Some items may be regarded as luxury products; customers may aspire to these and, when their incomes increase by a given percentage, there is a relatively large effect on demand (think Burberry, Blackberry, Dolce and Gabbana, and Jimmy Choo). Other products may be perceived more as necessities and so demand for them will increase with more income, but not necessarily very much. How much of any pay rise are you likely to spend on additional food flavourings, envelopes, or socks? Some items, known as inferior products, may actually see a fall in demand if income increases, as customers switch to what they regard as better products. If you win the National Lottery, you may find that you switch the moped for an Aston Martin, or a caravan holiday for an all-inclusive hotel holiday, so demand for mopeds and caravans falls as income increases.

Business Analysis   3.6

A survey by Ernst and Young in 2008 showed that UK spending power had fallen 'dramatically' due to a large rise in the cost of living over the previous five years. The average household was 15 per cent worse off than in 2003. After household bills and tax, it found that the typical family had less than 20 per cent of its gross income remaining, compared with 28 per cent in 2003.

Which types of product do you think are most likely to experience falling demand given the data above?

■ *The population size* In marketing terms, the 'population' is the total number of people in the target market. This is not necessarily the same as the whole population of a country; rather, it is the total number of potential buyers. If you can gain access to new regions of the world, the size of your target market could increase, significantly boosting the possible demand for your products. This is why many well-known brands are trying to sell their goods and services in emerging markets, such as China and India. Over 44 per cent of the income of Unilever, the food, household goods, and personal care products giant, now comes from emerging markets. Your target population will also increase if you target a new **market segment**: for example, if you promote your moisturiser at men as well as women, or your aspirins at people with heart conditions, as well as those with headaches.

■ *The time of day, week, and year* Sales of many products will tend to increase in the build-up to Christmas, for example. Sunglasses, travel insurance, and tennis equipment will tend to sell more in the summer. Clothes and music tend to sell more at the weekend; nightclubs will be busier on Friday evenings; and trains and buses will be busy at rush hour.

■ *The actions of competitors* The demand for your product will naturally be influenced by what your competitors are doing. After all, in many markets, you will be fighting for customers and your rivals will be eager to take away your demand. They will try to do this through their own marketing activities: updating products; launching new models; cutting prices; and increasing their promotion. BA and Virgin, for example, have fought very hard for many years to take customers off each other, to the extent that BA was accused in the early 1990s of dirty tricks, such as using Virgin's database to contact its customers with a better offer.

■ *The effects of changes in prices of* **complements** The demand for your products will depend on other products that are linked to yours. A highly successful new computer game designed specifically for a particular console system may boost demand for that system (and vice versa). A fall in the price of contact lenses may increase sales of contact lens solution.

■ *Changes in the law, or changes in government policy or advice* Smoking in public places was banned in the UK in 2007. This led to a surge in the demand for patio heaters as customers were forced to smoke outside. With less smoke inside pubs, the smell of sweat became much more noticeable and so demand from pubs for air fresheners also increased.

■ *The prices of other products* A fall in the price of a substitute product is likely to increase the quantity demanded of this product and reduce the quantity demanded of yours. An increase in the price of a complementary product is likely to reduce demand for this and for your product.

? *Think about it ...* 3.10

Which of the following are likely to decrease demand for your product?

A A fall in the price of a substitute product.

B A fall in the price of a complementary product.

C A decrease in income if your product is a normal good.

D An increase in the size of the buying population.

Shifts in demand

While a change in the price of a product can be shown as a movement along a demand curve, changes in any other factors leads to a shift in demand (see Figure 3.10). There is a change in the quantity demanded at each and every price. An increase in demand is shown by an outward shift in demand: more is demanded at each and every price (Figure 3.10a). A fall in demand is shown by an inward shift in demand: less is demanded at each and every price (Figure 3.10b).

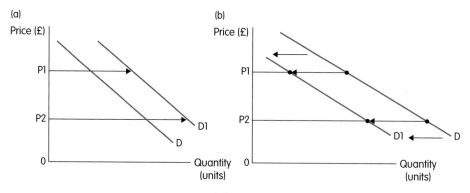

Figure 3.10 An increase (a) and a decrease (b) in demand

 ## Data Analysis: The Music Industry   3.4

- High-street sales of prerecorded music totalled £1,470 million in 2007. This was 29 per cent less than five years before.

- CD album sales dropped from £1,900 million in 2002 to £1,200 million in 2007.

- DVD sales have grown 13 per cent since 2002 to reach £2,100 million.

- Sales of album downloads increased 6,600 per cent to £66 million between 2004 and 2007. Sales of single downloads grew by 1,425 per cent over the same period.

- Specialist stores account for 40 per cent of music and video sales, while supermarkets and websites account for 27 per cent and 20 per cent, respectively.

Source: Adapted from Mintel

1. Discuss the factors that you think might account for the changes in demand within the music industry in recent years.

2. What are the possible implications of these changes for the managers of businesses that produce and sell albums?

 ## Business Analysis   3.7

The price of gold has increased rapidly over the last ten years. Its price has quadrupled since 1999 and, in March 2008, it reached US$1,000 an ounce for the first time ever. With uncertainty in financial markets, more people turned to gold as a 'safe' investment. Worries about whether banks, such as Northern Rock, would be able to pay its savers made people realize that money in banks might not always be there when they want it. As well as this, demand for gold for jewellery remained high. (This demand accounts for about two-thirds of the demand for gold worldwide.)

Figure 3.11 Average annual gold price

Source: BBC 2's *The Money Programme*, 13 June 2008.
Reproduced with kind permission.

What do you think might cause a fall in demand for gold in the future? Explain your answer.

Can you now answer question 1 from the opening case study?

How might a fall in demand affect a business?

A fall in demand for your product might occur for a variety of reasons, such as a fall in income, a fall in competitors' prices, or a fall in the number of people in the buying population.

With a fall in demand, sales are very likely to fall as well. In the short term, you may not take action: you may wait to see if the fall in demand is going to last or not. As a result, stocks may build up as you continue to produce even though demand has fallen. But if you do think that the fall in demand will be sustained, you are likely to try to find ways to get demand to increase again or you might try to reduce costs because of the fall in income to try to maintain your profits.

Actions to boost demand might include:

■ new promotional strategies to make more customers aware of the products;

■ a relaunch of the products aimed at new markets or market segments;

- finding new distribution channels to allow more people to access the products more easily.

Actions to reduce costs might include:

- not replacing staff who leave (and, if necessary, making people redundant);
- delaying new investment projects;
- looking for ways of reducing waste;
- looking to reduce capacity (for example, selling shops or shutting production).

The pressure on managers to take such action depends on how much demand has fallen and the existing financial position of the business.

>> **You Decide ...**

The Inspired Hotel, a four-star hotel near the centre of Oxford, has experienced a fall in demand in the last few months. Typically, over 55 per cent of its rooms are now empty on an average night and, as the manager of the hotel, you are under great pressure to boost profits.

Do you think that you should focus on increasing demand or reducing costs? Explain your answer.

Can you now answer question 4 from the opening case study?

The income elasticity of demand

One important factor influencing the demand for your products is likely to be the level of income of your customers. Changes in income will change demand and so you need to understand the relationship between the two.

The extent to which demand is affected by a given change in income is measured by the **income elasticity of demand**.

This is calculated using the equation:

$$\frac{\text{Percentage change in the quantity demanded}}{\text{Percentage change in income}}$$

Demand is said to be 'income elastic' if the percentage change in quantity demanded is greater than the percentage change in income. For example, if there is a 20 per cent increase in quantity demanded following a 10 per cent increase in income, this means that the income elasticity is:

$$\frac{+20}{+10} = +2$$

Demand is said to be 'income inelastic' if the percentage change in quantity demanded is less than the percentage change in income. For example, if there is a 2 per cent increase in quantity demanded following a 10 per cent increase in income, this means that the income elasticity is:

$$\frac{+2}{+10} = +0.2$$

In most cases, the demand for a product will increase with more income: hence the positive answer. But it is possible that demand might fall as customers switch to a more luxurious product: for example, there might be a fall of 20 per cent in quantity demanded when income increases by 10 per cent. In this case, the income elasticity of demand would be:

$$\frac{-20\%}{+10\%} = -2$$

Even though the number is negative, demand is still income elastic, because the change in quantity demanded is greater than the change in income (hence the value of 2).

If demand does fall with more income, the product is known as an **inferior good**. If demand increases with an increase in income, this is known as a 'normal good'. If demand is very sensitive to income (that is, a high value for the income elasticity), the product is known as a 'luxury product'. If demand is not very sensitive to income (that is, a low value for the income elasticity of demand), the product is known as a 'necessity product'. Following an income increase, the demand curve for a luxury good will shift more to the right than for a necessity; demand for an inferior good will shift to the left (see Figure 3.12).

The effects of an increase in income on different types of product is shown on an Engels curve (Figure 3.13).

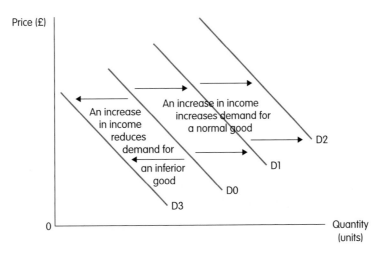

Figure 3.12 Income elasticity and shifts in demand

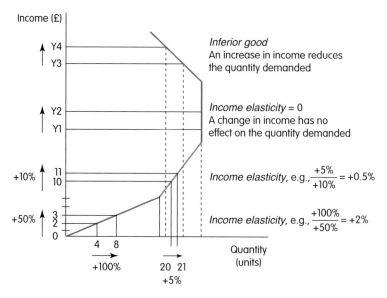

Figure 3.13 Example of an Engels curve

 Business Analysis 3.8

General Motors saw a fall in car sales in the USA of 30% in May 2008. This contrasts directly with Russia where the high oil prices have encouraged significant economic growth. Cars are no longer a luxury item in Russia and car ownership is growing quickly. Sales of new cars in Russia grew 36 per cent in terms of volume in 2007.

Interestingly, whilst sales of foreign car producers have increased to meet the growing demand, sales of Russian brands have actually stayed flat.

Sources: *The Economist*, 5 June 2008,
European Environment Agency, www.gm.com

Vroom

Russian passenger-car market, sales, m

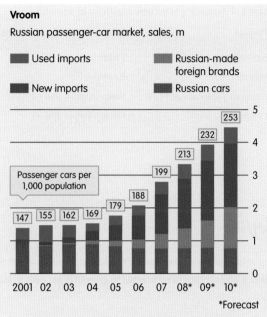

Figure 3.14 The russian passenger-car market

Source: *The Economist*, 5 June 2008.
Reproduced with kind permission.

1. If incomes in Russia are growing relatively quickly, what other products would you expect to experience a rapid increase in sales as well as cars?

2. Which products do you think might experience a fall in demand in Russia in the circumstances described above?

Data Analysis 3.5

1. If income levels increase from £20,000 to £24,000 and sales of your furniture increase from 300 units a week to 330, what is the income elasticity of demand?

2. If the income elasticity of demand is +0.1 and incomes increase 20 per cent, how much would the quantity demanded increase? If sales were originally 400 a week, how much would they be after the income increase?

3. If income levels increase from £20,000 to £24,000 and sales of your furniture fall from 300 units a week to 270, what is the income elasticity of demand?

Table 3.3 Summary of income elasticity of demand

Product	Income elasticity of demand
Normal product	Positive
Inferior product	Negative
Necessity and normal	Value positive and <1
Luxury and normal	Value positive and >1

Data Analysis   3.6

What do the following values of the income elasticity of demand tell us about the impact on the demand for the product if an economy is forecasted to grow at 3 per cent a year?

A +2.

B −2.

C 0.1.

Can you answer question 3 from the opening case study?

Why is the income elasticity of demand important to a manager?

If you can estimate the income elasticity of demand for your products, you can forecast the impact of expected changes in income. For example, if the income elasticity of demand for a product is +2 and an increase in income of 3 per cent is forecast, then you can expect an increase in the quantity demanded of 6 per cent. Based on this, you can order supplies, organize staffing, and decide whether this new level of demand is sufficient or whether you want additional promotions to boost sales further.

Marketing managers should therefore consider the income elasticity of their different products and consider the income growth in different regions; this may then lead to changes in the marketing approach. Imagine that you produce income elastic products, such as the latest washing machines and dishwashers: the fast economic growth in recent years of regions such as Brazil, Russia, India, and China (BRIC) would be appealing and may be a focus on future growth plans; if you were operating another country that was experiencing slower growth, you may change your product mix to concentrate on more basic, cheaper models that are less sensitive to income growth. Supermarkets, such as Tesco, have different ranges of products to meet different economic conditions. When incomes are growing fast, sales of the 'Tesco Finest' range will increase; when incomes are falling or growing slowly, the 'Tesco Value' range will do better.

Business Analysis 3.9

In one sense, food is recession-proof, because people have to eat whether the economy is doing well or not. Also, over the past thirty years, the share of food in US and European household spending has fallen from an average of 30 per cent to less than 10 per cent, so consumers do not care about price increases as much as they did in the past. But while we still need to eat, we can change what we eat, and where we buy it and eat it.

Those best positioned to weather an economic downturn include multinational companies with diversified customer bases, such as Nestlé, Unilever, and Danone, as well as retailers that focus on low prices, such as the US company Wal-Mart. Among the losers are upmarket grocers, such as Whole Foods Market, a firm based in Texas that specializes in fancy, often organic, food.

In response to the fall in incomes, many companies have been looking for cheap versions of their products to offer customers. In 2008, in response to a slowing economy, McDonald's responded by coming up with a menu of items that cost only US$1. Wendy's and Burger King followed suit, and offered double cheeseburgers for US$1. Starbucks introduced a US$1 coffee.

Can you think of examples of products that you think will not be sensitive to a fall in income in the economy?

 You Decide ...

You are eager to make your chain of clothes shops less vulnerable to changes in income in the economy. How might you do this?

The cross-price elasticity of demand

All businesses face competition. This means that you must be aware of what your rivals are doing and appreciate that your decisions will be affected by competitors' actions. This includes the effects of competitors changing their prices. At the same time, you must monitor changes in prices of products that are related to yours, because these will also have an impact on your demand.

Imagine that a customer is looking to buy a new digital camera: that customer is likely to look around at the various options, and compare models and prices. If a competitor offers a similar product at a lower price than yours, this is likely to reduce your sales; if the price of a complementary product falls, this might stimulate demand for your product. Lower prices of digital cameras may stimulate demand for photo printers, for example.

The extent to which your demand is sensitive to a change in the price of another product is measured by the **cross-price elasticity of demand**.

The cross-price elasticity of demand is calculated using the equation:

$$\frac{\text{Percentage change in the quantity demanded of product A}}{\text{Percentage change in the price of product B}}$$

If the price of another product increases and demand for your product increases, then the two products are substitutes: customers are switching from that product to yours (think Pepsi and Coca Cola, Haagen Dazs and Ben and Jerry's ice cream, or Mars and Kit Kat chocolate bars). The answer to the calculation will be positive, because the increase in the price of product B leads to an increase in quantity demanded of product A.

For example:

$$\frac{+20\%}{+10\%} = +2$$

The size of the answer (in this case, 2) shows the strength of the relationship. In this case, the products are fairly close substitutes, because an increase in the price of product B has twice the effect on the quantity demanded of product A.

Table 3.4 Summary of cross-price elasticity of demand

Product	Cross-price elasticity of demand
Substitutes	Positive
Complements	Negative

 Business Analysis   3.10

In 2008, the major UK supermarkets announced price offers to defend themselves against the discount stores, such as Aldi and Lidl, which have been growing in popularity. Asda announced that it was selling ten staple items, such as bread and eggs, for 50 pence; Tesco announced that it was cutting the cost of 3,000 items on Monday.

A business analyst said:

> In a competitive environment, they have to be aggressive in terms of pricing. If consumers
> have got less money in their pockets, they spend more money in discount supermarket
> groups. There is pressure on the major supermarket groups to compete with that.

But discount stores still only have a tiny market share. For example, Aldi has a 2.6 per cent
market share compared with Tesco, which has a 31 per cent market share.

1. What would you imagine to be the likely value of the cross-price elasticity between Asda and
   Tesco? Explain your answer.
2. Apart from price, what other activities do the supermarkets use to compete with each other?

If, however, the products were complements, the cross-price elasticity of demand would
be negative. An increase in the price of coffee-making machines might lead to a fall in
demand for coffee beans, for example. The size of the answer again shows the strength
of the relationship.

For example, if a 10 per cent increase in the price of product B leads to a 20 per cent
fall in the quantity demanded of product A, the cross-price elasticity is:

$$\frac{-20\%}{+10\%} = -2$$

In this case, the two products are quite close complements, because a price change for
product B has twice the effect on the quantity demanded of product A.

An example of the significance of substitutes and complements is given by Frank
(2008). Frank points out that many pubs and bars charge for water, but not for peanuts.
The reason is that peanuts are a complement for beer and spirits: by getting you to eat
more of these (which are usually salty), you will consume more alcohol—that is why they
are given away. Bottled water, however, is a substitute for alcohol and so bars charge for
this, otherwise they will lose income.

% Worked Example

The Bengal Tiger and the Old Curry House are two Indian restaurants on the high street of a large
town in south-west England. Last week, the Bengal Tiger introduced a special mid-week discount
that reduced the average price of a meal from £20 per person to £18. The number of customers
on that evening at the Old Curry House has fallen 20 per cent.

The price change at the Bengal Tiger is:

$$\frac{-2}{20} \times 100 = -10\%$$

The cross-price elasticity of demand for the Old Curry House is:

$$\frac{-20\%}{-10\%} = +2$$

This means that the products are substitutes (because a decrease in the price of one decreases demand for another) and closely related (because the change in quantity demanded is twice the change in price).

Data Analysis   3.7

1. Product A has increased in price from £2 to £2.50. Sales of your product have fallen as a result by 5 per cent. What is the cross-price elasticity of demand? Are the products complements or substitutes? Explain your answer.

2. The cross-price elasticity of demand for two products is −2. What is the effect on the quantity demanded of one if the price of the other decreases by 4 per cent?

Business Analysis   3.11

In Asia, the video games industry often gives away the software required for video games as a free download and users can therefore play for nothing. Revenue comes from small payments that eager players can pay to buy extras for their games, such as weapons. These devotees finance the game for everyone else. Meanwhile, PlayFirst, a San Francisco games business, has released *Diner Dash: Hometown Hero* and *Habbo*. *Diner Dash* is a game that involves setting up a chain of restaurants and allows players to buy extra levels, clothing, and decoration. *Habbo* is a 'hangout for teens' that takes the form of a virtual hotel and operates in thirty-one countries; it generates most of its revenue (nearly US$70 million last year) from sales of virtual clothing, furniture, and accessories.

Sources: www.playfirst.com, *The Economist*, 28 June 2008, CBS News May 2009

Can you think of any other businesses that give away an item (or charge relatively little for it) with the aim of making more money from related sales?

Why is the cross-price elasticity of demand important to a manager?

All managers need to scan their environment to understand how changes in the marketing of other products might affect their success. By calculating the cross-price elasticity, managers may understand the relationship between different products more effectively. The relationship may not always be immediately obvious: when one supermarket increased the price of its wine, it found that its sales of cheese also fell; customers who bought wine also ate cheese, and so the products were complements. Understanding these relationships may determine what stores stock and even where they are displayed. Soft drinks and crisps are complements (along with DVDs—think of nights on which you stay in watching a film), and so are often put opposite each other in the supermarket aisles; the close relationship of these products influenced PepsiCo's decision to expand from drinks into crisps.

Equally, the cross-price elasticity will show which products are substitutes. A major substitute for sweets, for example, is top-up phone cards: when children are deciding how to spend their money, they decide between these two products. A substitute for flowers is wine: people buy both as gifts for others. Understanding what is a substitute for your own products may influence how you promote your product, where you promote it, and with what messages.

? *Think about it ...*   3.11

Which of the following statements is true and which is false?

A The cross-price elasticity of demand measures the effect of the change in price of one product on the price of another.

B The cross-price elasticity of demand for two substitute products always has a value of < 1.

C The cross-price elasticity of demand for two complements are negative.

D A cross-price elasticity of +3 means that a 10 per cent increase in the price of the other product increases demand for your product by 30 per cent.

E A cross-price elasticity of demand of −0.8 means that an increase in the price of the other product of 20 per cent leads to a 16 per cent increase in demand for your product.

Other forms of elasticity of demand

The concept of elasticity of demand examines the relationship (or correlation) between the quantity demanded of a product and other variables.

■ The price elasticity of demand measures how sensitive demand is to changes in the price.

- The income elasticity measures how sensitive demand is to changes in income.
- The cross-price elasticity of demand measures how sensitive demand is to changes in the price of another product.

There are, of course, many other factors that can influence the demand for a particular product, such as changes in the temperature, interest rate changes, and the ages of your customers. The amount of boiled sweets consumed in the UK is linked to the amount of car journeys people take, for example.

Managers will want to know the correlation between a specific factor and the demand for their product. and will therefore use the relevant elasticity of demand. The quantity demanded of lager, for example, or the number of visitors to a garden centre, or the sales of sun cream, may be related to the temperature; in this case, the manager of these products may measure the temperature elasticity of demand.

This can be calculated using:

$$\frac{\text{Percentage change in the quantity demanded}}{\text{Percentage change in temperature}}$$

Similarly, managers might want to measure the relationship between the quantity demanded and spending on advertising. This could be measured by:

$$\frac{\text{Percentage change in quantity demanded}}{\text{Percentage change in advertising expenditure}}$$

The concept of elasticity of demand is therefore a powerful concept that can be used in a variety of situations to understand the drivers of demand for your product and the impact on demand as these variables change. Once these changes are predicted, a business can then plan in the different functional areas, such as producing a cash flow forecast, a workforce plan, or a marketing plan.

? *Think about it ...*   3.12

1. Think about the demand for the following products. What do you think are the main factors to which demand is likely to be related?

   A Pensions.
   B Shampoo.
   C Mobile phones.
   D Conservatories.

2. What other types of elasticity other than those mentioned in the text do you think would be useful?

Think about it ...   3.13

Which of the following statements are true and which are false?

A A change in price leads to a shift in the demand curve.

B A demand curve is usually downward-sloping because the quantity demanded rises as price increases.

C A change in income will shift the demand curve.

D A demand curve shows what people would like to buy at each and every price.

E An increase in the price of a substitute product will shift the demand curve for your product outwards.

How much should you care if you lose one of your customers?

The total demand for your product is simply all of the individual demands of customers added together. Diagrammatically, we add together all of the quantities demanded at each and every price (this is known as a 'horizontal summation'). In the same way, if we want the market demand for a product, we add up the demand for all of the individual firms (see Figure 3.15).

If you lose some customers, then there will be less demanded at each price, all other things being equal; this means the market demand shifts to the left. If you operate in a mass market, then the loss of one customer is unlikely to have much impact: one fewer person buying your chewing gum or drinking your smoothie may not affect the total sales very much. But, in some markets, one customer may be very significant indeed in terms of overall sales: if you produce military aircraft and lose an order from a particular government, for example, this may have a big impact.

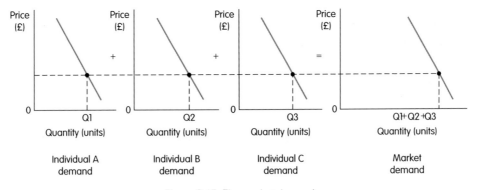

Figure 3.15 The market demand

The demand for a business and the market demand

Figure 3.15 can also be used to highlight the difference between the demand for one firm's products and the total market demand. A manager will be interested primarily in the demand for his or her products and how he or she can influence these. But the demand for all of the businesses combined will make up the overall demand for that product. The actions by one business to shift its own demand outwards—perhaps through a better use of its salesforce or improved packaging—may have relatively little effect on the overall demand in a market. If the effect is simply to take demand away from other businesses, the total demand would stay the same.

Business Analysis   3.12

Last year, BSM, the UK's biggest driving school, replaced its basic vehicle for learners—the Vauxhall Corsa—after signing a deal with Fiat. The Italian firm agreed to provide BSM with 14,000 cars over four years: mainly, its Fiat 500. The switch was a real loss to Vauxhall, because, according to BSM, about 70 per cent of learners buy the same car model as that in which they pass their test. A report said that the Corsa was no longer appealing to BSM's core customer—that is, women in their late teens and early 20s, who wanted to drive a more fashionable car. BSM has about 3,000 driving instructors who are franchisees and teaches more than 130,000 learners to drive each year.

1. If the average price of a Fiat 500 is £8,500, how much might this contract have been worth annually?

2. What might Fiat have offered to win this contract?

Summary

Marketing managers will be very interested in the revenue that they can generate through sales. Often, they will have sales targets; these may be set in absolute terms or as market share (that is, the sales of one product as a percentage of the total market). To achieve a given level of sales, marketing managers must understand the factors that influence the demand for their products and how sensitive demand is to changes in these. Through their marketing activities, they can try to influence the demand for their products.

The concept of the elasticity of demand measures the sensitivity of demand to changes in these different variables. A manager can change some factors, such as the price of the product, to influence demand; other factors, such as income, are not directly under a manager's control. Effective marketing involves not only understanding the influences of demand now, but also preparing for how demand might change in the future.

Checklist

Having read this chapter, you should now understand:

☐ what is shown by a demand curve;

☐ the difference between a movement along and a shift in a demand curve;

☐ the meaning of the price elasticity of demand;

☐ the determinants of the price elasticity of demand;

☐ the difference between price elastic and price inelastic demand;

☐ how demand varies at different prices along a straight-line demand curve;

☐ the relationship between price changes, the price elasticity of demand, and total revenue;

☐ the difference between a substitute and a complement, with reference to the cross-price elasticity of demand;

☐ the difference between a normal and an inferior product, with reference to the income elasticity of demand.

Case Study Review

Having read this chapter, you should now be able to answer the following questions.

1. Why do you think the demand for houses and apartments might have fallen so significantly?

2. How sensitive do you think demand for houses and apartments is likely to be in relation to changes in price?

3. How sensitive do you think demand for houses and apartments is likely to be in relation to changes in income?

4. What do you think the possible effects of the 30 per cent fall in sales might be on Fountains Construction plc?

5. What do you think determines the share price of a company such as Fountains Construction plc?

6. What actions do you think Alan should take in this situation?

Short Answer Questions

1. What is stated by the law of diminishing marginal utility?

2. Distinguish between a change in quantity demanded and a change in demand.

3. Which of the following statements are true and which are false?

   A A reduction in price always leads to an increase in total revenue.

   B Total revenue = Price + Quantity sold.

   C The price elasticity of demand for a downward-sloping demand curve is negative.

   D If the value of the price elasticity of demand is < 1, demand is price inelastic.

   E A price elasticity of −0.5 means that a 10 per cent increase in price leads to a 20 per cent fall in quantity demanded.

4. Which of the following statements are true for a downward-sloping demand curve and which are false?

   A An increase in price will increase revenue if demand is price elastic.

   B The price elasticity of demand is constant along a straight-line demand curve.

   C If the percentage change in quantity demanded is less than the percentage change in price, demand is price elastic.

   D A price elasticity of demand of −1.5 means that a 10 per cent increase in price will lead to a fall in quantity demanded of 15 per cent.

   E If demand is price inelastic, then the quantity demanded will not change with a change in price.

5. Explain two factors that influence the price elasticity of demand.

6. Distinguish between a substitute and a complement.

7. Distinguish between a normal good, an inferior good, and a luxury good.

8. If the income elasticity of demand is +1.5 and the income of a region increases by 20 per cent, and sales were 400 units, what will they be now? Is demand income elastic or income inelastic? Explain your answers.

Essay Questions

1. To what extent do you think that price is the most important determinant of demand?

2. Discuss the ways in which the concept of the elasticity of demand might be of value to the managing director of an international supermarket chain.

3. To what extent is the demand for low-cost airlines under the control of the companies' managers?

 One Step Further

Visit our Online Resource Centre at **www.oxfordtextbooks.co.uk/orc/gillespiebusiness/** for test questions, podcasts, and further information on topics covered in this chapter.

Supply

4

Learning Objectives

At the heart of the free market system are the elements of supply and demand. In Chapter 3, we examined the factors influencing demand. In this chapter, we examine the determinants of supply.

By the end of this chapter, you should:

- ☑ understand the influences on supply;
- ☑ understand the difference between a movement along, and a shift in, supply;
- ☑ understand the price elasticity of supply and factors influencing the price elasticity of supply;
- ☑ be able to explain the effect of an indirect tax on supply;
- ☑ be able to explain the effect of a subsidy to producers on supply.

Case Study

The world is likely to undergo major food shortages in the coming years as supply fails to meet growing demand. The supply of some crops has been affected because they are increasingly being used for biofuel. Biofuel uses the energy contained in organic matter—crops such as sugar cane and corn— to produce ethanol, which is an alternative to fossil-based fuels such as petrol. In an attempt to decrease the use of petrol, some governments have introduced subsidies for ethanol worth billions each year, which have diverted 100 million tonnes of cereals from human consumption. According to Oxfam: 'It takes the same amount of grain to fill a sports utility vehicle with ethanol as it does to feed a person. We don't want any more subsidies for biofuels.'

Meanwhile the chief executive of the UK Biotechnology and Biological Sciences Research Council (BBSRC) is calling for an additional £100 million a year to be spent on food research in the UK to help the world to meet growing demand:

> We have already seen riots in Indonesia and Mexico because of food shortages and what is undeniable is that the amount of food we are going to need to produce to deal with the world's population increases is an extra 50 per cent by 2030 and a doubling by 2050. We are going to have to do it on the same amount of land, because there isn't any more land, so we are going to have to increase agricultural yields to increase supply. We are going to have to do that without increasing the amount of oil-based fertilisers we put in because oil is a finite resource and of course produces greenhouse gases. And we are going to have to use no more water because water is a resource in short supply as well.

Questions

1. What do you think determines the world supply of food in any given year?
2. Do you think that it is easy to change the world supply of food or not? Do you think that supply is sensitive to price or not?
3. What do you think determines the world demand for food in any given year?
4. What do you think will happen to the world price of food if there are shortages?
5. How do you think governments could intervene in global food markets?
6. How do you think the supply of food will be affected by the subsidies for ethanol? Illustrate your answer with diagrams.
7. Do you think that the government should subsidize the growth of crops for ethanol production?

Introduction

Markets are important for managers to understand because that is where they buy their resources and sell their products. One aspect of a market is demand, which reflects what people are willing and able to buy at each price, all other things unchanged. The other element of a market is supply; this reflects what producers are willing and able to produce at each and every price. This chapter focuses on the determinants of, and influences on, supply.

The supply curve

A **supply curve** shows how much producers are willing and able to produce at any price, all other factors unchanged. To produce, suppliers will have to transform resources into the finished product.

Notice the key elements of the definition of a supply curve, as follows.

- It shows the amount that producers not only want to produce, but also are able to produce—that is, simply wanting to produce something is not enough; suppliers must have the capacity and skills to deliver it.

- It highlights changes in quantity supplied in relation only to price changes; it assumes that all other factors are constant. This is because if these 'other factors' change, then a new supply curve will have to be constructed, because more or less will be supplied at each price.

In Figure 4.1, the quantity supplied at P1 is Q1; at a higher price of P2, the quantity supplied is Q2—this is known as an 'extension of supply'. The supply curve is generally upward-sloping, which means that more is supplied at a higher price, all other factors unchanged.

In Figure 4.2, as the price falls from P1 to P2, less is supplied; this is known as a 'contraction of supply'.

A change in price therefore leads to a movement along the supply curve and a change in the quantity supplied.

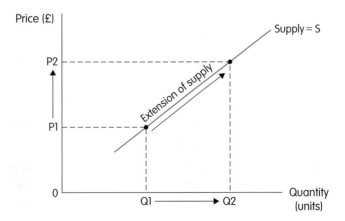

Figure 4.1 A movement along the supply curve—an extension of supply

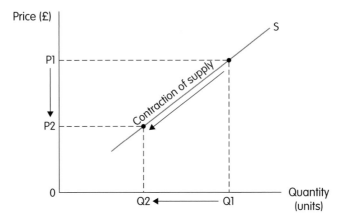

Figure 4.2 A movement along the supply curve—a contraction of supply

Why should a supply curve slope upwards?

To produce more units, a business will have to use more resources. As it demands more resources, the price of these is likely to be bid up, which increases the extra costs of production. This means that a higher price is usually needed to cover the higher extra (or marginal) costs—that is, an increase in the quantity supplied requires a higher price. The higher price means that businesses are able to produce more, because they can afford to cover higher extra costs: for example, if the price increases, oil producers can afford to extract oil from deeper down or in less-accessible locations, even though it is more expensive to do so. This means that, as the price increases, the quantity businesses are willing and able to supply increases and so the supply curve is usually upward-sloping.

The increase in the extra costs of production as more is supplied can also be linked to the law of diminishing returns (see Chapter 2). In the short run, when at least one factor of production is fixed, the extra output of additional variable factors will eventually fall. If each extra worker is less productive, then this has a direct effect on a firm's marginal costs: with less **productivity**, the marginal costs will rise. Imagine that you pay an extra worker the same amount of money as your existing staff, but he or she produces fewer units: this would mean that his or her wages are spread over fewer units of extra output and the cost of these extra units is higher than that of the previous ones. For example, if one extra employee is paid £50 a day and produces fifty units, then the labour cost is £1 a unit. If the next employee is paid £50 a day and produces twenty-five units, the cost of these extra units in terms of labour is now £2. As the productivity of the additional employee falls, the extra cost of the units produced in terms of labour therefore increases, and vice versa; the marginal cost curve is therefore the inverse of the marginal product curve in the short run. Given that the extra costs increase with more output, the price needs to be higher for firms to supply, and the supply curve is upward-sloping.

If, however, the extra costs of production fall with more output—perhaps due to the benefits of mass production—then it may be possible to produce more at a lower price; in this case, the supply curve may not be upward-sloping.

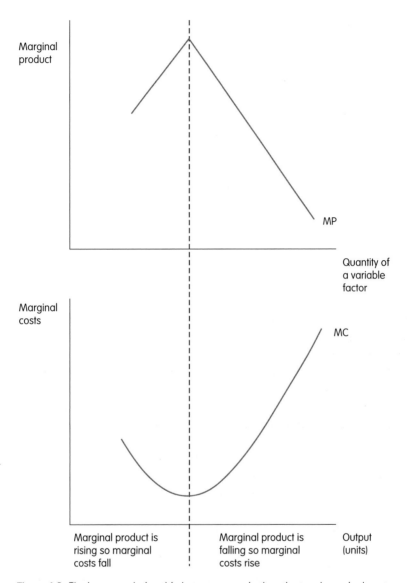

Figure 4.3 The inverse relationship between marginal product and marginal costs

Data Analysis   4.1

An additional employee produces 200 units. The next additional employee produces 400 units. They are both paid £6,000 a week.

Calculate the extra cost per unit in terms of labour as each of these employees is hired.

Producer surplus

As demonstrated in Figure 4.4, the supply curve shows how much a producer will supply at each price, all other factors unchanged. To supply Q1, for example, the supply needs a price of P1. But to supply more output, such as Q2, the supplier needs a higher price P2 to cover the higher marginal costs. If this price is paid on all units, then the supplier has gained an 'excess' on all units up to Q2, known as **producer surplus.**

A producer surplus occurs when the price paid for items is higher than the price for which suppliers would be willing and able to sell them. The customer is paying the price needed to cover the marginal costs of the last unit; this means that he or she is paying more than is needed for the units before creating this surplus for producers.

? *Think about it ...*   4.1

Imagine that you did not pay the same price for all units of the product, but insisted on paying a different price for each one. You bargain hard and pay the price for each unit that the supplier needs to supply it, but no more (that is, you pay the price for each one shown by the supply curve).

A powerful buyer such as this in a market is known as a 'monopsonist'.

What is the producer surplus equal to in this case?

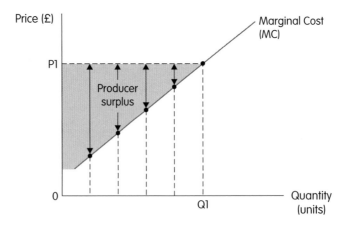

Figure 4.4 Producer surplus

Movements along versus shifts in supply

A change in price leads to a movement along the supply curve. It leads to a change in the quantity supplied. If, however, there is a change in 'other factors' apart from price, this will shift the supply curve (see Figure 4.5). This is because it will change the amount supplied at each and every price.

An increase in the amount supplied at each price (that is, an outward shift in supply) might occur in any of the following situations.

- If there are more producers in the industry—that is, if more firms enter an industry— then this increases the total capacity and shifts the supply to the right. This may occur when profits are high in an industry attracting other firms in from other sectors. For example, the success of organic food in recent years has led to more farmers switching to offer this type of product. The opening up of many international markets due to fewer restrictions on trade has also increased the supply in many markets. Just look at the products on your supermarket shelf to see how firms from all over the world now compete with each other. If, however, there are barriers to entry (for example, if the government limits the number of firms competing in a market, such as postal services), this would restrict the supply. How long it takes for supply to shift will depend on how easy it is to enter the market; with an industry that requires heavy investment, and specialist equipment and expertise, it may take some time for entry to occur.

- If technology improves, then more products can be produced at each price, shifting the supply curve to the right. This can be seen in industries such as car production and the computer industry, in which investment in technology over the years and improved production methods have increased the industry's capacity significantly. Similarly,

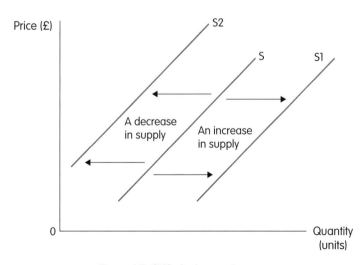

Figure 4.5 Shifts in the supply curve

better farming methods in many economies has meant that more can be produced from the same amount of land.

■ If the costs of producing and delivering the product fall, this means that more can be supplied at any price, which again shifts the supply curve to the right. This could be due to a fall in energy costs, materials costs, components, labour, or even a fall in the cost of borrowing money.

Business Analysis   4.1

An important factor behind the growth of international trade is the development of containerization. This enables products to be moved around the world cheaply on huge container ships. Now that standard sizes and designs have been adopted, products can be placed in containers, transported to the ship, and unloaded at the other end very efficiently. Some container ships can carry over 14,000 20-foot containers with a crew of fewer than fifteen people.

Containerization has reduced costs. What is the effect of this on the world supply of products at each and every price?

? Think about it...   4.2

What do you think might cause an inward shift of a supply curve?

Managers need to consider the supply conditions in the markets in which they operate (both the markets in which they acquire factors of production and those in which they sell) and think about how these might change in the future. A major increase in supply due to the entry of many producers from abroad, for example, would significantly change the market conditions and managers must prepare for this. The specific factors affecting supply will vary from market to market. For example, the primary sector is very dependent on the weather and natural conditions. Supply in these markets is very vulnerable to change: a disease can wipe out a crop and shift the supply curve to the left very significantly, and very rapidly. If you are relying on such inputs for your production, you may need to have contingency plans in case one supplier, or even a group of suppliers in one region, cannot supply you.

>> **You Decide ...**

Some businesses will want to stop others from entering their markets.

1. What actions do you think you might be able to take to stop others coming into your market?
2. Why might you want to do this?
3. Should you be allowed to do this?

 Business Analysis 4.2

Some of the world's largest chocolate-producing countries, such as the Ivory Coast in West Africa, could lose a third of their crop this year because of crop disease. Researchers are trying to map the DNA of the cacao tree to find genes that could be resistant to the most dangerous diseases, such as swollen shoot virus. Around 70 per cent of the world's chocolate comes from West Africa.

In recent years, a greater number of trees have been planted closer together as farmers try to keep up with increased demand and struggle to afford expensive fertilisers. In practice, this has meant that other types of tree, which would normally have grown between the cacao trees, have been cut down. This has encouraged the spread of disease, as has the trend to grow the plants in dry countries far from their native Amazon rainforest, where a lack of water makes them less able to stave off attack. Spread by common mealy bugs, swollen shoot virus is difficult to avoid, and the main defence against its encroachment has been has been to destroy infected trees and create 'firewalls' against the disease.

1. What do you think the consequence of a major crop disease affecting the supply of cocoa might have on businesses such as Cadbury's and Mars?
2. What actions can these companies take to protect themselves against this situation?

? **Think about it ...** 4.3

Which of the following statements are true and which are false?

A A supply curve shows how much producers would like to produce at each price.
B A supply curve shows how much customers want to buy.
C A reduction in costs should shift supply outwards.
D A change in price causes a shift in supply.
Can you now answer questions 1 and 6 from the opening case study?

The importance of labour productivity to supply

A key influence on a firm's costs, and therefore its supply, is the output per worker (that is, labour productivity). Managers are always eager to find ways of increasing the productivity of their workforce, because it can reduce costs and therefore increase the amount that they might want, and be able, to produce at a given price. This would shift the supply curve outwards. Improving productivity is a key operational objective in many organizations.

Methods of increasing labour productivity include:

- better training of employees so that they know exactly what they have to do and have the skills to do it more effectively;

- developing an open business culture within the business, so that employees feel able to contribute and suggest ideas that might lead to productivity gains;

- finding ways of motivating employees so that they try harder. Motivation is likely to depend on factors such as the management style, how jobs are designed, whether employees get feedback, and whether employees are given enough feedback on their efforts;

- greater investment in capital, such as new machinery and technology, which can provide employees with better tools to do the job, and can lead to faster and better quality production. The amount of investment that managers undertake will depend on their ability to raise finance and their expectations of future profits, which, in turn, will depend on their view of the business climate.

 Data Analysis 4.2

Labour productivity measures the output per employee. It can be calculated as:

$$\frac{\text{Output}}{\text{Number of employees}}$$

1. If you employ 200 employees and your output is 8,000 units a week, what is the labour productivity per week?

2. If the weekly wage is £400, what is the labour cost per unit?

3. If productivity increases by 20 per cent what will be:
   A the total output?
   B the labour cost per unit?

4. What does this show us about the relationship between productivity and the labour cost per unit?

Business Analysis 4.3

The UK has a long-standing productivity gap with its main industrialized competitors. French productivity is 29 per cent higher than that of the UK on an output-per-hour-worked basis, while the gap with both the USA and Germany is 16 per cent. On an output-per-worker basis, US productivity is 27 per cent higher than that of the UK, while French productivity is 11 per cent higher and German productivity is the same as that in the UK. The productivity gap with France and Germany has, however, narrowed over the past decade, and on the per-worker basis, the gap has now closed with Germany.

Source: Adapted from Office for National Statistics

1. Why do you think UK productivity in general might be lower than that of some other countries?

2. What are the possible implications of lower productivity for UK firms?

The impact of lean production on supply

As well as increasing productivity, managers will also try to reduce costs in other ways. By reducing costs, they can either make more profits at the same price or supply more. Primark, the low-cost clothes retailer, can only offer such low prices and make a profit by keeping its costs very low. The same is true of organizations such as Superdrug, EasyJet, Asda, and Poundstretcher, which use their low costs as a competitive weapon.

A major movement in operations management in recent years aimed at reducing costs is known as **lean production**. This involves efforts to reduce waste in all of its forms throughout the production process.

Waste can occur in many different ways such as:

■ when you are waiting around for work to be delivered to you;

■ when you have to rework items because they are faulty;

■ when you make too many items and therefore they have to be thrown away;

■ when stock is produced and is waiting around to be sold.

If these forms of waste can be reduced, then costs fall for any level of output and the business is more efficient. The supply curve can therefore shift to the right.

Lean production aims to reduce costs and increase the efficiency of businesses. The lean approach was pioneered in Japan by Taichi Ohno at Toyota and is one reason why Japanese companies have achieved large market shares in many markets, such as cameras,

Business Analysis 4.4

Ryanair was Europe's original low-fares airline and is still Europe's largest low-fares carrier. Ryanair carries over 58 million passengers on more than 800 low-fare routes across twenty-six European countries. It has achieved its success by incurring very low costs that have enabled it to offer extremely low prices to its customers.

Low costs have been achieved by:

- choosing local airports from which to fly rather than the major ones, such as Heathrow, because local airports are cheaper and are less congested, making it quicker to land and take off, wasting less time;

- having flexible staffing arrangements, so that employees have several different jobs, keeping staffing costs low—Ryanair pilots, for example, also tend to fly more hours than the pilots of other airlines and so have high productivity;

- having online booking and no reserved seats to make the booking process cheaper and quicker;

- focusing on short-haul flights, so that the planes can land and return the same day (often several times a day)—meaning that Ryanair does not need to pay for overnight stays for the crew and the plane does not need to sit idle;

- having a culture of keeping costs low throughout the business.

How difficult do you think it would be for other airlines to copy the Ryanair model?

cars, televisions, and consumer electronics: they have been able to offer products with many benefits for relatively low prices, out-competing many of their competitors.

One particular element of waste focused on by Ohno was stock: this was seen as a waste, because it represented materials sitting idle. This led to Ohno developing 'just in time' (JIT) production at Toyota. JIT involves producing to order and holding as little stock as possible.

Holding stock can be expensive because:

- it involves storage and warehousing costs;

- it involves opportunity costs, because money is tied up in the stock rather than earning interest in a bank;

- stock that has been produced may deteriorate or may not sell if demand is not there.

Lean production is also linked to *kaizen*. This is a Japanese word meaning 'continuous improvement' and involves working with employees to find ways of continuously improving the way in which things are being done. This approach believes that gradual incremental change will, if undertaken continuously, add up to major improvements in performance through better quality, but also cost reduction. It requires a positive working relationship between employers and employees, with a sense of them working towards the same goals.

 ## Business Analysis 4.5

The Japanese car company, Toyota, is famous for the Toyota production system. This is an approach that is 'steeped in the philosophy of the complete elimination of all waste and that all aspects of production with this philosophy in pursuit of the most efficient production method'. The objective is 'making the vehicles ordered by customers in the quickest and most efficient way, in order to deliver the vehicles as quickly as possible.' It is based on:

- *jidoka*—an approach that aims to highlight and make any problems visible as and where they occur, so that they can be prevented in future. If a defective part or equipment malfunction is discovered, the machine concerned automatically stops, and operators stop work and correct the problem;

- JIT production—that is, making only 'what is needed, when it is needed, and in the amount needed'.

1. Why might employees resist the introduction of a system like that of Toyota?
2. Why do many businesses have high levels of waste?

 ## You Decide ...

Imagine that you are the managing director of a cosmetics business that sells to leading department stores. Your operations director believes that you should introduce a JIT production process. You are used to holding high levels of stock, so that you can respond to customers' orders and to act as a buffer in case anything goes wrong.

Do you think that you should you now adopt JIT?

The price elasticity of supply

The extent to which the quantity supplied will change in response to a price change is measured by the **price elasticity of supply**. It is shown by the slope of the supply curve (Figure 4.6).

The price elasticity of supply measures the percentage change in the quantity supplied, given a percentage change in price. It can be calculated as:

$$\frac{\text{The percentage change in quantity supplied}}{\text{The percentage change in price}}$$

If supply is 'price elastic', this means that the percentage change in quantity supplied is greater than the percentage change in price—that is, the value of the answer will be > 1. For example, if the quantity supplied increases by 20 per cent following a 10 per cent increase in price, this means the price elasticity of supply is:

$$\frac{+20\%}{+10\%} = +2$$

The value of the price elasticity of supply here is 2, which means that the quantity supplied changes twice as much as the price has changed.

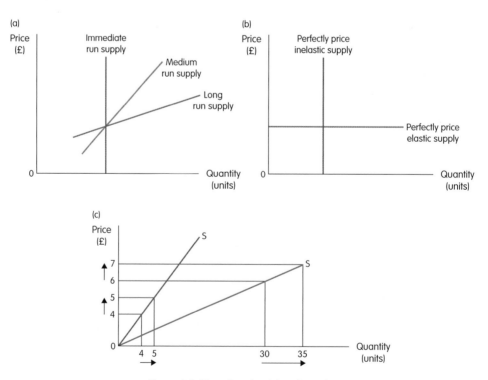

Figure 4.6 The price elasticity of supply

The sign of the price elasticity of supply is usually positive; this is because an increase in the price usually leads to an increase in the quantity supplied, so they have both moved in the same direction, which results in a positive answer. A negative answer would imply a downward sloping supply curve—for example, less was supplied at a higher price— which would be unusual.

If supply is price inelastic, this means that the percentage change in quantity supplied is less than the percentage change in price. For example, if quantity supplied increases by 2 per cent following a 10 per cent increase in price, this means that the price elasticity of supply is:

$$\frac{+2\%}{+10\%} = +0.2$$

Whenever the value of the price elasticity of supply is <1, it means that the percentage change in the quantity supplied is less than the percentage of price—that is, that supply is price inelastic.

 Data Analysis 4.3

1. Imagine that you are a small producer of bracelets and necklaces selling to a big retailer. At an average price of £10, the quantity supplied is 4,000 units a week. If the price increases to £12 and this leads to an increase in the quantity to 4,400 units, calculate the price elasticity of supply.

2. Imagine that you are the producer of homemade cakes to local stores. At a price of £3, you produce 500 a week. The price elasticity of supply is +0.8. How many will be produced if the price offered increases to £4?

Any straight-line supply curve that cuts through the origin has a unit price elasticity: any given change in price (in percentages) leads to the same percentage change in the quantity supplied. Any straight-line supply curve that cuts the X axis is price elastic and any straight-line supply curve that cuts the Y axis is price inelastic.

? **Think about it ...** 4.4

1. What will the value for the price elasticity of supply be if the curve is perfectly inelastic?

2. What will it be if it is perfectly elastic?

Determinants of the price elasticity of supply

The price elasticity of supply measures the ability of a business (or of all businesses in a sector if we are looking at the industry as a whole) to respond to changes in price. This depends on how easy it is to increase resources in the industry to increase output and how much the price has to increase to cover additional costs. If specialist skills and equipment are needed, or if it is a large-scale project, it may take time to increase supply when the price goes up (think nuclear power stations, football stadia, or motorways). This would make supply relatively price inelastic in the short term, compared to something such as the supply of cafes, which these can be set up relatively quickly. Within months, the supply could increase if the rewards were there. Over time, the supply of most products will become more price elastic as more resources are brought in.

If the price elasticity of supply has a value of 0, this means that supply is perfectly inelastic; there is a given amount of supply and this is not affected at all by price changes. This may be the case in the very short run in many industries: businesses cannot suddenly increase output and so supply is fixed. Cinemas, restaurants, and even schools have a limited supply of places at any moment. This can lead to queues and shortages if demand increases because supply is fixed; over time, more resources can be put into these areas and supply can become more price elastic.

If managers face a price inelastic supply in the markets for their resources, this means that increasing the quantity supplied of these inputs may require significant increases in the price paid for them; this would increase the buyer's costs and either squeeze profit margins or lead to an increase in the price of the final product. If specific resources can become available only at much higher prices, managers may look for alternative ways of producing.

?   ## Think about it ...   4.5

Organic food is grown without pesticides. It takes about two years for a farm to adjust from farming methods that use chemicals to be completely clear of pesticides. Up until the recession of 2008, the organic food industry was booming as consumers chose this type of more environmentally friendly and healthy food. But faced with falling incomes and redundancies, consumers look for cheaper options.

1. What do you think will happen to the supply of organic foods when the economy recovers?

2. Do you think that the supply of organic food is price elastic or inelastic? Why?

Can you now answer question 2 from the opening case study?

How can managers make their supply more price elastic?

Managers may want to ensure that they can respond to price changes effectively, that is, they may want to make supply more flexible. Supermarkets would like to be able to handle more or fewer customers according to the number of people visiting the store; airlines need to cope with more passengers at particular times of the year; and car producers have to be able to increase or decrease production according to levels of demand.

Attempts to increase the flexibility of production include:

- using temporary and part-time staff when demand is high—something that is common in sectors such as hotels, leisure, and fruit picking. It enables the labour input to be adjusted more easily to changes in requirements; when less has to be supplied, these staff can be laid off;
- having flexible contracts in which staff can easily be moved from one job to another as demand changes from one product to another—which include annualized-hours agreements under which employees' contracts determine the total number of hours that they will work in a year, while how many hours they work in any given week or month can be varied according to demand, as long as it stays within the total agreed;
- investing in new technology that is flexible enough to switch from producing one product to another easily and so has little 'downtime'.

Companies, such as Zara, have pioneered fast fashion, responding to changes in tastes by producing new clothes lines and getting them into the shops within weeks. By using its own designers, controlling its own production, and having flexible production equipment, it can turn out new designs and clothes very quickly. Each store orders small quantities, which are made just in time; every week, a new order is placed. This means that the company does not get left with stock and does not have to discount to get rid of **surplus** items. Some of Zara's competitors buy months of stock in one go, which may enable bulk discounts, but runs the risk of going out of fashion and being hard to sell. The responsive production system of Zara gives it a competitive advantage. Companies such as Domino's Pizza and Vision Express have also used the speed of their supply systems to gain market share.

The industry supply curve

The supply curve for an industry is the horizontal summation of the supply curves of each of the individual businesses (Figure 4.7). This simply means that it is the sum of all of the amounts that each firm can supply at each and every price. When more businesses enter the market, for example, this means that more is supplied at each price and the industry supply curve shifts to the right.

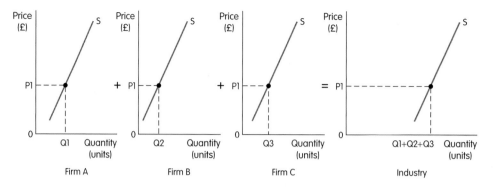

Figure 4.7 The industry supply curve

More firms are likely to come into an industry if:

- barriers to entry are reduced or removed—for example, a government may remove restrictions on foreign goods coming into its country, or developments in technology might make it easier to provide than services (such as online holidays);

- they are attracted by high rewards (or potential high rewards)—for example, the success of Facebook as a social networking site may bring in more providers of this type of service, such as LinkedIn.

Figure 4.7 highlights the difference between the supply of one firm and the total supply in an industry. Actions by managers to shift their own supply to the right (perhaps through investment in capital or more training) may have little effect on the overall supply in the industry if the business is relatively small.

? Think about it...   4.6

Which of the following statements are true and which are false?

A If a supply curve is upward-sloping, the price elasticity of supply is positive.

B If the price elasticity of supply is +0.5, then a 4 per cent increase in price leads to a 2 per cent increase in the quantity supplied.

C An increase in labour productivity should shift the supply curve to the left.

D The introduction of lean production should shift the supply curve to the right.

Joint supply

Some products will be provided together and this is known as 'joint supply'. If you produce more beef, you will also have more hides produced. An increase in supply of one increases supply of the other. This highlights that markets are interrelated—but these links may not always be desirable. Greater production of some products, for example, may also lead to more supply of pollution.

Government influences on supply conditions

A government may influence supply conditions by introducing indirect taxes and/or subsidies.

Indirect taxes

An 'indirect tax' is a charge tax placed on the producer, who is legally responsible to pay it to the government. This form of tax is used by a government to raise revenue for its spending projects and, in some cases, to discourage consumption (for example, of alcohol or cigarettes). Indirect taxes increase the costs of producing and shift the supply curve, as shown in Figure 4.8. For any given quantity, a higher price now has to be charged to cover the higher costs.

Some indirect taxes are a fixed amount per unit, in which case, the supply curve shifts parallel (see Figure 4.8a). Other indirect taxes are a percentage of the price (see Figure 4.8b), in which case, the supply curve will diverge (because 17.5 per cent of a high price is more than 17.5 per cent of a low price).

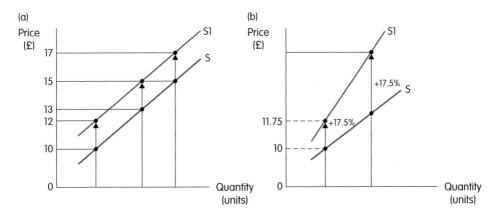

Figure 4.8 The effects of indirect taxes

Business Analysis   4.6

In 2009, Procter & Gamble had to pay tens of millions of pounds in value-added tax (VAT)—that is, a percentage indirect tax—after losing a legal battle over its Pringles snack. The Court of Appeal ruled in favour of HM Revenue & Customs (HMRC), which maintained that Pringles constitute a potato snack and are therefore liable for VAT.

Foods are usually exempt from VAT, but one of the few exceptions is the potato crisp.

A High Court judge ruled in July 2008 that Pringles' packaging, 'unnatural shape', and the fact that the potato content is less than 50 per cent meant that the snack was exempt from VAT. The Court of Appeal disagreed.

What would the effect of this tax be on the supply curve for Pringles?

Subsidies

A government may offer subsidies to producers to help an industry to produce more cheaply. It may, for example, want to encourage the consumption of particular products that it thinks are desirable (such as local bus services) and, to achieve this, it reduces the costs of producers via subsidies. For example, the European Union has subsidized dairy farmers in recent years to help keep these producers in business.

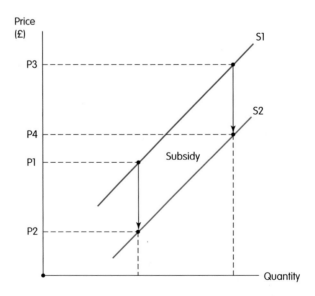

Figure 4.9 The effect of a subsidy

A subsidy shifts the supply curve downwards (see Figure 4.9): any given quantity can be supplied at a lower price. The extent to which the subsidy is passed on to the consumer as opposed to being kept by the business depends on the price elasticity of demand. The more price inelastic demand is, the greater the effect on price and the more the consumer benefits.

? Think about it ... 4.7

1. If a government is going to subsidize a business, from where will it get the money? What problems might raising the finance to subsidize an industry create?

2. Do you think that subsidizing an industry is a good way of increasing consumption?

Can you now answer question 5 from the opening case study?

>> You Decide ...

If you were a government minister, what would make you decide to subsidize one industry rather than another?

Summary

A supply curve shows the quantity supplied at each and every price, all other factors held constant. A change in price leads to a movement along the supply curve and a change in the quantity supplied; a change in the other factors, such as technology or the number of producers, leads to a shift in the supply curve. The sensitivity of the quantity supplied to a change in price is measured by the price elasticity of supply. An increase in indirect taxes adds to the costs of a supplier; a subsidy reduces the costs of a producer.

Managers need to understand the determinants of supply because an increase in supply might make the market much more competitive. Managers may also try to increase their ability to respond to price changes by making supply more price elastic.

Checklist

Having read this chapter, you should now understand:

☐ what is shown by a supply curve;

☐ the difference between a movement along, and a shift of, a supply curve;

☐ why a supply curve may slope upwards;

☐ why a supply curve might shift to the right;

☐ the effect of lean production and changes in productivity on supply;

☐ the meaning of the price elasticity of supply and an understanding of how to calculate it;

☐ how to derive the industry supply curve;

☐ the effect of an indirect tax on a supply curve;

☐ the effect of a subsidy on a supply curve.

Case Study Review

Having read this chapter, you should now be able to answer the following questions.

1. What do you think determines the world supply of food in any given year?

2. Do you think that it is easy to change the world supply of food or not? Do you think that supply is sensitive to price or not?

3. What do you think determines the world demand for food in any given year?

4. What do you think will happen to the world price of food if there are shortages?

5. How do you think governments could intervene in global food markets?

6. How do you think the supply of food will be affected by the subsidies for ethanol? Illustrate your answer with diagrams.

7. Do you think that the government should subsidize the growth of crops for ethanol production?

Short Answer Questions

1. Explain what is shown by a supply curve.

2. Explain three factors that influence the supply of a product.

3. Distinguish between a movement along, and a shift of, supply.

4. Explain how an increase in costs might affect the supply curve.

5. What is meant by the price elasticity of supply?

6. Explain what determines the price elasticity of supply.

7. Explain what is meant by a price elasticity of supply of +0.5.

8. Do improvements in technology lead to a movement along, or a shift of, the supply curve?

9. What is meant by producer surplus?

10. How is the supply curve for the industry derived?

Essay Questions

1. To what extent is productivity the main determinant of supply in a market?

2. Discuss the main determinants of the price elasticity of supply.

3. Discuss the ways in which managers can seek to shift supply to the right.

 One Step Further

Visit our Online Resource Centre at **www.oxfordtextbooks.co.uk/orc/gillespiebusiness/** for test questions, podcasts, and further information on topics covered in this chapter.

Markets

5

Learning Objectives

Much of economic analysis centres on markets. There are markets throughout economies, such as the market for products, for currencies, for money, and for factors of production. In this chapter, we examine how demand and supply interact in a market, and how the price mechanism adjusts to bring about equilibrium.

By the end of this chapter, you should:

- ☑ understand how the price mechanism works;

- ☑ understand the meaning of equilibrium;

- ☑ understand the meaning of excess demand and excess supply;

- ☑ understand how the price mechanism adjusts to equate supply and demand;

- ☑ be able to explain the effect on the equilibrium price and output in a market of a change in demand or supply conditions;

- ☑ be able to explain the effect on the equilibrium price and output in a market of the introduction of an indirect tax or subsidy;

- ☑ understand the meaning and importance of community surplus and allocative efficiency.

ⓒ Case Study

The United Nations Food and Agriculture Organization (UNFAO) says that the demand for tea exceeded the supply in 2008, driving up its price. Tea consumption reached 3.85 million tonnes last year, up 4.8 per cent from 2007. But production was only 3.78 million tonnes, according to the UNFAO's preliminary estimates. Tea was in **surplus** in 2007, but it seems that the recent shortfall can only get bigger.

Tea prices have soared as drought has hit Kenya hard in the past year, as well as Sri Lanka and India, which is the world's biggest producer of tea.

All of this has not gone unnoticed in Mombasa, a Kenyan coastal city of white sand and blue water that hosts tea auctions. These weekly auctions, which sell most of the tea produced in Africa, set the benchmark for the price of the crop throughout the world.

The average price of tea last year was US$2.33/kg, almost a third higher than US$1.76/kg in 2007, according to Kenya's Tea Board.

Black tea had jumped to a record of US$2.70 last August.

Tea traders worry that the production gap will get larger.

Kenya, which is Africa's largest grower of tea, will probably produce 328 million kg of the crop this year. That is well below the 345 million kg produced last year.

'If the shortfall turns out to be as deep as expected, then prices will go through the roof,' Mr Chang said.

But much in the same way as rising crude oil prices push up the cost of petrol at the pump, this too is likely to increase the price of high-street brand teas. The UK is the second biggest importer of tea in the world, behind Russia, so any costs of the raw materials will either have to be absorbed by the tea makers or passed on.

'Areas are certainly suffering drought and there is no reserve of tea, so shortages exist,' said Giles Hilton, Whittard's product director. 'Some prices might need reviewing soon.'

With global demand continuing to rise, there is little sign that production is going to be able to keep pace.

More expensive cups of tea may have to become a fact of life.

Sources: www.un.org, May 2008, BBC News, 'Tea prices are surging: Is your mug next?', available online at http://news.bbc.co.uk/go/pr/fr/-/1/hi/business/7973857.stm

Introduction

Managers oversee a transformation process. Resources such as labour, capital, and enterprise are transformed into final goods and services: take some food, some knives, whisks, pans, and an oven, add in a famous chef, and you have a meal worth a lot of money. Managers sell products to their customers and use resources acquired from suppliers. In both cases, they are operating in markets: one is a market for inputs; the other is a market for outputs. A market occurs when buyers and sellers come together to trade. If you have something to sell and you can find someone who wants to buy it, you have a market.

Understanding how markets work is clearly important to managers. Why are rents higher in some areas than others? What are they likely to be in the future? Do some employees need to be paid higher wages than others to keep them? Why can energy prices vary so much? These changes in input prices can all be explained by changes in supply and demand conditions in their markets, and an understanding of these elements should enable managers to analyse and anticipate the effects of changes in market conditions on the costs of the business.

Similarly, the price at which you can sell your products will also be affected by market forces. An increase in demand for your product or a change in supply conditions will affect the market price. A surge in demand for *High School Musical* merchandise, anti-bacterial handwash during a flu pandemic, or sun cream in a heat wave may all lead to more sales and pull up prices. Markets also affect many other factors that determine business success, such as the value of a country's currency and the value of a company's shares. In previous chapters, we have examined demand and supply conditions separately. In this chapter, we analyse how supply and demand interact, and the significance of this for business decision making.

Reaching equilibrium

A market consists of buyers and sellers who come together to trade. The demand curve shows what customers are willing and able to purchase at each and every price, all other things unchanged. The supply curve shows what producers are willing and able to produce at each and every price, all other things unchanged. The price acts as a signal, incentive, and rationing device to bring about equilibrium in the market. Equilibrium occurs when there is no incentive to change; the market position is stable.

If, for example, the price in a market is at P1, given the supply and demand conditions, then the quantity demanded is less than the quantity supplied (see Figure 5.1). This means that there is excess supply (equal to Q1, Q3), known as a 'surplus'. In this case, there will be downward pressure on the market price.

As the price falls, this reduces the quantity supplied (because there is less incentive for producers to produce) and increases the quantity demanded (because there are more units that are affordable for customers and which provide benefits worth this price).

This process of the price falling will continue until P2 is reached, at which point the quantity demanded equals the quantity supplied at Q2 and there is equilibrium—that is, at this price, there is no incentive for price and quantity to change.

If, however, the price in the market was originally at P3, the quantity supplied is less than the quantity demanded. This means that there is a shortage—that is, excess demand (see Figure 5.2). When there is a shortage, there will be upward pressure on prices. As the price increases, it rations demand, reducing the quantity demanded, while also acting as an incentive for producers to produce more, increasing the quantity supplied.

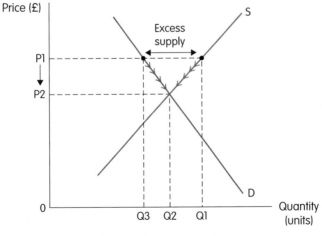

Figure 5.1 Excess supply

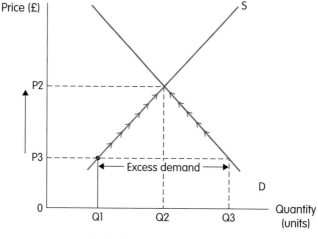

Figure 5.2 Excess demand

In a free market, the price mechanism should therefore adjust to match the supply and demand decisions made by producers and customers. Just look at the value of the pound in the currency market during any day and you will see it constantly changing as supply and demand conditions change. Alternatively, look at the share price of any major business over a few hours or weeks and, again, you will see it constantly moving as market conditions change. Both of these are examples of the price mechanism in action. In millions of markets every day, prices are adjusting to equate supply and demand, and to determine what is produced, how it is produced, and for whom. These markets are examined in more detail in Chapter 12.

In the free market, there is no overriding central authority: profit-maximizing firms and utility-maximizing consumers make independent decisions that bring about equilibrium via price changes, which is why it was called the 'invisible hand' by Adam Smith in 1776. Individuals focusing on their individual needs make their own decisions, but this is all pulled together and coordinated by the price mechanism. If you want something and are prepared to pay for it, there is likely to be a market for it.

? *Think about it ...*   *5.1*

The prices of most goods in the shops do not change every day. Does this mean that the price mechanism does not work in reality?

Data Analysis 5.1

Table 5.1

Price (£)	Quantity demanded (units)	Quantity supplied (units)
10	50	150
9	70	140
8	100	100
7	140	90
6	180	70
5	230	60

1. What is the equilibrium price in the above market?

2. If there were a tax on producers that meant that each quantity had to be supplied for £3 more, what would be the equilibrium price and quantity?

3. If, instead, there were a subsidy for producers that meant each quantity could be supplied for £2 less, what would be the new equilibrium quantity and price?

4. Illustrate the tax and subsidy scenarios above with supply and demand diagrams.

? Think about it … 5.2

1. Can you think of anything that would prevent the price from moving up or down to achieve equilibrium in any market?

2. Can you think of any market in which the price does not move up or down? Why not?

Much of what happens in the economic environment is determined by market forces, and so an understanding of supply and demand is essential for managers. Changes in rental prices, the prices of components, and the price of finished goods, for example, are all likely to be influenced by market forces and will all affect the success of a business. Understanding the underlying forces in a market allows managers to plan ahead and to react effectively to change. This is particularly important because market forces are not static: businesses are continually reshaping and moving into new markets; customers are often changing their purchasing patterns; new products are being developed; and new markets emerging. All of these factors are shifting demand and supply curves, and changing the equilibrium price and output.

? Think about it ...   5.3

Markets are continually changing: for example, new products are being developed, changing supply and demand conditions.

When do you think the following occurred?

A Google was launched.

B The first iPod was sold.

C The first Playstation was sold.

D Apple was set up.

E Facebook was set up.

Changes in demand conditions

Imagine that a market is in equilibrium at P1,Q1 in Figure 5.3. Given the demand and supply conditions in this market, there is no incentive to change at the moment at this price, because the quantity supplied equals the quantity demanded. But these conditions can change: incomes change; businesses change their marketing; competitors change their prices; and new substitutes emerge. Look at your lifestyles compared to those of your parents or grandparents and you will see how much consumption patterns have altered. How many products do you buy that simply did not exist when your grandparents were your age? How many brands would your great-grandparents recognize? How similar is your shopping basket to theirs?

If demand for a product increases—perhaps because of an increase in the number of buyers—this means that, at the given price, there is now excess demand. This will put upward pressure on prices, which, in turn, will reduce the quantity demanded and increase the quantity supplied. The new equilibrium occurs with a higher price in the market and a greater quantity demanded (see Figure 5.3). In 2009, for example, bad weather in the UK increased demand for holidays abroad. Demand in Spain increased so much that the prices of hire cars at airports doubled in price in the Balearic Islands.

If, however, demand falls, this leads to a fall in the equilibrium price and a lower equilibrium quantity (see Figure 5.4). With lower demand conditions, businesses face lower prices and output.

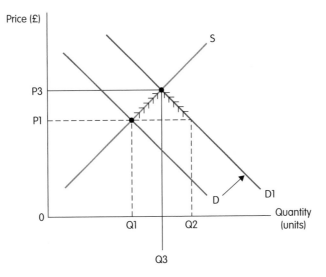

Figure 5.3 Impact of an outward shift in demand

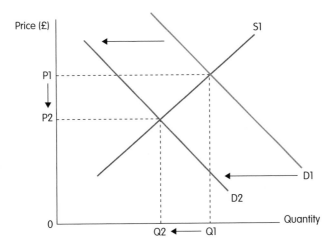

Figure 5.4 A decrease in demand

? Think about it ...   5.4

Which of the following might explain an increase in demand?

A An increase in the price of a substitute.

B An increase in the price of a complement.

C An increase in income for an inferior good.

D A decrease in the costs of production.

Data Analysis
5.2

1. Would the effect of an increase in demand on the equilibrium price relative to the equilibrium quantity be greater if the price elasticity of supply were 1.2 or 0.2? Explain your answer.

2. Given an increase in income of 10 per cent, would the shift in demand be greater or smaller if the income elasticity were 2 or 0.2? Explain your answer.

>> You Decide ...

You run a French restaurant in a large town in the UK. Demand has been falling for the past couple of years.

1. How does this affect your business in the different functional areas?

2. How might you react to the fall in demand?

Managers need to understand the consequences of reduced demand in their businesses, because it will reduce the quantity sold; this will affect decisions within many other areas of the business, including cash flow forecasts, workforce plans, and the ordering of supplies (see Figure 5.5). A general fall in demand in an economy may make businesses more wary when it comes to expansion and more focused on ensuring that they have the cash that they need to survive. This means that managers may be concerned about when they are going to be paid and may therefore delay payments to their own suppliers. They may also reduce the labour force and hold back on any expansion plans.

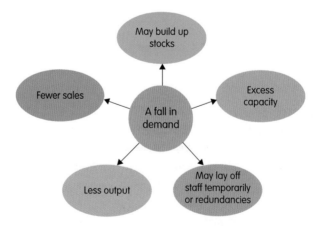

Figure 5.5 The effect of a fall in demand

Business Analysis 5.1

In 2009, Microsoft experienced a fall in demand for the first time in twenty-three years.

1. Why might this have happened?

2. What do you think Microsoft's managers might do in response to this fall in sales?

Think about it... 5.5

The Annual Social Trends published by the UK Office for National Statistics (ONS) in 2009 stated that the number of people in the UK is growing by 1,000 a day. There are 61 million people officially resident in the UK at present and this is expected to grow by 4.4 million by 2016. If trends continue, there will be 71 million people living in the UK by 2031. Longer term projections suggest that the UK could have 85 million inhabitants by 2081, and possibly 100 million by 2100, if current increases continue unchecked.

What effect is this growth in population likely to have on the following markets?

A Housing.

B Schools.

C Health care.

Changes in supply conditions

Just as changes in demand conditions will alter the equilibrium price and quantity in a market, so changes in supply will also affect the price and output in an industry. Imagine that a market is in equilibrium at P1,Q1: if there is an increase in supply, this will lead to a surplus at the existing price. In a free market, this will lead to a fall in the price. This, in turn, will lead to a fall in quantity supplied (because there is less incentive to produce) and an increase in quantity demanded (because products are cheaper) until the new equilibrium is reached at P2,Q2 (see Figure 5.6). An increase in supply, therefore, usually leads to a greater quantity being supplied at a lower price.

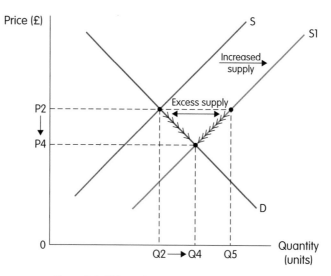

Figure 5.6 Effect of an outward shift in supply

Managers need to be aware of changes in the industry, such as new technology being adopted by other producers, because this can drive the overall market price down. Managers need to be able to adapt to these new conditions to produce at this lower price. Think of markets for consumer electronics, such as televisions, cameras, and DVDs, and how the price of these products has been driven down over the years.

By comparison, if supply in a market falls, then there will be excess demand at the existing price. This will lead to an upward pressure on prices, increasing the quantity supplied and reducing the quantity demanded, until the new equilibrium is reached with a lower quantity and a higher price. The lower quantity supplied will have implications for staffing and the amount of capacity needed.

? *Think about it ...* 5.6

1. Which of the following will increase supply?
   A An increase in income.
   B An improvement in technology.
   C An increase in production costs.
   D An increase in the price of a complement.

2. What will happen to the price of wheat in a year during which crops are poor?

3. Why might farmers welcome a poor year?

4. Would a shift in supply have a greater effect on the equilibrium price rather than the quantity if the price elasticity of demand were −0.1 or −1.1? Explain your answer using a supply and demand diagram.

Business Analysis   5.2

With the recession, the price of many commodities, such as copper, iron, nickel, and gold, fell. As economies seemed to be growing again in 2009, prices began to rise.

1. Show on a supply and demand diagram why prices would be rising again.

2. When drawing your diagram think about the price elasticity of demand and supply and explain whether you think these are price elastic or inelastic.

\# Data Analysis   5.3

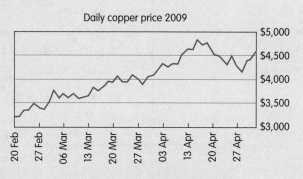

Figure 5.7 Daily copper price

Source: Yahoo! Finance. Reproduced with kind permission of Yahoo!

Figure 5.7 shows the daily price of copper over a three-month period. Copper is traded on world markets.

1. Using supply and demand analysis, explain the possible reasons why the price of copper may have changed in this way.

2. Outline the changes in the price of copper shown in the diagram above.

3. Discuss the possible implications of such changes for businesses.

Can you now answer question 3 from the opening case study?

Movements along versus shifts in supply and demand curves

If demand for a product increases, this means that, at each and every price, more is demanded. This means that, at the original equilibrium price, there is now excess demand and the price is pulled upwards. The result is a new equilibrium and a new quantity supplied, because of the higher price (see Figure 5.8). The shift in demand has led to a movement along the supply curve. The supply curve itself has not moved because supply conditions have not changed.

If supply increases (meaning that more is supplied at each price), perhaps because of an improvement in technology, this leads to an excess supply at the existing price. This causes a fall in price and, as the price falls, the quantity demanded increases. The shift in supply has led to a movement along the demand curve. The demand curve itself has not moved, because demand conditions have not changed.

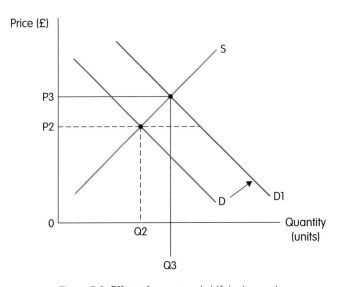

Figure 5.8 Effect of an outward shift in demand

Table 5.2

Causes of shifts in demand	Causes of shifts in supply
Changes in incomes	Changes in costs
Changes in the price of substitutes	Changes in technology
Changes in the price of complements	Changes in the number of producers
Changes in marketing activities	Changes in indirect taxes or subsidies
Changes in population size	Changes in productivity

? *Think about it...*   5.7

1. As a result of changes in demand or supply conditions, the equilibrium price and quantity have increased in your market. What change in market conditions might have caused this? Illustrate your answer with a supply and demand diagram.

2. As a result of changes in demand or supply conditions, the equilibrium price has increased and the quantity has decreased in your market. What change in market conditions might have caused this? Illustrate your answer with a supply and demand diagram.

3. As a result of changes in demand or supply conditions, the equilibrium price and the quantity have decreased in your market. What change in market conditions might have caused this? Illustrate your answer with a supply and demand diagram.

£ Business Analysis 5.3

In July 2008, global oil prices hit record highs above US$147 a barrel, but, within months, had fallen to close to US$100. The Organization of the Petroleum Exporting Countries (OPEC), the oil producers' cartel, responded to the lower price by cutting the amount of oil that it produced, reducing the world supply.

OPEC members had previously blamed rising prices on demand increases due to speculators and the weakening US dollar, which makes oil a more attractive investment. Demand for oil had been growing, because economies such as China and India needed to fuel their rapid expansion. At the same time, there were all sorts of worries about the supply of oil. A lot of the world's oil comes from potentially unstable countries, so, with concerns over security at Nigerian or Iraqi oil facilities, people became concerned about supplies.

In the oil market, the *perception* of supply and demand also matters as well as the *actual* supply and demand. This is because:

- nobody knows exactly how much oil there is in the ground;

- many producers are secretive over how much they have already extracted and governments won't declare how much they have in reserve; and

- speculators are buying on the basis of what they think will happen to the price.

1. Explain, using supply and demand analysis, why the price of oil might increase over time.

2. Explain two factors that would influence a speculator's decision to buy oil.

The relative effect on price and quantity resulting from a change in demand or supply conditions

As we have seen, a change in demand and supply conditions will lead to a change in the equilibrium market price and quantity. Whether the equilibrium price increases or decreases and whether the equilibrium quantity increases or decreases depends on what has changed and in what direction.

From a firm's perspective, an increase in demand creates the most favourable conditions and should lead to more output at a higher price. Customers are willing to pay more to get more. A fall in demand, by comparison, reduces the equilibrium price and quantity.

The precise effect of a change in demand on the equilibrium price and quantity will depend on the following.

- *How much demand shifts* For example, if income increases, this will shift demand outwards for a normal good. The amount that demand shifts to the right will depend, in this instance, on the income elasticity of demand. The more income elastic demand is, the more demand will shift to the right, given an increase in income.

- *The price elasticity of supply* If supply is very price inelastic, then the effect of a change in demand is mainly on price rather than quantity. The quantity supplied cannot change very much (in relation to changes in price). If supply were completely price inelastic, then a change in demand would have no effect on the quantity supplied and would affect only the price. The market for oil, for example, has a very price inelastic supply and therefore changes in demand have a significant effect on prices. If you are managing a business and demand increases, but you cannot increase supply easily, then the price will act as a rationing device.

? Think about it ...   5.8

Demand sometimes increases rapidly because of a 'craze' for something. Can you think of a craze in your economy in recent years that led to a major increase in demand?

 # Data Analysis   5.4

1. Which is more income elastic: a value for the income elasticity of +2 or +0.5? Explain your answer.

2. Which is more price elastic: a value for the price elasticity of demand of + 2 or +0.2? Explain your answer.

The effect of a change in supply on the equilibrium price and quantity will similarly depend on the extent of the shift and the price elasticity of demand. The more price inelastic demand is, the greater the effect on price rather than quantity (see Figure 5.9).

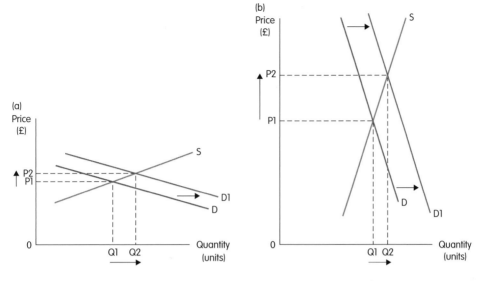

Figure 5.9 Impact of a shift in, and price elasticity of, demand

>> You Decide ...

As the manager of a business, would you prefer there to be an increase in demand or an increase in the supply in the industry? Explain your reasoning.

£ Business Analysis 5.4

In 2009, the cost of both coffee and sugar rose sharply, because of poor crops and strong demand, despite the slump in the economy.

The crop in Colombia was damaged by heavy rains creating a shortage.

Kraft, owner of the Maxwell House coffee brands, raised retail prices on its Colombian blend by almost 19 per cent due to the rising prices of Colombian coffee beans.

1. Do you think that the demand and supply of coffee beans are likely to be price inelastic or price elastic? Explain your reasoning.

2. Illustrate, using supply and demand, why the price of Colombian coffee went up. What do you think determines the demand for coffee?

3. How might producers of instant or bagged coffee, such as Nescafé, respond to the increase in the price of coffee beans?

Business Analysis 5.5

In the first three months of 2009, 2,462,700 flat-screen televisions were sold in the UK—up an impressive 17.5 per cent on the same period of the year before, according to figures from GfK Retail and Technology.

Despite the big increase in unit sales, the amount of money paid by customers for flat-screen televisions actually fell 1 per cent to £980 million.

Nick Simon from GfK says:

> Prices have declined, particularly in the most important category, 32" LCD, from £502 in April 2008 to £391 in April 2009. But sluggish value performance can also be attributed to the popularity of 19" and 22" TVs as we gradually switch over from analogue to digital broadcasting and people replace smaller second and third TVs or acquire them for the first time.

There was the same picture in low-energy light bulbs, with unit sales growing 38.8 per cent, but sales by value falling 3 per cent, because the average price for a bulb fell from £1.25 to 87 pence.

Explain, using supply and demand, how even though there was a big increase in unit sales, the amount of money paid by customers for flat-screen televisions actually fell 1 per cent to £980 million.

The speed of market adjustment

The speed with which the price changes following a change in supply or demand to restore equilibrium may vary from market to market. Share prices and currency prices, for example, change very quickly according to market conditions. This is because there are millions of transactions occurring regularly in these markets, so any change in demand or supply is quickly reflected in the equilibrium price and quantity. Similarly, commodities, such as gold, wheat, and silver, are traded on a worldwide market with prices fluctuating all of the time. This, in itself, creates a 'futures' market, in which people are speculating by agreeing to buy and sell these products at a future date—that is, they are trading in something that has not even been produced yet.

In other markets, however, the price may be slower to adjust. In the labour market, for example, salaries are often negotiated for a year or even more, and so cannot instantaneously adjust to a change in demand and supply. In other markets, prices may be agreed as part of a contract set for several months in advance at least. This means that prices will not change immediately, which can prevent markets from reaching equilibrium in the short run. Similarly, the costs and effort required to reprint brochures and alter price lists may mean that prices move occasionally, rather than instantaneously, to bring about equilibrium. Also businesses are often buying every several weeks or even months, and so any price changes caused by input costs may take time to work through the transformation process.

This means that the effect on price and quantity in the short run may be different from the long-run impact (see Figure 5.10).

In Figure 5.11, the effect in the short run of an increase in demand is mainly an increase in price, because supply is price inelastic. Initially, the price rises to P2 and the new equilibrium quantity is Q2. Over time, supply becomes more price elastic, and the price falls to P3 and the quantity increases to Q3.

There may also be other barriers that prevent the price adjusting to equate supply and demand. In the labour market, for example, employees may be reluctant to accept a reduction in their wages even if there is a fall in demand for labour. They might simply refuse a pay cut and threaten industrial action. The result is that those in work maintain a relatively high wage, but fewer people are employed than would be if the market were to 'clear'.

In Figure 5.11, there is a fall in demand for labour, perhaps because of a fall in demand for products in the economy. If market forces worked efficiently, the wage should fall to W2 and the equilibrium number of people employed would then be L2. If, however, employees insist on still receiving W1, then the quantity demanded of labour would be L3 and there would be excess supply of labour equal to L3, L1. Those employed retain their earnings at the original wage W1, but, by keeping the wage higher than equilibrium, the number employed falls to L1.

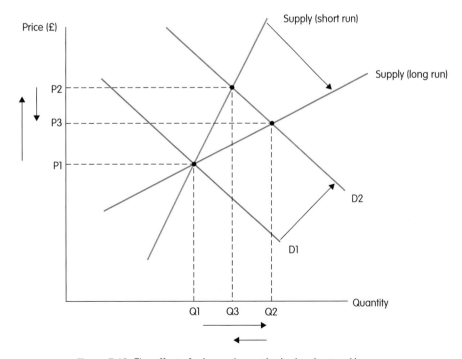

Figure 5.10 The effect of price and quantity in the short and long run

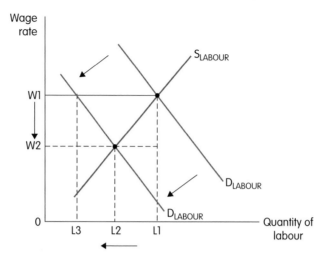

Figure 5.11 A fall in demand for labour

? **Think about it ...**   5.9

Which of the following statements are true and which are false?

A If there is excess demand in a market, the price is likely to increase.

B An increase in demand will usually lead to a higher equilibrium price and lower quantity.

C An increase in supply will usually lead to a lower equilibrium price and lower equilibrium quantity.

D If there is excess supply in a market, the equilibrium price is likely to rise.

>> **You Decide ...**

Demand for your nightclub is high and you have queues waiting outside most evenings. You are considering putting the price up to get into the club. Why might you decide not to do this?

Data Analysis 5.5

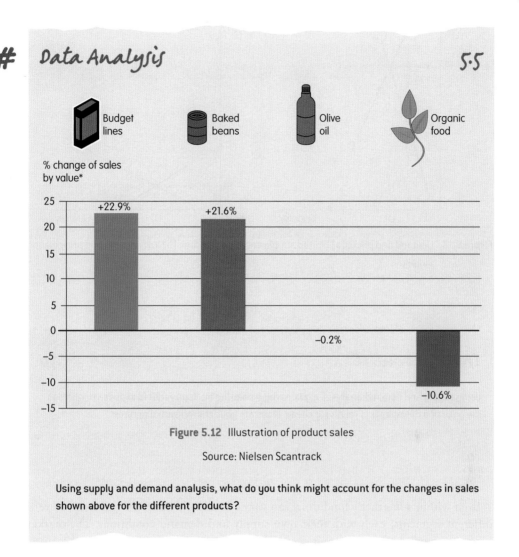

Figure 5.12 Illustration of product sales

Source: Nielsen Scantrack

Using supply and demand analysis, what do you think might account for the changes in sales shown above for the different products?

Different market conditions

Prices will differ in markets because of differences in supply and demand conditions. If the demand for an item is high and supply is limited, the market price will be relatively high (think of the price of Ferraris). If demand for an item is low and/or supply is higher, the price is likely to be relatively low (think of the price of milk).

In theory, producers of milk may be attracted into production of Ferraris because of the higher price—but the particular skills, expertise, and experience required for the production of Ferraris limits the numbers of firms that can compete in this market niche.

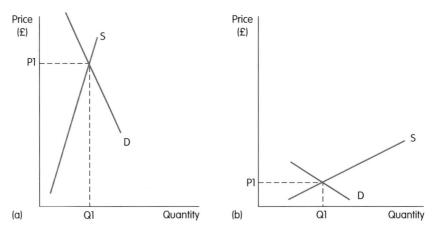

Figure 5.13. Demand and price, (a) limited supply and high demand, (b) low demand and price elastic supply.

? *Think about it ...*   5.10

Using supply and demand analysis, explain why a painting by Rembrandt is expensive, whereas the price of a newspaper is relatively cheap. Illustrate your answer with diagrams.

Even within a 'market', conditions can vary considerably because there can be very different segments, each with their own supply and demand conditions. The market for housing will be very different across the country depending on a range of factors, such as the availability of jobs, the facilities, the crime rates, and the ease of building. Even within one region, the demand will vary between types of housing, such as small flats and family homes, because demand and supply will differ so much. Similarly, consider the market for confectionery in the UK: this is growing as a whole in the UK, but, within it, the demand for bubble gum is falling (partly due to restrictions on advertising to young children that are now in place) and the demand for boiled sweets is falling (due to a lack of innovation), while the demand for chewing gum is booming (due to heavy investment in new product development). The different segments are performing very differently within one overall 'market'. Marketing managers are, of course, well aware of the difference between segments (for example, chocolate bought to eat for yourself is different from chocolate bought to share watching a film, which is different from chocolate bought to give as a gift) and adapt their marketing mix accordingly.

>> You Decide ...

You are the manager of a business supplying materials for decorating and household repairs, such as plumbing. Your business has targeted small building companies so far, but now you want to expand and target enthusiastic DIY homeowners (that is, amateurs).

How might you change your marketing mix for this new segment?

Data Analysis   5.6

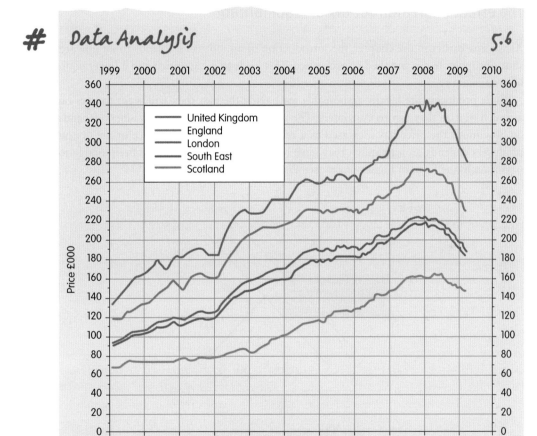

Figure 5.14 Demand and price

Source: HousePrices.uk.net

1. Summarize the key trends in the housing market shown in Figure 5.14.

2. What do you think determines the supply of housing available to sell at any moment in a region?

3. Do you think that the supply of housing for sale is likely to be price elastic or inelastic? Explain your answer.

4. What do you think determines the demand for housing in London? Why might there be competing demands for property?

5. Why do think the price of housing might change over time?

6. Why do you think house prices differ between regions in the UK?

7. What do you think is likely to be the long-term trend of house prices in London in the future? Explain your answer.

8. Do you think that prices in the housing market are quick to adjust to bring about equilibrium?

The effect of an indirect tax on equilibrium

As we saw earlier in the chapter, the introduction of an indirect tax leads to an upward shift of supply: less is supplied at each price. This leads to a high price and a lower equilibrium quantity.

While producers are legally responsible for paying the tax, they will want to pass on as much of it as they can to customers. The incidence of the tax on consumers depends on how much the price has increased as a result of the tax; the incidence of the tax on producers depends on how much they have to absorb because they have been unable to pass it on in the form of higher prices (see Figure 5.15).

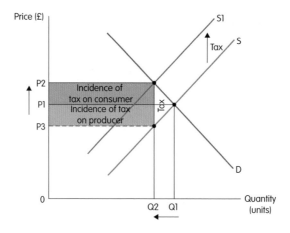

Figure 5.15 Average house prices

Source: HousePrices.uk.net

The ability of a business to pass on an indirect tax to customers depends on the relative price elasticity of demand and supply. If demand is more price inelastic than supply, the consumer will bear the greater proportion of the tax. If demand is more price elastic than supply, the producer will pay the greater proportion of tax (see Figure 5.16).

The importance of the relative price elasticity highlights why managers are often eager to make demand more price inelastic (that is, less sensitive to price), so that they can pass on indirect tax increases onto the consumer.

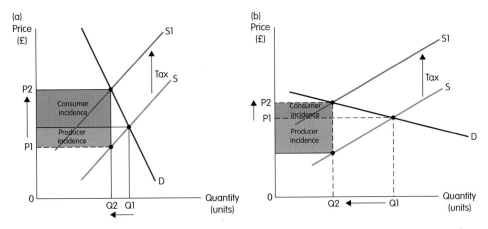

Figure 5.16 The incidence of an indirect tax on consumers and producers

? Think about it ...   5.11

1. How might you, as a manager, try to prevent indirect taxes being increased?

2. If an indirect tax is increased, how could you try to shift more of the incidence of this tax on to customers?

3. If the government would like to raise as much revenue as possible, would it prefer demand to be price elastic or inelastic? Explain your answer with a diagram.

4. What indirect taxes exist in your economy? Why do you think these have been introduced?

>> You Decide ...

As a manager, would you prefer the government to tax people's incomes or to place a tax on products?

The effect of a subsidy on equilibrium

As we saw in Chapter 4, a subsidy to producers reduces their costs and leads to a downward shift in the supply curve. Each quantity can be supplied at a lower price. The effect of a subsidy is to reduce the equilibrium price and increase the equilibrium quantity (see Figure 5.17). The effect on price relative to quantity will be greater the more price inelastic demand is.

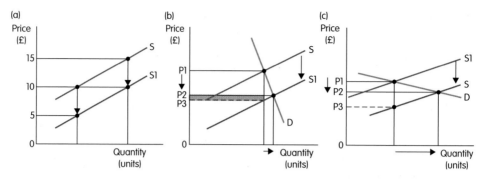

Figure 5.17 The effect of a subsidy on equilibrium

Data Analysis   5.7

Table 5.3

Price	Quantity demanded	Quantity supplied
£1.50	200	200
£1.40	210	180
£1.30	240	160
£1.20	250	120

1. What is the original equilibrium price and quantity in the above market?
2. As a result of a fall in production costs, supply rises by 50 per cent at all prices. What would be the new equilibrium price and quantity?

Markets and managers

Managers are operating in hundreds, if not thousands, of markets. For example, they trade in the different markets for factors of production, the markets for their different products in different regions, the money market in which they may raise money, and the currency market if they trade overseas. By understanding market conditions and the effects of changes in supply and demand, managers can anticipate possible changes in areas such as the price of land, the price of labour, the cost of borrowing money, and the price of inputs bought abroad. This should aid planning and lead to better decision making.

Equilibrium, social welfare, and community surplus

One of the benefits of the free market system is that market forces bring about equilibrium and this equilibrium maximizes the welfare of society.

A demand curve shows the marginal benefits (also called utility) of consuming a product; it shows how much customers are willing to pay for an additional unit, which therefore reflects its extra benefit to society. This means that it can also be labelled a social marginal benefit (SMB) curve. The supply curve reflects the marginal costs of producing another unit, because these need to be covered by the price. It can, therefore, be called a social marginal costs (SMC) curve (see Figure 5.18).

In the free market, equilibrium occurs at P1,Q1. This means that all of the units in relation to which the extra benefit to society is greater than the extra cost to society are produced, up to the point at which the SMB equals the SMC. In other words, all of the units that represent a net gain to society (because the extra benefit exceeds the extra costs) are produced up to the point at which society would not gain overall from another unit; as a result, the welfare of society must be maximized and the economy is said to have achieved **allocative efficiency**.

This can also be shown by the fact that the area of the consumer surplus plus the producer surplus—which is known as the **community surplus**—is maximized at this point. Any other combination of price and output would lead to less community surplus overall. If, for example, the price were set higher than P1, this would reduce the quantity demanded. This situation might occur if one business dominated the market and used its power to push up prices. As can be seen in Figure 5.19, this would increase the producer surplus (which is why the dominant producer pushes up prices in the first place), but, at the same time, reduce consumer surplus and the overall community surplus.

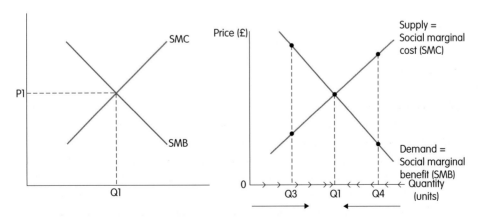

Figure 5.18 The social marginal benefit and social marginal costs curves

Producer surplus is now shown by the area P2,abc; consumer surplus is shown by the area P2,ae and community surplus overall is reduced by the area abf, which is known as a 'welfare loss (or deadweight) social burden area'. On units Q1,Q2, the marginal benefit is greater than the marginal cost, so society would benefit if these units were produced. This means that the business is not allocatively efficient, because the community surplus is not maximized and a deadweight social burden loss area exists.

The appeal of the free market, when it works, is that it brings about a price and quantity outcome that maximizes society's welfare. This is why market forces are encouraged in many countries: no other combination of price and output could achieve the same level of community surplus. But to maximize community surplus, market failures (such as a dominant firm) may need to be avoided—and this may require government intervention.

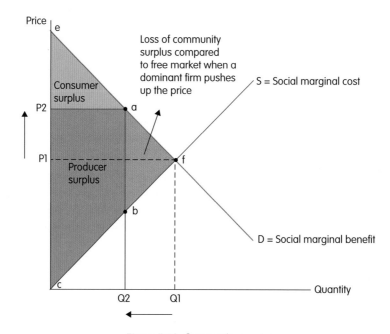

Figure 5.19 Community surplus

Summary

Equilibrium occurs at the price and quantity at which demand equals supply, and at which there is no incentive to change. In a free market, the price mechanism should adjust to bring about equilibrium. At this point, the extra benefit to society of a unit equals the extra cost to society; this maximizes the welfare of society and is allocatively efficient. The speed at which a market moves from one equilibrium to another following a change in demand or supply depends on the flexibility of price and will vary from market to market.

Governments may, however, intervene in several ways to influence the market system, and this affects the equilibrium price and quantity.

Checklist

Having read this chapter, you should now understand:

- [ ] how equilibrium is reached in a market economy;
- [ ] the meaning of shortage and surplus;
- [ ] the effects of shifts in supply and demand on the equilibrium price and quantity;
- [ ] the significance of the price elasticity of supply and demand of a shift in supply or demand;
- [ ] the effect of an indirect tax on the equilibrium price and quantity;
- [ ] the effect of a subsidy on the equilibrium price and quantity;
- [ ] the meaning of producer surplus;
- [ ] the meaning of consumer surplus;
- [ ] the meaning of community surplus;
- [ ] the meaning of allocative efficiency and welfare loss.

Case Study Review

Having read this chapter, you should now be able to answer the following questions.

1. Explain what factors are likely to determine the supply of tea in any given year.

2. Explain what factors are likely to determine the demand for tea in any given year.

3. Explain why the price of tea has been increasing. Illustrate this using supply and demand analysis.

4. How might the importers of tea respond to an increase in the price of tea? What factors might determine the actions that they take?

5. How might the increased price of tea affect demand for other drinks, such as coffee? Illustrate this using supply and demand analysis. What factors determine how much the demand for coffee might be affected?

Short Answer Questions

1. What is the difference between a movement along, and a shift of, demand?

2. Identify three factors that might influence demand for a product.

3. Identify three factors that might affect the supply of a product.

4. Explain how the price mechanism adjusts to bring about equilibrium.

5. What is the likely effect of an increase in demand on the equilibrium price and output?

6. What is the likely effect of a decrease in supply on the equilibrium price and output?

7. What determines how much the price of a product falls if there is a fall in demand for the product?

8. What is meant by consumer surplus?

9. What is meant by community surplus?

10. Explain what is meant by a deadweight social burden loss?

Essay Questions

1. Discuss the factors that influence the impact of a new indirect tax on the market price.

2. Evaluate the effects of a minimum wage on an economy.

3. Discuss the benefits of the free market system as a way of analysing resources.

 ## @ One Step Further

Visit our Online Resource Centre at **www.oxfordtextbooks.co.uk/orc/gillespiebusiness/** for test questions, podcasts, and further information on topics covered in this chapter.

Market analysis: shares, currency, and labour markets

6

Learning Objectives

In this chapter, we illustrate the workings of the market mechanism by examining the determinants of supply and demand, and the effects of changes in demand and supply in some important markets. This analysis will highlight the importance of the market mechanism to managers. We will also examine government intervention in markets.

By the end of this chapter, you should:

✓ understand the key factors influencing supply and demand in the labour, share, capital goods, and currency markets;

✓ understand the consequences of changes in supply and demand conditions in these markets;

✓ be able to explain the effects of changes in these variables;

✓ understand how the government intervenes in markets and the effect of such intervention.

Case Study

The chief executive of Brixton, the industrial property landlord, was recently voted out by his board of directors after the value of the company fell significantly. He had been with the business for twenty-four years and been chief executive for nine of these. This was not enough to save him, however, when the share price fell 79 per cent in the first two months of 2009. Investors felt that Brixton had been too slow to strengthen its financial position by raising funds. The company's market capitalization had fallen to only £74 million.

Share issues worth more than £2,000 billion had already been sold by three of the UK's largest property groups—Land Securities, British Land, and Hammerson—and there were concerns that Brixton might not be able to gain the financial backing that it needed.

Brixton's board said that it had decided to change the chief executive to 'ensure that it has the most appropriate leadership in place for the long-term future of the company'. The shares rose by over 10 pc following the announcement, before closing down 1.5 at 27 pence.

Questions

1. What is a company?
2. Who owns a company?
3. What is the role of the board of directors?
4. What do you think determines the price of a share?
5. What is meant by market capitalization?
6. Why does the price of a share matter to a business?
7. Why do you think the chief executive was asked to leave his job?
8. What might be considered when making the new appointment?
9. What factors might the directors take into account when making a large scale investment?

Introduction

There can be many different types of market in an economy: for example, there can be markets for goods, services, people, land, currency, shares, and money. These markets are driven by the same fundamental forces of supply and demand, but they can differ significantly, for the following reasons.

- *The relative importance of different factors affecting demand or supply will vary.* For example, the demand for education and nappies is heavily related to demographic factors; the demand for ice cream and thermal underwear depends more on the weather.

The supply of PCs will depend heavily on technology; the supply of ballet performances often depends more on government subsidies.

■ *Markets vary in terms of how much demand and supply shift over time.* Demand for clothing may be vulnerable to sudden changes in fashion; demand for salt may be more stable. The supply of gold can depend on the ability to find new sources; the supply of Mars bars may depend more on investment in production facilities.

■ *Markets vary in terms of the price sensitivity of demand and supply.* The demand for Ferraris may not be particularly sensitive to the price; the demand for washing machines may be more price elastic. The supply of power stations may be more price inelastic, whereas the supply of newspapers may be more price elastic.

■ *The extent of intervention by the government may vary from market to market.* In the UK, the National Lottery is a **monopoly** with the sole rights to supply this service granted by the government; similarly, the government grants franchises to run railway services. But the market for cafes has millions of suppliers, many of whom are located close to each other with very similar offerings and who are not regulated particularly heavily by the government.

As a result of these differences in market conditions, the extent and frequency to which the equilibrium price and quantities change in markets can vary considerably. The prices of shares of public limited companies, for example, are changing every few seconds due to constant changes in demand, whereas the price of a postage stamp does not change as often.

In this chapter, we examine the nature of several important markets in an economy, and the causes and effects of changes within them, to highlight the importance of supply and demand analysis.

? Think about it... 6.1

Can you think of two markets in your economy in which supply is likely to be price inelastic and two markets in which demand is likely to be price inelastic?

The foreign exchange market

The value of one currency in terms of other currencies is determined by market forces of supply and demand in the currency markets (unless the government intervenes to fix a price). If the value of a currency is high in relation to other currencies, it is called a 'strong' currency; this could be because of a high level of demand or a fall in supply. If the value of the currency is low, it is called 'weak'. When a currency increases in value, it 'appreciates'; when it falls in value, it 'depreciates'.

The value of a currency affects the price of a firm's products abroad, which will affect sales abroad (that is, exports). It will also affect the cost of buying supplies from abroad (that is, imports). Changes in the value of a currency are particularly significant now that so many businesses operate globally. There are, in fact, many different markets for currency: for example, the value of the pound sterling compared to the US dollar, the yen, the renminbi, or the rouble. In each of these markets, supply and demand interact to determine the value of one currency against another.

This means that it is possible for the pound to increase in value against one currency while decreasing in value against another. When analysing currency changes, managers will focus on the changes in markets in which they sell their products or those from which they buy materials or resources.

 ## Data Analysis   6.1

1. If the equilibrium value of £1 changes from US$1.5 to US$1.1, is the pound getting weaker or stronger?

2. What would happen to the price of a £200 product in dollars if the exchange rate were to change in this way?

3. What is the value of your currency? Do you know how much it has changed in value against another currency in the last year? Two years? Do you know if it has got stronger or weaker?

Demand for pounds

The external demand for UK currency comes from foreign individuals and organizations, which want to change their currency into pounds to buy UK goods and services. The more expensive the price of a pound, the more foreign currency has to be changed to buy it (that is, the more expensive UK products will be in terms of foreign currency). Assuming that all else remains constant, this will reduce the quantity demanded of pounds. The demand for pounds will therefore be a downward-sloping curve: the more expensive the pound is, the lower the quantity demanded of pounds.

The slope of the demand curve for pounds will depend on the price elasticity of demand for UK products in foreign currencies. If demand for UK exports is very price sensitive, then a given increase in the price of UK products abroad following an increase in the value of the pound will lead to a relatively large fall in the quantity demanded of products and therefore the quantity demanded of pounds. In other words, the more price elastic demand for the products, the more price elastic demand for pounds (see Figure 6.1). This is because the demand for pounds is derived from the demand for UK products. The price elasticity of demand for UK products will depend on factors such as how unique they are, the power of the brand, the quality, and the reliability.

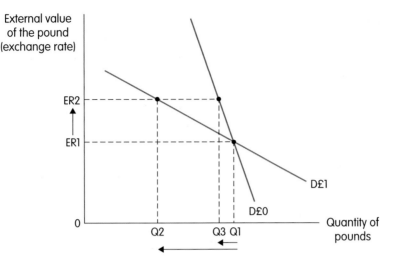

Figure 6.1 The demand for pounds in the currency market

 Data Analysis 6.2

Your handmade designer furniture sells for around £3,000 per piece in the UK. Your main export market is the USA, where you sell 500 units a week.

1. If the value of the UK currency were to change from US$1.2 to US$1.4, what would happen to the price of your products in the USA?

2. What actions could you take to prevent your sales from falling in this situation?

3. If the price elasticity of demand for your products in the USA were −1.5, what would happen to your sales and your revenue following the increase of the exchange rate?

4. If your business were to keep the same price in dollars following the exchange rate change, how much would it earn in pounds for each item?

Supply of pounds

The supply of pounds to the foreign currency market depends on the desire of individuals and organizations to change pounds into foreign currency (for example, if they plan to visit these countries or buy goods and services there). If the value of the pound increases in terms of foreign currency, this means that the pound has more purchasing power abroad. This makes foreign goods and services cheaper, because fewer pounds are required for any given amount of foreign currency. For example, if you want to buy a €600 suit and the exchange rate is €1:£1, the suit costs £600; if the pound appreciates to €1.2:£1, it will cost £500.

This means that an increase in the value of the pound should lead to an increase in the quantity demanded of foreign products. If demand for foreign products is price

Business economics

elastic, this means that the total spending on imports increases: although the price is lower in pounds, a significant increase in the quantity demanded increases the overall amount spent. Instead of buying forty suits at £600 spending £24,000, you might buy 60 at £500, spending £30,000 overall. In this case, the supply of pounds to the foreign currency market is upward-sloping: a higher value of the pound increases the quantity supplied.

If, however, the demand for imports is price inelastic, then the lower price of imports will lead to a relatively smaller increase in the quantity demanded of products from abroad and the total spending on imports will fall. If you were only to buy forty-two suits at £500, spending would have fallen to £21,000. In this case, the supply of pounds is downward-sloping, because an increase in the price of pounds leads to fewer being supplied (see Figure 6.2).

 Data Analysis 6.3

The price of a bottle of Italian olive oil is €12.
The exchange rate is £1:€1 and you import 30,000 bottles a month.

1. What is the price in pounds of the product?

2. How much do you spend in pounds a year on this product?

The exchange rate rises to £1:€1.2 and you import 40,000 bottles a month.

3. What is the price in pounds of the product now?

4. How much do you spend in pounds a year on this product now?

5. Calculate the price elasticity of supply for this product. Given an increase in the exchange rate has the supply of pounds risen or fallen?

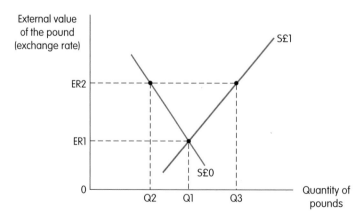

Figure 6.2 The supply of pounds in the currency market

Reaching equilibrium in the currency markets

In a free market, the price of the currency will adjust until the quantity supplied equals the quantity demanded. The price mechanism adjusts to bring about equilibrium. As illustrated in Figure 6.3, if the exchange rate is ER3, for example, there is an excess supply of the currency. In this case, the value of the pound falls, reducing the quantity supplied (if the supply curve is upward-sloping) and the quantity demanded falls. This process continues until equilibrium at ER1.

At ER2, there is excess demand (a shortage) of Q3,Q2 and the price of the currency will rise. This increases the quantity supplied and reduces the quantity demanded until the equilibrium is reached at ER1. Currencies are being bought and sold all of the time, with many buyers and sellers, meaning that the price changes rapidly, which should bring about equilibrium rapidly.

Shifts in demand for a currency

An increase in the demand for a currency will shift the demand curve outwards and will usually lead to a higher exchange rate. The demand for pounds in the foreign currency markets may increase because of:

- an increase in incomes overseas, leading to more demand for UK products (assuming that they are normal products);

- an increase in UK interest rates relative to the returns available elsewhere, which attracts foreign investors searching for high returns in UK banks and other financial institutions, and wanting to save pounds in the UK;

- a belief by speculators that the pound will increase in value against other currencies in the future, which means that these speculators will buy pounds now in the hope of selling later at a higher price.

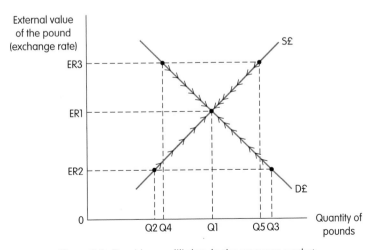

Figure 6.3 Reaching equilibrium in the currency market

Shifts in supply of the currency

An increase in the supply of pounds may be due to:

- an increase in UK incomes, leading to more demand for imports, meaning that more pounds will have to be supplied to change into foreign currency;
- an increase in overseas interest rates, leading to money flowing out of the UK in search of higher returns abroad;
- speculators selling pounds in the belief that the pound is going to fall in value in the future.

Changes in supply of and demand for a currency

An increase in demand for a currency will lead to an increase in price and an increase in the equilibrium, assuming that supply is upward-sloping (see Figure 6.4a). A decrease in supply of a currency will lead to an increase in the price, but a fall in the equilibrium quantity (see Figure 6.4b).

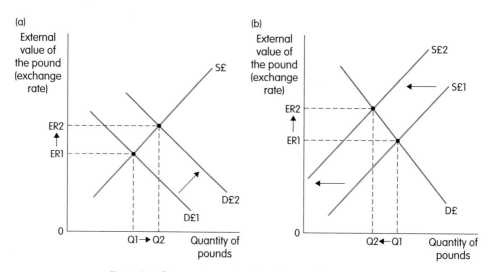

Figure 6.4 Changes in supply of and demand for a currency

Data Analysis   6.4

1. Imagine the exchange rate changes from £1:US$1.5 to £1:US$2 and that a UK product sold in the USA sells for £100 in the UK. What is the price in dollars before and after the change in the value of the pound?

2. Originally, 500 units were sold; if the price elasticity of demand for this product were −2, what would the new level of sales be? What was the original spending in pounds on the product? What would it be after the change in the exchange rate?

3. The exchange rate changes from £1:US$1.5 to £1:US$2 and a UK business buys a US$300 product from the USA. What is the price in pounds before and after the change in the value of the pound?

4. Originally, 200 units were bought.

    A How much was originally spent in pounds buying these products?

    B If the price elasticity of demand for the product is −2, what will be the new sales and the new level of spending in pounds? Has the spending increased or decreased, and what does this mean in terms of the supply curve for pounds? Will it be upward or downward-sloping?

    C If the price elasticity of demand for the product is −0.2, what will be the new sales and the new level of spending in pounds? Has the spending increased or decreased, and what does this mean in terms of the supply curve for pounds? Will it be upward or downward-sloping?

5. Illustrate the effect of an inward shift in the demands for a currency and an outward shift of the supply of a currency on the equilibrium price and quantity in a currency market.

? *Think about it ...* 6.2

What might make you think that a currency is going to lose value in the future?

Why do changes in exchange rates matter?

If the pound falls in value on the foreign currency markets, this means that it is cheaper relative to the relevant foreign currency. If the UK business keeps its prices the same in pounds, the prices in overseas currencies will be less. This should increase the quantity of products demanded from abroad. This means that a UK business needs to be ready and able to export more.

Alternatively, managers of UK businesses may decide to maintain the same price in terms of the foreign currency (perhaps because contracts have been negotiated or price lists printed already), which leads to a high profit margin being earned. This may lead to higher investment into the business or higher returns for investors.

By contrast, if the pound increases in value, then, if the price in pounds is kept the same, the price in foreign currency is now higher than it was, which is likely to reduce sales. Alternatively, the business might keep the overseas price the same, which would reduce its profit margins.

Data Analysis   6.5

1. What is likely to happen to the US price of a £100 product if the exchange rate rises from £1:US$1.5 to £1:US$2?

2. If the business were to keep the price at the original US price despite the increase in the currency, what would happen to the amount of pounds that it receives?

Think about it ...   6.3

How might a fall in the value of a currency in its major trading markets affect the different functions of a business?

Changes in the value of the pound will also affect import prices. If a UK business buys in supplies and the pound strengthens, this will reduce its import costs. This may lead to higher profit margins or enable the firm to reduce its prices. But the strong pound also means that customers can buy products from overseas competitors more cheaply, which might reduce the UK's firms' domestic sales as customers switch to overseas producers.

Given the high amount of international trade today, managers are almost certainly buying products from abroad and/or selling products abroad. An understanding of the exchange rate is crucial to modern-day business. It is particularly important to monitor and try to anticipate changes because the exchange rate is out of the control of any one business: the price is determined by millions of transactions happening all of the time and one manager cannot influence this.

The demand and supply conditions in currency markets can change suddenly, and this can lead to major movements in the value of a currency. In particular, the markets can be heavily influenced by speculators, which can make it hard to predict what the currency will be worth in the future. This makes financial planning difficult and can quickly change the competitive position of a business.

Data Analysis   6.6

1. Briefly summarize changes in the value of the pound against the US dollar in the period 2005–09 shown in Figure 6.5.

2. Explain, using supply and demand diagrams, what might have caused the changes in the value of the pound.

3. Discuss the possible effects of such changes for UK businesses.

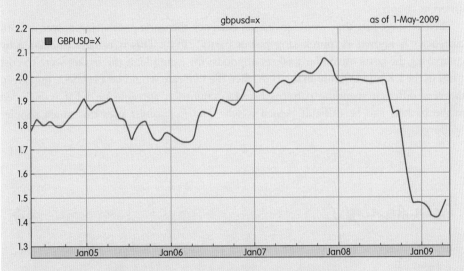

Figure 6.5 The value of the pound against the dollar

Source: Reprinted with kind permission of Yahoo!

 Business Analysis   6.1

In 2009, the Italian clothing retailer Benetton reported a 38 per cent fall in first-quarter profits, after being hit by a drop in demand and unfavourable exchange rates. The firm also said that its 2009 Autumn/Winter collection would be delayed. It is reorganizing its sourcing, production, and shipment schedule for the collection.

Benetton said that its first-quarter results had been affected by 'unfavourable euro exchange rate trends with the currencies of emerging countries' and singled out the Korean won, the Indian rupee, the Turkish lira, and the Russian rouble.

How do you think Benetton could make itself less vulnerable to exchange rate changes?

The McBurger index

Sometimes, currencies may be overvalued or undervalued compare to the long-term value that would be reached with the underlying demand and supply conditions. Pressure from speculators or government policy may push the value high or low in the short term. To identify the long-term underlying value of a currency, *The Economist* magazine uses the 'McBurger index'; this helps it to decide whether a currency is overvalued or undervalued. The McBurger index compares the actual exchange rate with what it would need to be to keep the prices of burgers in the different countries comparable. A McDonald's burger is chosen because it is a fairly standardized product in different countries.

The exchange rate that would give each currency the same purchasing power in both currencies is known as 'purchasing power parity' (PPP). This is usually calculated by comparing the costs of similar baskets of goods: for example, if the basket were to cost £150 in the UK and US$300 in the USA, then the PPP rate would be £1: US$2. But, given the very different spending patterns between countries, agreeing on what is included in the baskets can be difficult, which is why *The Economist* uses this much simpler McBurger index.

 ## Data Analysis   6.7

1. Identify three currencies that were overvalued according to the McBurger index illustrated in Figure 6.6.

2. Identify three currencies that were undervalued.

3. Why do you think a McDonald's burger might be a good product to use to work out what the exchange rate should be? What other products might you use?

| | Big mac prices | | Implied PPP* of the dollar | Actual exchange rate: Jan 30th | Under ( )/ over ( ) valuation against the dollar, % |
	In local currency	In dollars			
United States	3.54	3.54	–	–	
Argentina	Peso 11.50	3.30	3.25	3.49	–7
Australia	A $ 3.45	2.19	0.97	1.57	–38
Brazil	Real 8.02	3.45	2.27	2.32	–2
Britain	£2.29	3.30	1.55‡	1.44‡	–7
Canada	C $ 4.16	3.36	1.18	1.24	–5

Chile	Peso 1.550	2.51	438	617	−29
China	Yuan 12.5	1.83	3.53	6.84	−48
Czech Republic	Koruna 65.94	3.02	18.6	21.9	−15
Denmark	DK 29.5	5.07	8.33	5.82	43
Egypt	Pound 13.0	2.34	3.67	5.57	−34
Euro area§	3.42	4.38	1.04**	1.25**	24
Hong Kong	Hk $ 13.3	1.72	3.76	7.75	−52
Hungary	Forint 680	2.92	192	233	−18
Indonesia	Rupiah 19.880	1.74	5.593	11.380	−51
Israel	Shekel 15.0	3.69	4.24	4.07	4
Japan	¥290	3.23	81.9	89.8	−9
Malaysia	Ringgit 5.50	1.52	1.55	3.61	−57
Mexico	Peso 33.0	2.30	9.32	14.4	−35
New Zealand	NZ $ 4.90	2.48	1.38	1.97	−30
Norway	Kroner 40.0	5.79	11.3	6.91	63
Peru	Sol 8.06	2.54	2.28	3.18	−28
Philippines	Peso 98.0	2.07	27.7	47.4	−42
Poland	Zloty 7.00	2.01	1.98	3.48	−43
Russia	Ruble 62.0	1.73	17.5	35.7	−51
Saudi Arabia	Riyal 10.0	2.66	2.82	3.75	−25
Singapore	S $ 3.95	2.61	1.12	1.51	−26
South Africa	Rand 16.95	1.66	4.79	10.2	−53
South Korea	Won 3.300	2.39	932	1.380	−32
Sweden	SKR 38.0	4.58	10.7	8.30	29
Switzerland	CHF 6.50	5.60	1.84	1.16	58
Taiwan	NT $ 75.0	2.23	21.2	33.6	−37
Thailand	Baht 62.0	1.77	17.5	35.0	−50
Turkey	Lire 5.15	3.13	1.45	1.64	−12

*Purchasing power parity; local price divided by price in the United States
‡Average of New York, Chicago, Atlanta and San Francisco
‡Dollars per pound
§ Weighted average of prices in euro area
**Dollars per euro

Figure 6.6 The Hamburger standard

Sources: McDonald's; *The Economist*. Reproduced with kind permission.

Overcoming exchange rate problems

Exchange rate changes clearly make planning difficult and can change the cost position of a business or its competitiveness abroad very quickly. There are also administration costs of changing currency, which reduce the profits that can be made from overseas trade. While managers cannot themselves directly influence the exchange rate, they can take steps to reduce the impact.

To overcome some of the problems of fluctuating exchanges rates, managers may decide to:

■ target markets that use the same currency—a US producer, for example, may find that there is enough demand within that country to meet its targets; a French producer may decide to concentrate on countries such as Germany and Italy, which use the euro as their currency—but a decision to do this may reduce export opportunities and the ability to buy the best inputs at the best prices;

■ operate in several overseas markets, so that unfavourable changes in the currency of one market may be offset by more favourable changes in the currency of another country;

■ buy currency in advance at a set price, so that they know what their exchange rate will be (this is known as a 'futures market');

■ speculate in currencies to try to offset any movements.

Again, it must be remembered that one currency may be moving in different directions against others, so it is important to analyse with which markets a particular business is trading (that is, buying from and/or selling to) and the relevant currency movements in these markets.

>> **You Decide ...**

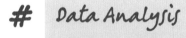

1. As the marketing director of Jaguar cars (which exports a high proportion of its sales), would you prefer the pound to be strong or weak? Justify your answer.

2. What would the operations director prefer?

\# *Data Analysis*   6.8

1. Imagine that the pound has fallen in value against the US dollar from US\$1.6:£1 to US\$1.2:£1. What is the effect of this on the price of a £200 product in the USA? If sales were originally 500 units a week and the price elasticity of demand were −2, what would be the effect on sales?

2. Imagine that a UK company was buying components from the USA priced at US$400. What would be the effect of the fall in the pound's value on the price of imports? If purchases were originally 200 units a week and the price elasticity of demand for imports were −0.8, what would be the effect on the number of imported products purchased?

The impact of an exchange rate change

The impact of a change in the exchange rate on a business depends on:

- what proportion of its sales are exported;
- what proportion of its inputs are imported;
- the degree of competition in the market from overseas businesses;
- how much the value of the currency has changed (and in what direction) against the currencies in its export and import markets;
- the price elasticity of demand for exports and imports.

? *Think about it ...* 6.4

The euro is a currency now used by many countries within Europe. What do you think are the benefits for a group of countries of having the same currency?

>> *You Decide ...*

Given that the exchange rate may fluctuate a great deal, should your business avoid overseas trade?

Of course, the exchange rate is only one factor that affects the competitiveness of a business. A strong pound may make it more difficult to export, but not impossible. Sales depend on the overall value for money, which, in turn, depends on factors such as the design, the quality, the effectiveness of the marketing, and the speed of delivery. Managers can therefore take steps to overcome adverse exchange rate changes or to protect themselves against them. Adopting leaner production techniques to drive down costs, for example, may enable businesses to remain price competitive abroad even if the currency is strong. Alternatively, they may try to develop features that differentiate their products, so that demand becomes price inelastic.

Government intervention in the foreign currency markets

If the value of a currency is determined entirely by market forces of supply and demand, this is known as a 'floating exchange rate'. Given the significant impact of currency changes on businesses and households, however, a government may want to influence the value of its currency. It may even want to stabilize the value of its currency and fix its value. This is known as a 'fixed (or pegged) exchange rate', and can be achieved by buying and selling currency and/or using interest rates.

To increase the value of its currency, a government can undertake the following.

■ *Buy its own currency using foreign currency reserves that it will have acquired in other periods*—that is, when selling its currency to bring the value down. By buying its own currency, the government shifts the demand for it to the right, increasing the equilibrium price (see Figure 6.7). The limit to such intervention is the amount of foreign currency that the government holds or is willing to borrow from foreign banks or governments.

■ *Increase interest rates* The interest rate is the return given to savers in a country's banks and can be influenced by the government (see Chapter 10). A high interest rate will attract investors into the country in search of high returns (although it is likely to reduce demand domestically, due to the higher costs of borrowing).

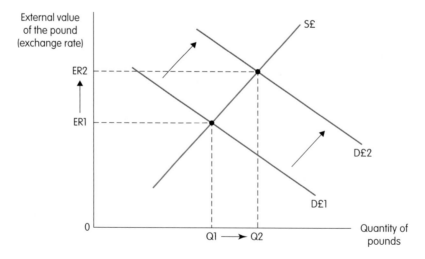

Figure 6.7 Government intervention to increase demand for a currency and increase its external value

? Think about it ...   6.5

1. What do you think might be the effects on the domestic economy of an increase in interest rates?

2. How could a government reduce the value of its currency? Illustrate your answer using supply and demand diagrams.

£ Business Analysis   6.2

The European Exchange Rate Mechanism (ERM) was an exchange rate system in which member currencies were fixed against each other. The ERM gave national currencies an upper and lower limit on either side of a central rate within which they could fluctuate (6 per cent, in the case of the UK). The UK joined the ERM in 1990, but, in 1992, struggled to keep within the set boundaries. Speculators kept selling pounds, forcing the UK government to buy its own currency (using around £27,000 million to do so) and increase interest rates.

On 16 September 1992, the crisis became clear and despite billions of pounds worth of foreign currency reserves being used by the UK government to buy its currency, and despite interest rates being increased from 10 per cent to 12 per cent and then to 15 per cent in one day, the downward pressure was too great and the UK withdrew from the ERM. The pound fell immediately and this day became known as 'Black Wednesday'. The Italian lira also left the ERM and the Spanish peseta was devalued.

During this period, some speculators made fortunes. George Soros , for example, is believed to have made over US$1,000 million by speculating. He sold huge quantities of pounds at the relatively high price at which the government was trying to keep it. When the pound did eventually fall in price, Soros could buy them all back again at much lower prices.

How do you think being a member of the ERM might have helped UK businesses?

The euro

The euro is the official currency of sixteen of the twenty-seven countries in the European Union (EU); euro notes and coins first started being used on 1 January 2002. The euro is managed and administered by the European Central Bank (ECB) in Frankfurt. These countries have given up their own currencies, such as the German mark and French franc, to adopt the euro. The benefits of belonging to the 'eurozone' include:

- there are no transaction costs converting one currency to another;
- managers do not have to worry about the effects of currency fluctuations with other eurozone countries, which provides greater stability and makes planning easier;
- it is easier to compare prices of suppliers, which may allow a manager to find a better deal and force suppliers to be price competitive.

But joining the eurozone does involve:

- giving up your own currency, which can be politically unpopular;
- accepting a eurozone interest rate set by the ECB, which may be changed to alter the value of the euro relative to other currencies. A particular government may find that the ECB increases the interest rate to increase demand for the euro even though, within its own country, it would want to reduce the interest rate to stimulate demand. Governments must therefore be prepared to give up control over their domestic interest rates.

The UK is not a member of the eurozone, although there has been interest in joining at various points in the past. At the moment, the position of the UK government is that five tests must be passed before the UK would join the euro. These focus on whether the UK's economic structure and the state of the economy is compatible with European interest rates, whether joining would create better conditions for long-term investment in the UK, and the impact on UK financial markets, growth, stability, and jobs.

?   Think about it ...   6.6

Which of the following statements are true and which are false?

A An increase in the demand for a currency is likely to increase its value.
B Higher interest rates in an economy are likely to reduce its value.
C An appreciation of the currency occurs when it decreases in value.
D A stronger currency is usually beneficial for importers, rather than exporters.

The market for shares

A company is a business organization that has its own legal identity in law and which is owned by shareholders. Each share represents part-ownership of the business. There are different types of share, but 'ordinary shares' are the most common.
    Holders of ordinary shares:

- have one vote per share, so the more shares they have, the more votes they have;
- can vote on what happens to any profits that are made—that is, they can decide how much is retained for investment and how much is paid out as dividends each year;

- can benefit (or suffer) from changes in the share price between when they buy them and when they sell them;

- have limited liability, which means that investors are liable for the amount that they have invested and can lose this, but their personal possessions are safe.

? *Think about it ...* 6.7

Why do you think limited liability is vital to enable companies to raise large sums of finance via selling shares?

The shares of public limited companies (plcs) can be traded on the stock exchange. A stock exchange provides a huge market for buyers and sellers of shares. Shares of private limited (ltd) companies can be traded, but not on the stock exchange: they must be sold privately.

The price of shares in both private and public companies are determined by demand and supply conditions.

The demand for shares in a company is determined by the following factors.

- *The extent to which individuals or organizations want a vote to influence the company's policy* Generally, there is one vote per share, so the more shares you accumulate, the more control you have over the company's activities. When a business is taking over another, for example, it will want to gain control of enough shares to influence decisions.

- *The expected* **dividend** Each year, the shareholders vote on what they want to happen to the profits of a business. They need to decide how much profit is retained within the business to finance future growth and how much is paid out to the investors as dividends. The 'dividend per share' shows the amount of money paid out to investors. The 'dividend yield' shows the dividend as a percentage of the market price of a share.

- *The expected change in the price of the shares* If potential investors believe that the share price will increase in value (for example, if they think that, in future, other investors will want to buy the shares), then the demand will increase now, which is likely to bring about the increase in the share price that was originally anticipated. This increase in the value of a share is known as a 'capital gain'.

The supply of shares in a company at any given moment is fixed. All companies have an agreed number of shares that can be issued; more may be sold in the future, but this requires the permission of the existing shareholders. When new shares are issued, they are usually offered to existing owners who have the right to buy them; this is known as a 'rights issue'. In the market for existing shares, however, the number that people are willing to sell is likely to be upward-sloping: as the price increases, so does the amount supplied to the market.

The price of a share will determine the overall value of the company. The total value of all of the shares in the company (that is, the price that would have to be paid to buy all of the shares) is known as the **market capitalization** of the business and can be calculated as follows.

Market capitalization = Current share price × Number of shares available

If the market capitalization of a business is perceived to be low at present relative to what an investor believes is the true potential value of the company, then some investors may want to buy shares or even try to take over and gain control of the company.

Can you now answer questions 1, 2, and 5 from the opening case study?

£ Business Analysis 6.3

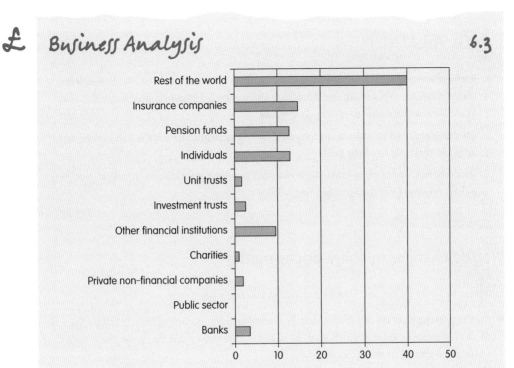

Figure 6.8 Share ownership (% of plc shares owned by different groups)

To be traded on the stock exchange, plcs must meet various criteria and follow the stock exchange's rules. At the end of 2006, the UK stock market was valued at £1,858,000 million. Investors from outside the UK owned 40 per cent of UK shares listed on the UK stock exchange at the end of 2006; investors from the 'rest of the world' held £742,000 million of UK shares. Of this, £245,000 million (33 per cent) was held by investors based in North America.

- UK individuals owned £239,000 million of shares.

- Insurance companies owned £273,000 million.

- Pension funds held 13 per cent (£236,000 million).

- Banks owned £63,000 million (3 per cent) of UK shares.

But the pattern of share ownership does change over time: for example, foreign ownership within the UK has increased, with more takeovers of UK companies by overseas investors. Also government ownership increased in 2008, when the UK government bought shares in Royal Bank of Scotland (RBS) and Lloyds to gain control over the banking system.

Source: Adapted from Office for National Statistics (ONS). Reproduced with kind permission.

In what ways do you think that who owns a company's shares might affect its objectives?

Data Analysis 6.10

1. The dividend yield measures the dividend per share as a percentage of the share price. If the dividend is 5 pence per share and the market share price is 150 pence, what is the dividend yield? What would make the dividend increase?

2. If the dividend yield for a share is 10 per cent and the current share price is 250 pence, what is the dividend that has been paid?

3. The dividend for a company is usually announced in two stages during the financial year. Why will the dividend yield change many times daily?

Why do changes in share prices matter?

Changes in share prices are significant in the UK because:

- they represent part of the assets that households own, meaning that a fall in the value of shares reduces their wealth and, as a result, they may cut back on their spending, reducing demand in the economy;

- a significant proportion of shares are owned by pension funds, meaning that a fall in share prices reduces individuals' pensions and so is likely to reduce spending now, as individuals worry about their future;

- they reflect the confidence that investors have in a company and an economy, meaning that if share prices generally fall, this may suggest that investors are concerned about growth in the economy.

To senior managers, the company's share price is important because it reflects how much investors value the business. An increase in the share price increases the wealth of the investors and this should mean that they are happy with the managers' performance; managers may, of course, also hold shares in the business.

The share price will also influence the amount of money that can be raised if the investors agree to sell more shares; this therefore influences a company's access to finance through shares as opposed to loans.

 Business Analysis 6.4

In May 2009, investors seemed to think that the worst of the recession might be over and started to invest again in shares both in the UK and the USA. This led to an increase in share prices after months of falling prices. In London, all of the losses since the start of the year were reversed. Positive signs in the world economies included the fact that US employers cut fewer jobs the month before than for the six months before that. Lord Mandelson, the UK Business Secretary, said: 'We have to maintain a sense of perspective and I think ... we are through the worst.'

In what ways do you think an increase in share prices could help an economy to recover?

Can you now answer questions 4, 6 and 7 from the opening case study?

The market for capital goods

Capital goods are products that are used to help produce in the future, such as new equipment; they represent an investment. Businesses invest in capital goods to help them to produce more efficiently and to enable them to produce more products in the future. For example, managers buy factories, machinery, and new IT systems: look at the impact that investment in technology can have on a Formula One racing team and you can appreciate the benefits of investment in terms of improving a firm's competitiveness. Gross investment is the total investment in capital goods in an economy. Some of this investment will be used to replace and update capital equipment that has worn out (called 'depreciation'). Net investment can be calculated as follows:

$$\text{Net investment} = \text{Gross investment} - \text{Depreciation}$$

An economy that has high gross investment, but low net investment, is simply replacing capital rather than increasing its capital resources.

When considering whether to invest in more capital goods, managers will consider the extra returns generated by an investment. This is known as the **marginal efficiency of capital (MEC)**. The MEC represents the rate of return from each additional unit of investment: for example, the expected profit from a project could be 10 per cent a year, meaning that a £200,000 investment would be expected to generate a profit of £20,000 a year. This return depends on managers' expectations of future levels of demand and costs. Projects can be ranked according to their returns, from the most profitable to the least.

Managers will compare the expected marginal benefits (the MEC) with the marginal costs of investing (which is generally the interest rate paid to borrow money). If the MEC is greater than the marginal cost, then an additional project generates a higher return than the cost of undertaking it and a profit is made. For example, if the cost of borrowing money from a bank were 10 per cent, then every investment project that was expected to earn more than 10 per cent would be desirable, up to the point at which a project earned 10 per cent itself—that is, the same as the cost of borrowing—at which point, no extra profit could be made. The profit-maximizing level of investment therefore occurs when the MEC equals the marginal cost. Again, we can see the marginal condition in action: if the marginal benefit exceeds the marginal cost, then going ahead with this means a net gain for the individual or business. Where the marginal benefit equals the marginal cost, the net gains are maximized.

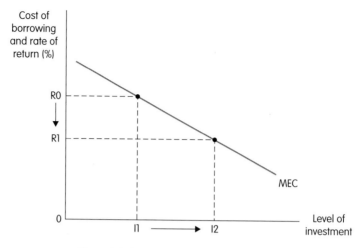

Figure 6.9 The marginal efficiency of capital

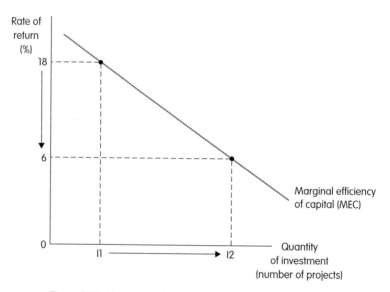

Figure 6.10 Movement along the marginal efficiency of capital

If the marginal cost falls (for example, if the extra cost of borrowing money falls), more projects have a higher return than the marginal cost and therefore the quantity of investment should increase. A change in interest rates is shown by a movement along the MEC schedule (see Figure 6.10).

A shift in the MEC schedule occurs when there is a change in expectations: if managers expect that sales are likely to be higher in the future than first thought, then the expected return on projects increases and the MEC shifts outwards. This means that, at

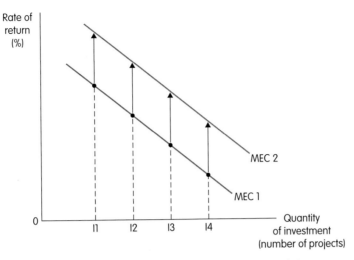

Figure 6.11 A shift in the marginal efficiency of capital

any given interest rate, there are now more projects that generate a higher return than the cost of borrowing and investment should increase. The MEC may be highly volatile, and constantly shifting inwards and outwards, because of changes in expectations. Greater optimism shifts the MEC outwards, increasing investment for any given interest rate; whereas less optimism shifts the MEC inwards, reducing investment for any given interest rate (see Figure 6.11).

The level of investment for any given interest rate therefore largely depends on expectations of the future and companies' forecasts of expected profits. The importance of expectations can be seen in the number of surveys of business confidence that appear in the media.

? *Think about it ...*   *6.9*

1. Using a diagram, illustrate how a fall in interest rates might not lead to an increase in investment even if the MEC is downward-sloping.

2. What could have changed to lead to less investment?

Why is investment important?

Spending on capital goods is an injection into an economy, and therefore affects the total level of demand and spending. Falls in the level of investment reduce demand in certain industries, and can lead to less employment and growth.

Investment is also important on the supply side of the economy, because it enables firms to produce more: an increase in investment shifts the production possibility frontier (PPF) outwards and leads to an increase in supply over time.

The level of investment is therefore important because of its impact on current spending and future growth. Governments will want to influence investment because it can be so volatile, due to expectations: sudden falls in the level of optimism in the economy can shift the MEC inwards and reduce investment. This volatility means that governments will keep a close watch on the total level of investment in an economy because of its impact on total demand.

? *Think about it ...*   6.10

1. How do you think a government could influence the level of investment in an economy?

2. Governments are often keen to talk of the investment that they are putting into areas such as education and health. Is all investment desirable?

The labour market

One of the key resources of a business is its employees. Indeed, many companies, such as Intel, state that their 'employees are [their] greatest asset'. Like any other asset, employees have to be acquired and retained. How this is done is part of the human resources (HR) function of a business. Employees need to be managed effectively because they are a cost: they have to be paid for and this will affect the profits of the business. This is particularly important in labour-intensive organizations, such as hairdressers, accountancy firms, football clubs, and insurance companies. In the UK, which is predominantly a service economy, labour costs as a whole are a very significant part of the total costs of a business. Of course, employees also generate revenue: both directly and indirectly, their actions determine the nature and quantity of the product provided, as well as the quality of customer service and the degree of innovation that occurs. When deciding how many employees to hire, managers will therefore be trying to compare the likely gains from employing an extra employee to the potential costs of doing so.

A business would want to hire any employee where the extra benefit of employment exceeds the extra cost up to the point at which the marginal benefit equals the extra cost. Again, economic analysis focuses on what happens at the margin in order to maximize returns.

What determines the price of labour?

The price of labour is known as the 'wage' (if paid weekly) or the 'salary' (if paid monthly). Wages and salaries are often (but not always) determined by market forces—that is, the demand for labour and the supply of labour.

The demand for labour

The demand for labour depends on the benefits that employees generate for a given business. The demand for labour is a derived demand; this means that it is derived from the demand for the final product. Employees help to add value for the business by developing new features, improving customer service, coming up with new approaches, and actually producing the product and providing the services. The value of an extra employee to a business will depend on:

- the extra output that he or she helps to produce, which is the 'marginal product';
- the revenue generated by selling this extra output, which is the **marginal revenue.**

The **marginal revenue product (MRP)** shows the revenue earned by the extra output produced by an employee and can be calculated as:

$$\text{MRP} = \text{Marginal product} \times \text{Marginal revenue}$$

This determines the additional financial benefit that an additional employee brings to the business.

The MRP curve will usually be downward-sloping because:

- the revenue earned by selling extra employees' output is likely to fall as more employees are hired—to sell more, the price is likely to have to be lowered and so less is earned by selling additional units;
- the marginal product of labour is likely to fall in the short run, due to the law of diminishing returns.

The demand for labour will shift if:

- demand for the product changes—for example, if demand for the product increases, this will increase the value of the output produced and therefore increase the MRP of employees, which shifts demand for labour to the right;
- productivity increases—that is, if employees produce more units, they are adding more value to the business and this again shifts the MRP to the right (see Figure 6.12).

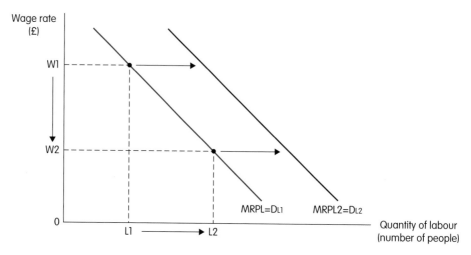

Figure 6.12 A movement along versus a shift in demand for labour

>> *You Decide ...*

What is the best way in which to increase the productivity of your workforce?

The wage elasticity of demand

The wage elasticity of demand for labour shows how sensitive demand for labour is to changes in the wage level. This depends on the following factors.

- *How easy it is to substitute other factors of production for labour* If it is relatively easy to replace employees with computer systems or to automate their jobs, for example, then the demand for labour will be wage elastic; copywriters in an advertising agency, designers in a computer games company, or star basketball players may be more difficult to replace with machines, so demand would be wage inelastic.

- *How sensitive the demand for the final product is relative to changes in price (that is, the price elasticity of demand for the final product)* An increase in wages will increase costs and push up the price of the final product. If demand for the final product is price elastic, this will lead to a relatively large fall in the quantity demanded of it and therefore the quantity demanded of labour. If demand for the final product is insensitive to price changes, then the demand for labour is also likely to be insensitive to wage increases (see Figure 6.13).

- *Labour costs as a percentage of the total costs* If a wage increase for employees has a significant impact on the firm's total costs (for example, in an accountancy firm)

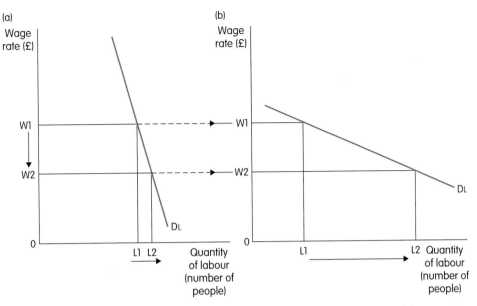

Figure 6.13 The impact of a change in wages, (a) demand for labour is wage inelastic, (b) demand for labour is wage elastic.

and therefore the price of the product, then the fall in the quantity demanded of the product is likely to be relatively high and this will lead to a relatively significant fall in the quantity demanded of labour. If, however, labour costs are only a small percentage of the total costs of the business (for example, in an aircraft manufacturing business), then an increase in wages is not likely to have significant impact on the final price and therefore the quantity demanded of labour is not likely to fall significantly.

? *Think about it ...*   *6.11*

1. State two types of business in which you think labour costs are likely to be:

   A a small percentage of total costs;

   B a large percentage of total costs.

2. Explain two factors that can influence the price elasticity of demand for a product.

The supply of labour

The supply of labour to an industry shows the number of people who are willing and able to work at the given wage, all other factors held constant. Generally, the higher the wage, the more people will want to work, because of the higher rewards and the higher opportunity cost of staying at home. This means that the supply of labour is usually upward-sloping in relation to wages (see Figure 16.14a).

The supply of labour to an industry depends on:

- the number of people in the working population, which determines the maximum number of people who could work in an industry. The size of the working population will be affected by factors such as school leaving age and retirement age. In the UK, the State Pension age is 65 years for men and 60 years for women (which will be equalized at 65 years by 2020, rising to 66 years by 2026, to 67 years by 2036, and to 68 years by 2046);

- The appeal of the jobs in the industry, which might relate to the working conditions, the status of the jobs, and the nature of the tasks involved—for example, there may be more people willing and able to be shop assistants than surgeons;

- the degree of training and experience required—that is, what skills, qualifications, and previous achievements are required—for example, there may be many people wanting to be professional footballers, but they may lack the necessary skills, while a job, such as learning to fly a plane, takes time to master, which would limit the supply of labour at any moment;

- the availability of information about jobs in the industry, so that people know that they exist (if you don't know what opportunities there are, you cannot supply your labour);

- the cost and ease of people moving to the area to take the jobs, which is known as 'geographical immobility'—that is, the cost of living can be higher in some areas than others, which can act as a barrier to movement, as can big differences in costs such as house prices;

- the incentives to accept these jobs relative to the incentives to not work—for example, a high rate of income tax may deter people from working, whereas low levels of unemployment benefits may increase the desire to work. The 'unemployment trap' occurs when people are worse off working than they are on benefits and so do not make an effort to work.

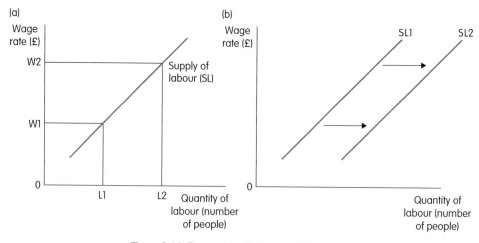

Figure 6.14 The supply of labour to an industry

A shift in the supply of labour (see Figure 6.14b) might occur if the following occurs.

■ *The working population increases, perhaps due to an increase in net immigration* In 2004, the expansion of the EU led to an inflow of over half a million workers to the UK from Eastern Europe, providing an increase in the labour supply in sectors such as construction, leisure, and retail.

■ *The tax rates on income are reduced, so that employees get to keep more of their earnings* Lower tax rates provide an incentive to work at each wage rate whereas higher income tax rates might shift the supply of labour to the left. In 2009, when the UK government announced a 50 per cent income tax for earnings over £150,000; following this several footballers announced that they would have to leave the country to earn enough. Some clubs decided to pay their players in the form of interest-free loans rather than salaries, because this avoided the extra tax.

■ *Education and training improves* Improvements in education and training may mean that more people have the skills to accept the jobs.

Data Analysis   6.11

When an individual is considering how many hours to work in relation to the wage rate, there are two effects to consider:

• the substitution effect; and

• the income effect.

With a higher wage, it is more expensive not to work, so the 'substitution effect' encourages more hours to be worked. But with higher wages, an individual can work fewer hours and still earn the same amount of money (known as the 'income effect').

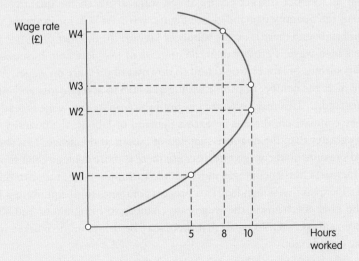

Figure 6.15 The effect of a change in wages on the number of hours worked

Look at Figure 6.15. What can you deduce about the relative size of the income and substitution effects when the following wage rate changes occur?

A From W1 to W2.

B From W2 to W3.

C From W3 to W4.

 ## Business Analysis 6.5

In 2009, youth unemployment in the UK increased above the average for Europe after many years of being below it. Rational teenagers decided to delay entering the world of work, and stay on for sixth form and university. Despite a demographic decline in the number of 16-year-olds, sixth-form colleges experienced an increase in the demand for places of 35,000. Applications to university increased by 34,000 (nearly 8 per cent).

Source: *Times Higher Education*, February 2009

What is the likely consequence for business of this trend?

Equilibrium in the labour market

Equilibrium in a labour market occurs at the wage at which the quantity supplied of labour equals the quantity demanded (see Figure 6.16). At W2, for example, the wage is above equilibrium and there is excess supply of labour: the number of people wanting to work at this high wage is greater than the number of people whom businesses want to employ. This surplus of labour would lead to downward pressure on wages. As the wage falls, this reduces the number of people willing and able to accept a job, and increases the quantity demanded. This process continues until the equilibrium wage is reached.

At W3, by comparison, there is an excess demand of labour: the quantity demanded of labour is greater than the quantity supplied of labour at this wage. This shortage will put upward pressure on the wage rate, because there is more demand than supply. As the wage rate increases, this encourages more people to supply their labour to this industry and reduces the quantity demanded. This process continues until equilibrium is reached. Just like the price mechanism, the wage rate changes to bring about equilibrium. But annual agreements on salaries mean that there may be delays in the market adjusting to reach a new equilibrium.

In a perfectly competitive labour market, each business would be a wage taker. This means that each firm is small relative to the market and therefore cannot influence the

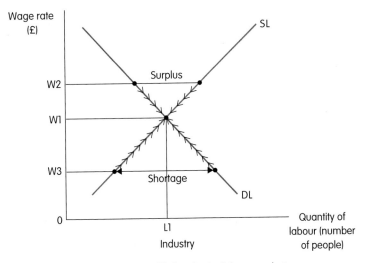

Figure 6.16 Equilibrium in the labour market

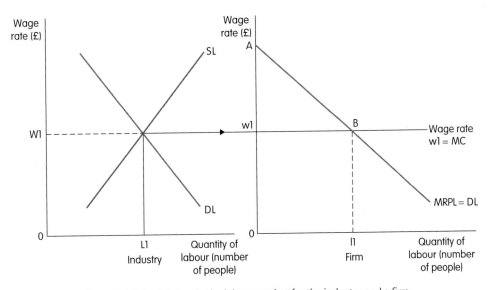

Figure 6.17 Equilibrium in the labour market for the industry and a firm

market wage. A decision by the business to employ more or fewer workers is insignificant to the market as a whole, and therefore cannot shift the market demand for labour and the equilibrium wage. Each firm can therefore hire as many employees as it wishes at the given wage rate. The marginal cost of labour (MC of labour) equals the wage. The firm employs staff up to the point at which the value of employing an extra employee—known as the 'marginal revenue productivity of labour' (MRP of labour)—equals the marginal cost (see Figure 6.17). This is the profit-maximizing employment decision.

Of course, this is an extreme model in which labour markets are assumed to be competitive and businesses are wage takers. In reality, labour markets may be uncompetitive, with employees trying to restrict supply (perhaps through a **trade union**) to push up the wage and managers trying to use their power as a major employer to push down wages.

?   *Think about it ...*   6.12

Illustrate the effect of an increase in the supply of labour, and show its effect on the equilibrium wage and quantity employed.

Wage differences

Wage differences will occur in labour markets if supply and demand conditions vary. For example, in Figure 6.18a, the demand for labour is high because of the amount of money that football players earn for their clubs via merchandising and attendance fees. Supply is limited, due to the high levels of natural ability required to compete at this level. In the case of cleaners (see Figure 6.18b), the supply of labour is much higher, because the job is relatively unskilled and easy to do, and demand is low because cleaners do not directly earn a business much money. The result is that some football players are paid much more than cleaners.

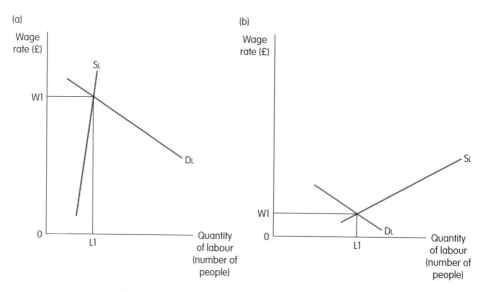

Figure 6.18 Wage levels in different labour markets

Business Analysis 6.6

This year, EU governments met to decide whether to cap the bonuses paid to bankers. Banks had been heavily criticized for their role in the global recession and public opinion was strongly against high rewards to bankers as economies began to recover.

1. Do you think that a limit to bonuses would help the economy?

2. Do you think that it could be effective?

Changes in labour market conditions

If the demand for labour increases in a market, perhaps because of an increase in demand for the product, this means that, at the old wage W1, there is an excess demand of labour. This puts upward pressure on wages. As wages increase, this leads to an increase in the number of people wanting to work and a reduction in the quantity demanded. This process continues until the new equilibrium at W2,L2 (see Figure 6.19). The increase in demand has led to more people being employed at a higher wage.

The effect of any shift in the demand of labour on the equilibrium wage and quantity depends on the extent of the shift and the wage elasticity of labour supply. The sensitivity of the supply of labour to wage changes depends on how easy it is to recruit employees into this industry, which, in turn, depends on the mobility of labour. The more inelastic supply is, the greater the effect of a shift in demand in wages rather than the quantity of labour (see Figure 6.20).

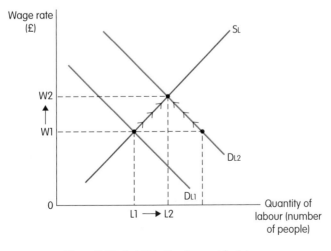

Figure 6.19 A shift in the demand for labour

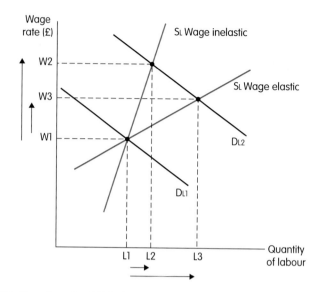

Figure 6.20 The effect of a shift in demand for labour on equilibrium wage and quantity

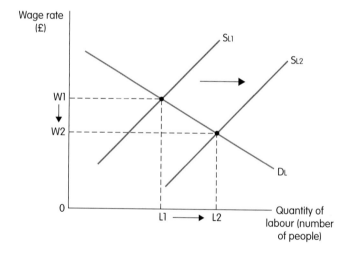

Figure 6.21 A shift in the supply of labour

If the supply of labour increases, perhaps due to immigration, this means that there is excess supply at the previous equilibrium wage. This puts downward pressure on wages. As wages fall, this reduces the number of people willing to work and increases the quantity demanded. This process continues until a new equilibrium is reached at W2,L2 (see Figure 6.21). The increase in the supply of labour leads to more people being employed at a lower wage.

The effect of any shift in the supply of labour on the equilibrium wage and quantity of people employed depends on the extent of the shift and the wage elasticity of labour demand. The more inelastic demand for labour is, the greater the impact on the wage rather than the quantity of labour employed.

Data Analysis 6.12

Show the effect on the equilibrium wage and the quantity employed of an increase in the supply of labour when the demand for labour is:

A wage inelastic;

B wage elastic.

? Think about it ... 6.13

In which of the following industries is the supply of labour likely to be most wage inelastic? Explain your reasoning.

A Doctors.

B Plumbers.

C Stockbrokers.

D University lecturers.

E Airline pilots.

F Cleaners.

 ## Business Analysis 6.7

In 2009, there were over 6 million students graduating from Chinese universities—nearly six times as many as in 2000. In 2010, it was around 7 million according to the *Beijing Evening* newspaper. To reduce the possible effects of this major graduate surplus, the government is offering loans to graduates to start up their own businesses, as well as a variety of tax breaks. In addition, graduates who join the army, or who accept jobs in poorer and remote areas of China, will have their tuition fees refunded. Interestingly, the proportion of students joining the Communist Party has risen from 1 per cent in 1990 to 8 per cent last year. This may well be a way in which they hope to help their job prospects.

What do you think the effect of such a labour surplus will be on wages in China?

Trade unions

The wage level in a business or industry may also be affected by trade unions. A trade union is an organization that represents and bargains for employees' rights. The aims of unions are to protect employees' interests and to ensure that they are properly rewarded. This may involve restricting the supply of labour to an industry so that only union members can gain employment; this would lead to higher wages and less employment. Unions may also push wages above the equilibrium level, leading to an excess supply of labour. They could, for example, try to insist on L1 employees being employed at a wage of W2; this forces the employer off his or her demand curve (see Figure 6.22).

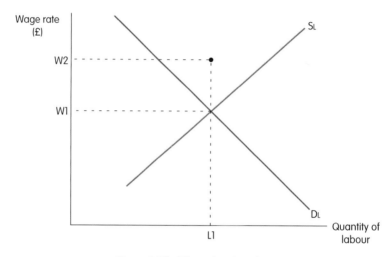

Figure 6.22 Effect of trade unions

Other factors influencing wages

While market forces of supply and demand are undoubtedly important influences on many labour markets, not all labour markets are competitive and not all earnings are directly determined by market forces.

For example, in the public sector, employees do not always produce output that is sold (for example, in the health service and education), and therefore the monetary value of what they produce is difficult to estimate and the demand curve cannot be the MRP. In such situations, employers may try to match the jobs with those in the private sector and therefore arrive at the appropriate level of earnings; there will, however, inevitably be financial pressures in the public sector because these jobs do not produce saleable output and this may limit the amount that may be awarded to employees.

A government may also intervene to influence wages. The UK's Minimum Wage Act 1998, for example, prevents the wage level from falling below a certain level. This is because it is felt that, in some markets, such as unskilled factory workers, wages might be

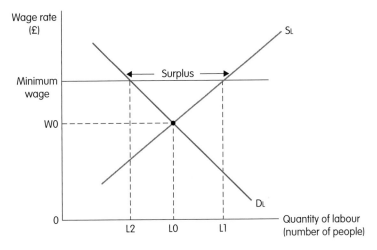

Figure 6.23 The effect of a minimum wage in the labour market

so low in the free market that is perceived as unfair (even if it is economically efficient). To prevent this from occurring, a government may ensure that everyone is paid what it regards as a 'fair' wage. The result of this is that those in work earn at least the minimum wage. But fewer people will be employed compared to in a free market, because wages have been pushed above equilibrium (see Figure 6.23).

? Think about it... 6.14

1. The effect of the minimum wage in Figure 6.23 is to reduce the quantity demanded of labour. What is the effect of the total earnings of the workforce? Explain your answer.

2. What would the effect be of a minimum wage below W0?

>> You Decide ...

Your workforce has demanded a pay increase. Should you agree to it?

Also, when examining wage levels, it is important to realize that there are many different labour markets. Supply and demand conditions may vary considerably between regions, for example. There are also differences between different jobs in an industry and even between the same jobs: there may be many sales managers in the tourism industry, for example, but within this, there may be markets for managers at different levels of seniority and focusing on different types of tourism. This means that while the principles of market forces are very important, each market must be carefully defined when analysing it.

The equi-marginal condition

Labour is only one input into the transformation process and managers must consider the right combinations of resources to use. As you would expect , this will be influenced by the productivity and costs of these factors of production relative to each other.

If the price of labour increases (perhaps because of a decrease in supply), this is likely to make managers reconsider the mix of resources that they use in their transformation process. With all other things unchanged, managers will want to switch away from labour towards other relatively cheaper factors of production. Whether this is possible will depend on factors such as the price and productivity of the other factors.

A profit-maximizing producer will employ different factors of production up to the point at which:

$$\frac{\text{Marginal product of factor A}}{\text{Price of factor A}} = \frac{\text{Marginal product factor B}}{\text{Price of factor B}} = \dots \frac{\text{Marginal product factor X}}{\text{Price of factor X}}$$

This is known as the 'equi-marginal condition'. If the marginal product per pound spent of factor A were higher than other factors, this would mean that it would be better value for money. The manager would switch to this factor and away from the other options. As this happens, the marginal product is likely to fall due to the law of diminishing returns and the price of the factor may increase with more demand. This process of switching resources should continue until each one offers the same extra productivity per pound. At this point, the manager is employing resources efficiently.

The effect of an increase in the price of labour, by comparison, will reduce the marginal product per pound spent on labour, which should therefore lead managers to switch away towards other factors, such as capital, until the equi-marginal condition is fulfilled.

? *Think about it ...*   6.15

Which of the following statements are true and which are false?

A An increase in labour productivity shifts the supply of labour outwards.

B An increase in demand for the final product shifts the demand for labour outwards.

C An increase in the supply of labour should increase the equilibrium wage and quantity of people employed.

Price controls

So far in this book we have seen how markets work and how the price changes to bring about equilibrium. This can maximize community surplus and society's welfare. However there are many potential problems with markets and this is why government intervention occurs. A government may intervene in a market to control the price at which some products are sold. For example, a government may set a maximum price to prevent prices from going too high. This may occur if the government feels that a high price would be unfair: for example, a government may want to make sure that certain medicines are affordable for the vast majority of people and so it might decide to keep prescription prices down below the equilibrium market price. The effect of such intervention is to create excess demand (see Figure 6.24). This is when queues and waiting lists can develop, and acts as a rationing device because the price mechanism is not being allowed to work properly.

If a government decides to set a maximum price below equilibrium, a black market may develop. A black market is one in which products are traded illegally at a price that is higher than the set price. Given the high levels of demand, people are willing to pay more than the 'official' price to buy the item; those who bought it at the set price can resell at a higher one and make a profit on the black market.

Alternatively, a government might set a minimum price to prevent prices from falling too far. For example, in the labour market, the government may feel that employees are exploited if wages are too low. As a result, the government may set a minimum wage above equilibrium that all employers must pay. The result of this is that there is excess supply (see Figure 6.25).

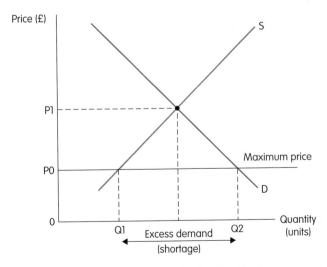

Figure 6.24 A maximum price below the equilibrium level leads to excess demand

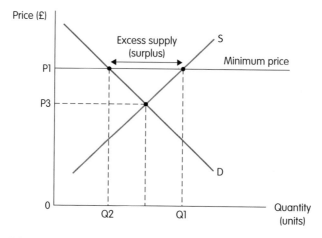

Figure 6.25 A minimum price above the equilibrium level leads to excess supply

? Think about it ...   6.16

1. What is the effect on a market if the government sets a maximum price above equilibrium?
2. What if the minimum price is below equilibrium?
3. Why do you think there is often a black market for tickets to major sports events or rock concerts?

Summary

Markets can differ considerably in terms of their demand and supply conditions, and the price elasticity of demand and supply. A change in demand or supply can have very different effects in terms of the equilibrium price and quantity. In this chapter, we have examined a number of important markets to highlight the importance of the market mechanism and to show how it varies from market to market. The potential effects of a maximum or minimum price have also been considered.

Checklist

Having read this chapter, you should now understand:

- ☐ the meaning of an exchange rate;
- ☐ the determinants of the supply of and demand for a currency;

<ul>
<li>☐ the impact of an increase or decrease in the value of a currency;</li>
<li>☐ why the demand for labour is a derived demand;</li>
<li>☐ the meaning of the marginal revenue product (MRP);</li>
<li>☐ causes of shifts in the demand and supply of labour;</li>
<li>☐ the possible impact of a trade union on the market wage;</li>
<li>☐ the factors affecting the share price of a company;</li>
<li>☐ the meaning and significance of market capitalization;</li>
<li>☐ the meaning and significance of the equi-marginal condition;</li>
<li>☐ the impact of a maximum or minimum price.</li>
</ul>

Case Study Review

Having read this chapter, you should now be able to answer the following questions.

1. What is a company?
2. Who owns a company?
3. What is the role of the board of directors?
4. What do you think determines the price of a share?
5. What is meant by market capitalization?
6. Why does the price of a share matter to a business?
7. Why do you think the chief executive was asked to leave his job?
8. What might be considered when making the new appointment?

Short Answer Questions

1. What determines demand for a currency?
2. What determines the supply of a currency?
3. What is meant by a 'strong' pound?
4. How might the government intervene to increase the value of its currency?
5. Why do investors buy shares?
6. What is meant by market capitalization?
7. What is meant by marginal revenue product?
8. What factors determine the supply of labour to an industry?
9. What determines the wage elasticity of demand for labour?
10. Why is demand for labour a derived demand?

Essay Questions

1. Discuss the main reasons why exchange rates are often so unstable.

2. Discuss the main factors influencing the level of investment in an economy.

3. To what extent does a change in share price of a company matter?

 One Step Further

Visit our Online Resource Centre at **www.oxfordtextbooks.co.uk/orc/gillespiebusiness/** for test questions, podcasts, and further information on topics covered in this chapter.

Market failures and imperfections

7

Learning Objectives

In Chapter 5, we examined the free market system and highlighted the benefits of leaving market forces to solve the fundamental economic problems. In this chapter, we examine some of the failures and imperfections in a free market that prevent an optimal allocation of resources.

By the end of this chapter, you should:

- ✓ understand different types of market failure and imperfection;
- ✓ be able to explain the effect of failures and imperfections on the allocation of resources;
- ✓ understand the ways in which a government might intervene in the economy to remedy market failures and imperfections.

© **Case Study**

In 2008, the UK economy was shrinking and the banking system was in chaos. Some of the banks had lent too much in the form of high-risk lending and had lost money when they were not paid back. They were now reluctant to lend to households and businesses for fear of losing more money. This reduction in lending contributed to a lack of demand in the economy. The situation was so severe that the UK government announced that it would pour billions of pounds of taxpayers' money into three UK banks in one of the UK's biggest nationalizations. The Royal Bank of Scotland (RBS), Lloyds TSB, and HBOS had a total of £37,000 million injected into them. In return for its investment, the government gained some control over the way in which the banks would be run, including a say on the bonuses paid to management. Under the government's plan, RBS would receive £20,000 million and a further £17,000 million was put into HBOS and Lloyds TSB.

Some analysts were critical of the government's plan and said that this type of intervention into the economy would not help the long-run competitiveness of the banks.

Chancellor Alistair Darling told members of Parliament that the rescue package contained: 'essential steps in helping the people and businesses of this country and supporting the economy as a whole'. The Prime Minister insisted the investments were assets and 'not just money being pumped in', adding that the government intended to sell its share at some point. The measures needed to be accompanied by international banking system reforms, he added. The year before, the UK government had nationalized Northern Rock bank, taking complete control of this bank.

Source: Adapted from BBC News, 'UK banks receive £37bn bail-out', available online at http://news.bbc.co.uk/go/pr/fr/-/1/hi/business/7666570.stm

Questions

1. What is nationalization? As part of its plan, the UK government gained some control over RBS and Lloyds Bank. Why was this different from nationalization?

2. Why do you think the banks ended up lending so much money that could not be repaid?

3. Why might the government intervene in this situation?

4. How might the government raise the money to finance this investment into the banks?

5. What do you think might have happened if the government had not intervened in the economy?

6. Do you think that the government will base its decisions on different factors from those of a private business?

7. In what areas of your economy does the government provide goods or services in your economy? Why do you think it provides these products, but not others?

8. What do you think could be the dangers of government intervention?

Introduction

In a free market, the equilibrium price and output is determined by market forces of supply and demand. In Figure 7.1, this is shown by P1,Q1. This maximizes the welfare of society—that is, the consumer surplus plus the producer surplus. In this case, the free market seems to be allocating resources efficiently.

An increase in demand raises the potential rewards in this industry, and resources should be switched into this sector and out of another. The free market therefore works to allocate and reallocate resources efficiently, and to maximize community surplus. Letting market forces operate can lead to an optimal outcome; this is why some economists believe that market forces should be allowed to operate as much as possible and that the government should not get too involved in an economy. If something is demanded, then people will pay for it and it will be created if a profit can be made. If something is not wanted, demand will fall and resources will move out of the industry. Millions of independent decisions by rational decision makers pursuing their own interests determine what is produced, how it is produced, and who gets what.

There are, however, various problems in the free market that prevent it from working effectively and efficiently. These are known as market 'imperfections' and 'failures'. In this chapter, we examine these failings of the free market and consider what the governments might do to intervene to overcome these.

Monopoly power

The free market system can achieve an efficient allocation of resources when markets work effectively. In reality, however, some firms may come to dominate their markets, reducing the degree of competition; this means that they have a high share of the market relative to that of their rivals. In the extreme case of a pure monopoly, there is only one firm in the market, so it has a market share of 100 per cent. More generally, the term 'monopoly' is

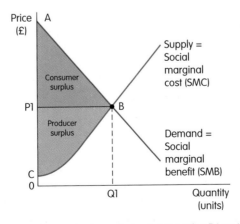

Figure 7.1 The community surplus is maximized at the price P1 and the quantity Q1

used when a business, such as Microsoft or Wrigley's, has a large market share (in UK law, more than 25 per cent).

A monopoly is able to set the price in its market due to a lack of competition. In a competitive market, if one firm were to increase its price, customers would simply switch to the cheaper alternatives; if there is a dominant firm, it may be able to charge significantly higher prices because its product is differentiated and customers have fewer alternatives. In a competitive market with many thousands of small firms, each firm has to follow the market price or it will lose business and make a loss. This means that market forces bring equilibrium at P1,Q1. A monopolist, however, can push up prices (for example, to P2) and is not susceptible to market forces, because it *is* the market.

The effect of this higher price is that the quantity demanded and sold in the market falls (for example, to Q2). Overall, the producer is better off (because the producer surplus has increased to P2, BCF, which is why the firm used its power to push up prices), while consumer surplus falls to ABP2 (see Figure 7.2). Society, as a whole, is worse off due to a deadweight social burden loss triangle of BEC. This occurs because, on units Q2, Q1, the extra benefit to society is greater than the extra cost and so society would benefit from having these produced. If the output Q2, Q1 could be produced, the extra benefit of these units is greater than the extra cost and so society's welfare would increase. Again, the optimal position is where the marginal condition is met. This is why governments regulate monopolies: to ensure that they are not abusing their power and to try to ensure that society as a whole is not worse off. This is known as 'competition policy'.

Competition policy may involve preventing companies from expanding or joining together if they are going to get too big, or it may involve fining companies that are already dominant for abusing their power. Managers who want to grow their businesses (to increase the producer surplus, for example, so that they can reward their owners) or those who already have monopoly power need to be aware that there may be government restrictions on their behaviour.

The price and output decisions in monopoly relative to competitive markets are examined in more detail in Chapter 9.

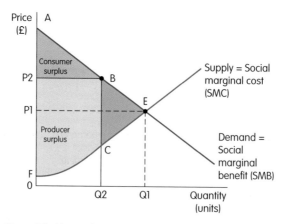

Figure 7.2 Monopoly power reduces the community surplus

Think about it ... 7.1

1. Can you think of any benefits for any stakeholder group that might occur if one firm were to dominate a market?

2. What percentage share of a market do you think it is acceptable for one firm to have? Explain your choice.

3. When might a fall in output increase revenue?

Business Analysis 7.1

In 2008, six retailers and tobacco firms—Asda, Somerfield, First Quench, TM Retail, One Stop Stores, and the tobacco firm Gallaher—agreed to pay up to £173.3 million in combined fines after admitting unlawful tobacco-pricing practices. The companies had used their dominance in the market to fix prices.

The OFT's [the Office of Fair Trading, which enforces competition policy in the UK] objective is to make markets work for consumers and the economy alike,' said the Chief Executive of the Office of Fair Trading (OFT). The OFT alleged that the retailers and tobacco groups arranged to swap information on future pricing. The OFT found that understandings between cigarette companies and retailers between 2000 and 2003 limited the retailers' ability 'to determine its selling price independently.

Source: *Guardian*, July 2008, BBC News, July 2008

Why might you not want producers and retailers to fix prices together?

Business Analysis 7.2

In 2009, Sports Direct's purchase of thirty-one stores from its rival JJB was referred to the Competition Commission by the OFT. This came after Sports Direct failed to sell stores in five areas in which there were competition concerns.

What might be the effect of Sports Direct being the main retailer of sportswear in a particular region?

Externalities

In a free market, managers will take account of the extra benefits that any action brings to the business (for example, the extent to which it helps increase revenue) and the extra costs to the business (for example, the cost of resources used to produce the output). But they will not take account of extra costs and benefits that might affect society as a whole, but which do not directly affect them as private businesses. If their actions happen to pollute the environment, why should they care unless they are made to care? Similarly if their business happens to help the local economy grow, this, in itself, would not be part of their thinking. As profit maximizers, it is assumed that managers focus on the extra private benefits and costs to the business to pursue private profits, but will not want to take account of any other benefits and costs unless they are made to do so.

In a free market, therefore, managers are assumed to ignore the external effects of what they do (which are called 'externalities'). This means that the factors considered by managers when making decisions about prices, output, and investment are not the same as the decisions that would be made if we were looking at them from the perspective of society as a whole, because they are based on different views of the relative costs and benefits. The result is that the free market does not lead to the same allocation of resources that society as a whole would want. This is highlighted by an analysis of negative and positive externalities.

Negative externalities

Figure 7.3 shows the supply curve for a product and reflects the private marginal costs to the business of producing more units. The demand curve, in this case, is assumed to reflect the marginal social benefits to the customer of consuming an additional unit. As we saw earlier, the equilibrium at P1,Q1 maximizes the community surplus. But if the business is generating external costs, then P1,Q1 is no longer going to be the socially optimal price and output. Imagine that businesses in this industry generate large amounts of pollution contributing to global warming, that their vans are causing congestion and creating traffic jams, and that their production processes are destroying the local wildlife. These actions are all imposing costs on others that are not included in the private costs of production—costs of which society would like the business to take account of, but ones that the manager will not consider unless he or she is made to do so. If we add on the external costs to the private costs, we can see a new supply curve reflecting the social marginal costs (SMC) and the socially optimal equilibrium (at Q2). On all of the units between Q1 and Q2, the extra cost of the unit to society exceeds the extra benefit and so overall society is worse off at Q1 than at Q2. The shaded area represents a dead weight social burden triangle and represents a loss of welfare due to overproduction.

When the social costs of production are greater than the private costs, this is called a 'negative **externality**'. In this situation, we might want a government to intervene and reduce production to Q2, which is the socially optimal level.

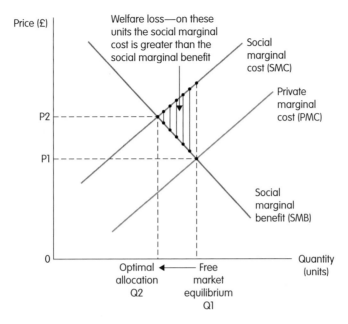

Figure 7.3 A negative externality

A government may do this in various ways, including the following.

- *Introducing indirect taxes to raise the private costs of the producer so that they match the social costs* The precise monetary cost of external effects, such as pollution, can be difficult to quantify in reality, but, in theory, if costs were increased to the social level, the market could settle naturally in equilibrium at P2,Q2. Taxes on alcohol, betting, air travel, petrol, landfill, vehicles, and congestion charges are all examples of the government trying to reduce the effects of negative externalities.

- *Legislating to control production to the level of Q2* Again, it is difficult for a government to estimate social costs accurately and so limit the production to exactly the right level, but the aim of such legislation would be to place restrictions on production to Q2. For example, legislation on clean air or pollution emissions are designed to combat negative externalities. Since 2009, only energy-efficient light bulbs could be sold in the UK; energy-inefficient ones were prohibited.

- *Highlighting the importance of issues, such as global warming, to try to encourage business to take into account the effects of its actions on society as a whole* There have been an increasing number of businesses that have tried to adopt a more socially responsible approach rather than only to focus on profits. '**Corporate social responsibility**' (CSR) refers to an approach in which the needs and interests of different groups, such as the community, employees, society in general, and even future generations, are taken into account when making decisions rather than only those of the shareholders. With more interest in the need to view the business as a corporate citizen and not just a profit-maximizing organization, some owners and directors are trying to take into account the external costs of their actions and are attempting to reduce them even without government intervention.

- *Subsidizing other options* By subsidizing the purchase of fuel-efficient vehicles, for example, the government could bring about a fall in demand for 'gas guzzlers' and increase the purchase of energy-efficient cars.

- *Taking control of production and provide the product itself* When a government takes over a business, this is known as 'nationalization'. By nationalizing, a government can control what is produced, how it is produced, and how it is allocated. In the past, the UK government nationalized many industries, such as coal, trains, airlines, water, and gas. The political belief at the time was that these 'commanding heights' of the economy were best run by a government, which could ensure that the provision of them was fair and available to all who needed it at a reasonable price. The private sector, it was felt, pursues profit and not social objectives, and would ignore the social benefits of the consumption of these products. But a counter-argument is that the pressure of market forces and shareholders will force managers to be more efficient and push costs down.

 ## Business Analysis   7.3

In 2009, the French government introduced a law enabling it to take legal action against kidnap victims who have been deemed to ignore official advice about travelling to dangerous parts of the world. The government said that if people chose to travel to such places and got into trouble, then it was reasonable to charge them for any action taken to save them. The costs of rescue operations that can involve navy vessels, air force helicopters, commandos, and secret service agents can run into millions of euros.

Why is the above case an example of a government intervening in an economy because of a negative externality?

 ## Business Analysis   7.4

In 2009, US President Barack Obama announced tough targets for new fuel-efficient vehicles to cut pollution and lower dependence on oil imports. Describing the move as 'historic', Mr Obama said that the country's first-ever national standards would reduce vehicle emissions by about a third by 2016. Under the proposed standards, manufacturers must reach an average of 39 miles per gallon for passenger cars by 2016, and 30 miles per gallon for light lorries.

The new standards are expected to raise the price of new vehicles by about US$1,300 [£839] per vehicle by 2016. But the president said that this would be offset by lower fuel costs within three years. The USA is the biggest car market in the world, with more than 250 million cars and light lorries on the road.

The President said: 'As a result of this agreement we will save 1.8 billion barrels of oil over the lifetime of the vehicles sold in the next five years.'

He said that this amounted to removing 177 million cars from the roads by 2016.

Sources: BBC News, 'Obama moves to curb car emissions', available online at
http://news.bbc.co.uk/go/pr/fr/-/1/hi/world/americas/8056908.stm,
The Guardian, May 2009, www.reuters.com, May 2009

How might the US government decide what level of emission standards to set?

Positive externalities

As well as external marginal costs that managers do not take account of in the free market, there may also be external marginal benefits arising from the activities of a business. These are gains that do not directly earn income for the business, but which benefit society as a whole. These are called 'positive externalities' (see Figure 7.4). For example, the setting up of a business in a deprived area helps to create jobs and incomes, which might improve the quality of life and reduce crime for those living there. Because

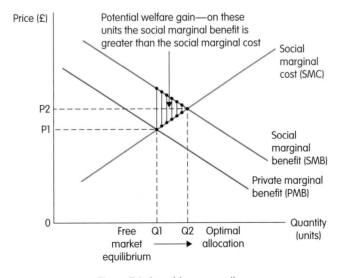

Figure 7.4 A positive externality

these external marginal benefits do not directly generate revenue, they are not taken into account by profit-maximizing managers. As a result, the free market produces at P1,Q1, whereas if the full benefits of the business's activities were taken into account, the socially optimal level of output is Q2. On units Q1,Q2, the extra benefit to society is greater than the extra costs and so society would benefit from these units being produced. There is a potential welfare gain from producing Q1,Q2; society is losing out by underproducing, because the benefits of units is undervalued.

To encourage the production of products with a positive externality, a government might:

- subsidize production, which would lower costs and therefore increase the profit-maximizing output—for example, the government may subsidize the arts, opera, sports provision, and museums;

- regulate—for example, in the UK, there are private train, bus, and telecommunications operators, but they are regulated by the government; train prices, for example, are only allowed to increase by 1 per cent more than prices are rising in general;

- take over supply to increase output and consumption—for example, the government may provide education and health care.

▶▶ You Decide ...

1. Do you think that the UK government should subsidize the BBC (the British Broadcasting Corporation)?

2. What other products do you think a government might subsidize to encourage consumption?

Can you now answer questions 2 and 3 from the opening case study?

Business Analysis   7.5

In 2009, US President Barack Obama faced massive opposition when he proposed an overhaul of the US healthcare system. The US system is primarily a market system in which individuals take out private insurance to pay for health care. Although some basic provision is available to all regardless of income, most treatments require funds to pay for them. Obama wanted to move the system towards the UK model, whereby health care is essentially free to all—that is, it is heavily subsidized by the government rather than provided privately.

Do you think that Obama is right to change the system in the USA?

>> **You Decide ...**

As the managing director of a public limited company, do you think that you should take negative and positive externalities into account?

Cost–benefit analysis

When undertaking its investments, such as building a new school or motorway, a government will take account of any external costs and benefits, as well as the private costs and benefits, to achieve the socially optimal level. This is known as **cost–benefit analysis** and involves putting a monetary value on externalities. This means that the government has to try to value, in pounds, the external costs and benefits of any investment: for example, it would place a monetary value on the impact of a road-building project on wildlife, on the environment, on the quality of life, on congestion, on noise, and on the well-being on those using the road and living nearby.

Cost–benefit analysis often has to be used to make difficult decisions and involves the use of scientific techniques; it does, however, require a manager to make estimates of factors that are, in reality, very difficult to quantify. In the area of health care, for example, there are limited budgets available because any money used in health care is not being used somewhere else in the economy, and the costs and benefits of any investment must be weighed up. Healthcare administrators must decide on how to use the money available, which means deciding which treatments and which patients justify the use of funds. This involves numerous calculations regarding, for example, the impact of spending on life expectancy and the likelihood of improvement in someone's quality of life. Inevitably, a price has to be put on health, injury, and illness, and while more people could be saved with more investment, it is not always economic to do so.

? **Think about it ...** 7.2

Do you think that it is right to try to put a monetary value on quality of life?

Can you now answer question 6 from the opening case study?

Business Analysis   7.6

In 1970, Ford discovered that its Pinto car had a major design flaw, which meant that it burst into flames if another car hit it from behind. Rather than immediately recall the cars, Ford's managers undertook a cost–benefit analysis talking into account:

- the number of cars that it had sold at that point;
- the likelihood of an accident occurring;
- the likely number of deaths if the cars it had sold were left on the road.

The amount that Ford might have to pay in damages if it did not recall its cars was calculated to be around US$49 million; this was less than the likely cost of recalling the cars, which was estimated to be US$137 million.

When this cost–benefit analysis was discovered by the media, there was considerable outrage, which led to the cars being recalled and serious damage to the company's image.

Do you think that Ford was right to undertake a cost–benefit analysis in these circumstances?

? **Think about it …**   7.3

1. What are the potential external costs of building a motorway?
2. How might a government estimate these external costs?

Property rights

According to the economist Ronald Coase, the problem of externalities arises because the external costs and benefits are not traded in a market; this is because of a lack of clearly defined 'property' rights (that is, it is not clear who has the right to do what). If, for example, you were to have a clear right to silence, then those wanting to make a noise (which generates an external cost) would have to pay you to get you to allow them to do this. They would consider the extra benefit of making more noise and the extra cost of paying for your agreement to allow them to do this, and this would lead to the optimal level of noise output (at which the marginal benefit equals the marginal cost). Noise would therefore be traded.

Alternatively, if the people making a noise were to have the right to do so, you would consider the cost of paying them to be quiet and the impact of their noise on your well-being.

? *Think about it ...*   7.4

Why is the socially optimal level of noise not zero?

Similarly, if you have a right to no pollution, then any firm wanting to pollute more must consider the extra benefits of doing so (for example, the benefits from the extra production) and the extra costs of gaining the acceptance of others to be allowed to do so. It will therefore consider the extra costs and benefits of more pollution, and keep producing up to the output level at which the extra benefits equal the extra costs. Alternatively, if it has a right to pollute, you would consider how much you were willing to pay to reduce its emissions. By clearly establishing property rights, this enables externalities to be traded and valued in a market economy, and a value is placed on the external effects.

? *Think about it ...*   7.5

Which of the following statements are true and which are false?

A Negative externalities occur when the social benefit is greater than the private benefit.
B Some products are overproduced in the free market due to negative externalities.
C Governments may want to subsidize products with positive externalities to encourage their consumption.
D A deadweight social burden area occurs when the social marginal cost is greater than the marginal benefit.
E If production of a product generates a negative externality, then production should be stopped.

Merit and demerit goods

A **merit good** is a product that the government thinks provides a benefit to society that is greater than the individual appreciates. Examples of merit goods include education and health care. By being educated, you can increase your earnings, you can contribute to the success of businesses, and thereby help others, and you are likely to have a better standard of living; you may not fully appreciate these benefits when you are younger and so are likely to underconsume merit goods if left to yourself. This is why the government provides merit goods directly or subsidizes them to encourage consumption or production.

A 'demerit good' is one that is more harmful to you than you might realize. An example of this is drugs: you may not appreciate the long-term damaging effects of these to you and others, and so overconsume them. This is why the government regulates and restricts the consumption of demerit goods.

In the free market, merit goods would be underprovided, because the individual undervalues them, and demerit goods would be overprovided, because the individual does not realize how bad they are. To achieve a socially optimal output, a government will therefore provide or subsidize merit goods and tax or discourage demerit goods. In the UK, for example, students must stay in education until they are at least 16 years old (to be raised to 18 years old by 2013) and this is provided free of charge by the state; drugs such as heroin and cocaine are illegal.

? Think about it ...   7.6

Will all governments have the same view of what are merit and demerit goods? Can you think of examples where they might differ?

Business Analysis   7.7

In Dundee, smokers are being offered £12.50 a week by the National Health Service (NHS) if they can prove that they have given up smoking. In other parts of the country, pregnant women can claim food vouchers from the NHS if they stop smoking.

Overweight patients in Kent are being offered incentives for losing weight.

Do you think that financial incentives are a good way of changing the way in which people look after themselves?

Can you now answer questions 6 and 7 from the opening case study?

Public goods

Public goods are products that, once provided, offer a benefit to everyone. For example, if you build a lighthouse, then every ship that passes will benefit from it; you cannot prevent any ship from benefiting from the light, because consumption is non-excludable. Another significant aspect of public goods is that they are non-diminishable. With most products, if one person consumes them, this means that there is less for everyone else: for example, if you buy one of the bottles of water on the shelf of the supermarket, there is one bottle fewer for someone else to buy. The consumption of the product by one person reduces the amount left for others. In the case of a public good, no matter how many people consume it, it does not reduce how much is available: there could be thousands of ships passing by and there is still the same amount of light available.

In a free market, public goods would not be provided, because the producer would not be able to make a profit from doing so; this is because it could not prevent people from consuming the product and therefore they would be able to get it for free (known as the 'freerider problem'). As a result, no one would volunteer to pay for a public good, because consumers would ride for free on the back of anyone who paid for it. For these products to be provided, a government needs to step in and provide them itself.

Factor immobility

In theory, resources can reallocate from one market to another very easily in the free market. As demand for smoothies increases and the demand for cabbage declines, producers move out of the latter sector and into the former. As they do so, they shift labour, land, and capital equipment from one industry to the next, in which the potential rewards are higher. This reallocation of resources can be shown on a production possibility frontier (PPF) as the economy moves from X to Y due to changes in demand (see Figure 7.5).

In reality, resources may not be perfectly mobile: they may struggle to reallocate, which means the economy ends up at point Z (see Figure 7.6), at which resources are underutilized and the resource allocation is inefficient. Resources have come out of cabbages, but have not been able to shift into smoothie production.

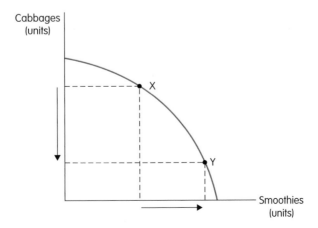

Figure 7.5 The reallocation of resources

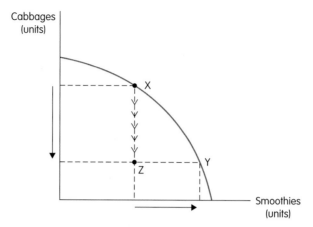

Figure 7.6 The inefficient reallocation of resources

The immobility of capital resources may arise because they are specialized and suitable for one type of production, but cannot easily be reset, reprogrammed, or moved to produce something else. The immobility of some land resources is also clear: demand may be high for pineapples, but land in the UK cannot easily be adapted to grow these.

In the case of the labour market, immobility may occur because:

■ employees lack the necessary training and skills to transfer from one industry to another, meaning that there may be a delay (possibly a very long delay) before they can move into new jobs;

■ employees may be located in one area and find it difficult to move because of family ties, friends, or school arrangements with their children, or it may simply be very expensive to move, perhaps because of the differences in house prices, which acts as a barrier (known as 'geographical immobility');

■ employees may also lack information of what vacancies exist—that is, if they do not know what jobs there are, they will not be able to transfer.

To reduce labour immobility, a government might:

■ try to promote better information of vacancies that exist—for example, via jobcentres;

■ offer training schemes and subsidize or encourage training within business, so that employees have the skills that they need;

■ offer subsidies to help people to relocate.

>> **You Decide ...**

How can you make your business more flexible and adaptable to change so that it can switch into the production of new products easily?

Instability

Another problem of the free market is that, with changes in demand and supply, there can be major movements in the prices of some products and resources. This instability can make planning difficult for managers. The prices of commodities, for example, are particularly vulnerable to shifts in supply (for example, due to changes in the weather). These shifts can have significant effects on the price because both supply and demand are so price inelastic; this is highlighted by the 'cobweb' model.

Imagine an agricultural market in which supply is totally price inelastic at any moment in time. This is because, no matter what the price is, there is only a certain amount of the crop available at any given moment. Over time, more crop can be planted and more land can be allocated to this crop, so supply will become more price elastic, but in the immediate run, there is a fixed amount available regardless of price.

Imagine that the market is originally in equilibrium at P0,Q0 and then there is a shock to supply that reduces the quantity available to Q1. Given the fall in quantity available, this leads to a higher equilibrium price of P1. This high price sends a signal to farmers to produce more because of the higher rewards that they think they can now earn. When this larger crop is eventually harvested, the increased supply will lower the equilibrium price. The low supply price will then send a signal to farmers to reduce the quantity supplied; when this low quantity is produced and harvested, it will lead to a high price to clear the market.

If demand is more price inelastic than supply, the changes in price each session are moving the market away from equilibrium. This is known as an 'exploding cobweb' (see Figure 7.7).

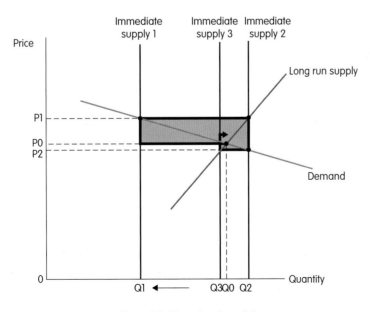

Figure 7.7 The cobweb model

? Think about it ... 7.7

1. The cobweb model assumes that farmers continually base next year's planting decision on this year's prices. Do you think that this is a realistic assumption? On what else might they base their decisions?

2. If demand is more price elastic than supply, the cobweb is imploding—that is, the price changes each year move back towards equilibrium. Can you illustrate this using supply and demand diagrams?

? Think about it ... 7.8

Illustrate the effect of a shift in supply on the equilibrium price and output if supply and demand are both price elastic. Is the effect of a shift mainly on output or price?

>> You Decide ...

If the price of your inputs are unstable (for example, food products), what could you do to try to reduce the damaging effects of this?

In markets such as agriculture, in which prices can change a great deal, the government may intervene to stabilize prices. To do this, they might adopt a buffer stock scheme (see Figure 7.8). In this system, when there is an increase in supply (perhaps due to good weather), the government can buy up the excess supply to prevent the price from falling. In periods during which supply is low, the government can release the stocks that it has built up from the good periods. This can help to keep the price at the same level.

There are, however, problems with the buffer stock system, including that:

- it incurs stockholding costs to store the products in 'good' years;
- there may be more good periods than bad over a period of time, in which case, the government is left holding stocks for long periods, or there may be more bad periods than good periods, in which case, the surplus does not meet the shortages;
- there are administration costs to running the scheme.

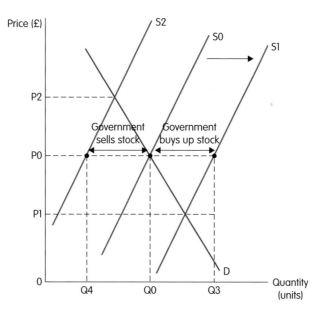

Figure 7.8 A buffer stock scheme

Instability means that producers are uncertain of the revenue that they will generate. It also creates problems further down the production chain. A cereal manufacturer, such as Kellogg's, for example, will have to make plans based on forecasts of grain prices. Unexpected falls in supply can increase the price of its materials significantly, which can reduce profit margins and/or force it to pass on increased costs, which may damage sales. The same problems face airlines uncertain about petrol prices, manufacturers uncertain about energy prices, and chocolate companies uncertain about cocoa prices.

>> You Decide ...

Given the instability in the agricultural market, should you invest in any business in this sector?

? Think about it ...   7.9

1. Do you think that the government should intervene to stabilize the prices of shares? Could it do this?

2. Do you think that the government should fix the prices of agricultural products to prevent instability?

Imperfect information

In a perfect free market, each of the different groups involved in transactions, such as firms, employees, and customers, make rational decisions to maximize their returns and have perfect information about the options open to them. If demand were to increase, for example, firms would immediately realize that there was excess demand at the old price and begin to increase the price until a new equilibrium was reached. In reality, information is far from perfect and customers do not always know their options when it comes to suppliers, employees do not always know their work and leisure options, and suppliers do not always know the relevant demand conditions. For example, a manager of a restaurant business would like to be able to change the prices of its food according to the likely levels of demand; if he or she was sure of a busy lunch period, he or she might push up its prices, because he or she cannot fit everyone in. But anticipating exactly what demand will be is difficult and therefore managers will tend to set prices based on 'average' levels of demand. The result is that, sometimes, a restaurant has empty tables, because the price is too high for the demand; at other times, there are queues, because the price is too low given the levels of demand.

The problems of imperfect information were examined by George Akerlof in his analysis of the second-hand car market. A 'lemon' is the name given to a poor-quality second-hand car. Akerlof highlighted that buyers of second-hand cars are never sure if they will be buying a lemon or not and so are only willing to offer average prices for what might actually be better-than-average second-hand cars. This then means that people with better-than-average second-hand cars decide not to sell them; therefore the average price becomes too high for what is actually on the market and the price falls. This could potentially lead to the collapse of the market entirely.

?   *Think about it ...*   7.10

How can sellers of second-hand cars that are not lemons convince buyers of the quality of their cars?

The problem of the lemons is common because there is **asymmetric information** in many markets. This occurs when one party has more information than another: for example, a garage may recommend that certain parts are changed without the customer knowing whether they are actually needed or not. In the private healthcare market, doctors know more than patients about health care, so could be tempted to diagnose treatments that are not needed.

? Think about it ... 7.11

Insurers typically add about £44 to every car insurance policy to cover fraudulent claims. Why is this caused by asymmetric information?

>> You Decide

What can you do as a manager to limit the risk of trading with suppliers to make sure that you choose ones on which you can rely?

The failure of government intervention

Although government intervention is generally intended to remove market failures and imperfections, intervening can, in itself, cause more problems. 'Government failure' occurs when intervention creates more inefficiencies in the market and can occur for the following reasons.

- *Politicians may intervene for political reasons (for example, to win votes) rather than to remedy a market failure* This may lead to inappropriate decisions being made: for example, inefficient businesses may be subsidized in an area to keep jobs and win votes.

- *Regulatory capture* This occurs when a government organization set up to monitor an industry or business begins to work in its interests, rather than those of society as a whole. Years of working with managers in a declining industry, for example, may lead ministers to start sympathizing with their interests—especially if managers and employees in this industry are well organized in terms of lobbying support.

- *Imperfect information* Just as managers and households lack perfect information, so does the government. This may mean that intervention is mistimed or inappropriate because the government has misunderstood the nature of the problem. Intervention may make the situation worse: for example, by overtaxing a negative externality, resulting in less than the socially optimal output being produced.

Can you now answer question 8 from the opening case study?

Business Analysis   7.8

James Murdoch , the chairman and chief executive of News Corporation in Europe and Asia, launched a scathing attack on the BBC in 2009, describing the corporation's size and ambitions as 'chilling'. He also heavily criticized media industry regulator Ofcom, the European Union (EU), and the government, accusing the latter of 'dithering' and failing to protect British companies from the threat of online piracy.

Murdoch complained about the 'astonishing' burden of regulation placed on BSkyB, the pay-television giant that he chairs. 'Every year, roughly half a million words are devoted to telling broadcasters what they can and cannot say,' he said. But his most withering comments were reserved for the BBC:

> 'The corporation is incapable of distinguishing between what is good for it, and what is good for the country. ... Funded by a hypothecated tax, the BBC feels empowered to offer something for everyone, even in areas well served by the market. The scope of its activities and ambitions is chilling.'

He described the BBC's purchase of the travel guide publisher Lonely Planet as a 'particularly egregious example of the expansion of the state'.

Murdoch added that the BBC's news operation was 'throttling' the market, preventing its competitors from launching or expanding their own services, particularly online. News International, the News Corp subsidiary that owns the company's British newspapers, including *The Sun* and *The Times*, is currently considering introducing charges for all of its websites.

> 'Dumping free, state-sponsored news on the market makes it incredibly difficult for journalism to flourish on the Internet. Yet it is essential for the future of independent journalism that a fair price can be charged for news to people who value it. ... We seem to have decided to let independence and plurality wither. To let the BBC throttle the news market, and get bigger to compensate.'

The BBC is a government-funded broadcaster in the UK. Viewers pay a licence fee, which is paid to the BBC News Corporation—a private business, the interests of which include broadcasting and publishing newspapers.

Sources: *The Guardian*, August 2009, *The Independent*, August 2009

1. Summarize Murdoch's criticisms of the BBC.

2. Why do you think the BBC is state-financed?

3. Discuss the case for government intervention in the light of the above case.

Inequality

In a free market, your earnings are determined by the supply and demand for your labour. If you are highly able and talented, and work in an industry that generates high returns, you are likely to be paid a lot. If, however, you lack training and there are many others with a similar level of skills, your earnings will be low. If you are unemployed, you will earn nothing. In the free market, therefore, there are likely to be great differences between the incomes of different individuals. This means that there will be income inequality. Whether this is regarded as fair or not and whether the government should make it a priority to intervene to change the distribution of income is a question of normative economics, rather than positive economics. An efficient allocation of resources in the free market may mean that there is inequality. It is up to society to decide whether this is acceptable.

The level of incomes earned and the distribution of incomes in an economy can be considered by looking at the following factors.

- *Absolute and relative poverty* 'Absolute poverty' measures the number of people living below a given income level. 'Relative poverty' measures the extent to which a household's income falls below the average income for the economy.

- *The income distribution in an economy* This is shown by the **Lorenz curve** and the **Gini coefficient**.

The Lorenz curve shows the cumulative income share on the vertical axis compared to the distribution of the population on the horizontal axis. In Figure 7.9, 40 per cent of the population earns around 20 per cent of the total income. If each individual were to have the same income (that is, if there were total equality in the economy), the income distribution curve would be the straight line in the graph: the line of total equality.

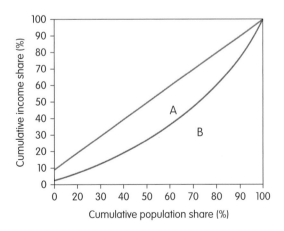

Figure 7.9 Lorenz curve of income distribution

To measure how far away we are from total equality—that is, how unequal the income distribution is within an economy—you can use the Gini coefficient. This coefficient is calculated as:

Area A / Area A + Area B

If income is distributed completely equally, then the Lorenz curve and the line of total equality are the same, and the Gini coefficient is 0. If one individual receives all of the income, the Lorenz curve would pass through the points (0,0), (100,0), and (100,100), and the surfaces A and B would be similar, leading to a value of 1 for the Gini coefficient. The Gini coefficient therefore lies between 0 and 1, sometimes expressed as a percentage (that is, between 0 per cent and 100 per cent); the higher its value, the more unequal the income distribution is within the economy.

? Think about it   7.12

Why might the distribution of income within an economy be of interest to a manager?

To change the distribution of income in an economy, a government can use:

■ the tax system—for example, a progressive tax system is one in which the marginal (extra) rate of tax increases as income increases, which reduces the difference between the highest earners and the lower income earners;

■ the benefit system—for example, higher benefits could be given to low-income earners and those who are unemployed to reduce the differences between high and low-income earners.

? Think about it   7.13

Which of the following statements are true and which are false?

A Public goods will be overprovided in a free market.
B A high Gini coefficient suggests a high level of income inequality.
C A monopoly may create a welfare loss in society.
D A merit good is underprovided in the free market.

Financing intervention

If a government wants to intervene in a market, it may need funds to do so. For example, it may need funds to:

■ take over and nationalize an industry;

■ subsidize merit goods and positive externalities;

■ fund organizations to regulate markets, such as competition policy.

These funds may be generated through different types of taxation. For example, direct taxes are taken direct from the earnings of individuals and companies, such as income tax and corporation tax. Indirect taxes are paid when products are purchased, such as value added tax (VAT). By introducing such taxes, the government will affect consumers and business behaviour. Higher income taxes may reduce the incentive to work. Higher corporation taxes may reduce the incentive to invest. VAT may deter consumption of some products.

Governments can also borrow money by selling bonds (effectively, IOUs). The government agrees to pay a return each year and repay the initial sum on a given date. Selling such bonds may affect markets because, if large sums of money are spent buying bonds, they cannot be used for anything else. A large sale of government bonds may 'crowd out' private investment projects, because the money that would have been used for these is now with the government.

The ways in which governments raise funds is explained in more detail in Chapter 10.

The benefits and problems of government intervention

There are clearly a number of reasons why governments might intervene in an economy and ways in which they may do so. One of these is for the government to provide goods and services directly.

The benefits of this are that:

■ it can pursue social objectives, rather than focus only on profit—for example, rural bus services may be desirable, but not profitable;

■ it can ensure access to everyone, rather than only those who can afford it—which may be seen as important when it comes to products such as water, energy, and health.

But critics of government-run organizations argue that:

■ they are often bureaucratic, involving too much centralized decision making, rather than letting local markets decide what is provided and how it is provided;

■ they can be inefficient, because they are not owned by private individuals and organizations, so the pressure to be more efficient or innovative is not there;

■ they do not necessarily deliver what is wanted in the most efficient way.

Views of the role of government vary between countries and over time. In the 1980s and 1990s, the view in many European countries was for less intervention, but recent economic problems has called for more government controls.

 Business Analysis   7.9

In 2009, President Hugo Chavez of Venezuela took control of the country's leading food company's rice-processing plants after a price dispute. Chavez accused the company of overcharging and warned that they could be nationalized if they did not bring prices down.

Since 2006, Hugo Chavez's government has taken into state ownership Venezuela's largest telecommunications, electricity, and steel companies, and four major oil projects, as it aims to create a state-run socialist economy. He argues: 'This government is here to protect the people, not the bourgeoisie or the rich.'

In Venezuela, the government provides basic foodstuffs at low prices in state-run markets known as *mercales*. In 2009, Venezuela also nationalized its third largest lender, Banco de Venezuela, paying US$1,050 million (£660 million) to Spanish owner Banco Santander. The Venezuelan Vice-President said that the move would allow the government to assert greater state control over the economy.

1. What problems might there be when nationalizing an industry?
2. How might a business be run differently under a government compared to private ownership?
3. Do you agree with Chavez's view of the role of government?

The theory of the second best

There are, as we have seen, many potential failures and imperfections in a free market system; this is why governments intervene in economies to rectify these problems. But governments must be careful not to create more failures by trying to solve the ones that already exist. In raising finance to subsidize merit goods, for example, the government may create distortions elsewhere, such as higher income taxes, leading to less incentive to work.

In fact, the 'theory of the second best' argues that it may be better to leave some failures, because this may lead to a better outcome for society. A monopolist may restrict output, for example, but in the case of a negative externality, this may be desirable because, otherwise, there would be overproduction in a free market.

Failures, imperfection, and managers

The existence of failures and imperfections all influence managers' behaviour. A lack of perfect knowledge means that, sometimes, there may be shortages or surpluses in a market. The existence of monopolies may mean that a business buying from such a seller pays a higher price than it would in a free market. Instability makes planning difficult. At the same time, it is useful to understand and anticipate possible government intervention, because of its potential impact on costs, regulations, and even market structure.

Summary

A perfect free market would maximize the welfare of society. In reality, however, there are numerous imperfections and market failures, which move the economy away from the socially optimal position. In these situations, the government may intervene. Intervention can occur via taxation, subsidies, legislation, or direct provision.

The extent to which a government intervenes will depend on its political philosophy and the extent to which it believes the free market can work unaided. The recent collapse of many banks across the world due to high-risk lending and the consequent downturn in many economies has led many governments to reconsider the extent to which they leave markets unregulated.

Checklist

Having read this chapter, you should now understand:

- [ ] what is meant by market failure;
- [ ] what is meant by monopoly power;
- [ ] what is meant by a negative externality;
- [ ] what is meant by the deadweight social burden triangle;
- [ ] what is meant by a positive externality;
- [ ] what is meant by a merit good and a demerit good;
- [ ] what is meant by the immobility of labour;
- [ ] what is meant by public goods;
- [ ] what is meant by regulatory capture;
- [ ] what is meant by asymmetric information;
- [ ] what is meant by crowding out.

Case Study Review

Having read this chapter, you should now be able to answer the following questions.

1. What is nationalization? As part of its plan, the UK government gained some control over RBS and Lloyds Bank. Why was this different from nationalization?

2. Why do you think the banks ended up lending so much money that could not be repaid?

3. Why might the government intervene in this situation?

4. How might the government raise the money to finance this investment into the banks?

5. What do you think might have happened if the government had not intervened in the economy?

6. Do you think that the government will base its decisions on different factors from those of a private business?

7. In what areas of your economy does the government provide goods or services in your economy? Why do you think it provides these products, but not others?

8. What do you think could be the dangers of government intervention?

Short Answer Questions

1. Explain what is meant by a negative externality.

2. How might the government intervene in an economy to rectify the problems of negative externalities?

3. Explain what is meant by a welfare loss.

4. What are the key features of a public good?

5. What is meant by a merit good?

6. Explain two causes of labour immobility.

7. Explain two actions that the government might take to reduce labour immobility.

8. What is meant by a buffer stock scheme?

9. Why do queues occur at cinemas?

10. What is meant by monopoly power?

Essay Questions

1. Discuss the reasons why governments need to intervene in the free market.

2. Discuss the ways in which the government may intervene in the free market.

3. Can the free market be trusted?

 One Step Further

Visit our Online Resource Centre at **www.oxfordtextbooks.co.uk/orc/gillespiebusiness/** for test questions, podcasts, and further information on topics covered in this chapter.

Costs and revenues

8

Learning Objectives

In this chapter, we examine the factors that determine the costs and revenues of a business, and how these might affect a manager's decision making.

By the end of this chapter, you should:

- ✓ understand the difference between fixed and variable costs;
- ✓ understand the difference between average variable, average fixed, and average costs;
- ✓ understand marginal, average, and total revenue;
- ✓ understand the difference between normal and abnormal profits;
- ✓ be able to explain what is meant by profit maximization;
- ✓ understand the marginal condition of profit maximization;
- ✓ understand alternative theories of the firm.

ⓒ Case Study

Susannah is expecting a bleak Christmas. In the past, she had always hoped for a jump in sales in December as customers bought last-minute presents from her book shop. This year has been very quiet, however, and if things do not improve, she will have to think about selling up. She has owned the Summercity Book Shop for fifteen years and built up a good number of loyal customers. Then, three years ago, Borders, a national book chain, opened up nearby; a few months ago, a major supermarket opened just a few minutes away and is selling all of the bestsellers at prices that Susannah cannot match. Susannah just cannot see a way of competing with these larger businesses.

In the past, Susannah had considered expanding her own business and opening up more shops in the region, but she had always decided against this. She had worried about her ability to control a much bigger business and decided that she was happy running only the one shop, provided that it made her enough money on which to live. Now, she is sure that she has left any plans for expansion far too late: survival is the key issue at the moment. If only she had expanded years ago, she might have been in a much better position now.

Susannah has written to her local member of Parliament, complaining about the seemingly non-stop growth of the big stores at the expense of smaller businesses. The MP has been understanding, but has said that there is little that she can do to interfere with the plans of private businesses.

Questions

1. What problems will Susannah have competing against the bigger stores?
2. Is there anything that you think she could do to keep in business?
3. Do you think that expanding her business would have made good business sense?
4. What are Susannah's objectives? Do you think that these are typical business objectives?
5. What do you think influences the objectives of the owners of a business?
6. Do you think that the government should intervene to change business behaviour?
7. Is there anything else that Susannah could do to try to get the government to intervene to protect her business?

Introduction

An objective is a target for which to aim. To be effective an objective should be 'SMART'—this means it should have the following features:

- specific—it defines exactly what is being measured;
- measurable—it sets out the amount to be achieved or the desired rate of return;

- agreed—between superior and subordinate;
- realistic—capable of being achieved;
- timely—it sets out the time period within which the target needs to be achieved.

The objective of many businesses is to make profits. For example, a business might have an objective of increasing profits by £2 million over the next five years or achieving a return on investment (ROI) of 10 per cent a year over the next five years.

The profits of a business are determined by the difference between its revenue and its costs. Revenue measures the value of its sales; costs measure the value of the inputs used up. The difference between revenues and costs represents the excess earnings generated from being in business; these belong to the owners of the business. In this chapter, we examine the factors that influence revenues and costs, and therefore the profit of a business.

Profits

Profits are important to many businesses because they:

- are used to reward the owners for taking the risk of investing;
- affect the value of the business—for example, high profits may boost demand for shares, thereby increasing the share price and increasing shareholders' wealth;
- can be used as an internal source of finance for further expansion, which is cheaper than borrowing money, because the business does not have to pay interest.

For managers, profits are often used as an indicator of their own performance and so, by increasing profits, they are helping their own careers (and possibly earning a bonus).

Economic profit versus accounting profit

The profit of a business depends on the revenue it can earn and the costs it incurs. There are many different costs that a business has to pay: for example, staff costs, rent, and the costs of energy, materials, and equipment. These would all be measured by an accountant. But when economists think of costs, they also include the opportunity cost of the resources being used. They consider what these people, with these skills and this land, and this machinery and this finance, and all of the other resources that they have available, could be earning elsewhere and build this into the calculation of the costs. This is where accountants and economists differ in their calculations: an accountant measures the costs being paid (such as rent, wages, interest, and materials), but an economist includes opportunity costs as well.

As a result of this, if a business is only covering its costs, in economics, it is actually making enough profits in accounting terms to keep resources in their present use. This level of profit is called **normal profit**. There is no incentive for a business making normal profits to leave the industry for another one and there is no incentive for other firms to enter this industry: the profit being earned only covers the accounting costs and the opportunity cost of being there. Imagine that Tesco makes a profit of £1,000 million. This is obviously a large sum of money, but it may simply be the amount of profit that these resources need to make to keep them being used by Tesco in the markets in which it operates. After all, Tesco is an extremely large organization with over 440,000 employees and around 4,000 stores worldwide. It could, in theory, use these resources to provide a completely different type of service and needs to consider how much it would then earn.

If the revenue being earned is greater than the economic costs, this means that an **abnormal profit** is being earned; this acts as an incentive or signal for other firms to try to come into this industry, because the existing businesses earn more than the opportunity cost of being there. In 2007, Tesco's accounting profits before tax were £2,800 million; an economist would want to estimate how much of this was normal profit and how much was abnormal. If, for example, we estimated £1,000 million as opportunity cost, then the abnormal element would be £1,800 million. This would then suggest that other firms, such as international operators, would want to attack this market. Abnormal profits act as a signal for outside firms to switch their efforts and enter new regions or develop new products to benefit from high returns. Whether they can actually enter the market depends on whether there are any barriers to entry.

Data Analysis   8.1

In 2007, the clothing company, Gap, had sales of US$14,500 million and profits of US$967 million.

Do you think that this amount of profit represents 'abnormal profits'? What other data might help you to make this decision?

If the revenue of a business is less than its economic costs, this means that a loss is being made. Businesses will want to leave this sector, because it is not earning enough to justify being there. In 2008, many businesses in the UK, such as MFI, Zavvi, Whittards, Waterford Wedgewood, and Adams, had to close; given the low levels of demand due to the poor state of the economy, they were unable to cover the costs of being in their industries. Resources could be more efficiently used elsewhere.

Think about it ...   8.1

There are many property programmes on television at the moment in which people redevelop and sell houses. Imagine a couple who give up their jobs and spend a year working very hard, six days a week, developing a house for an accounting profit of £30,000.

Why might an economist argue that this is a loss?

The short run and long run

The cost and revenue conditions of any business, and the decisions that managers take as a result of these, will depend on the time period involved. This is because, over time, managers can be more flexible in terms of the decisions that they can take and are, therefore, able to change more of their resources: for example, they can recruit new staff and find new suppliers.

Also, in the long run, it is possible for the structure of their markets to change around them as new firms enter the market and as technology changes. Nokia, for example, started off producing paper before transforming itself into a telecommunications business, attracted by the higher rewards in this growing sector. 3M turned itself over time from 'Mining in Minnesota' to become a producer of products such as the Post-It®.

It is important, therefore, to distinguish between short-term (short-run) and long-term (long-run) decisions. The short term is defined in terms of production as the period during which at least one factor is fixed; in the long run, all factors of production are variable.

In the short run, therefore, at least one factor of production acts as a constraint and managers may not be able to choose the factors of production in exactly the combination that they want. This means that, in the short run, the costs of the business may not be as low as they can be in the long run; this is because, in the short run, managers may have to try to minimize costs, given the technology and equipment that they have, whereas in the long run, they can update this. In the long run, the manager can, therefore, choose the optimal mix of resources to minimize costs.

Another difference between the short and long run is that it may be possible for firms to enter or exit an industry over time. This means that managers may face more competition over time if other businesses enter the industry. It also means that managers may choose to reallocate their own resources to move into a different industry or market segment if they wish.

How long the short run actually is will vary from industry to industry: for example, retail store managers may be committed to pay the rent on a building and not be able to change the firm's location for at least one year. Alternatively, transferring data from an existing database system to a new one might take nine months, while opening a new factory might take eighteen months.

? Think about it... 8.2

The long run is the period during which all factors of productions are variable. How long it takes to change factors of production will vary from industry to industry.

How long do you think it is likely to take to introduce a new production line in a car factory? What about the length of time to open a new hotel? Justify your answers.

Classifying costs

One of the most common ways of classifying costs is to examine what happens to them as output changes—that is, to distinguish between variable costs and **fixed costs**. 'Fixed costs' are costs that do not change with output: for example, the interest being paid on a debt or the rent on facilities may be fixed for any given period and are not related to amount produced. Fixed costs can change over time, but they are not affected directly by how much you produce. By comparison, 'variable costs' do vary with the level of output: for example, the costs of materials and components used in providing the product would increase as more is produced. As you build more houses, you use more bricks, wood, slates, and electrical wire, for example.

The total costs of a business can therefore be analysed in terms of the fixed costs and variable costs combined, and calculated as:

$$\text{Total costs} = \text{Fixed costs} + \text{Variable costs}$$

As output increases, variable costs will increase as more of these resources are used up; fixed costs will not. The difference between total costs and fixed costs at any output is the amount of variable costs.

When running their businesses, managers must consider their cost structure. If, for example, they have high fixed costs (perhaps because of expensive office locations or high salaries for staff), then even if output falls to zero (meaning that no revenue will be coming in), the fixed costs still have to be paid in the short run. High fixed costs therefore create a high risk if sales are lower than expected. Imagine that you have high levels of debt with high interest payments: if revenue falls, you may struggle to meet your loan commitments. Eurotunnel, the cross-Channel Tunnel operator, has suffered enormous financial problems due to high interest repayments and a failure to hit its initial sales targets, thanks to low-cost airlines and the ferry companies.

The high risk caused by fixed costs explains why some businesses have tried to become more flexible in their operations. They have tried to limit the number of salaried staff to the key employees and they have outsourced elements of production. If demand increases, more work is subcontracted; if demand falls, less work is subcontracted. This makes the costs of the business more flexible and more responsive to changes in demand. A reduction in revenue is matched by a reduction in costs as the business quickly scales down. If, however, many costs are fixed, then a fall in demand can cause far more difficulties. One of the advantages of the Internet is that it has allowed many businesses to set up and trade online with relatively few fixed costs.

Even if most of the costs of a business are variable, managers will still be interested in controlling them. This may be by searching around to find the best-value supplier or finding ways of reducing waste. But, when reducing costs, they must be careful not to reduce the quality of the product and service or they may end up reducing sales as a result. Cutting the number of crisps in your packet, the amount of cereal in your pack, or the quantity of soup in your can may lead to customer dissatisfaction.

>> **You Decide ...**

You have been working with a design and advertising agency for several years, and have generally been happy with its work. A new company has approached you, offering to do similar work for 20 per cent less money. What would you need to consider before deciding to switch agencies?

 Business Analysis   8.1

In 2009, British Airways (BA) followed its low-cost rivals and took free meals off the menu for passengers in the UK and Europe. This was to make savings of £22 million—an important saving for the loss-making airline. The company lost £401 million in 2008. The company's chief executive said that the business was fighting for survival after a downturn in demand. BA is also making cuts elsewhere and has cut its workforce by 2,500 to about 41,000. It is negotiating with unions to cut another 3,400 jobs, and wants to renegotiate pay and allowances.

What problems might BA have in making these cost savings?

Average and marginal costs

As well as total costs, managers will also be interested in analysing the following.

- *Average costs* These are the costs per unit. Average cost is calculated as:

$$\frac{\text{Total costs}}{\text{Output}}$$

Managers will want to make sure that the price that they charge covers the average costs in the long run. If the price is higher than the average cost, abnormal profits are made on each unit. But when setting the price, the manager will consider the volume of sales, as well as the profit per item. It may be better to make less profit per item and sell more than to have a high profit per item with low sales. The profit per sale for Tesco is around 5 per cent, but it is able to generate high total profits because it has such a high level of sales overall.

- *Marginal costs* These represent the extra cost per unit. Marginal cost is calculated as:

$$\frac{\text{Total costs}}{\text{Change in output}}$$

If the marginal cost of the tenth unit is £5, for example, this means that the total costs have increased by £5 when the tenth unit is produced. In some industries, the marginal costs of production will be significant (for example, the cost of producing another gourmet meal in a top-class restaurant); in other industries, the costs of an additional customer (for example, another person on the bus or plane) will be negligible because the majority of the costs are fixed. Marginal costs are important because, as we will see later, the profit-maximizing output can be found by comparing marginal costs and marginal revenue.

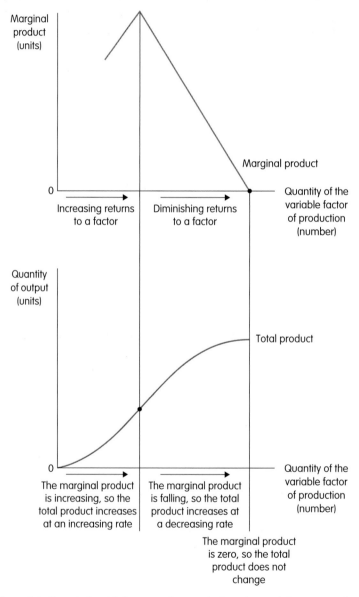

Figure 8.1 The relationship between the marginal product and the total product

The law of diminishing returns and marginal costs

In the short run, marginal costs are often influenced by the law of diminishing returns. This law states that the extra output (also called the 'marginal product') from adding a variable factor, such as labour, to a fixed factor, such as machinery, will eventually diminish (see Figure 8.1). This means that total output will be increasing as more variable factors of production are added, but it increases at a slower rate. With less productivity, the marginal costs of production will rise (see Figure 8.2). If each extra worker produces fewer units, but is paid the same amount of money as the original workers, the extra cost of the units in terms of labour will go up. If one extra employee is paid £50 a day and produces fifty units, then this costs £1 a unit. If the next employee is paid £50 a

Data Analysis   8.2

Table 8.1 The relationship between marginal and total costs.

Output (units)	Total cost (£)	Marginal costs (£)
1	20	n/a
2	50	30
3	90	
4	140	
5		60
6		80
7	400	

Complete the missing figures for total cost and marginal cost in the table above. Explain the relationship between marginal and total costs.

? Think about it ...   8.3

Which of the following statements are true and which are false?

A Fixed costs never change.

B If marginal costs are zero, total costs are zero.

C If marginal costs are positive, but falling, total cost is rising at a slower rate.

D If output is zero, total costs are equal to fixed costs.

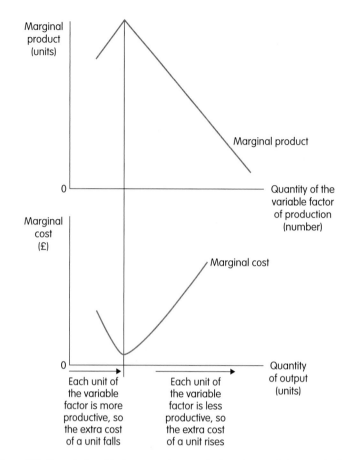

Figure 8.2 The relationship between the marginal product and the marginal cost

day and produces twenty-five units, the cost of these extra units in terms of labour is now £2. As the productivity of the additional employee falls, the extra cost of the units produced in terms of labour increases; the marginal cost curve is therefore the inverse of the marginal product curve in the short run.

Given the impact of the law of diminishing returns, the marginal costs will rise as the marginal product declines. This means that total costs will rise at a slower rate at first, due to falling marginal costs, then start to rise at an increasing rate, due to increasing marginal costs (see Figure 8.3).

The relationship between average and marginal costs

If the marginal cost of another unit is below the existing average cost, then the average cost will fall (see Figure 8.4). Imagine that the average cost per unit is £10 and then you make an extra unit for £1: this will bring the average cost down.

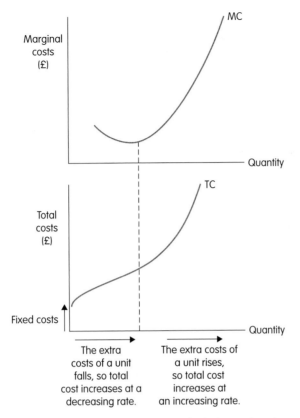

The extra costs of a unit falls, so total cost increases at a decreasing rate.

The extra costs of a unit rises, so total cost increases at an increasing rate.

Figure 8.3 The relationship between marginal costs and total costs

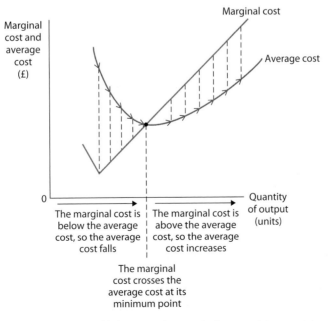

The marginal cost is below the average cost, so the average cost falls

The marginal cost is above the average cost, so the average cost increases

The marginal cost crosses the average cost at its minimum point

Figure 8.4 The relationship between the marginal cost and the average cost

Table 8.2

Output (units)	Total cost (£)	Average cost (£)*	Marginal cost (£)	Consequence
1	100	100		
2	180	90	80	The marginal cost is below the average cost, so the average cost falls
3	240	80	60	The marginal cost is below the average cost, so the average falls
4	280	70	40	The marginal cost is below the average cost, so the average falls
5	400	80	120	The marginal cost is above the average, so the average rises
6	600	100	200	The marginal cost is above the average so the average rises

* Calculated as Total cost/Output

If, however, the marginal cost is above the average cost, the average will increase. Imagine that the average cost per unit is £10 and then you make an extra unit for £12: this will pull the average cost up.

The table above demonstrates the relationship between the marginal cost and the average cost.

Managers will continually be trying to find ways of controlling their marginal and average costs to ensure that they remain competitive. An increase in costs is likely to mean fewer profits (or even a loss) or may require the business to try to push up prices if it can. Lower costs, by comparison, may increase profit margins and/or enable the business to reduce its prices, making it more price competitive.

Analysing average costs

The average cost (the cost per unit) is made up of the fixed cost per unit and the variable cost per unit. In this next section, we analyse the factors that determine the shape of these curves and how they influence the overall cost per unit.

Average fixed costs

The average fixed cost will continually fall as more units are produced. This is because the fixed costs can be 'shared out' over more units. Fixed costs of £100,000 with an output of one unit are £100,000 per unit; if 50,000 units are produced, they are only £2 per unit; if 100,000 units are produced, they are only £1 per unit. This explains why, in industries in which there are high fixed costs (such as the car industry, telecommunications, and transport companies), managers are very keen to keep outputs high so that the fixed costs are spread over more units.

If sales are low, managers will need to consider discounting their prices to promote sales; higher sales would reduce the average fixed cost and therefore may enable more profits to be made, even at the lower price. But the danger is that, if sales do not increase, the business will make a loss due to the low price. The success of a price-cutting policy in these circumstances depends on the price elasticity of demand.

? Think about it ...   8.4

1. Can you think of three types of business likely to have high fixed costs?
2. If you were cutting price to increase sales significantly, would you want demand to be price elastic or inelastic?

Average variable costs

The average variable cost shows the variable cost per unit and its shape depends on the productivity of the variable factors. In the short run, the average product of the variable factor will tend to decrease at some point due to the law of diminishing returns. Employees are, at first, more productive on average, but at some point, they become less productive because more workers are being added to fixed factors that limit their ability to produce. The average variable cost is the inverse of this: when employees are becoming more productive, the variable cost per unit falls and vice versa.

When the marginal product is above the average product, this pulls up the average product; when it is below, it pulls down the average product (see Figure 8.5). For example, if, on average, your employees handle fifty enquiries a day in your call centre and then the extra person only handles forty, this will bring down the average; if, on average, your employees handle fifty enquiries a day in your call centre and then the extra person handles sixty, this will bring up the average. The marginal product therefore cuts the average product at its maximum point. Similarly, if marginal cost is below the average variable cost, the latter will fall; if marginal cost is above the average variable cost, the latter will rise. This means that the marginal cost cuts the average variable cost at its minimum point.

Figure 8.6 highlights the inverse relationship between productivity and costs on a marginal and an average level. Essentially, if your variable factors are more productive, this reduces unit costs; if they are less productive, your unit costs rise. This explains again why managers should focus on productivity and make sure that this is improving, if possible.

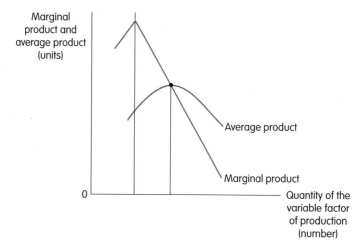

Figure 8.5 The relationship between the marginal product and the average product

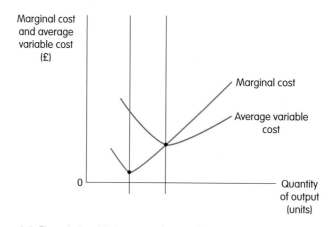

Figure 8.6 The relationship between the marginal cost and the average variable cost

Data Analysis   8.3

1. You employ ten employees who produce 500 units. What is the average product? If the marginal product of an eleventh worker is 100 units, what is the new average product?

2. If the marginal product of additional employees is falling, what is happening to total output?

Short-run average costs

Given that average fixed costs continually fall as output increases, this means that the average variable cost and average total costs get closer to each other as a business expands. At low output levels, costs are dominated by the fixed costs, but as output increases, the variable costs become more significant (see Figure 8.7). Again, this highlights the risk of having high fixed costs if sales are low: the cost per unit will be high because of your fixed costs, meaning that you will be making a loss.

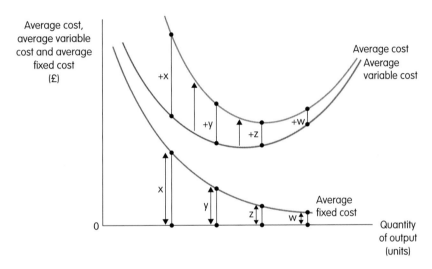

Figure 8.7 The relationship between the average cost, the average variable cost, and the average fixed cost

Data Analysis 8.4

The fixed costs of a business are £80,000 a week. The variable costs are £20 a unit.

1. What is the average fixed cost and the average cost if:

   A output is 200 units?
   B output is 1,000 units?
   C output is 5,000 units?
2. Would the business make a profit if the price per unit were £50? Explain your findings.

Long-run average costs

In the long run, managers can change all of the factors of production; they are no longer constrained by having at least one factor fixed. With all of the factors being variable, they can choose the ideal combination to minimize the average cost for any level of output. The lowest average cost for any output level is shown by the long-run average cost curve. This curve is derived from the short-run average cost curves.

A short-run average cost curve is constructed on this basis and shows the lowest cost per unit given a level of fixed factor(s). Over time, the fixed factor can be changed (for example, more equipment can be acquired or bigger premises found) and another short-run curve is constructed with a new level of fixed factors (for example, twelve machines rather than eleven). If the fixed factors are changed again, there is another short-run average cost curve, and so on. This means that there are different average costs curves in the short run for all of the different levels of the fixed factor. The long-run average cost curve is derived from moving from one short-run average costs curve to another.

Figure 8.8 demonstrates internal **economies of scale** and **diseconomies of scale**. Imagine that a business is producing at Q1 and has the optimal amount of capital equipment, so that its average costs are the lowest possible and it is therefore on the long-run average cost curve. If the business expands to Q2 in the short run, it is constrained by its capital and, in the short run, produces at X on SRAC1. Over time, it can increase its capital equipment to the optimal level and move on to a new short-run average cost curve at 'Y'. If it expands again to Q3 in the short run, it moves along SRAC2, but over time, adjusts its capital equipment to reduce the unit costs to 'W' on a new short-run average cost curve SRAC3.

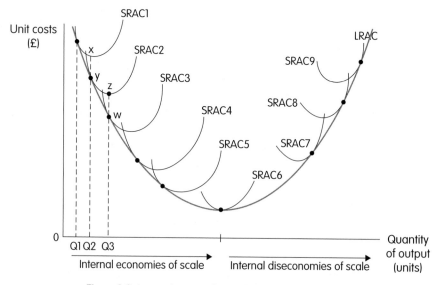

Figure 8.8 Internal economies and diseconomies of scale

The shape of the long-run average cost curve is important for managers when deciding whether or not to expand the business. If the long-run average cost falls, then there will be an incentive to produce more over time, although this decision will obviously depend on demand as well.

?   *Think about it ...*   8.5

If the unit cost of producing, say, 20,000 shirts a month is significantly less than that of producing 5,000 a month, why do you think a business might continue to produce 5,000 rather than expand its facilities?

Internal economies of scale

As a business moves to a larger scale of operations in the long run, it may experience falling average (unit) costs (as it moves from one short-run average cost curve to another). If the unit cost falls as the scale of operations increases, the business is said to be benefiting from 'internal economies of scale'.

These internal economies of scale may be due to the following factors.

- *Technical economies of scale* A business may invest in capital equipment, such as a production line. If this equipment is used only on a small scale, this will be expensive (for example, the high costs of the production line may be spread only over a few hundred units of production). If production occurs on a larger scale, the cost per unit is likely to be lower, because the costs of the investment are spread over more units. Some technology is therefore designed for large-scale production and will be inefficient if used on a small scale. Think of farming: if you have only one field, but buy a tractor, this equipment is not used to its full potential. As you expand your farm, your tractor can be used more efficiently. This helps explain why farming production is increasingly undertaken by fewer bigger farms that are able to use their technology efficiently and spread costs in a way with which small farms cannot compete. Similarly, a production line will be inefficient if it is not used for the scale for which it has been designed: the production line at Coca Cola in Milton Keynes can produce 2,000 cans per minute; imagine the impact on the cost per unit if it were to produce only one can per minute.

- *The law of increased dimensions* This economy of scale is most appropriate to businesses involved in transportation or warehousing. If the dimensions of a warehouse or container lorry are doubled, the volume that it can contain increases eight times (see Figure 8.9). This means the cost per unit of storage or delivery is reduced. To build a container ship twice as big may cost twice as much in material costs but given that it can hold eight times as much cargo the cost per unit being transported falls.

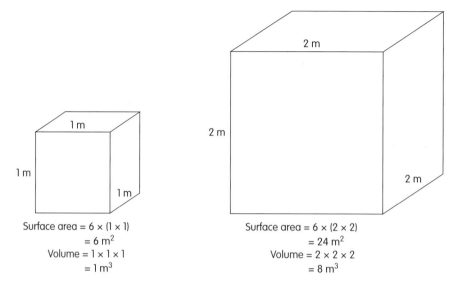

Figure 8.9 Economies of scale through increased dimensions

- *Managerial economies of scale* These occur as a business grows, allowing it to use specialist managers. For example, larger organizations are more likely to be able to afford and justify specialist human resource (HR) managers. This may help to ensure that people are managed effectively, are motivated, and are used efficiently. For example, they may be more likely to turn up and less likely to leave, which will reduce costs compared to a business that lacks such specialist advice and guidance. Other areas in which specialists may be used might include finance and marketing. Entrepreneurs are often trying to manage all of the areas of the business themselves and are unlikely to be experts in all of these different fields. The employment of specialists can lead to better decisions and fewer mistakes being made.

- *Financial economies of scale* These occur if larger businesses are able to raise finance more cheaply than smaller businesses. Larger businesses are likely to have more collateral than small firms and this might mean that a bank believes they are less risk and therefore can be given lower rates of interest. The credit rating of a business (which is assessed by companies such as Standard and Poor, and Moody's) has a big impact on the interest rate that it is charged; this does not depend only on the size of a business, but a bigger firm with more collateral may be asked to pay less back overall.

- *Purchasing economies of scale* These occur when larger firms can negotiate better terms from suppliers and distributors. Given the scale of the orders, they can push prices down and achieve a lower cost per unit. They are the cost benefits that occur due to bulk buying. Large orders also enable suppliers to benefit from their own economies of scale, which can lead to lower unit costs, which can be passed on as lower prices.

The existence of internal economies of scale provides a reason for a business to expand to benefit from the cost advantages of large-scale operations.

? **Think about it ...**   **8.6**

As markets become more global, why do you think seeking to benefit from internal economies of scale may play an even more significant role in business planning?

£ **Business Analysis**   **8.2**

Discount retailers such as Lidl—and Aldi, another German chain—are increasingly taking market share in Europe. They generally charge some 30–50 per cent less for groceries than ordinary supermarkets.

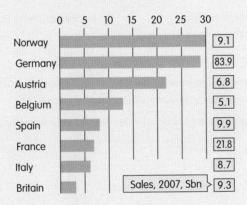

Discount stores, market share, 2007, %

Figure 8.10 Room for expansion

Source: Planet Retail. Reproduced with kind permission.

Discounters hold a far narrower range of goods than a normal supermarket offers, resulting in fewer suppliers, a high volume of purchases and sales, and massive economies of scale. Whereas Tesco might hold sixteen brands of tomato ketchup, Lidl will hold one.

Aldi and Lidl, which dominate the world of discounting, have annual sales estimated at €43,000 million (US$64,000 million) and €35,000 million, respectively. They are privately owned and can take a long-term approach to expanding abroad.

1. Do you think that all retailers will eventually follow the Aldi and Lidl model?
2. What do you think is meant by a 'long-term approach to expanding abroad'?

Data Analysis 8.5

Table 8.3

Rank	Company	Revenues (US$m)	Profits (US$m)
1	WalMart Stores	378,799	12,731
2	ExxonMobil	372,824	40,610
3	Royal Dutch Shell	355,782	31,331
4	BP	291,438	20,845
5	Toyota Motor	230,201	15,042
6	Chevron	210,783	18,688
7	ING Group	201,516	12,649
8	Total	187,280	18,042
9	General Motors	182,347	−38,732
10	ConocoPhillips	178,558	11,891

The companies above were the biggest in the world in 2008 according to *Forbes* magazine. Their size has been measured in terms of their revenues.

1. How else do you think you might measure the size of a business?

2. Choose one of the top ten companies shown above. What types of economy of scale do you think are most important to this business? Explain your reasoning.

3. Why do you think so many large firms are either American, European, or Japanese?

Economies of scope

As well as internal economies of scale, larger businesses may benefit from 'economies of scope'. These are factors that make it cheaper per unit to produce a range of products in one business rather than for each of them to be produced by individual businesses. These economies include cost savings from centralized functions such as marketing. For example, Cadbury's markets all of its chocolate under the one brand name, which means that it may need to spend less to get a new product tried by customers, because the brand is known; it will also be cheaper to distribute all of its products together. Economies of scope will also include shared research into different products or processes.

Another advantage comes through cross-selling products from one business to others. For example, a travel company might sell travel insurance from one of its other divisions. This enables firms to access customers more cheaply: just look at how banks have diversified into areas such as insurance, pensions, life assurance, and share trading.

A desire for economies of scope might encourage managers to diversify into different areas to share its skills in new areas. Historically, companies such as BTR and Hanson, in the UK, and ITT, in the USA, aggressively pursued expansion through acquisition, buying companies in very different markets, believing that there were gains from shared resources however different the products. In recent years, however, the problems of running many different types of business have tended to make conglomerates unpopular with managers and investors.

Internal diseconomies of scale

At some level of output, if managers keep expanding the business, the long-run average costs may start to increase. If the average costs rise with an increase in scale, the business is experiencing internal *dis*economies of scale.

The reasons why average costs might increase with a larger scale are generally linked to the problems of managing a bigger business, which include the following.

- *Coordination and control problems* Managing a small business is relatively simple, in that there may be relatively few people to organize, and a limited number of products and customers with which to deal. As a business grows, it usually operates in more markets, with more products, more suppliers, and more decisions to make. Simply keeping track of what is happening when, who is doing what, and who is in charge of what can be increasingly difficult.

- *Motivational problems* With more people working within an organization, keeping everyone feeling as though they are part of the business and working towards the same aims can be difficult. Different departments, different divisions, and different regions can form their own ways of doing things, set their own priorities, and have their own values. This can lead to conflict between parts of the business and can lead to some people feeling as if their views are neglected. Absenteeism and labour turnover tend to be higher in larger organizations than smaller ones because of these problems of alienation.

? Think about it ... 8.7

Unilever is a major manufacturer of food, homecare, healthcare, and personal care products. It has 400 brands spanning fourteen categories of home, personal care, and foods products. Its brand portfolio includes global brands, such as Lipton, Knorr, Dove, and Omo, to trusted local brands, such as Blue Band and Suave.

1. To what extent do you think Unilever can develop a common set of values among all of its employees and brands?

2. What problems might it face in achieving this?

To avoid diseconomies of scale, managers may adopt many management techniques, such as:

- the use of target setting to agree on objectives throughout the organization;
- the use of budgets to set financial targets for different parts of the business;
- the use of appraisals to review individuals' performance;
- ensuring that any one unit within the business is not too big—a policy adopted by the Virgin Group and Swedish company ABB;
- producing a mission statement to make it clear in what the business believes and what it values, to try to get everyone thinking, believing, and acting in the same way. A mission statement is meant to reflect the purpose of the business and the core values of its employees. It can provide a useful focus point for employees by defining what the business represents.

All of these techniques aim to try to ensure that all employees are aiming for the same goals and that they feel part of the business; this, hopefully, can prevent diseconomies of scale from emerging.

The Minimum Efficient Scale

The level of output at which internal economies of scale stop occurring is known as the **Minimum Efficient Scale (MES)** (see Figure 8.11). To benefit fully from internal economies of scale without incurring diseconomies, managers would want to produce at the MES. This level of output is likely to influence the number of firms competing in a market. If the MES is high relative to the total market sales, then the market is likely to be dominated by a few firms only operating efficiently; if each firm becomes efficient and produces at the MES, it means that a few firms can supply the whole market. This may occur in markets such as banking, insurance, the car industry, pharmaceuticals, and aircraft manufacture.

If, however, the MES is only a small proportion of the total market, then the industry can have many relatively small, but nevertheless efficient, producers. This will result in a more competitive industry and there may be no advantages—and, potentially, cost

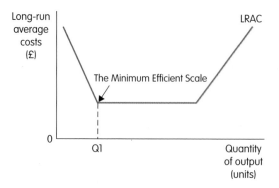

Figure 8.11 The Minimum Efficient Scale

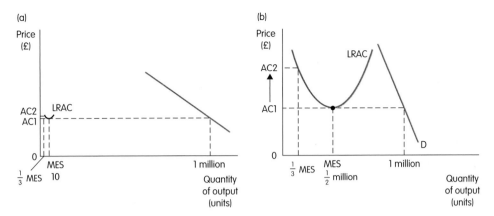

Figure 8.12 The relationship between the Minimum Efficient Scale and market structure

disadvantages—to becoming too big. This may occur in markets such as hairdressing, plumbing, and electricians.

But the market structure will also depend on the cost disadvantage of *not* producing at the MES level (see Figure 8.12). If, for example, the unit costs of producing at one tenth of the MES level are only 0.01 per cent higher than being at the MES, the disadvantage of remaining small is not a major problem. You might find many inefficient firms surviving in this industry, and it might be possible to enter the market and compete even if you are relatively small.

If, however, the cost disadvantage of operating at one tenth of MES is 50 per cent, then it is unlikely that inefficient firms will survive; trying to compete in this industry on a relatively small scale is likely to be difficult unless your product is different enough to justify a high price to cover the costs. In the diagram above on the left there is a low Minimum Efficient Scale relative to demand and a low cost disadvantage of operating below the MES; you would therefore expect many firms operating in this industry. In the industry on the right-hand side the MES is high relative to the industry and the cost disadvantage of operating below this is high; this suggests there will be relatively few businesses in this industry.

Understanding internal economies and diseconomies of scale is therefore important for managers because it will influence:

■ at what level of output they might want to produce;

■ the likely structure of any market that they enter.

Think about it ...   8.8

1. In the car industry there are significant internal economies of scale. But some smaller producers continue to exist even if their unit costs are much higher than the mass producers. How can they survive?

2. What else do you think might, or should, influence the size of a business as well as the existence of internal economies and diseconomies of scale?

You Decide ...

Innocent Ltd produces smoothies, water drinks, and food that are free of artificial ingredients. It has grown very fast since it was set up. To what extent do you think such fast growth will bring benefits?

 ## Business Analysis   8.3

The world's biggest printing plant was opened by News International in 2008. This company publishes *The Times*, *Sunday Times*, and *The Sun*. Twelve state-of-the-art colour printing presses cover an area the size of twenty-three football pitches in Hertfordshire. Up to 70,000 papers an hour can be printed in full colour. This is compared with 30,000 at Wapping, its previous printing press, which, in its day, was also state-of-the-art and revolutionized the newspaper industry. The new presses require even fewer people to run them: 200 instead of 600.

Source: Adapted from BBC News, 'World's biggest print plant opens', available online at
http://news.bbc.co.uk/go/pr/fr/-/1/hi/uk/7299941.stm

What factors do you think News International would have considered before expanding its printing production?

Can you now answer question 1 from the opening case study?

External economies and diseconomies of scale

As well as internal economies and diseconomies of scale, there are also external economies and diseconomies. These occur when a firm benefits from an external factor that increases or decreases the average costs at every level of output.

External economies of scale occur when the average costs fall at every level of output, for one of the following reasons.

- *A location decision*   By locating in a particular area near other similar businesses, this creates a demand for specialist services. Suppliers may locate nearby and local colleges may provide specialized training courses for this industry. This can reduce your own costs. These cost savings are also known as 'economies of agglomeration'. In the UK, for example, Northampton has been an area in which many shoe producers used to locate and Sheffield has attracted many steel companies, sharing resources and skills.

■ *The expansion of the industry*   This creates more demand for suppliers, who might then benefit from internal economies of scale. As the suppliers gain lower unit costs, this may be passed on to their customers via lower prices.

External diseconomies of scale may occur if the industry expands, and this causes suppliers to grow and experience internal diseconomies of scale; they may then pass their higher average costs on in the form of higher prices.

Problems reducing costs

Controlling costs is important to maximize profits—but this may require some painful decisions. A reduction in output, for example, may require a reduction in the labour force—that is, some staff may need to be made redundant. In 2008, the Royal Bank of Scotland (RBS) made a loss of £24,100 million, the biggest corporate loss in UK corporate history; this led to major changes at the bank to cut costs. In the first nine months of 2009, for example, the size of the business was reduced by 26 per cent, which involved selling businesses and cutting thousands of jobs. Such changes require consultation with employee representatives and may involve difficult decisions regarding who is to be made redundant. Managers will probably not want to rush to lay employees off if they can help it; after all, if demand increases again, they may need those staff again. The business may try to negotiate wage freezes or temporary layoffs in the short term.

Business Analysis   8.4

In 2008, two major US car producers, General Motors (GM) and Chrysler, approached the US government for financial aid amounting to US$25,000 million. The companies had been performing poorly for many years, but the problems became even more severe when the US recession hit sales. The falling revenue was a particular problem, because of the high level of fixed costs that the companies had. This was due, in part, to the wage deals that they had agreed with trade unions. These deals included good healthcare and pensions benefits. With employees living longer, these costs had become extremely high. Healthcare costs account for US$1,500 of each new car for GM compared to about $200 for its rival Toyota.

Even before asking for government funding, the companies had been taking action to reduce their costs. GM, for example, had closed twelve plants and cut more than 34,000 jobs in a bid to cut US$9,000 million (£4,600 million) from its operating costs. The chief executive of GM, Rick Wagoner, recognized the need to improve productivity and profitability, to try to regain GM's competitive edge.

GM reported an operating loss of US$4,200 million (£2,660 million) in the third quarter of 2008, and said that it would be in very severe financial difficulties if economic and market conditions were not to improve.

1. Identify two fixed costs and two variable costs likely to be incurred by GM.
2. What factors would it be difficult for GM to change in the short run?
3. What problems might GM have faced when cutting costs by closing twelve plants?
4. Why do you think the government might have agreed to subsidize these car companies?

Summary table

Table 8.4

Item	Meaning	Equation	Label
Total product	Total output	n/a	TP
Marginal product	Extra output gained by employing an additional factor of production	Change in output/change in factor of production	MP
Average product	The output per factor of production, e.g. output per employee	Total output/number of units of the factor of production	AP
Marginal cost	The extra cost of a unit	Change in total costs/ change in output	MC
Average cost	The cost per unit	Total costs/output	AC
Average fixed cost	The fixed cost per unit	Fixed costs/output	AFC
Average variable cost	The variable cost per unit	Variable costs/output	AVC

Revenue

Controlling costs is obviously an important aspect of management and will affect all areas of the business. For example, the overall levels of spending that a business can afford will affect the marketing budget, the amount spent on supplies, the production costs, and the firm's approach to managing people. But the other element of profit is revenue, and managers will want to consider the likely revenue at different levels of output and compare this with the costs to decide on the profit-maximizing level of output. When analysing the accounts of a business, the revenue is called the 'top line'; the profits are called the 'bottom line', because this is the final figure after costs are deducted.

Producing very low levels of output may have low costs, but if there is relatively little to sell, the profits may not be very high. Producing on a larger scale will cost more in total, but if sales are high and the business benefits from internal economies of scale, profits might increase as well. The optimal output therefore depends not only on an analysis of costs, but also of revenue.

The revenue of a business measures the value of its sales. It is also called the 'total revenue' or 'turnover', and is calculated as:

$$\text{Total revenue} = \text{Price} \times \text{Quantity sold}$$

If, for example, a business sells 1,000 units at £20 each, then its revenue is £20,000 (see Figure 8.13).

Most businesses have a range of products and these are often sold at different prices in different markets. The total revenue of the business is the combination of all of the different revenues from the various products.

Costs then have to be deducted to calculate the profit that has been made:

$$\text{Total revenue} - \text{Total costs} = \text{Profit}$$

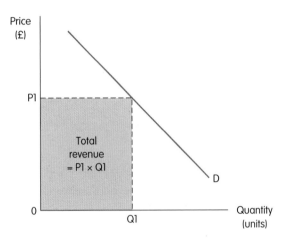

Figure 8.13 Total revenue

Data Analysis 8.6

Procter and Gamble has three business units: beauty; health and well-being; and home care. Its sales in 2008 totalled US$83,503 million; its net earnings (i.e. its profits) in 2008 were US$12,075 million.

Table 8.5

Business unit		Products include	Brands include	% sales	% net earnings
Beauty	Beauty	Cosmetics; deodorants; hair care; personal	Head & Shoulders; Olay; Pantene; Wella	22	23
	Grooming	Blades and razors; electric hair removal devices; face and shaving products; home appliances	Braun; Gillette	10	13

(Continued)

Table 8.5   (*Continued*)

Business unit		Products include	Brands include	% sales	% net earnings
Health and well-being	Health care	Feminine care; oral care; personal health care; pharmaceuticals	Actonel; Always; Crest; Oral-B	17	20
	Snacks, coffee, and pet care	Coffee; pet food; snacks	Folgers; Iams; Pringles	6	4
Home care	Fabric care and home care	Air care; batteries; dish care; fabric care; surface care	Ariel; Dawn; Downy; Duracell; Gain and Tide	28	27
	Baby care and family care	Baby wipes; bath tissue; diapers; facial tissue; paper towels	Bounty; Charmin; Pampers	16	14

1. Which division of Procter and Gamble do you think is performing best? Explain your choice.

2. What other data would you want to assess Procter and Gamble's overall performance in 2008 more fully?

Marginal and average revenue

Managers will be interested in total revenue for any level of sales, but they will also be interested in analysing marginal and average revenue. Managers need to understand marginal and average revenue to decide whether to produce an additional unit, and to calculate their profits for any level of sales.

■ Average revenue is the amount of income per unit—that is, the price. If each unit is sold for £20, then the average revenue per unit is £20.

■ Marginal revenue is the extra revenue generated from selling another unit. If all units are sold at the same price, the marginal revenue is the same as the average revenue. For example, if all units are sold at £20, then the extra revenue is £20; when the price has to be cut to sell more, the marginal revenue and average revenue start to diverge.

Imagine that you were able to sell one unit at £20, but you want to sell two units instead. If you are facing a downward-sloping demand curve, then, to sell more, you will need to lower the price. Imagine that, to sell two units, you have to lower the price to £18. The average revenue (that is, the price) is now £18 per unit, but the marginal revenue is only £16. This is because you lowered the price to £18 for the second unit; you also had to reduce the price of the first unit down from £20 to £18. The extra revenue is therefore:

£18 (the second unit price) – £2 (the 'loss' or lost revenue on the first unit) = £16

Alternatively, you can see this from calculating the change in total revenue:

Total revenue for one unit = £20 x 1 = £20

Total revenue from two units = £18 x 2 = £36

The marginal revenue from selling the second unit is the extra revenue generated:

£36 – £20 = £16

What if you were to want to sell three units rather than two and, to do so, you have to lower the price to £16?

The extra revenue from the third unit is £16, but you have lowered the price on the first two by £2 each. The marginal revenue is:

£16 – £4 = £12

Calculating the total revenue, we can see:

Total revenue for two units = £18 x 2 = £36

Total revenue for three units = £16 x 3 = £48

The marginal revenue from selling the third unit is therefore:

£48 – £36 = £12

You can see from this that, as you lower the price to sell more units, the marginal revenue starts to diverge from the average revenue (that is, it gets further and further away). This is because you are lowering the price on the last unit and all of the previous units. The more you sell, the more units that will have their prices reduced. Marginal revenue therefore equals the price of the last unit less the reductions in price on all of the units before.

This is important for managers to remember: if they are going to set a higher sales target, they may have to reduce the price and sell all of the units at the same price; the extra benefit should recognize that the prices will be lower on all of the previous units than they were before. Think of a bank manager wanting to offer lower interest rates to new borrowers: if this has to be extended to the existing borrowers as well as the new ones, the lost revenue must be taken into account.

Data Analysis   8.7

You run a car dealership in Scotland. Imagine that you can sell twenty cars this week at £10,000 each. To sell twenty-one cars and hit your sales target, you estimate that you will need to drop the price to £9,000.

1. What is the marginal revenue of the twenty-first car? What is the total revenue?
2. You calculate that, to sell twenty-two cars, you would need to drop the price as low as £6,000. What is the total revenue of twenty-two cars?
3. What is the marginal revenue of the twenty-second car?

 Think about it ...   8.9

If all products were sold at the same price—for example, £10—what would be the marginal revenue?

Calculating marginal average revenue and total revenue

Table 8.6

Output	Average revenue = price	Total revenue = price × quantity	Marginal revenue = change in total revenue/ change in output
1	£10	£10	n/a
2	£9	£18	£8
3	£8	£24	£6
4	£7	£28	£4
5	£6	£30	£2
6	£5	£30	£0
7	£4	£28	−£2
8	£3	£24	−£4

Between one and five units in the table above, the price is lowered to sell more and is lowered on all previous units, meaning that marginal revenue falls. The more units being sold, the more units affected by the price cut, and the bigger the difference between price and marginal revenue. As marginal revenue falls, total revenue is increasing at a slower rate. At the output of six units, marginal revenue is 0, meaning that total revenue does not change. To sell the seventh unit, the price cut on the previous unit exceeds the gain from the last unit and overall revenue falls (that is, marginal revenue is negative).

The divergence of average and marginal revenue can be seen in the table. You can also see the relationship between total revenue and marginal revenue (see Figure 8.14). When marginal revenue is positive, but falling, the total revenue will be increasing, but at a slower rate. When marginal revenue is zero, total revenue does not change and is at its maximum point. When marginal revenue is negative, the total revenue will be falling. (A negative marginal revenue occurs when the price is reduced by so much or on so many previous units that this outweighs the gains of the extra unit.)

The marginal revenue shows how much the total revenue changes and is therefore the gradient of the total revenue curve.

In the case of a price elastic demand, a cut in price leads to a bigger percentage increase in the quantity demanded, so the gains from the new sales outweigh the revenue lost on the ones before. Marginal revenue is therefore positive and total revenue increases with a price cut (see Figure 8.15).

In the case of a price inelastic demand, a price cut has relatively little effect on the quantity demanded and so the gain from new sales does not outweigh the lost revenue on the previous units. Marginal revenue is therefore negative and total revenue falls.

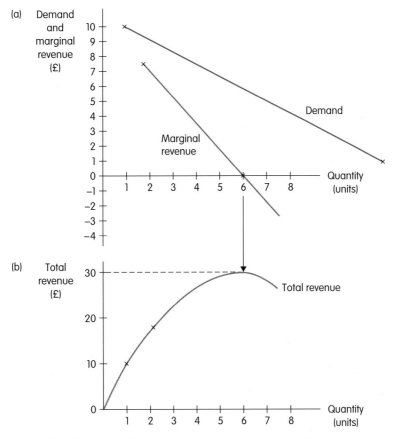

Figure 8.14 The relationship between the marginal revenue and the total revenue

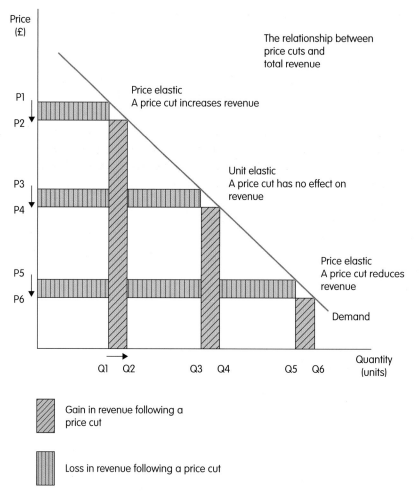

Figure 8.15 The relationship between price cuts and total revenue

---

? **Think about it ...** 8.10

Which of the following statements are true and which are false?

A If marginal revenue is zero, total revenue will not increase if the unit is sold.

B If all units are sold at the same price, the marginal revenue is the same as the price (that is, the average revenue).

C If the price is lowered to sell another unit, the average revenue is less than the marginal revenue.

D If marginal revenue is positive, but falling, total revenue is falling.

Determining the profit-maximizing price and output—the marginal condition

Having analysed the costs and demand conditions at different levels of output, managers can determine the price at which they want to sell, and the output that they want to produce and sell.

The 'right' price and output will depend on managers' objectives. If the aim is to profit maximize, then this means that the manager will want the biggest positive difference between total revenue and costs. This level of output can be identified by using what is known as the 'marginal condition' (see Figure 8.16).

The marginal revenue is the extra revenue earned by selling another unit; the marginal cost is the extra cost of producing another unit.

If a firm is producing at the point at which the marginal revenue is greater than the marginal cost, this means that selling another unit would earn additional profits. This means that this unit and any others like it should be produced and sold to increase profits.

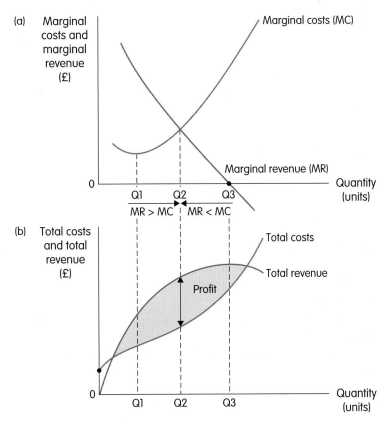

Figure 8.16 The profit-maximizing output

If the marginal revenue of selling another unit is less than the marginal cost, this means that a loss would be made on this extra unit; as a result, this extra unit should not be sold, because the overall profits would fall. If the marginal revenue of an extra unit equals the marginal cost, profit would not change and would be maximized.

To maximize profits, a manager therefore needs to make sure that the business is selling all of the units for which marginal revenue is greater than the marginal cost, up until the point at which the marginal revenue equals the marginal cost; this means that every unit for which there is extra profit to be gained has been sold, up until the point at which there is no extra profit and so profits are the greatest that they can be.

Profit maximization occurs when there is the biggest positive difference between revenue and costs—that is, when marginal revenue equals marginal cost. This is the output for which there will be the biggest positive difference between revenue and total costs.

When marginal costs fall, the total cost rises at a slower rate (see Figure 8.17). This occurs up to Q1; after this, marginal cost rises and the total cost increases at a faster rate (the slope of the total cost, which reflects the marginal costs, gets steeper). Marginal revenue is falling as more output is sold, which means that total revenue increases at a slower rate up until Q3. At Q3, marginal revenue is zero, so there is no extra revenue and total revenue is maximized. After Q3, marginal revenue is negative and this means that total revenue falls. A business profit maximizes when marginal revenue equals the marginal cost, which is the point at which there is the biggest positive difference between total revenue and total cost at Q2.

Measuring the profits or losses made—the average condition

When a firm produces at the point at which marginal revenue equals marginal cost, this means that it is profit maximizing (or loss minimizing); it is making the highest profit that it could make given the demand and cost conditions. To calculate the profit (or loss) actually made, managers should measure the profit per unit, calculated as:

$$\text{Average revenue (the price)} - \text{Average cost}$$

when this profit per unit is multiplied by the sales, the total profit can be seen. The marginal condition therefore shows where to produce; the average condition shows how much profit is being made.

Producing in the short run—the shutdown point

In the short run, a business will be committed to pay fixed costs whether or not it produces. Even if output is zero and there are no sales, fixed costs still have to be paid (so a loss is made at zero output equal to the fixed costs of the business). Once the organization starts to produce, variable costs will be incurred. Provided that the revenue generated from the

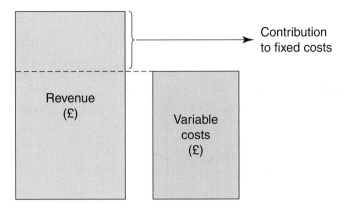

Figure 8.17 A contribution to fixed costs

sales at least covers the variable costs, the business should produce in the short run, even if a loss is made.

Imagine, for example, that the variable costs at a given level of output are £10,000, the fixed costs are £20,000, and the revenue is £11,000. Overall, if the business decides to produce, it will make a loss of £19,000, because the revenue of £11,000 does not cover the costs of £30,000. But the firm should still produce in these circumstances, because the revenue covers the variable costs and generates an excess of £1,000; this £1,000 is called a 'contribution' because it contributes to the fixed costs of £20,000 (see Figure 8.18). This means that the loss is only £19,000 if the firm produces, whereas if it were to shut down, it would still have to pay all of the fixed costs and make a loss of £20,000. By producing, the loss is smaller than the loss it would have made were it not to produce.

A manager should, therefore, keep producing in the short run provided that revenue is greater than the variable costs. If he or she can reduce the variable costs (for example, through cost cutting), this can make it more feasible to keep going with a lower revenue.

If this situation is analysed in terms of individual units, then a business should continue producing provided that the revenue per unit (the price) is greater than the average variable costs (that is, the variable cost per unit). This means that there is a contribution per unit, which can be put towards fixed costs.

The point at which there is no difference in terms of losses whether or not the firm produces is called the **shutdown point** (see Figure 8.19). This occurs when the total revenue equals the variable cost (which is the same as the price being equal to the average variable cost).

In Figure 8.19, the units are all sold at the same price, so the revenue per unit can be calculated as:

$$\text{Average revenue} = \text{Price} = \text{Marginal revenue}$$

If the price is less than the average variable cost, the firm not only has to pay its fixed costs, but is also unable to pay its variable costs and so would be better shutting down.

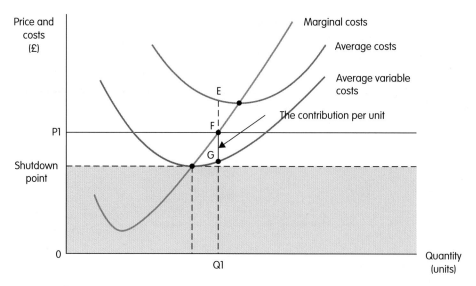

Figure 8.18 Shutdown point. At P1 the best output to produce at is where MR = MC i.e. Q1. At this output the price more than covers the average variable costs and makes a contribution of FG towards the fixed costs. Overall a loss is made because the price does not cover the average costs but the loss is smaller than if the business shut down.

Imagine that the price is £10, the average variable costs are £12, the fixed costs are £10,000, and the output is 1,000 units. If the firm decides to produce, the revenue fails to cover the variable costs by £2 a unit; this is a £2,000 loss. The fixed costs also have to be paid so the overall loss is:

$$£10,000 + £2,000 = £12,000$$

If the business were shut down, the losses would be only £10,000 (the fixed costs).

Overall, therefore, a firm should produce in the short run provided that the price is greater or equal to the average variable cost, but not if it is less. This highlights how important it is for managers to distinguish between the variable and fixed costs. If they were to scale right back in the short run, they would need to know the costs to which they would still be committed.

Contribution

The importance of understanding the concept of contribution can be seen in many business situations in which managers may be seeking to minimize their losses. Imagine a hotel is half empty and you ring up late in the day wanting to book a room. The price for the room is normally £100 a night, but you offer £60: should the manager accept this offer? The answer is that he or she might—provided that the £60 covers the variable costs (such as the food provided at breakfast and the cost of cleaning your room). In this case, what you are offering contributes to the fixed costs that have to be paid anyway. The hotel may still make a loss, but it will be less of a loss than if the offer was not accepted. The same approach to pricing occurs in many industries, such as the airline business and holiday sector.

If, however, a business regularly accepts prices below its published price, customers will all start to ask for the lower price and this may drive the price ever further downwards, removing any profits being made. Also, if the fixed costs are not fully covered, the business will not be able to sustain this sort of approach in the long run.

>> **You Decide ...**

The revenue of a business measures the value of the sales, but does not necessarily mean that the items have been paid for in cash. You may 'sell' something at the beginning of a month and this counts as revenue even if the actual payment (the cash) arrives weeks later. This is why managers are interested in the 'cash in', as well as the revenue.

Imagine that you are manager of a soup business. You have estimated the unit cost at 80 pence a carton. You have orders at the moment with relatively small outlets, such as delicatessens, selling for £1.40, with payment three weeks after delivery. You are operating at 80 per cent capacity. You have been approached by a major supermarket wanting to buy your products for £1.20 with payment seven weeks after delivery. If you accept the order, you will need to triple capacity.

Do you accept the order?

Producing in the long run—the breakeven point

In the long run, if a business cannot at least cover its total costs, it should transfer resources out of this sector and into another, or simply stop producing, because it is making a loss. In the long run, therefore, the total revenue must cover the total costs for a business to stay in this industry. This means that the price per unit (the average revenue) must equal the average cost (see Figure 8.20).

If the price falls below the average cost, the business will have to shut down in the long run.

If a business is making a loss in the short run, then the manager will need to try to change this position to stay in the industry, by using one of the following strategies.

- *Trying to increase revenue* For example, managers might launch a marketing campaign to try to increase demand. This will, of course, increase costs as well, but the aim would be to boost revenue by more than costs.

- *Trying to reduce costs* For example, the manager might try to reduce the amount of resources used in the production process. The danger of this approach is that the quality of the offering suffers and therefore demand falls, and the overall financial position may be worsened.

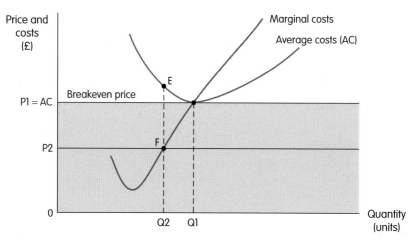

Figure 8.19 Breakeven point

 Business Analysis   8.5

The confectionery business, Cadbury, was recently accused of cheating customers by replacing favourite sweet ranges with less popular dark chocolates. The company removed four ranges—Time Outs, Picnics, Dreams, and Crunchies—from its tins of Heroes and replaced them with only two—Bournvilles and Eclairs. It is claimed that this was done to reduce costs. The company had issued a warning to the stock market earlier about falling profits and consumers are cutting spending across the board.

A Cadbury spokesperson rejected claims that the sweet changes were a cost-cutting measure and said that they swap ranges every year.

What are the long-term dangers to Cadbury of cutting costs?

? *Think about it ...*   8.11

Which of the following statements are true and which are false?

A A business should produce in the short run only if the price covers the average costs.

B A business should produce in the long run only if total revenue covers the variable costs.

C A business will profit maximize when there is the biggest positive difference between marginal revenue and marginal costs.

D Even if a business shuts down, it must still pay fixed costs in the short run.

Business objectives

In economics, it is often assumed that managers will be aiming to maximize profits for their owners. But while there are many good reasons why managers will want to maximize profits (or at least why their investors want profits maximized), they may also have other objectives, for the following reasons.

■ We often assess the performance of a business in terms of its size or revenue, rather than its profits. We may be impressed by a business with many stores or with a very visible brand even if we do not know much about its profitability. A manager may therefore want to be running a bigger business with more output or more sales revenue, in order to be seen as being successful by the general public and the media, even if this growth reduces profit because of diseconomies of scale.

■ Managers' rewards are often linked to targets set for them that are not necessarily linked to profits: for example, they may have sales-based bonuses or bonuses linked to the successful growth of the business. Again, this would make managers focus on objectives other than profits. According to Williamson (1964), managers will try to maximize their own utility, not their investors' rewards. Their own utility, he argues, is linked to their salary, their job security, their power, and their professional status. They may therefore pursue their own interests rather than those of investors. For example, many takeovers and mergers do not lead to the cost savings that they promised because they are actually driven by the desire of the managers to achieve something for themselves rather than by profits. The relationship between investors and managers is an interesting one, and has been studied a great deal. This is because there is a 'divorce between ownership and control' (Berle and Means, 1933). The investors who own the business appoint the managers to control and run it in their best interests. On a day-to-day basis, however, managers know far more about what is happening in the business than the investors; there is an asymmetry of information. The investors are known as the 'principals' in this relationship and the managers are their 'agents'.

In reality, managers are likely to have their own challenges, their own values, and their own agenda, and may not always be working towards the same goals as those of the investors. In 2008, for example, Michael Frenzel (chief executive of TUI, Europe's biggest travel agency) was forced to change his strategy of focusing on travel and shipping. He argued that the shipping provided a good safety net given how volatile the travel business can be. His shareholders disagreed and, in March 2008, Frenzel announced that TUI would sell its shipping division.

To try to bring shareholders and managers closer together, many managers have been given shares in the business or have been given profit-related bonuses. To monitor managers' behaviour, shareholders elect directors to review the plans and work of managers, and are provided with an annual report at the annual general meeting (AGM). Shareholders have also insisted on more outside directors being appointed (rather than the directors also being managers, which can lead to a conflict of interest). But the effectiveness of directors is sometimes called into question and, in some cases, the shareholders have had to organize themselves to force the directors to resign. The ways in which shareholders try to monitor managers' behaviour and actions is known as 'corporate governance'.

Possible objectives of managers apart from profit maximization may therefore include the following.

- *Sales revenue maximization* (Baumol, 1956)   This occurs when a firm produces at an output level when the total revenue cannot increase any more. This occurs when

 Business Analysis   8.6

Sir Stelios Haji-Ionannou, the founder of the budget airline Easyjet, had to argue hard to get the other directors to agree to cut the company's growth targets in 2009. The company's passenger numbers had been growing at 15 per cent per year as it tried to gain market share across Europe. Stelios argued for 7.5 per cent. His family controls 38 per cent of the business. Stelios was worried about this rate of growth in an economic downturn.

As part of its review, Easyjet has reassessed delivery of new aircraft to ensure that it does not have excess capacity. It has ninety-one planes on order from Airbus, but will increase its fleet size by only thirty to 207 in the next three years. Some older planes will be sold and leased aircraft will be returned to their owners; even so, some of the ninety-one on order may need to be cancelled or delayed.

Why might there have been differences in opinion between Stelios and the rest of the board of directors?

>> *You Decide ...*

In 2008, Sir Stuart Rose, chief executive of Marks and Spencer plc (M&S), who had been responsible for the turnaround of the company in recent years, insisted on becoming chairman of the board of directors as well. This went completely against best practice, which kept the role of executive and chair of the board separate so that the latter acted as an effective control mechanism.

1. Why do you think Sir Stuart Rose insisted on both roles?

2. How might it affect the objectives of the business?

3. Should M&S have given him these roles?

marginal revenue is zero (that is, there is no extra revenue to be made). This approach does not focus on costs; managers are simply interested in the value of sales. But to keep shareholders satisfied, in reality a certain level of profits might need to be made and therefore managers might seek to maximize revenue subject to making a given level of profit.

■ *Growth maximization* (Marris, 1964)   This occurs at the highest level of output at which a firm can produce without making a loss. This occurs when the average revenue (price) is equal to the average cost.

A business will maximize profits at the point at which the marginal revenue equals the marginal cost (that is, Q2 in Figure 8.20); at this output, there is the biggest positive difference between revenue and costs.

A business will maximize revenue when marginal revenue equals zero (that is, at Q3); this is the highest level on the total revenue curve.

A business will produce the highest output possible without making a loss (that is, maximize its growth) by producing at Q4. At this output, the total revenue equals the total costs (that is, the price per unit equals the average cost per unit).

In reality, in both the revenue and growth maximization models, managers may have to achieve a minimum level of profit to satisfy their investors. In this case, they may aim for the output for which marginal revenue equals zero or for which average revenue equals average cost, but have to be as close to this as they can, while making a given level of profit. For example, to achieve a given level of abnormal profit to satisfy investors, managers pursuing growth may have to produce slightly below Q4. Similarly, for managers trying to maximize revenue, if the profit is not high enough for investors at Q3, they may have to produce slightly nearer to Q2.

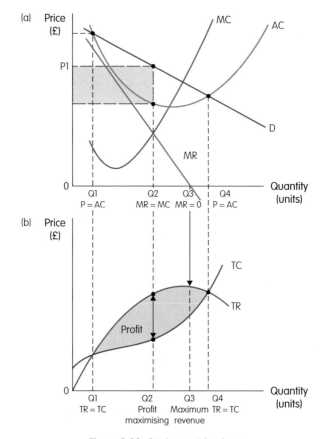

Figure 8.20 Business objectives

 Business Analysis   8.7

In February 2008, Takao Kitabata, Japanese Vice Minister of Economy, Trade, and Industry, said: 'To be blunt, shareholders in general do not have the ability to run a company. They are fickle and irresponsible. They only take on a limited responsibility, but they greedily demand high dividend payments.'

His comments were aimed at Steel Partners, a US investment fund that questioned the management of Sapporo, a beermaker, in which it holds a 19 per cent stake.

Questioning what managers do is very rare in Japan. Steel Partners also demanded that the managers of Aderans, a wigmaker in which it owns 24 per cent, resign. Even though the share price of Aderans has fallen by 50 per cent in two years, the managers insist on keeping non-core assets, such as a loss-making golf course.

Do you agree with Takao Kitabata's view?

Forms of growth

Managers may want their business to grow because of the potential gains from internal economies of scale. This growth may be organic (internal) or external. Internal growth is achieved by generating more sales from the existing business. This type of growth is usually relatively slow and therefore may be relatively easy to manage. External growth occurs when one business joins together with another (this is called a 'merger') or one business takes over another one (called a 'takeover' or 'acquisition'). External growth can lead to a sudden change in the scale of a business. This can be difficult to manage because it involves two different enterprises coming together and rapid transitions in size. This can cause cultural clashes, because employees have different ways of doing things, different priorities, and different procedures. Studies suggest that most mergers and acquisitions actually end up performing worse than the companies would have done had they remained separate. This is due to the problems of diseconomies of scale and cultural clashes.

When undertaking a merger or takeover, managers may look to join with one of the following.

- *A supplier* This is known as 'backward vertical integration', because the business is joining with another organization at an earlier stage of the same production process. By joining with a supplier, you can remove or reduce its profit margin, and may be able to guarantee the volume and quality of supplies you want. Tyrrell's, the crisp manufacturer, highlights the fact that it uses its own potatoes, for example and turns this into a marketing point because it can rely on the quality of home-grown inputs.

- *A distributor or a retailer of their products* This is known as 'forward vertical integration' and occurs when one business joins with another at a later stage of the same process (that is, at a stage nearer to the final customer). A business may undertake this form of integration to guarantee access to the market. Music equipment producers Bose and Bang Olufsen sell through their own outlets to ensure that the buying experience fits with the overall brand values. In 2009, Pepsi bought its top two bottlers for US$7,800 million (£4,600 million) in an effort to save money and get its products to market more quickly. In the oil industry, companies such as Shell and BP have undertaken forward and backward integration, so that they control every aspect of the supply chain, from exploration, refining, and transport, through to retail. This gives these businesses complete control over the production and marketing processes, but requires heavy investment and many different skills to understand and operate in these different markets. This is why many businesses prefer to specialize in a particular stage of the process rather than to control the whole process.

- *A business at the same stage of the same type of production process* This is known as 'horizontal integration', and is often undertaken to achieve greater market power and economies of scale. For example, the businesses may share research and development facilities, IT resources, their HR departments, or their marketing teams. Horizontal integration can enable a business to increase its market share rapidly. In February 2008, for example, Microsoft made a US$44,600 million bid for Yahoo!, the online business that had previously been struggling. This was part of Microsoft's strategy to gain power to compete with Google. At that time, Microsoft's market share of online advertising was estimated to be around 2.9 per cent, compared to Google's 62.4 per cent and Yahoo!'s 12.8 per cent. Google had recently acquired another online advertising business, DoubleClick, which would enable it to pull even further ahead. Yahoo! resisted the bid at the time, but, months later, asked Microsoft to buy it. Horizontal integration may also help a business to expand into different regional markets quickly: for example, Morrisons, a supermarket based mainly in the north of England, bought a competitor, Safeways, in 2004, which was stronger in the south. In 2006, Nippon Sheet Glass, a glass producer that had a strong presence in Asia, bought Pilkington, a UK glass producer that sold more in Europe. These companies were able to share their expertise and distribution channels in different regions.

■ *A business that operates in a different market* This is known as 'conglomerate integration' and may be undertaken because a business wants to operate in different markets; this may reduce the risk if demand falls or slows in one market. In 2008, for example, Mars paid US$23,000 million for Wrigley's; the company

 Business Analysis 8.8

In 2006, the beauty products retailer Body Shop agreed to be taken over by the large French cosmetics company L'Oreal for £652 million. The offer price of 300 pence per share was a significant premium on the closing price of Body Shop shares of 268 pence. L'Oreal makes a wide range of cosmetics, including Ambre Solaire sun cream and Lancome lipsticks. Body Shop is famous for its ethically sourced products, and its campaigns against animal testing and to protect the environment. In 2006, the Body Shop had more than 2,000 stores in fifty-three countries. 'A partnership between our companies makes perfect sense,' said L'Oreal's chairman. L'Oreal said that it planned to operate the British company as a stand-alone business.

1. Why would Body Shop sell to L'Oreal?

2. Why do you think L'Oreal would want to buy Body Shop?

3. What do you think will determine the price offered for the Body Shop and the long-run success of this takeover?

? Think about it ... 8.12

If the majority of mergers and takeovers have led to poor performance, why do so many still occur?

wanted to diversify out of chocolate, which is slowing in growth, and move into the faster-growing gum market. But managing a conglomerate may be difficult, because it means bringing together very different types of business.

What can prevent a business from growing?

While many managers may want to expand their business, they may not be able to raise the money to finance the desired growth. Both external growth (for example, taking over another business) and internal growth (for example, opening new stores) will require money. If you do not want to sell shares or use loans to raise the funds externally, or if you do not have the profits that you need to finance this growth internally, then it may not be possible to expand even if you feel that it is desirable.

Business Analysis 8.9

In 2008, the Competition Commission blocked the proposed acquisition by BOC Ltd (BOC) of the packaged chlorine business and assets of Ineos Chlor Ltd (Ineos Chlor). The Commission concluded that the merger would result in a substantial lessening of competition in the markets for the distribution of packaged chlorine in cylinders and in drums in the UK. It found that the proposed merger would reduce the number of competing distributors, and would end the rivalry between BOC and Ineos Chlor, which are currently each other's closest competitors in these markets. It felt that the merger would be anti-competitive, and would lead to customers paying higher prices and having less choice than would otherwise be the case.

How do you think BOC might have tried to defend this merger?

Can you now answer questions 4 and 5 from the opening case study?

There may also be restrictions on your growth. Governments are often concerned about the power that large firms can have and therefore have legislation to control monopolies. In the UK, the Competition Commission has the right to investigate any business that has a market share of more than 25 per cent. The Competition Commission may prevent a merger or takeover on the grounds that it will lead to one organization holding over 25 per cent share of the market if it fears that this power may be abused and may not work in the public interest. (The role of the Competition Commission is examined in Chapter 9.) Companies found to be abusing their dominant position can be fined up to 10 per cent of their turnover and takeovers or mergers that might lead to more than 25 per cent market share may be prevented or conditions may be imposed upon them.

Limitations of models that assume maximization

In reality, managers may not actually maximize anything. This is partly because they will not necessarily know exactly what costs and demand conditions are or what they will be in the future. Gathering information in itself is expensive and time-consuming, and even if you undertake market research, it cannot be guaranteed to be 100 per cent accurate. Simon (1955) claims therefore that managers have 'bounded rationality' and make decisions by 'satisficing' rather than maximizing. They reach a decision that is 'good enough' and with which they are happy, given the uncertainties that exist, even though this may not be the optimal decision. It is the best decision that can be made in the circumstances and with the information available, but may not maximize anything.

Managers also face many different interest groups within the business, all of whom may want different things. They will need to balance the different needs of these stakeholders rather than maximizing anything. The sales department may be desperate to hit its sales targets, the finance department may be worried about cash flow and financing expansion, and the local community may be worried about congestion if the business does expand and has more deliveries. The final price and quantity outcome may be a combination of different profit, size, and profit targets from different stakeholders. The managers will, therefore, have different forces acting on them and may end with a form of compromise.

Managers may also avoid maximizing profits because they want a certain degree of 'organizational slack' within their business. If managers allow costs to be higher than they could be in 'good' years, it means that they can make cutbacks relatively quickly and easily when demand conditions are less favourable. Having slack, such as excess labour and stocks, also allows them to meet changes in demand easily. Another phenomenon that may prevent maximization is that managers may set targets that are relatively easy to achieve rather than ones that maximize results, but which may be difficult to achieve. Setting conservative targets may enable them to look better when reporting to investors on what they have achieved.

A further problem with the maximization model is that decisions to maximize, say, profit will vary depending on the time period involved. If a manager were aiming to maximize profits in the immediate run, for example, he or she might cut back on training and investing in new products. These would be unnecessary expenditure because he or she is looking for quick rewards. But to achieve longer term profits, a manager may invest heavily in research and development to build a portfolio for the future. He or she might also reduce price to gain market share to develop a strong market position for the future. Short-term profits may suffer in search of higher long-term profits. When deciding whether to maximize profits, a real problem is to know over what period to try to achieve this.

In defence of the concept of maximization, however, is the idea that, whether managers know it or not, if finally they end up with the biggest sales or the highest possible profits, then, by definition, they are maximizing these. A manager may not know cost and revenue conditions precisely, and may not compare marginal costs and revenues, but if he or she continually adjusts his or her decisions to boost profits, then he or she is moving towards the output at which marginal revenue equals marginal costs even if he or she does not know it. Managers may well experiment with prices and outputs, and gradually move towards the maximization position.

? Think about it... 8.13

Which of the following statements are true and which are false?

A A business maximizes its revenue when marginal costs are zero.

B A business maximizes profits when marginal revenue equals marginal costs.

C A business produces the highest level of output without making a loss when the average revenue equals the average variable cost.

D A normal profit is made when average revenue is greater than average costs.

Profits and risk

In 2008, the global banking system hit major problems. Banks all over the world had been lending excessively and making high-risk loans. Once the dangers of this were exposed, it became clear that their loans lacked the collateral that it had been assumed that they had and that banks were dangerously exposed. When this combined with a global **recession,** which drove down asset prices, it became clear that banks had overextended themselves and their loans were, in some cases, worthless because the individual or organization could not repay. To protect the banking system, governments had to intervene and provide more finance. In the UK, the government bought control of the Royal Bank of Scotland (RBS) and Lloyds Bank, and provided billions of pounds of extra support.

What had gone wrong? Directors and managers had been pursuing profit to such an extent that they had taken excessive risks in search of more rewards. The banking system had not been regulated enough, enabling behaviour that proved to be dangerous to investors and customers; as a result of lending excessively, banks responded by cutting back lending to such an extent that this halted growth in many economies. Many analysts who had previously argued that governments should leave markets to work for themselves now wanted the state to take greater control. Alan Greenspan, who had been the head of the US Federal Reserve (the US central bank) for eighteen years, wrote, in his book *The Age of Turbulence* in 2007: 'Why would we wish to control the pollinating behaviour of Wall Street bees?' At that stage, he was in favour of the actions that banks were taking to make more profits. In 2008, in front of a US government committee, he said:

> I made a mistake in presuming that the self-interests of organizations, specifically banks and others, were such as that they were best capable of protecting their own shareholders and their equity in the firms. ... [T]he reason I was shocked [was] because I have been going for forty years or more with very considerable evidence that it was working exceptionally well.

Profit-maximizing behaviour may therefore lead to firms taking too many risks; the lessons of the recent crisis may curb the desire of some managers to pursue profit so aggressively.

Summary

Managers must make decisions regarding the output that they want to produce and the prices that they want to charge. In some cases, they must make decisions about whether to produce at all. To make such decisions, they need to know what happens to costs and revenues at different output levels. In the short run, they can produce provided that the price at least equals the average variable costs. In the long run, the price must at least equal the average cost—that is, normal profits must be made. The precise price and output decision will depend on the objectives of managers. We tend to assume that managers profit maximize, meaning that they will produce when marginal revenue is equal to marginal costs. But it is possible that, due to a lack of information, they do not actually maximize profits; rather, they end up aiming to make what they and their owners regard as a satisfactory level. Also given the nature of the way in which managers are often rewarded, and the divorce between the ownership and control of many businesses, managers may end up pursing other aims, such as growth and revenue targets.

Checklist

Having read this chapter, you should now understand:

- [ ] the different types of cost and the relationship between them;
- [ ] the link between costs and productivity;
- [ ] why managers want to keep costs low and how they might do this;
- [ ] the different types of revenue (for example, total revenue, marginal revenue, and average revenue);
- [ ] the difference between the short run and the long run, and why it matters;
- [ ] the marginal condition for profit maximization;
- [ ] alternative theories of the firm.

Case Study Review

Having read this chapter, you should now be able to answer the following questions.

1. What problems will Susannah have competing against the bigger stores?

2. Is there anything that you think she could do to keep in business?

3. Do you think that expanding her business would have made good business sense?

4. What are Susannah's objectives? Do you think that these are typical business objectives?

5. What do you think influences the objectives of the owners of a business?

6. Do you think that the government should intervene to change business behaviour?

7. Is there anything else that Susannah could do to try to get the government to intervene to protect her business?

Short Answer Questions

1. Define profit. Explain why an accountant's understanding of profit is different from that of an economist.

2. Is it true or false that fixed costs never change? Explain your answer.

3. Is it true or false that the shutdown point for a business in the short run occurs when the price equals the average variable cost? Explain your answer.

4. Explain three types of internal economy of scale.

5. Explain two reasons why internal diseconomies of scale might occur.

6. If marginal costs are below average costs, what will happen to average costs?

7. Distinguish between horizontal and forward vertical integration.

8. Explain one reason why a business might undertake a conglomerate merger.

9. What is meant by contribution?

10. Explain two ways in which a manager might try to reduce the cost per unit.

Essay Questions

1. To what extent do economies of scale matter?

2. Discuss the potential cost advantages and disadvantages to a business of expanding.

3. Is external growth better than internal growth?

 ## One Step Further

Visit our Online Resource Centre at **www.oxfordtextbooks.co.uk/orc/gillespiebusiness/** for test questions, podcasts, and further information on topics covered in this chapter.

Analysing market structure

9

Learning Objectives

In this chapter, we consider the different forms of market structure that exist and the implications of these structures for managers.

By the end of this chapter, you should:

- ✓ understand different market conditions and the impact on price and output decisions;

- ✓ understand the meaning and significance of barriers to entry;

- ✓ understand the price and output decisions in a perfectly competitive market in the short and long runs;

- ✓ understand the price and output decisions in a monopoly market in the short and long runs;

- ✓ understand the price and output decisions in the short and long runs in monopolistic competition;

- ✓ understand the price and output decisions in an oligopoly market in the short and long runs.

© **Case Study**

Manufacturers of liquid crystal display (LCD) panels have been charged by Europe's top competition regulator with running a cartel. The European Commission did not identify the suspected cartel members, but Philips, the Dutch electronics company, acknowledged that it had received the formal statement of objections in respect of LG Display, a jointly owned business in which it has since sold its remaining stake.

Philips said that it intended to contest 'vigorously' the Commission's allegation. 'It is important to note that the statement of objections does not allege that Philips was directly involved in the infringement,' it said.

The Commission's charges comes three years after it was revealed that authorities in the USA, Japan, South Korea, and Europe had launched an international investigation into alleged price-fixing by LCD screen manufacturers.

LCD panels are used widely in mobile phones, televisions, computers, MP3 players, digital watches, and pocket calculators.

In late 2006, when the industry was struggling with falling prices and oversupply, Philips said that it was—along with a number of other companies—being investigated by international regulators for 'possible anti-competitive conduct'.

Since then, LG Display, Sharp, and Chunghwa Picture Tubes have agreed to plead guilty and pay a total of US$585 million in fines following from the US probe into the sector.

Unlike some competition regulators, the European Commission cannot impose criminal penalties, but it can levy heavy fines for price fixing. In theory, the fines can be as much as 10 per cent of annual turnover—and while that limit is rarely approached, European fines for anti-trust breaches have been rising sharply during the past couple of years because of changes in guidelines.

The policy has run into criticism, but European officials defend it on the grounds that effective deterrents are needed to prevent price fixing.

Source: Adapted from *Financial Times*, 'LCD makers face cartel claim', available online at
http://www.ft.com/cms/s/7eaf9b66-6f9e-11de-bfc5-00144feabdc0.html

Questions

1. What is a cartel?
2. Why might the producers of LCD displays want to form a cartel?

3. What do you think are the conditions necessary for a cartel to be successful?

4. Why might the European Commission want to take action against a cartel?

5. Do you think that a fine is an effective deterrent against cartels?

6. Can you think of markets other than consumer electronics in which cartels are likely to be created?

Introduction

There are many different types of market in the business world. Some are local, such as the supply and demand for taxis within a city; others are global, such as the market for oil or wheat. The structure of these markets can vary considerably in terms of the number of firms competing and their size. In some markets, such as hairdressing and newsagents, there are hundreds of thousands of small providers of very similar products. In other markets, such as insurance, banking, and pharmaceuticals, there are relatively few, large producers. In this chapter, we examine the different market conditions and their implications for managers.

The concentration ratio

One key element of the structure of a market is the extent to which it is dominated by a few firms. The **concentration ratio** measures the market share of the largest firms in a market. For example, the 'four-firm concentration ratio' measures the market share of the largest four firms in the market. This ratio varies significantly between markets in the UK. In the case of sugar, oil, and cars, for example, it is very high; in the case of hairdressing, web design, and plumbing, it is low, highlighting that there are many small firms in these industries. The higher the concentration ratio, the more a market is dominated by a few firms. This influences the degree of competition.

If one firm dominates a market (that is, if it has a high market share), it is called a 'monopoly'. If a few firms dominate it, is an **oligopoly**. If there are many thousands of firms and none of them are particularly large, it is known as a 'competitive market'. Of course, when analysing the competition, managers must be clear what they mean by the 'market'. A retailer may be interested in the competition within a 20-minute drive, because this is where their shoppers come from; a shampoo producer may be interested in competition nationally or even globally.

Data Analysis 9.1

The product sales of the top five businesses as a percentage of the total market sales can be summarized as follows.

Table 9.1

Product	%
Tobacco	99%
Sugar	99%
Confectionery	81%
Soft drinks and bottled water	75%
Coal extraction	79%
Telecommunications	61%
Pharmaceuticals	57%
Alcoholic beverages	51%
Soap and toilet preparations	40%
Accountancy services	36%
Jewellery and related products	20%
Fishing	16%
Hotels, catering and pubs	13%
Advertising	10%
Market research, management consultancy	10%
Wood and wood products	9%
Legal activities	9%

Source: Adapted from Economic Trends, 2006

1. Why do you think concentration ratios differ so much from one industry to another?

2. What do you think are the possible effects on:
   A customers?
   B investors of a high concentration ratio?

3. Do you think that these ratios would be the same in other countries?

4. Why might they change over time?

? *Think about it...* 9.1

Can you think of any markets in your economy in which you think the concentration ratio has changed in recent years? Why and how has it changed?

Managers will be interested in the market share of their business and the market share of other businesses, because this will influence their power relative to that of their competitors. For example, Microsoft dominates the software market, which offers it various advantages, such as:

- it may be able to negotiate better prices with suppliers;
- some programmers will be keen to work for it because of its leading status;
- it may have a brand loyalty and recognition that makes launching a new product easier than it might be for an unknown business;
- it has huge resources that may be used to deter anyone else entering the market and it can therefore protect its position.

A smaller producer may be in a much weaker position and be trading on less favourable terms, making it more difficult for it to survive and grow. In some markets, two firms (think Coca Cola and Pepsi, McDonald's and Burger King, Playstation and XBox, Google and Microsoft) fight it out to win orders—that is, two giant companies fight for dominance mainly through product development. In other markets, such as advertising agencies and hairdressers, there are many small businesses, but no single firm has a significant share of the market.

The conditions within a market will affect a manager's ability to control the price, the likely level of output that a business will be producing, and how it competes. These decisions will, in turn, affect many other aspects of the business, such as:

- its workforce planning (for example, whether it needs to recruit or make redundancies);
- the likely profits of the business (for example, whether it needs to warn shareholders of a likely fall in their rewards in the future);
- the desired level of capacity (for example, whether it is time to expand);
- the level of investment in marketing, and research and development.

Understanding the market is therefore very important for a manager. This means not only understanding the implications of the present concentration ratio, but also considering how easy it is for other firms to enter the market.

The threat of entry may influence a firm's behaviour as much as its existing rivals: for example, it may force a business to ensure that it remains competitive in what it offers and the level of service provided.

Think about it ...   9.2

Why do you think there are so many taxi businesses and hairdressers in the UK, but relatively few electricity companies or train companies?

Business Analysis   9.1

In recent years, there has been considerable consolidation within the retail market for electrical goods. The high-street market is now dominated by DSGi and Kesa. Between them, they operate Currys, Dixons, PC World, and Comet. Currys has 27.1 per cent and Comet has 17.5 per cent share of electrical specialists' sales.

In 2007, the leading retailers' share of specialist sales was as follows.

Table 9.2

Company	Market share (%)
DSG International	42.7
Of which:	
PC World	*14.6*
Currys/Currys.digital	*27.1*
UK e-commerce	*1.0*
Comet (Kesa Electricals)	17.5
Jessops	1.3
Apple Retail UK (Apple Inc, US)	3.3
Richer Sounds	1.0
Maplin	0.8
Evesham	0.7
Bose	0.7
Bennetts	0.6
Bang & Olufsen	0.6

Sources: Adapted from Company Reports and Accounts/Mintel

1. What problems do you think smaller retailers, such as Bose and Maplin, faced compared to the bigger firms?

2. How do they survive?

Barriers to entry

The number of businesses competing in a market will depend, in part, on how easy or difficult it is to enter. 'Barriers to entry' are factors that make it difficult for new firms to enter the market and include the following.

- *Access to suppliers and distributors* New businesses need to be able to access the required materials or components; without them, they cannot produce or sell. If most of the land that can be farmed in the champagne region of France is already growing grapes, then starting up as a champagne producer could be difficult. Similarly, if a business cannot get its products on the shelves of stores because the retailers prefer to stick with brands that they know or are worried about upsetting the bigger producers, then newcomers will find it difficult to gain any market share. In 1998, Walls ice cream was prosecuted for giving chilled cabinets to independent retailers and, in return, insisting that they stock Walls' products. Given the physical size of these stores, if they were to accept Walls' gift, they would not have space for another freezer cabinet and so, in effect, Walls was preventing competitors from accessing the market. Vertical integration by existing firms is another way of creating barriers to entry by controlling elements of supply and distribution.

>> You Decide ...

As the manager of a company producing luxury chocolates, should you try to buy a chain of retail outlets to help to sell your products?

- *The costs of entering a market* The set-up costs for some industries can be so high that it will deter entrants. For example, imagine trying to compete in the aircraft manufacturing business: the design costs and costs needed to set up a production system would be huge. This market is dominated by Boeing and Airbus, and it is difficult for other firms to enter. Similarly, think of the costs required to start up as a pharmaceutical business in terms of the investment in research and development, and trialling and testing. These will be prohibitive for many organizations. Even consumer markets, such as perfume, are very difficult to enter because of the marketing costs. The cost of simply promoting a new perfume in the UK is estimated to be £1 million if you want any chance of success; this amount is too much for small producers, thereby blocking their entry. Chanel spends over £7 million a year on promoting its products.

- *Legal requirements* In some markets, the existing firms are legally protected and entry by other businesses is prevented. For example, some countries use protectionist measures to protect their domestic industries against foreign competition. **Quotas** or tariffs are often used. Quotas limit the amount of units that foreign producers can sell in a country; a tariff places a tax on foreign goods, making it relatively expensive compared to domestic products. This makes it difficult for overseas firms to enter these markets. The pressure on governments to protect their own businesses was seen in 2008 when Boeing (a US aircraft manufacturer) and EADS (an European aircraft manufacturer) were bidding for orders from the US airforce worth nearly US$100,000 million. Patty Murray, a US senator, said: 'American taxpayers should not reward a company that has spent decades hurting American workers, and we should not turn a critical military contract that is unfairly supported and subsidized by foreign powers'. She was not alone in this view in the USA.

■ *Legal restrictions* Legal restrictions can also make it difficult to access a market. In India, for example, foreign companies cannot invest in retail outlets except for single brand stores in which they can own 51 per cent. This means that a business such as Reebok can open a store, but a supermarket such as the French chain Carrefour cannot. Trading is made more difficult by numerous taxes charged if you move goods between states and even within some states. Small, family-owned, retail outlets dominate this market and big Western retailers cannot get to the customers.

■ *Fear of retaliation* Firms may be wary of entering a market if they are afraid of what existing firms might do: for example, if they were worried that they would start a price war. If the existing firms react aggressively whenever anyone enters, this may act as deterrent over time and stop more from coming in. The way in which firms react will depend in part on the size of the market and whether it is growing or not. In a shrinking market, any further competition would be strongly resisted because it would take away even more sales at a time when winning and maintaining sales is difficult (whereas, in a growing market, it is possible that all can sell more). Also, the extent to which established firms have money invested in an industry that cannot easily be transferred will affect how fiercely they resist entry. A 'sunk cost' represents spending that cannot be recovered if a business leaves the market: for example, investment in specialized equipment that cannot be transferred to another industry. If there are high sunk costs, existing firms will fight harder to protect their market share.

■ *The learning curve* As a firm gains experience in a market, it is likely to become better at producing: it will learn by doing. Imagine that you start a job at a new business; it will take time for you to get up to speed—that is, to work out how things are done, to find out who you ask for various things, to find out where you buy supplies from, and so on. Those people who have been there a while should know the answers to many of these questions because they will have learnt along the way. A new person has much to learn and will therefore be less efficient at first. The same is true for businesses: if managers have been in an industry for a while and have expanded, they will have more experience than newcomers, should make fewer mistakes, and should make better decisions. As a result of the learning curve, entering a market can be difficult and this therefore acts as a barrier to entry.

>> You Decide ...

You are the government minister in charge of business advice, support, and regulation. The car industry has been failing for many years and many jobs are likely to be lost as closures are made. The senior managers of the major domestic car companies have asked you to protect them from foreign competition.

Do you think that you should help?

Business Analysis   9.2

In 2007, the European Union (EU) Commission blocked a €1,480 million bid by Ryanair to take over rival Irish carrier Aer Lingus, saying that the lack of competition would lead to higher ticket prices. The budget carrier Ryanair would have assumed a monopoly on twenty-two routes and more than a 60 per cent market share on thirteen others, affecting a total of more than 14 million passengers. Both carriers account for about 80 per cent of the airline passenger traffic in and out of Dublin, the report said. The Commission argued that other carriers would be unlikely to compete against a merged Ryanair and Aer Lingus.

This is not only because the merged entity would be able to operate from the very large bases of Ryanair and Aer Lingus in Ireland ... but because Ryanair has a reputation of aggressive retaliation against any entry attempt by competitors.

It was the first time that the Commission had blocked an aviation merger and only the twentieth time overall in 3,000 cases since 1990. The Aer Lingus chairman said that the ruling was good for competition: 'Consumer choice is at the core of every competitive market and the creation of one dominant player out of Ireland, despite the protestations of Ryanair, just cannot be in the interest of consumers.'

1. What do you think are the long-term consequences of Ryanair reacting aggressively to any new entrant?
2. How do you think Ryanair might have defended its proposed takeover of Aer Lingus?

The barriers to entry in a market can change over time. For example, additional investment in advertising by existing firms can raise the costs for new entrants, making it more difficult to enter. But the Internet has reduced the costs for businesses of entering many markets; this is because a physical presence is no longer required (think of travel agents, insurance, and banking). Similarly, to enter the 'book' market, you used to have to print the books physically; books are now increasingly being stored electronically and more digital book readers are being launched on the market.

?   *Think about it...*   9.3

Can you think of markets other than those mentioned above in which the barriers to entry have been reduced by the Internet?

The effectiveness of barriers to entry depends, in part, on who wants to enter. Wrigley's dominated the chewing gum market for many years in the UK, with a market share of over 90 per cent. Many firms considered entering this market, but rejected the idea on the basis that:

■ it would be expensive to develop a chewing gum product;

■ marketing costs would be too high to try to gain any market share off Wrigley's;

■ Wrigley's would be likely to fight back, and had considerable resources and power in the market, which would make survival difficult.

In 2007, however, Cadbury's entered the UK chewing gum market with Trident gum. Cadbury's already had links with retailers and had considerable power over them, because of its chocolate products. It also had the financial resources to sustain a battle against Wrigley's and had experience in chewing gum from companies that it owned elsewhere in the world. What had been barriers to entry for many were not enough to discourage Cadbury's in the long run.

Barriers to entry may also be avoided or made obsolete by technology. For many years, Kodak dominated the camera and film industry, only to be by-passed by digital camera makers, such as Canon and Sony, which were big in completely different industries. Technology revolutionized the industry, making the existing businesses the laggards and firms from other sectors created a new market. The producers of pianos used to be traditional music instrument makers until the development of the electronic keyboard revolutionized this sector.

The extent to which barriers to entry exist will influence the level of profits that a business can make. If you are making high profits, this will attract other firms into the industry. If they are able to enter easily, they will compete away the abnormal profits. Porter (1985) talked of a 'pool of profits' being available in any industry: with more firms competing, these profits have to be shared out. But if there are barriers to entry, this means that an established business should be able to earn high profits for longer; although other firms may be attracted by the higher returns and want to switch resources into this market, they will not be able to enter.

Business Analysis 9.3

For over twenty years, the only big Western fast food companies in China were McDonald's and Yum! brands, which operate the Kentucky Fried Chicken (KFC) and Pizza Hut brands. They were fighting over a market worth around 200,000 million renminbi (RMB) (US$29,000 million) a year.

In 2005, Burger King entered the market; by 2008, Burger King had only twelve outlets, but announced plans to open another 250 in the next five years. Of these, 90 per cent will be franchised. KFC already had 2,200 outlets and McDonald's had 950.

One difficulty for Burger King is that its menu is based around beef. Chinese customers prefer chicken and so the company has had to invest heavily in marketing to convince customers of the healthy benefits of eating beef. Also, it has not gone as far as KFC in terms of adjusting its menu for local tastes. KFC offers pumpkin porridge, Beijing chicken rolls, and a Chinese deep-fried twisted dough stick (*youtiao*).

What barriers do you think a business such as Burger King might face entering a new market such as China?

Data Analysis 9.2

Companies often develop their brands so that you recognize their products more easily, so that you trust the product, and so that you identify with the brand's values. This makes it more difficult for others to enter the market because of the brand loyalty to existing brands.

According to Interbrand, the biggest global brands in 2008 were:

- Coca Cola (beverages), with a revenue of US$66,667 million;
- IBM (computer services), with a revenue of US$59,031 million;
- Microsoft (computer software), with a revenue of US$59,007 million;
- GE (diversified), with a revenue of US$53,086 million;
- Nokia (consumer electronics), with a revenue of US$35,942 million.

Sources: Adapted from Interbrand, Best Global Brands 2008

1. **What do you think are the main benefits of investing in a brand?**
2. **What do you think that the Coca Cola brand represents?**
3. **Do you think that the cola market would be difficult to enter or not? Explain your reasons.**

Types of market

There are many different types of market structure. In some, there are relatively few businesses and it is difficult to enter; in others, there are many firms and it is easy to start up. Each market structure leads to different price and quantity outcomes. In the next section, we examine the short-run and long-run outcomes in different market structures, and the impact of these in terms of efficiency.

Perfect competition

One type of market structure in economics is known as 'perfect competition'. In perfect competition, we imagine a market in which there are hundreds of thousands of providers of similar products. You manage one business, which offers goods or services that are exactly the same as the others. For example, it may be the wheat or milk market, in which there are thousands of farmers producing similar outputs, or it could be the market for shares or currencies markets, in which there are many organizations or individuals buying and selling exactly the same thing. This means that the product is a 'commodity'—that is, it is not differentiated from other products. There is no difference in what each producer is offering.

The assumptions of a perfectly competitive market are that:

- there are many producers offering similar products (also called 'homogenous products'), each of which is a small part of the market—that is, its supply is insignificant relative to the total supply in the market;
- customers have perfect information, which means that they know what is on offer from all of the producers and what prices are being offered, allowing them to switch easily;
- there is freedom of movement of other providers into and out of this market.

This last assumption is important, because it means that there are no barriers to entry. This means that, if existing businesses are making abnormal profit (that is, if revenue is greater than costs), this will attract firms in from other industries. Managers operating elsewhere will want to make the high returns available in this sector, and will look to reallocate resources and enter this market. We can see in the UK, over the years, how resources have moved out of industries such as coal and manufacturing, and into sectors such as leisure, hospitality, finance, and the media, which have been growing and offering higher returns.

By examining the outcomes of perfect competition, you can see the effects of an extremely high level of competition: although very few markets come close to anything like perfectly competitive, by analysing this form of market structure, it provides a benchmark against which to assess the effects of competition and a point of comparison when considering less competitive markets. It is therefore a model, as described in Chapter 1—that is, it has a set of assumptions that lead to particular outcomes. These may not exactly reflect reality, because no market is fully perfectly competitive, but it shows what happens as markets move towards this and therefore policymakers can decide whether this is desirable or not.

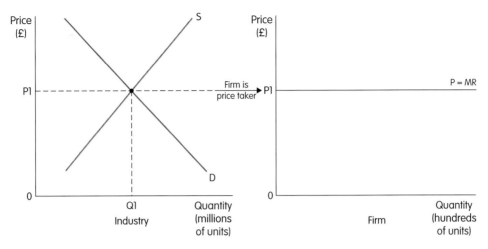

Figure 9.1 The firm in perfect competition is a price taker

In Figure 9.1, the market supply and demand is shown on the left-hand side. On the right-hand side, we see the position of one individual firm. Each firm is very small in relation to the industry as a whole, so it is producing, say, hundreds of units, while the market produces millions. Each firm is a price taker; this means that it can sell as much as it wants at the given market price. A firm is a price taker because it is so small relative to the industry as a whole that changes in its output do not shift the total supply in the industry to any significant extent and so its output decisions do not change the market equilibrium price.

If every unit can be sold at the same price, this means that the price is equal to the marginal revenue. If every unit can be sold at £10, then the extra revenue from selling a unit is £10. The price (which is the average revenue) equals marginal revenue.

Each business will profit maximize at the output at which the marginal revenue equals the marginal costs (see Chapter 8). At this point, there is no extra profit to be made. In perfect competition, the price equals the marginal revenue, so a business profit maximizes where:

Price = Marginal revenue = Marginal cost

In Figure 9.2, the firm is making abnormal profit. This is because the price is greater than the average cost. This sends a signal to businesses in other industries that they should reallocate their resources and move into this one because of the high returns available. They can do this because there are no barriers to entry.

The entry of new firms into the industry means that existing managers will face more competition and customers will have more choice. With more firms providing the products, the market price is driven down. Whereas changes in output by one firm on its own cannot shift the industry supply curve enough to move the equilibrium price, if many firms enter the market producing more output, this will shift the industry supply curve to the right. This increase in supply in the industry will lead to a fall in the price. As an existing business, what you are experiencing is more firms entering your market, competing away

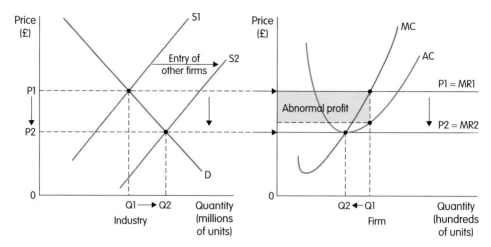

Figure 9.2 The adjustment process from short-run abnormal profits to long-run equilibrium in a perfectly competitive market

your profits; unfortunately, with similar products, ease of entry, and perfect knowledge on behalf of the customers, there is nothing that you can do about this.

The long-run equilibrium in perfect competition

The freedom of entry into the market is good for the customers, but competes away the abnormal profits of existing businesses. Firms will keep entering this market until normal profits are earned (when the price or average revenue equals the average costs which means that total revenue equals total costs). Once this level of profits is achieved, firms are earning the level of rewards that they would expect to make given the risk and resources involved; there is no further incentive for businesses to move into this industry. The industry will be in long-run equilibrium.

If, however, businesses were making a loss in this industry, firms would leave (because they were not covering the opportunity cost of being in there). As they leave the industry, this reduces the total number of suppliers. Again, whereas one firm cannot shift the supply curve, if many firms leave the market, the industry supply will shift to the left (see Figure 9.3). With less being supplied in the industry, the market price increases (as the product becomes scarcer); this process continues until the price has risen sufficiently to enable those firms that are left to make normal profits.

In the long-run equilibrium in perfect competition, firms therefore make normal profits. They are also efficient, which is why this market structure appeals to many analysts. There are two main types of efficiency: allocative and productive. In long-run equilibrium in perfect competition, businesses are both allocatively efficient and productively efficient.

■ Allocative efficiency occurs when the number of units being produced maximizes the welfare of society. To see where this occurs, we consider the extra benefit to society of a unit being produced (shown by how much consumers are willing to pay for it—that is, the price) and the extra cost to society of producing it. If the extra benefit is greater than the extra cost, society will benefit from the unit being made. So, for allocative

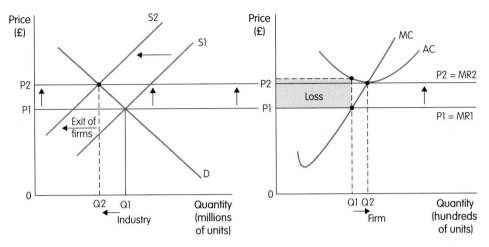

Figure 9.3 The adjustment process from short-run losses to long-run equilibrium in a perfectly competitive market

efficiency, every unit for which the extra benefit (price) is greater than the extra cost should be made up to the output at which the extra benefit equals the extra cost—that is, a firm should produce when price equals marginal cost. As we will see later, this does not happen in many markets, but in perfect competition, the profit-maximizing output is also the output for which social welfare is maximized.

■ Productive efficiency occurs when firms produce at the minimum of the average cost curve—that is, at the lowest possible cost per unit.

The fact that perfect competition leads to an efficient solution without government intervention highlights why society might like competitive markets. Businesses make normal profits, production is productively efficient, and the welfare of society is maximized. A business, however, may not necessarily want this situation: you are more likely to want to differentiate your products and gain some control over the market, so that your business gains, even if society as a whole suffers.

? *Think about it...* 9.4

Which of the following statements are true and which are false?

A In perfect competition, businesses must make normal profits in the short run.

B In perfect competition, the marginal revenue curve for a business equals the price.

C In perfect competition, an individual firm is small relative to the industry as a whole.

D In perfect competition, a business is a price taker.

E In perfect competition in the long run, the price equals the marginal revenue equals the marginal costs equals the average cost.

Monopoly

A very different type of market structure from perfect competition is a monopoly. This occurs when one firm dominates the industry. Under UK competition law, a monopoly is defined as a business that has a market share of over 25 per cent, but, in its most extreme version, a monopolist would have a 100 per cent market share. This could happen, for example, if the government were to insist there were only one provider of a service, such as water, gas, or electricity: for example, in the UK, only Camelot is allowed to provide the National Lottery. While a single-firm monopoly is not common, the model is useful to show the effects of a dominant firm, which can be compared with the outcome in perfect competition.

In a monopoly market structure, it is assumed that:

- there are barriers to entry—that is, that the existing firm is protected from competition by mechanisms such as legal protection, the need for specialist skills, or high costs of entry;
- the firm's product is differentiated from the competition—that is, that there are no providers of a similar product, which means that the business is in a much more powerful position than in perfect competition, when the business is just one of many.

In a monopoly, it is possible for a business to earn abnormal profits in the long run as well as the short run. Although other firms will be attracted by these high returns (as in perfect competition), they will not be able to enter the market due to the barriers to entry. This means that the monopolist can continue to enjoy high rewards even in the long run.

Not surprisingly, then, many managers will be looking for ways in which to create a monopoly position for their business: for example, by trying to stress the brand differences between their product and others, and by developing brand loyalty. Coca Cola, for example, stresses that it is the 'real thing' and promotes its heritage, to try to differentiate it from other cola drinks. Jack Daniels, the bourbon producer, stresses its use of special casks and the length of time for which it ferments its drink to promote it as a premium drink. Innocent stresses that its drinks do not include any artificial additives. The desire for a dominant position is why firms are continually fighting for market share. Virgin and British Airways, for example, have competed vigorously (and in the case of British Airways, sometimes illegally) to have dominance on transatlantic routes. Microsoft is fighting hard to catch up in the search engine market and to gain market share from Google. Google, meanwhile, is attacking Microsoft's dominance of the word-processing market.

? *Think about it ...*   9.5

1. Can you think of any other brands that clearly try to differentiate themselves from the competition? How do they do this?

2. If they are successful, how easy is it for others to copy what they are doing?

In a monopoly, the business is a price maker; it does not have to charge what everyone else is charging (that is, it does not have to be a price taker), because it has a monopoly position. This generally leads to higher prices and lower outputs than in a perfectly competitive industry. The lack of competition means that the business can drive up price by restricting what is on offer.

In Figure 9.4, the monopolist is profit maximizing (that is, producing when marginal revenue equals marginal cost). This means that it charges price P1 and sells quantity Q1.

The lack of competition in a monopoly market may lead to a poor-quality service for the customer. If the customer does not have much choice, then managers may decide that it does not matter how they are treated. This is why governments worry about monopolies: they are concerned that monopolies may exploit customers and not act in the interests of the general public.

Most governments therefore have regulations in place to oversee the behaviour of monopolies. In the UK, competition policy does not assume that the monopoly is always acting against the public interest, but it reserves the right to check on its behaviour or possible behaviour. In 2008, for example, the Competition Commission ordered BAA (British Airports Authority) to sell off Gatwick, Stansted, and Edinburgh airports because of a lack of competition at UK airports. BAA ran seven UK airports at the time. The Competition Commission argued that, 'under separate ownership, the airport operators,

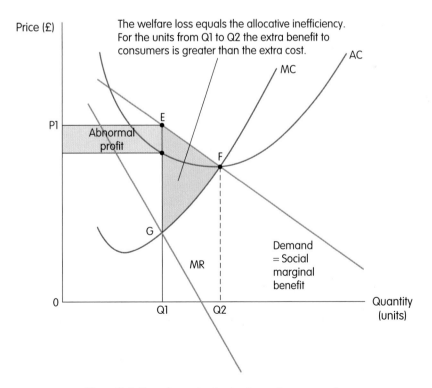

Figure 9.4 The price and output outcome in a monopoly

including BAA, will have a much greater incentive to be far more responsive to their customers, both airlines and passengers'.

The possible need to investigate monopolies is reinforced by the fact that monopolies are allocatively inefficient; this is because, at output Q1, the price paid by the customer is greater than the marginal cost of providing it. The price represents the extra benefit to the customer of consuming this unit; this is greater than the extra cost of providing it, and so the welfare of society could increase if this unit were produced. In fact, on all of the units Q1,Q2, the extra benefit is greater than the extra cost and so society's welfare would be increased if these were produced. The socially optimal (or allocatively efficient) output is Q2; the shaded area EFG represents a deadweight social burden area, which is allocatively inefficient.

The reason that a monopolist does not provide these additional units (Q1,Q2) is because the impact of lowering the price on these and on all of the ones before would be reduced profit. Profits are maximized where marginal revenue equals marginal cost, so that is where the monopolist wants to be, regardless of social welfare.

As well as being allocatively inefficient a monopolist is also productively inefficient, because it is not producing at the minimum of the average cost curve. Although it could produce at a lower average cost, to sell these units would involve lowering prices and it would end up with lower profits; as a result, the business restricts output and pushes up the price to compensate for the higher costs.

? **Think about it ...** 9.6

1. As a manager, would you prefer your business to be in a monopoly position or a perfectly competitive market? Why?

2. In what ways do you think a monopolist might exploit its customers?

However some would argue monopolies need to be prevented from being inefficient. Other economists, such as Schumpeter (1942), argue that monopolies may actually lead to lower prices and higher outputs than more competitive markets. The one firm in a monopoly may produce on a much larger scale than any one firm in perfect competition; this may mean that it benefits from internal economies of scale and that therefore the average costs are lower than they would be in a competitive market, and this can bring the price down.

It is also worth considering that the higher profits of monopolies may provide the finance needed for expensive investment in research and development. In industries such as cars, pharmaceuticals, and computers, developing new products is a hugely expensive business requiring major investment. GlaxoSmithkline Beecham, the pharmaceutical business, claims that developing a new medicine costs over US$500 million and takes over twelve years because of the amount of testing required. It might be that abnormal profits help to finance this, and that this can bring about innovations that improve the choice available to customers, reduce costs, and bring down prices. This is Microsoft's defence of its actions when it is accused of abusing its monopoly power: it would argue that it has pushed technology forward and that this is why it is so successful. Its profits are either reinvested into the business, funding further research, or are paid out to the investors, many of whom are likely to be pension funds and banks. Smaller businesses and customers may take a different view of the desirability of monopolies making high profits.

Schumpeter's argument in defence of monopolies also highlights that their profits are often generated by offering a better service or product than those of their rivals; in many cases, they sustained this profit only by continuing to be better than the competition. If this view is correct, then the profits of monopolies are the sign of excellent customer service; if they were to fail to provide this level of service, others would enter and take away customers. Schumpeter calls this 'creative destruction'—that is, a monopoly position may be created by innovation, but will be swept away by further innovation unless the original firm keeps developing and improving its offering to stay ahead of the competition. Many markets that are dominated by large firms clearly experience a high level of innovation: for example, razor blades, toothpaste, and soaps. Research into British manufacturing firms by Blundell, Griffith, and Van Reenen, of the Institute for Fiscal Studies, found that higher market shares were associated with higher investment in research and development, and innovation. However few firms are ever safe; as one firm establishes a lead, Schumpeter argued that others would follow. In 2007, Apple launched the iPhone, which proved that consumers would use a phone to browse the Internet. The iPhone was followed by a rush of product development and launches by other producers, such as Rim, which produces the Blackberry, to provide similar technology for their 'smartphones'. A year later, Google launched its Android software, making Internet access available on a whole range of cheaper mobiles.

More market power may, therefore, be used in such a way that the public gains. While it is true that many brands have dominated their markets for years (think Kellogg's, Marlboro, Heinz, and Colgate), it is also true that new products are being developed each year, that many products die each year, and that companies also die as they fail to keep up with the competition. Kwik Save supermarkets, Woolworth's the retailer, and Zavvi all suffered and disappeared, because they could not keep up and were removed by competition or substitutes. Gaining market share may give firms power in the short run, but in the long term, this may spur on more competition and in this situation, to keep alive, you have to keep looking for ways of staying ahead of rivals.

There is, therefore, considerable debate over the desirability of monopolies and the extent to which they are good for customers or not. From the perspective of a manager, however, the advantage of creating a monopoly position is that it enables him or her to earn abnormal profits to reward investors (and presumably him or herself). The manager of a perfectly competitive firm is subject to market forces and has to accept the market price. A monopolist, however, can influence demand through its operations and marketing activities; it can try to shape the demand and make it less sensitive to price, to try to boost its profits.

Think about it...   9.7

Do you think it is unethical if managers aim to achieve a monopoly position in a market?

Business Analysis   9.4

In 2007, the European Court of First Instance (CFI) upheld a major anti-trust (anti-monopoly) ruling against Microsoft, the world's largest software firm.

Microsoft was prosecuted in Europe and the USA because it tried to protect and extend its Windows monopoly in two ways. One was by bundling together other types of software along with Windows so that companies were buying several software programmes together, rather than choosing which parts they wanted. Microsoft was also said to hold back information from rivals that would have enabled their software to work well with Windows software. This made it difficult for other software firms to compete.

The European Commission's initial ruling against Microsoft in 2004 ordered Microsoft to sell a version of Windows without its media player software. It ruled that the firm had to provide information on how to interoperate with Windows servers. The Commission also imposed a fine of €497 million (US$613 million), which has since grown to €777 million (US$990 million) because it claimed that Microsoft was not fully complying with its decision.

These decisions were upheld in 2007.

1. How might Microsoft have defended its actions?
2. Should a business such as Microsoft have to share information with its competitors?

How can a business create a monopoly position?

To build a monopoly position, you must differentiate your product significantly from the competition and protect your market from others entering. You might differentiate your product by:

- developing new technology, which can then be patented, providing legal protection;
- developing a unique selling proposition (USP), such as 'one-hour delivery' or '24-hour opening'—but the problem with these sort of offerings is that, over time, they can be imitated by others and so maintaining a monopoly position may be a continuous process of continually raising the barrier.

- building brand loyalty, so that customers perceive your product as different from the rest; this is likely to require heavy investment;
- gaining government protection—for example, you may lobby government to prevent other business from competing in your market, arguing that your monopoly is important to keep jobs in the country, for example, or that it is such a vital industry that it cannot be open to foreign competition (such as the defence or energy industries);
- forcing competitors out of business via a price war or through takeover and making it clear that further entry will be responded to aggressively—but the competition authorities will probably prevent this behaviour.

? Think about it ...   9.8

Which of the following statements about a monopoly are true and which are false?

A The marginal revenue curve equals the average revenue.

B The monopolist profit maximizes when marginal revenue equals marginal cost.

C A monopolist can make abnormal profits in the long run as well as in the short run.

D A monopolist is allocatively efficient in the long run.

>> You Decide ...

What could you do to try to build a monopoly position in a market for your sports retail business?

Monopolistic competition

Monopolistic competition is another market structure in which managers have some control over their markets, but, unlike monopoly, there is freedom of entry and exit into and out of the market. Examples of monopolistic competitive markets are hairdressers, shoe shops, and coffee shops. Each business is different in some way from its rivals, so the demand curve for each one is downward-sloping. A price increase will lead to a loss of some customers, who switch to competitors, but will not lead to the loss of all customers; some will stay because of the particular features of this business. Similarly, a price decrease will attract some customers from competitors, but not all of them, because each business is different in some way.

In the short run, a monopolistic competitive firm can make abnormal profits or losses. But there can be entry and exit into and out of the market in the long run, unlike a monopoly market. This means that it is not difficult for other businesses to set up in these markets, perhaps because the start-up costs are not that high and there are limited specialized skills required; also, closing down is not that difficult (for example, the premises can easily be reused for something else and so should be fairly easy to sell). This means that if existing firms are making abnormal profits, this will attract other businesses into the market. These new businesses will attract some customers, taking these away from the existing firm; this will shift demand inwards for the established firms, thereby reducing their profits. Entry will stop when the profits being made are only normal profits and so there is no further incentive for firms to enter.

Think of what happens when a new feature is offered on mobile phones by one provider: it is not long before others follow. Manufacturers then seek new ways of differentiating themselves to push their demand outwards again.

If, however, the established firms were making losses (perhaps because of a fall in demand), some of them would leave; this would increase demand for the ones left and this process continues until those left make normal profit.

In Figure 9.5a, the established firm is profit maximizing at P1,Q1. It is making abnormal profits (because the price is greater than the average cost). More firms enter the market, which reduces the demand for the established business and shifts its demand curve inwards until only normal profits are made.

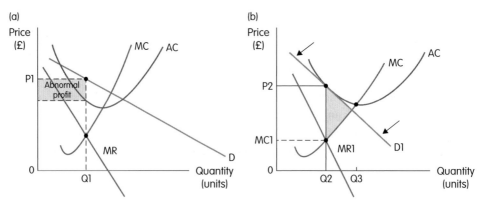

Figure 9.5 Profits in monopolistic competition. Short run abnormal profits (a) are competed away by the entry of other firms so normal profits are earned in the long run (b).

In Figure 9.5b, a loss is being made; firms leave and demand for those left increases, shifting demand to the right until only normal profits are made.

In a monopolistically competitive market, managers will try to differentiate their products and gain even more monopoly power. In the short run, it is possible to earn abnormal profits, but this will lead to more entry into the market; to regain abnormal profits, the manager will want to try to shift demand for his or her own business outwards again and regain more control over the market or develop barriers to entry to stop others entering.

? Think about it ...   9.10

1. What do you think determines the slope of the demand curve in a monopolistically competitive market?

2. What makes you choose one restaurant rather than another? How loyal are you?

From society's view, monopolistic competition is inefficient, like monopoly. In the long-run equilibrium, the price is above the marginal costs, so the business is allocatively inefficient. The shaded area of Figure 9.5 is a deadweight social burden triangle representing allocative inefficiency; on these units, the extra benefit to society is greater than marginal cost.

The business is also productively inefficient because it is not producing the output for which the average cost is minimized. As with monopoly, the firm is more interested in profit maximizing than serving society's interests and this means pushing the price up by restricting output to the point at which marginal revenue equals marginal cost.

? Think about it ...   9.11

In 2008, the furniture retailer MFI ceased trading, with the loss of 1,400 jobs. The company's 111 stores were all closed.

MFI went into administration due to the downturn in the housing market, which affected the demand for new kitchens and bedrooms. Sales also fell due to competition from rivals such as Ikea.

What do you think the business might have been able to do to avoid shutting down?

Oligopoly

Another form of market structure is known as oligopoly. This describes a market that is dominated by a few large firms. This type of market structure is quite common: for example, the banking sector, travel business, and petrol market in the UK are all oligopolistic markets. In these sectors, the firms are interdependent; this means that managers realize that the actions of one business affect the others, and that therefore they must take into account each other's possible actions and reactions when making decisions.

 ## Business Analysis   9.5

The following are examples of markets dominated by a few firms in the UK.

Table 9.3

Oil and gas extraction	British Gas; BP; ConocoPhillips; ExxonMobil; Shell
Sugar	British Sugar; Tate & Lyle
Soft drinks	Cadbury Schweppes; Coca Cola
Brewers	Allied Domecq; Carlsberg Tetley; Diageo; Interbrew; Scottish & Newcastle
Tobacco	BAT; Gallaher Group; Imperial Tobacco Group
Pharmaceuticals	Astra-Zeneca; Eli Lilly; GlaxoSmithKline; Pfizer
Food and personal care products	Procter & Gamble; Unilever
Electrical retail	Currys; Dixons; Kesa (Comet)
Food retail	Asda/WalMart; Morrisons; Sainsbury; Tesco
Motorway service operators	Macquarie (Moto); Roadchef; Welcome Break
Fast food	Burger King; KFC; McDonalds
Home DIY	B&Q; Focus; Homebase
Mobile phone networks	O2; Orange; T-Mobile; Vodafone
Accountancy	Deloitte; Ernst & Young; KPMG; PricewaterhouseCoopers

1. Can you think of any other oligopoly markets in your economy?
2. Why do you think these markets are oligopolistic rather than more competitive?

The price and quantity outcomes in oligopoly therefore depend on the assumptions that managers make about their rivals and how they will behave.

Possible outcomes are shown by different models such as the following.

The kinked demand curve model

The kinked demand curve model was developed by Sweezy in 1939. It assumes that managers are pessimistic about how their rivals might act and believe that their competitors will not collaborate with them. Managers assume that if they cut their prices, their rivals will follow because they will be worried about losing sales. Therefore, they assume that demand will be price inelastic if they cut price (the increase in quantity demanded will be less than the increase in price in percentage terms).

They assume, however, that if they push the price up, their rivals will be happy for them to be the only ones doing so and will not follow. This means that demand will be price elastic if they put the price up, because the fall in quantity demanded will be larger than the rise in price (in percentage terms).

These assumptions mean that the demand curve is kinked around the existing prices and that there is no incentive to change price (see Figure 9.6). A price cut leads to a relatively small increase in quantity demanded, so revenue would fall; a price increase leads to a relatively large decrease in quantity demanded, so revenue would fall. It is therefore better to keep price where it is.

This model helps to explain why prices of producers in oligopoly are often similar and do not change much (this is called 'price stickiness'). Rather than start price cutting, firms often compete in ways other than price. For example, investing in technology to add features or investing in marketing to build the brand is common in oligopolies, as firms try to avoid price wars and reducing all of their margins.

? *Think about it ...*   9.12

Imagine that you are managing a chain of juice bars stores across the UK. You are reluctant to cut price in case it simply leads to everyone cutting price and sales do not increase significantly. How else could you compete?

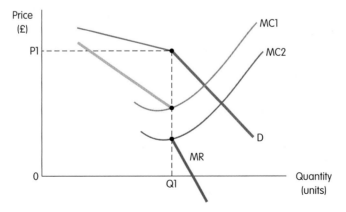

Figure 9.6 The kinked demand curve in an oligopoly The kinked demand curve model also highlights that costs can change from MC1 to MC2 and the profit maximizing price and output are P1Q1.

The cartel

The cartel model of oligopoly assumes that firms will collude and work together. They will try to maximize the profits available to them by restricting output and pushing up price. It is exactly this sort of behaviour that governments worry about and usually try to prevent, for fear that the customers will lose out due to monopoly power. Under a cartel arrangement, the member firms may decide how much output each one will make (called a 'quota') and at what price this will be sold. In effect, the individual businesses are joining together to act like a single monopolist. Customers may end up paying more for less compared to a competitive market. The result is that a cartel can maximize the total profits of the members.

Cartels will differ in terms of the nature of the agreements, but typically involve deals involving the choice of area in which members will sell, to which customers different members will sell, prices, and terms and conditions, and even who will gain which contract.

In a cartel, the members combined maximize profits at the point at which the marginal revenue in the industry equals the marginal cost (that is, P1,Q1 in Figure 9.7). This determines the profit-maximizing price (P1). The total quantity (Q1) will be divided among members, which will be given a quota each. For example, a firm might be told to produce at q1 and sell at price P1. Under these circumstances, it makes a profit equal to the shaded area in Figure 9.7 on the right-hand side.

Given that the product is all being sold at P1, this means the marginal revenue also equals P1; the firm would profit maximize by producing at q2. This would increase its own profits, but would lead to more output in the industry as a whole and move the industry from the profit-maximizing position. This firm would gain at the expense of others. There is therefore a temptation for individual firms to break the cartel and ignore the quota. The more that do this, the more that will be produced, driving down the industry price and reducing the total profits of the industry; this is likely to lead to the end of the

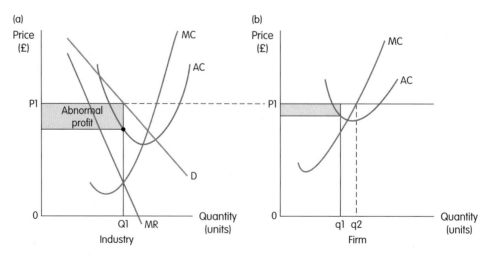

Figure 9.7 The cartel model

cartel unless it can be effectively policed to prevent this from happening. Those cheating need to face a significant threat if they pursue their own interests to the detriment of the cartel as a whole.

Cartels have been found in many sectors, such the cement industry, private schools, and airlines. In 2007, for example, the Office of Fair Trading (OFT) fined British Airways £121.5 million for trying to fix fuel surcharges with Virgin Atlantic. In the same year, several supermarkets and dairies owned up to fixing milk prices, and agreed to pay fines of £116 million; between 2000 and 2003, the OFT accused eleven retailers and two tobacco companies of fixing the price of cigarettes.

The factors that make collusion more likely include:

- relatively few businesses that can monitor each others' actions easily;
- significant barriers to entry providing existing firms with a strong control over the market;
- similar costs, so that they will gain similar rewards and there are less likely to be disputes;
- stable market conditions so that any agreements will remain valid.

Cartel agreements are, however, often unstable. This is because individual members of the agreement might try to increase their own rewards at the expense of others in the cartel. If they have agreed a price and quotas, for example, individual members may start to overproduce and try to sell their additional output. By doing this, they increase the total amount of products on the market and this starts to drive the price down. The cheating firms may benefit and increase their own rewards because of their extra output, but the other members and the industry overall will make fewer profits if they have stuck to their original quota because the price has now fallen. Some members might also object to the set price and quantities if they think that they are unfair. If, for example, one producer has higher costs than the others, its profits will be less per unit than the others if they all charge the same price. Cartels, therefore, have to be closely monitored by their members to make sure that cheating is not happening and/or to find those responsible.

Governments are naturally eager to find out when cartels are occurring because of the potential exploitation of customers. In the UK, anti-competitive agreements are prohibited by the Cartels and the Competition Act 1998 and Arts 81 and 82 of the EC Treaty. Many governments have now adopted a policy that encourages members to inform on any other cartel members. In the USA, for example, the first member to inform on its partners automatically gets full immunity from criminal prosecution.

 Business Analysis   9.6

In 2005, six of the leading hotels in Paris were fined for sharing commercial information that helped to keep prices artificially high. The Crillon, Bristol, Meurice, Piazza Athenee, Ritz, and

George V hotels were accused by competition regulators of operating a cartel. A four-year investigation found that they shared details of room rates averaging more than €700 (£480) a night. The six establishments were fined a total of €709,000. The establishments were in a league of their own due to their central location, exceptional accommodation, high-class restaurants, facilities such as swimming pools, and high staff numbers.

Source: BBC News 2005, *The New York Times* 2005, *The Guardian* 2005

1. How might you decide on the fine given to businesses that have been found to be colluding?
2. Do you think it is right that if one firm informs on the others, it is given immunity from prosecution?

>> You Decide ...

You are the marketing director of a major airline. Your main competitor on a popular route rings you up and suggests that you both increase prices on this route by 15 per cent to help to compensate for the recent increases in oil prices that the industry has experienced.

Do you agree to this?

The interdependence of firms within an oligopolistic market and the importance of considering the reactions of other firms is highlighted in **game theory**. This stresses that the strategy of one business will depend on its assumptions about the behaviour of other firms. The essence of game theory is shown in the 'prisoner's dilemma', in which two individuals have both been arrested for a crime. The question is whether they should confess to the crime or not and that, in turn, depends on what they think the other person will do. Unfortunately, they are locked up in separate rooms and cannot communicate, so they have to make assumptions about the other person's behaviour. It is assumed that if they both confess, they will be imprisoned for a long time; if they both refuse to confess, the police cannot prove anything and they will be released. The problem comes if one person refuses to confess and the other one does so: the latter person gets a light sentence and the one who refused to talk gets a very long sentence for non-cooperation. The ideal solution, from the prisoners' point of view, is not to confess and then they would both get off. But if you do not trust your fellow prisoner and think that he or she will confess. you are better confessing as well. On this basis, they will both confess because they do not trust each other.

The prisoner's dilemma highlights how your decisions about what to do depend on your relationship with other prisoners (or businesses in an oligopoly) and your view of whether you think you can trust them or not. It also shows the dangers of oligopoly from a manager's view: a lack of trust may lead to an outcome in which firms are worse off than if they trusted each other.

The prisoner's dilemma in a business context is highlighted in Figure 9.8. Two businesses are considering what level of output to produce: high or low. If they both produce low outputs, this will push the price up and both will win. But if one produces relatively little and its competitor produces a lot, this will increase supply and drive the price down; the first producer will do badly because its rival wins the market and is selling more. As a result, both producers might flood the market fearing that each other will do this anyway; the total output in the market ends up very high and the market price is low, meaning that both are both worse off compared to a situation in which both had restricted their output.

Figure 9.8 shows the financial results of each possible outcome: if both firms produce high levels of output, they will gain £1 million each; if both restrict output, they will earn £2 million each.

This model shows the importance of managers' assumptions about what other businesses will do. The past behaviour of businesses becomes very important here: how they have behaved in the past may influence assumptions about what they will do in the future.

Game theory can become much more complex depending on the assumptions that are made. Imagine that, in relation to Figure 9.9, you are the manager of Firm A thinking about your pricing options. Assume that you are pessimistic and look at the worst possible outcome of any decision. If you choose a price of £2, the worst that can happen is that B will charge £1 and you will make profits of £5,000. If you were to charge £1, the worst that could happen is that B would do the same and you would end up with £6,000. If you decide to choose the 'best of the worst', then you choose a £1 price. This is called a 'maximin' strategy because you are maximizing the minimum outcomes. If Firm B were to do the same, it would choose £1 as well and you would both end up with £6,000, when you could have had £10,000 had you agreed to charge £2 and believed each other.

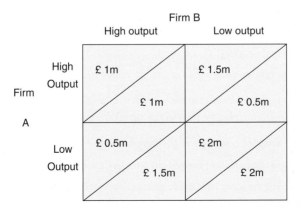

Figure 9.8 The prisoner's dilemma in a business context (The top area of each quadrant shows the payoff for A; the bottom area shows the payoff for B).

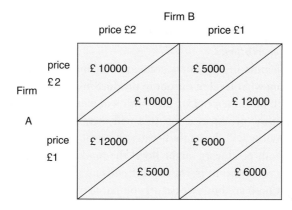

Figure 9.9 Pricing options (The top area of each of the quadrants shows the payoff for A; the bottom area shows the payoff for B).

A 'maximax' strategy occurs when a manager is optimistic and bases decisions on the 'best of the best' outcomes.

Decision making in business can therefore be like a chess game in which you are anticipating what your opponents will do next. Interestingly, world chess champion Gary Kasparov has written a book on business strategy called *How Life Imitates Chess*, in which he argues the importance of planning, but also the need, at times, to trust your instincts when making business decisions.

 Business Analysis   9.7

In December 2008, holiday firms cut their rates and offered a range of deals, including free children's places, extra weeks, and no flight supplements. Thomas Cook offered 10 per cent off all holidays booked by February, plus early booking savings of up to £400, while First Choice offered up to £200 off next year's summer holidays.

Airlines are also fighting hard to attract customers given the poor economic conditions, with British Airways and Virgin reducing prices to a range of long-haul destinations.

The holiday companies have already cut back on the number of holidays that they are offering due to the recession. The supply next year will be down by around a million holidays.

1. Why are holiday companies so eager to get early bookings?

2. If you are a holiday company that has not cut price yet, should you do so now?

3. If you were asked by the other holiday companies later in the year to agree to an across-the-board increase of 20 per cent in price, would you do this?

? *Think about it ...*   9.13

Which of the following statements about oligopoly are true and which are false?

A The kinked demand curve is a model in which firms cooperate.

B In a cartel, the industry produces at the point at which marginal revenue equals marginal costs.

C In game theory, businesses base their decisions about what to do on assumptions about what others are doing.

D In oligopoly, a few firms dominate the market.

Can you now answer questions 1, 2, and 3 from the opening case study?

How to protect your success

While governments are wary of the possible abuse of power by businesses that gain a monopoly position, they also recognize that individuals and firms should be able to protect their ideas. This is why legislation exists to protect intellectual property (IP) rights. Intellectual property refers to the ownership of a brand, invention, design, or other kind of creation.

The protection that managers can gain for their IP includes the following.

- *Patents* A patent protects new inventions and covers how things work, what they do, how they do it, what they are made of, and how they are made. It gives the owner the right to prevent others from making, using, importing, or selling the invention without permission. To gain a patent, an invention must be new, have an inventive step that is not obvious to someone with knowledge and experience of the subject, and must be capable of being made and used.

- **Trademarks** A trademark is a sign that can distinguish your goods and services from those of your competitors. It can be, for example, words, logos, or a combination of both. To be registered, a trademark must be distinctive (that is, it must differentiate your goods and services from those of competitors).

- **Copyright** Copyrights protect literary works (including novels, instruction manuals, computer programs, song lyrics, newspaper articles, and some types of database), dramatic works, musical works, artistic works, recordings, and broadcasts. The originator of these works automatically has a copyright on it; he or she does not need to register it.

- *Registering a design* This is a legal right that protects the overall visual appearance of a product in the geographical area in which you register it. The visual features that form the design include such things as the lines, contours, colours, shape, texture, materials, and the ornamentation of the product that, when applied, give it a unique appearance.

Think about it ...   9.14

What do you think are the long-term consequences for the industry of illegally downloading music?

 Business Analysis   9.8

Historically, China has not been known as a country in which IP rights are respected; piracy and copycat products have been rife. Since 2003, however, the number of trademark applications in China has increased by 60 per cent and the number of patents has nearly doubled, as have the number of IP lawsuits. The first laws to protect patents were only introduced in China in 1985 and it only began to enforce them in 2001 as part of the agreement to join the **World Trade Organization (WTO)**.

To encourage competition, however, China introduced a major set of anti-trust (anti-monopoly) laws in 2008. This could bring about significant changes in a country in which many markets, such as energy, telecoms, transport, and steel, lack competition. Even what were thought to be more competitive industries, such as rice flour and instant noodles, were recently reported to have seen price fixing and collusion. The new competition laws are expected to give more protection to consumers, and to allow them to benefit from lower prices and higher quality. The new laws will also apply to the state-owned monopolies, although there is an exemption when economic or national security is threatened, which could be an important get-out clause for the government.

Sources: *The Economist*, 17 July 2008, *Bloomberg* 30 August 2007, *Reuters* May 2009

1. What do you think the consequences of the new anti-trust laws might be in China?
2. What might be the consequences for business of not having IP protection laws?

 Business Analysis   9.9

eBay, the online trading site, was recently ordered to pay €38.6 million in damages to the luxury goods group LVMH for negligence in allowing the sale of fake bags, lipsticks, and designer clothes on its site. LVMH argued that eBay had committed 'serious errors' by not doing enough to prevent the sales of fake goods in 2006, including Louis Vuitton bags and Christian Dior products. It also argued that eBay had allowed unauthorized sales of perfume brands owned by the group, including Christian Dior, Kenzo, Givenchy, and Guerlain.

Do you think it is fair that eBay is held to blame for negligence?

Contestability

When making decisions about price and output, managers will not only consider how many firms are in the market already, but will also consider the likelihood of entry and exit in the future. This affects the contestability of a market. For example, there is an obvious difference between operating exclusively in a market and knowing that the government prevents any other entrants at all, and having a short-term monopoly position, but suspecting that other firms might and could enter at any moment.

The importance of possible future entry is highlighted in the theory of contestable markets. If markets are heavily contestable, that is, if entry is relatively easy, this puts more pressure on the existing firm (or firms) to be competitive, whereas if the market is very protected, managers are able to be more inefficient and survive. What matters when managers are considering how to set price and output is not only the present situation, but also how likely it is that others could enter in the future, i.e. what barriers to entry exist. With low barriers to entry abnormal profits will be competed away, for example.

Summary of market structures

Table 9.4

	Perfect competition	Monopolistic competition	Oligopoly	Monopoly
Differentiated products	No	Yes	Yes	Yes
Number of firms	Many	Many	Few	One
Entry and exist in the long run	Yes	Yes	No	No

Price discrimination

The analysis has so far focused on the behaviour of businesses in relation to a single market. In reality, businesses operate in many market segments. A 'segment' is a group of similar needs within an overall market. Managers can segment a market in many different ways, including by:

■ age: for example, developing different toys for different age groups (such as Lego for younger children and the Playstation for older children);

■ region: for example, producing different versions of a newspaper for different regions to reflect the local news;

- reason for purchase: for example, some people buy chocolate to reward themselves, some people buy it because they feel that they need cheering up, some buy it to share, and some buy it to give to others; chocolate companies therefore develop different products to target these different needs and promote them in different ways (a Mars bar is a snack product, After Eights are a gift, and Celebrations are for sharing);

- income: for example, some products clearly target higher income earners than others and the promotional channels are chosen accordingly (a Ferrari is unlikely to be promoted in a local newspaper, for example).

?   *Think about it ...*   *9.15*

Can you think of three different brands of chocolate and the particular reason for purchase that they are targeting?

Each of these segments may face its own demand and conditions: the demand may be higher or lower, and more or less price elastic. In some of these cases, different products will be developed for the different segments and, therefore, the cost conditions will also differ; in this case, with different costs and revenue conditions, the profit-maximizing price and output will clearly vary.

In some cases, however, it may be the same product being sold, but demand may still differ between different segments. For example, the demand for sandwiches at a train station is different from the demand for sandwiches once you are on the train, even though the sandwiches themselves are the same product. If demand conditions do vary (for example, demand for taxis in the city centre at 2 a.m. compared to 2 p.m.), then managers will be able to increase profits by charging different prices in the different segments rather than having one price fits all. Charging a different price for the same product is known as 'price discrimination'. (Note that this is different from producing different products for the different segments.)

 Business Analysis   *9.10*

JSTOR, a non-profit organization that makes available online back copies of scholarly journals, analyses the electronic data to charge libraries and academic institutions different fees, depending on their use and circumstances.

As a customer, do you think that you benefit or suffer from price discrimination?

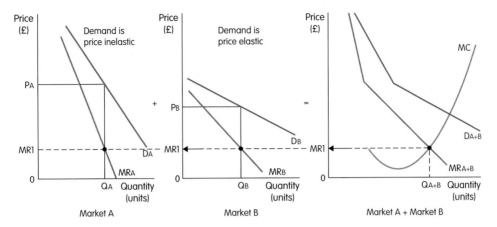

Figure 9.10 Profit maximizing by setting different prices in markets with different demand conditions

When demand conditions vary in different markets, the profit-maximizing price and output occurs when the overall marginal revenue equals marginal cost *and* when the marginal revenue in each market is equal. If the marginal revenue of selling another unit were higher in market segment A than in market segment B, for example, then the business would be better reallocating its products and selling more in A and fewer in B: the extra revenue gained in A outweighs the revenue lost in B, so the business gains overall (see Figure 9.10).

The combined marginal revenue in the two market segments is calculated by horizontally adding the marginal revenue in each of the markets. The profit-maximizing output is found where the combined marginal revenue equals the marginal cost. This determines the level of marginal revenue in each market. From this, the relevant price can be identified. The higher price occurs in the market in which demand is more price inelastic.

This form of price discrimination (that is, charging different prices in different markets for the same product) is called 'third-degree discrimination'.

? Think about it... 9.16

1. What is meant by a price inelastic demand?

2. Why would you expect the higher price to be in the price inelastic market?

3. Which of the following are examples of third-degree price discrimination?

   A Lower prices at cinemas for children and older audiences.
   B Happy hours for cheap drinks in pubs.
   C Cheap weekend holiday breaks.
   D Lower fares in the off-peak periods.
   E A book publisher having a cheap international edition of a book.
   F Discounts for members (for example, loyalty card holders).

For third-degree price discrimination to work, markets must be kept separate—that is, you need to avoid someone buying at the low price and then reselling at the higher price in the other segment. The separation of markets may be based on factors such as time, status (for example, whether the customer is a loyalty card holder or not), region, or age.

Price discrimination boosts the profits of the business by reducing consumer surplus. Managers would, ideally, like to charge each customer exactly what they are willing to pay. This would mean that they completely remove all of the consumer surplus, but charge a different price for every unit sold. This is called 'first-degree price discrimination'. Think of street traders haggling with you to find out exactly what you are willing to pay. In what is known as a 'Dutch auction', the price starts high and is gradually reduced until someone bids; the price paid should be close to the maximum that they are willing to pay and therefore there would be no consumer surplus.

In Figure 9.11, a firm charges a different price for every unit sold; to sell more, the price is lowered on the last unit, but not on the ones before. The extra revenue from the sale is therefore the same as the price and the demand curve in this case is the same as the marginal revenue curve. A business will profit maximize where marginal revenue equals marginal cost (that is, Q1). At this output, the cost per unit is AC1 and therefore the total cost is shown by the area 0AC1EQ1. Given that the cost per unit is higher than any price, a business charging one price for all its units would make a loss and would not provide this product in the long run. But by perfectly price discriminating, the revenue is all of the shaded area under the demand curve (0FGQ1). This revenue is greater than the total costs and therefore the perfect price discriminator can provide products that would not be provided otherwise. By removing all consumer surplus, the business makes more profits than a single price producer, which may mean that it can cover high costs.

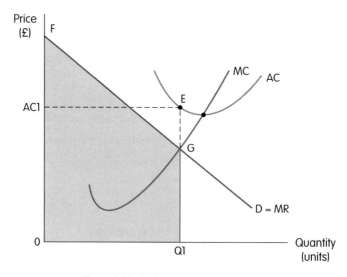

Figure 9.11 Perfect price discrimination

With first-degree price discrimination, the business maximizes its own producer surplus and completely removes all consumer surplus.

There is also another form of price discrimination called 'second-degree discrimination'. This occurs when a business is trying to use up any excess capacity that it has, such as last-minute deals in the airline and hotel industries, or in end-of-season sales. In these sectors, fixed costs are high, but the marginal cost of serving a customer or passenger is very low, so the price can fall a lot and the business can still make a contribution to its fixed costs.

By price discriminating, a business can make more profits, but consumer surplus is reduced. One possible benefit for the consumer is, however, that businesses may cross-subsidize using profits made in one segment to finance losses in other segments. In theory, for example, higher prices in developed markets could subsidize lower prices for drugs in developing economies. It may also mean that some products are provided that would not otherwise be because a profit could not be made if only one price were charged.

? *Think about it ...* 9.17

Which of the following statements about price discrimination are true and which are false?

A To maximize profits, the marginal revenue in each market should be equal.

B In perfect price discrimination (first-degree discrimination), consumer surplus is zero.

C Prices will be higher in the price elastic markets.

D With perfect price discrimination, consumer surplus is zero.

Market structure and profits

The importance of the structure of an industry was analysed by Michael Porter (1985) in his 'five forces' model (see Figure 9.12). This highlighted the importance of five factors in determining how the profits of an industry are shared between firms, their suppliers, their distributors, their competitors, and their customers.

The five forces are as follows.

- *Rivalry* This describes the extent to which firms are competing with each other. The greater the rivalry, the fewer profits any one firm is likely to make. The degree of rivalry will depend on factors such as the number of firms in the industry and their relative size, market growth: (because if a market is shrinking, firms are likely to be very competitive as they struggle to survive) and how they compete (for example is it by cutting price or trying to differentiate themselves).

- *The entry threat* If there is a high entry threat, then competitors are able to enter the market and take away profits. As we have seen, the entry threat depends on factors

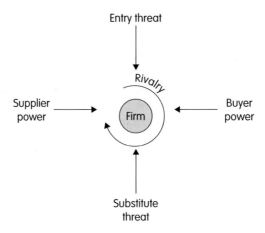

Figure 9.12 Porter's 'five forces'

such as the entry costs and likely retaliation from the existing firms, and refers to the contestability of a market.

■ *Substitutes* These are alternative goods and services that perform a similar function in the eyes of the customer. For example, you may buy wine or flowers as a thank you gift; you may buy a card or an e-card; you may buy a new sofa or a holiday. Although these are very different products, customers choose between them and so they are substitutes. The more substitutes that are available, the more pressure on a business to keep prices down or risk losing customers.

■ *Buyer power* If you are heavily reliant on one or two buyers (for example, you sell healthcare products to the National Health Service), then the buyer is likely to push down the price and negotiate very favourable terms, giving it more of the profit available.

■ *Supplier power* If you are heavily reliant on suppliers (for example, airlines are reliant on the oil companies), then they have the power to push up prices and 'take away' your profit. The greater the supplier power, the lower your profits are likely to be.

Porter highlighted that the average return on investment (ROI) was much higher in some industries than others and had been for many years. His analysis suggested that this was because of unfavourable forces acting on firms in the industry: for example, high rivalry, a low entry threat, high buyer and supplier power and a high substitute threat.

This does not mean that a business must accept the forces acting upon it; rather, it could try to change the forces to make them more favourable. For example, it could change its strategy to:

■ join with others in the industry to have more power when negotiating with suppliers;

■ take over others in the market to reduce the degree of rivalry;

■ differentiate the product to make the product different from anything else and reduce the degree of substitution.

Data Analysis 9.3

During 1992–2006, the average rate of return in various US industries was as follows.

Table 9.5

Soft drinks	37.6%
Prepackaged software	37.6%
Pharmaceuticals	31.7%
Perfume, cosmetics, and toiletries	28.6%
Tyres	19.5%
Household appliances	19.2%
Book publishing	13.4%
Laboratory equipment	13.4%
Hotels	10.4%
Airlines	5.9%

Source: Adapted from Porter (1985)

With reference to Porter's five forces model, why do you think the rates of return might have differed so much between these industries?

Regulation of markets

Managers wanting to grow or considering working with other businesses need to consider competition legislation. Competition laws are established to protect consumers and to ensure that they are not exploited.

In the UK, competition laws are overseen by the OFT. The OFT declares itself:

responsible for making markets work well for consumers. We achieve this by promoting and protecting consumer interests throughout the UK, while ensuring that businesses are fair and competitive.

It aims to make sure that consumers have as much choice as possible, believing that 'When consumers have choice they have genuine and enduring power'.

The OFT implements many pieces of legislation and has a range of enforcement options. At one level, it provides advice and guidance; at another level, it prosecutes and can levy fines of up to 10 per cent of a firm's turnover.

Business Analysis 9.11

Consumer protection legislation includes:

- the Consumer Credit Act 1974, as amended by the Consumer Credit Act 2006;
- the Estate Agents Act 1979, as amended by the Consumers, Estate Agents and Redress Act 2007;
- the Unfair Terms in Consumer Contracts Regulations 1999;
- the Consumer Protection (Distance Selling) Regulations 2000;
- the Consumer Protection from Unfair Trading Regulations 2008;
- the Business Protection from Misleading Marketing Regulations 2008;
- the Enterprise Act 2002.

Are there any areas in which you think consumers still need protection?

Can you now answer questions 4 and 5 from the opening case study?

Summary

There are several different types of market structure, ranging from a monopoly to a perfectly competitive industry. The structure depends on the number of firms in a market, the relative size of these, and the ease of entry and exit. The structure of a market will affect the behaviour and performance of businesses, and the price and quantity outcomes that a manager chooses. If managers can create a monopoly position, for example, their business can earn abnormal profits even in the long run. In an oligopoly, the decisions facing a manager are particularly complex, because there are other large firms in the market and he or she needs to think about what they will do. Oligopoly highlights the complexity of business strategic planning.

Checklist

Having read this chapter, you should now understand:

- [ ] the assumptions behind the different market structures;
- [ ] the short and long-run outcomes in perfect competition;
- [ ] allocative and productive efficiency;
- [ ] the arguments against and for monopoly;
- [ ] why the government allows firms to protect their intellectual property;
- [ ] the importance of barriers to entry;
- [ ] why the price and quantity outcomes depend on the assumptions that a manager makes about his or her competitors;

☐ what will happen to the price and quantity outcomes in the short and long run of different market structures;

☐ how Porter's five forces model helps to analyse market structure and influences business strategy.

Case Study Review

Having read this chapter, you should now be able to answer the following questions.

1. What is a cartel?
2. Why might the producers of LCD displays want to form a cartel?
3. What do you think are the conditions necessary for a cartel to be successful?
4. Why might the European Commission want to take action against a cartel?
5. Do you think that a fine is an effective deterrent against cartels?
6. Can you think of markets other than consumer electronics in which cartels are likely to be created?

Short Answer Questions

1. What is meant by abnormal profit? Does normal profit mean that the company makes no profits in accounting terms?
2. What is meant by allocative efficiency?
3. Explain, with examples, what is meant by barriers to entry.
4. How does a profit-maximizing manager know how much to produce?
5. Does a firm in perfect competition make abnormal or normal profits? Explain your answer.
6. Does a monopolist make abnormal or normal profits? Explain your answer.
7. Why are prices 'sticky' in the kinked demand curve model of oligopoly?
8. Why might cartels be unstable?
9. If a business is making abnormal profits in monopolistic competition, what will happen in the industry?
10. What is meant by price discrimination?

Essay Questions

1. Are monopolies undesirable?
2. To what extent do you think managers can prevent entry into their market?
3. Is price discrimination a good thing?

 One Step Further

Visit our Online Resource Centre at **www.oxfordtextbooks.co.uk/orc/gillespiebusiness/** for test questions, podcasts, and further information on topics covered in this chapter.

Macroeconomics

10

Learning Objectives

In this chapter, we examine the macroeconomy, and the workings of aggregate demand and aggregate supply.

By the end of this chapter, you should:

- ☑ understand the meaning of aggregate demand and influences on it;
- ☑ understand the meaning of aggregate supply and influences on it;
- ☑ understand equilibrium in the economy;
- ☑ be able to explain the effect of a shift in aggregate demand or aggregate supply on equilibrium in the economy.

Case Study

In the last few months, Toyota has replaced its bosses, halted pet projects, and temporarily cut production in Japan almost in half. Toshiba said that it would shut down unprofitable businesses. Sony plans to halve the number of its suppliers to save 500 billion yen (US$5,200 million) this year alone.

All have cut back their part-time and temporary workers, who had only ever been promised a pay cheque, not a job for life.
The actions of these prominent Japanese companies have encouraged others to follow suit.

During the 'lost decade' of 1991–2002, when economic growth was very slow, Japanese firms dithered rather than adopted the harsh measures that might have prevented a drawn-out stagnation. But this time around, the response has been much faster and deeper. After all, if any country ought to know how to respond to a low or no-growth environment, it is Japan: it has had plenty of practice.

It helps that, this time, the crisis originated outside Japan and all unpleasant measures could be blamed on the US bankers whom many Japanese held responsible for it. And the sudden collapse of export sales, which happened in tandem with a spike in commodity prices and an appreciation of the yen (which makes Japan's exports more expensive), meant that corporate Japan had no choice but to act.

All of this is quite a turnaround. During the lost decade, corporate reforms were introduced slowly and imperfectly. Jobs, sacrosanct in Japan, were eventually shed. The reaction, this time, is notable because it capitalizes on the changes introduced back then and provides an opportunity to push for even more restructuring.

Source: Adapted from *The Economist*, 18 June 2009

Questions

1. Why do you think Japan may have experienced a fall in demand in its economy in the 1990s and in 2008–09?

2. How do you think the different functions of a business such as Toyota might be affected by a major fall in demand in the economy?

3. Why might managers in Japan have been slow to make redundancies in the past?

4. Why is the value of the currency important to the level of demand in an economy? Explain your answer.

5. What could the Japanese government do to try to increase aggregate demand?

6. Do you think that an increase in demand in the circumstances described above would be likely to increase output or prices? Illustrate your answer using an aggregate demand and supply diagram.

Introduction

So far, we have focused on what happens in particular markets: for example, we have analysed the influences on the demand and supply of labour, shares, and foreign currency. We have examined issues such as the impact of a change in demand or supply conditions in these individual markets, and have considered the effects on the price and output decisions of firms operating in different market structures, such as monopoly and oligopoly. But each individual market is a part of the whole economy.

In this chapter, we analyse factors in the overall economy and consider their significance for business decision making. This is known as 'macroeconomic analysis' (looking at the big picture) as opposed to 'microeconomic analysis' (looking at a small part of the picture). Variables such as interest rates, exchange rates, inflation, and national income affect businesses throughout the economy, and are therefore macroeconomic factors.

Understanding macroeconomics is vital to managers because of the impact of changes in macroeconomic factors on both supply and demand conditions. Just listen to the news every day and you will get some sense of the ever-shifting macroeconomic landscape. A fall in the value of the currency, a fall in the growth of the economy, and higher prices, for example, will affect a firm's costs and demand. In the last few years in the UK economy, interest rates have fallen to their lowest level ever, the economy has shrunk in size, the currency has been weak in value, unemployment has increased significantly, and house prices have fallen. Managers need to understand what determines changes in macro conditions and how they might change in the future, so that they can plan for these. Whereas managers have some control over micro conditions (for example, their costs, their marketing, and their strategy in relation to their competitors), they have little influence over the macroeconomic climate. Although the collection of decisions by millions of businesses will affect the economy, the decisions of any one firm will have limited effect.

Macroeconomics therefore shapes the arena in which businesses compete and yet they cannot control macroeconomic factors: all the more reason to understand the causes and consequences of macroeconomic change. This is particularly true given the dynamic nature of economics: on a day-to-day level, this can be seen by the constant movement in the value of most currencies; on a bigger scale, it can be seen in major changes such as the rise of Chinese and Indian economies in the recent years. Understanding the macro economy is therefore an important part of external analysis and strategic planning. When analysing the macroeconomic environment, it is essential to understand **aggregate demand** and aggregate supply.

Aggregate demand and aggregate supply

When examining a particular market, managers have to consider the demand for, and supply of, that product. The same type of analysis can be used for the whole economy except that this time we are interested in:

- aggregate demand—that is, the demand for all final goods and services in an economy, which are the products at the end of the transformation process, such as a newly completed house or laptop, demand for which includes the demand for all of the components and materials that go into the final product;

■ aggregate supply—that is, the supply of all final goods and services in an economy.

In an individual market, equilibrium occurs at the price at which demand equals supply; in the economy as a whole, equilibrium occurs when aggregate demand equals aggregate supply. The interrelationship between aggregate demand and supply determines the output and income of the economy.

? *Think about it ...* 10.1

1. Why would a manager be concerned about the overall level of income in an economy?

2. As a marketing manager of a consumer electronics business, why might it be useful for you to consider the average income in an economy and its expected growth rate?

Aggregate demand

Aggregate demand shows the quantity of final goods and services in an economy that customers are willing and able to buy at each and every price, when everything other than the price level is held constant (see Figure 10.1).

The total planned demand in the economy is made up of the desired spending of four different sectors—that is, households, businesses, the government, and overseas trade (see Figure 10.2).

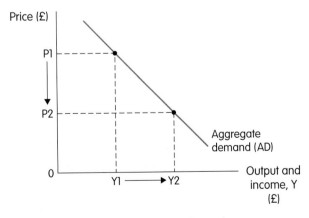

Figure 10.1 The aggregate demand curve

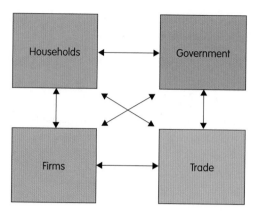

Figure 10.2 The four sectors of the economy

Aggregate demand is made up of:

- consumption demand (C)—that is, the demand from households for final goods and services, and the largest element of aggregate demand. It includes spending on items such as food, clothing, and holidays;

- investment demand (I)—that is, the demand from businesses for final goods and services, such as equipment and machinery;

- government spending (G)—that is, the demand from the government for final goods and services, such as spending on education and health;

- exports (X)—that is, the demand from abroad for final goods and services in the economy, such as sales of British-made Jaguar cars in the USA;

- imports (M)—that is, spending by domestic households, businesses, and government on foreign goods and services. This is part of the spending of households, firms, or the government that leaves the domestic economy and so has to be deducted from the overall spending to show the demand for domestic goods and services. For example, if a household spends £10,000 in total, but £3,000 is on foreign goods, the spending domestically can be calculated as:

$$£10,000 - £3,000 = £7,000$$

- The equation for aggregate demand (AD) can therefore be calculated as:

$$AD = C + I + G + X - M$$

?   *Think about it...*   *10.2*

How might a significant increase in aggregate demand affect a business's workforce and operational planning?

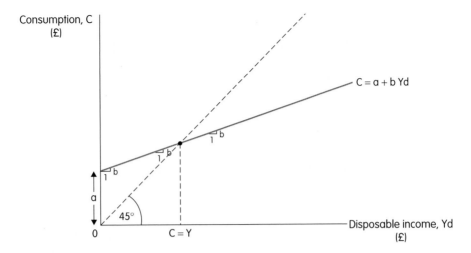

Figure 10.3 The consumption function

The determinants of aggregate demand

The level of aggregate demand in an economy depends on the various elements within it. The determinants of the different types of spending within an economy are as follows.

- *Consumption spending* (C) This is likely to depend heavily on the level of households' current income. With more income, consumption is likely to increase (see Figure 10.3). The importance of current income as a determinant of consumption was highlighted by the economist Keynes. According to Keynes:

$$C = a + bYd$$

where:

- 'a' represents an autonomous level of consumption spending—even if income were zero, consumers would dis-save and spend this amount of money to survive;
- 'b' represents the marginal propensity to consume—that is, the amount spent out of each extra pound—which determines the slope of the consumption function;
- 'Yd' represents disposable income—that is, the income after tax that consumers have available.

 Data Analysis 10.1

$$C = 10 + 0.8Yd$$

$$Yd = £500 \text{ million}$$

1. What is the level of consumption in this economy?
2. What is the level of saving (given that households' income is used either for consumption or saving)?

3. How much is saved out of each extra pound? (This is called the 'marginal propensity to save'.)

4. How much would be spent if income were zero? (This is called 'dis-saving'.)

5. What do you think the equation would be for the savings function?

As well as disposable income, however, the level of consumption spending in an economy may be affected by the following.

■ *Expectations of future income* What households spend may be influenced by what they think they are going to earn over the long term, not only their present income. Imagine that an individual loses his or her job, but expects to find a new one fairly soon: his or her present level of consumption would not necessarily drop significantly, even though his or her current income has, because of his or her long-term projected earnings. This highlights the importance of expectations in influencing household spending decisions. The economist Milton Friedman argued that households' consumption is related more to their 'permanent income'—that is, their expected average income over their lifespan—rather than what they are actually earning at any given moment.

■ *Interest rates* This is because the interest rate affects the return that households receive on their savings. With higher returns, there is more incentive for households to save and less desire to borrow, so that the level of consumption is likely to fall.

■ *The prices of assets* If assets (such as houses) increase in value, this will influence households' views of their wealth and therefore their confidence when it comes to spending. With greater wealth, more spending is likely.

? **Think about it ...**   10.3

Which of the following might increase the level of consumption in the economy?

A A rise in house prices.

B A decrease in interest rates.

C A rise in taxes on expenditure.

D A rise in taxes on income.

 Business Analysis   10.1

Recently, the Chinese government has asked its people to spend a little more and save a little less to help get the country through the global economic downturn. The Chinese are prolific savers, putting away at least 30 per cent of their disposable income each month.

For many Chinese, it is a form of 'self-insurance'. The money is saved in case it is needed to meet medical bills, the costs of education, or in case someone in the family loses his or her job.

China does not have the same kind of welfare systems that you see in the USA, or in Europe or Japan, so there is not much of a 'safety net' if the family falls on hard times. It may be difficult therefore to change the savings habits of Chinese people.

If China's leaders want families to spend more, they need to help them to worry less. Discount schemes on home appliances or cars are persuading some to head for the shops. Real and substantial changes to the country's welfare system would make much more of a difference, but that is much more expensive and much harder to get right.

Sources: BBC News, 'Can China's frugal savers help the economy?', available online at http:// news.bbc.co.uk/go/pr/fr/-/1/hi/world/asia-pacific/8153469.stm, Reuters, November 2009

1. The Chinese are savers; UK households tend to spend far more. Why do you think this is?

2. What do you think might lead to a change in spending habits?

3. What might the effect on businesses be if the domestic population are savers?

■ *Investment in capital goods* (I) This represents spending by businesses for future production: for example, it might involve the purchase of new capital equipment or transport. As we saw in Chapter 6, investment is likely to be heavily influenced by interest rates and estimates of future returns. Lower interest rates reduce the cost of borrowing and make more projects look financially attractive. This is shown by a movement along the marginal efficiency of capital (MEC) schedule as the price of investment has changed (see Figures 10.4 and 10.5).

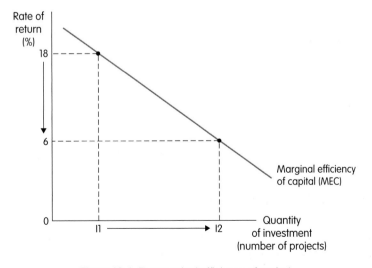

Figure 10.4 The marginal efficiency of capital

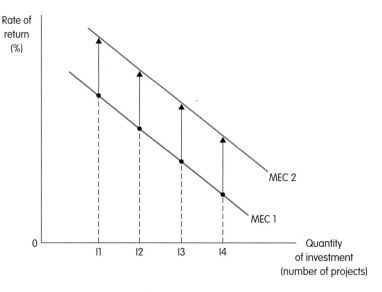

Figure 10.5 A shift in the marginal efficiency of capital

You Decide ...

Your company produces computer games. Your new products division has estimated that the launch of a new game in Japan, a market that you have not targeted before, will generate a rate of return of 10 per cent a year. Should you go ahead with the launch?

£ **Business Analysis**   **10.2**

In 2009, British Airways (BA) announced that it was going to cut its investment in 2009–10 by one fifth as a result of the economic downturn and a fall in the number of passengers. The airline cut spending by 20 per cent to £580 million (US$952 million) from £725 million and delayed its orders for twelve Airbus A380 aircraft.

BA said:

Market conditions continue to be very challenging with trading at levels well below last year. The firm is looking for 3,000 redundancies among crew and administrative staff.

Another 4,000 employees are taking unpaid leave, 1,400 people have volunteered to work part-time, and a further 740 overseas workers have also agreed to the cost-cutting measures.

1. What factors do you think are most likely to influence the volume of air passenger travel in the future?

2. What other factors are likely to influence BA's future investment levels?

Greater confidence in the expected level of sales or a fall in the expected costs of projects will increase the forecasted returns and should therefore lead to more investment. The importance of expectations when making investment decisions explains why you often see confidence surveys in the media in which managers are asked what they think of the present economic condition: more confidence should lead to more investment.

■ *Government spending* (G) This represents spending by a government on final goods and services, such as public services, including education, health care, and the armed forces. The level of this spending will be heavily influenced by government policy and the perceived position of the economy at any given time. An interventionist government is likely to spend more than a government that is more laissez-faire wants to leave the market system to function.

The amount of spending by a government will also depend on how much it thinks it can afford to intervene. To spend more, it must borrow more and/or increase taxes; the consequence of this may have negative effects on the economy. For example, raising more finance by selling bonds may require higher interest rates, which may reduce household borrowing and spending; higher income taxes may reduce the incentive of employees to work. The government must weigh up the costs and benefits of more spending in any situation.

■ *Export spending* (X) This spending will be determined by the consumption patterns abroad. The levels of income overseas, the cost of borrowing, and the expectations of foreign businesses and households of their future income levels will all be important determinants of demand for UK exports. Other key factors affecting a country's exports include the extent to which its firms are allowed to trade abroad (sometimes, there are barriers put on this by other governments) and the cost of one currency in terms of another (that is, the exchange rate). If the pound is low in value against other currencies, for example, this makes UK products cheaper in other currencies, which should stimulate export demand.

■ *Import spending* (M) This spending is linked to the overall levels of consumption in a country, because it represents the spending that 'leaks' from an economy abroad. The amount of money that goes abroad depends on factors such as the range and quality of products produced domestically compared to products produced overseas, the exchange rate, and whether barriers to trade exist.

Business Analysis   10.3

Export sales of Scottish whisky have boomed recently despite the recession in the UK.

There is robust growth in most of the major markets, including North America. Total Scotch sales in China have risen dramatically, from just £1 million in 2000 to £40 million last year. Distilling capacity is being increased at its fastest rate since the early 1970s. A new malt distillery was opened in Girvan by William Grant and Sons last year; Diageo is planning a major new plant on Speyside. Mothballed plants are also coming back into operation. More than £500 million of new investment has been announced over the last eighteen months, according to the Scotch Whisky Association.

The industry says that there are just over 9,000 people directly employed and another 31,000 in related trades, such as bottle manufacture.

The weaker pound can only help to lift spirits even higher.

Sources: BBC News, 'Scotch whisky exports buck downturn', available online at http://news.bbc.co.uk/go/pr/fr/-/1/hi/business/7611214.stm, *Forbes*, May 2009

1. Explain why the weak pound is good for exports.
2. What do you think might cause increased export sales apart from the weak pound?

>> You Decide ...

1. As a manager, would you prefer to buy supplies from domestic producers or to buy from abroad? On what does your answer depend?
2. Your business exports toasters and kettles that have been designed and produced in the UK. What do you think determines the export demand for your products?

Movements along versus shifts in aggregate demand

Aggregate demand is inversely related to price. As the general price level in an economy falls, then, given a level of nominal income and wealth, customers can afford more products. In real terms, households are better off if prices fall and so the quantity demanded of products increases. A change in prices therefore leads to a movement along the aggregate demand.

A shift in aggregate demand will occur if, at each and every price, there is a change in quantity that individuals or organizations are willing and able to spend on products in the economy.

A shift in aggregate demand may occur for the following reasons.

- *An increase in consumption* This may occur if households have greater confidence in the future of the economy, making them more willing to spend money. If the government is perceived to have effective economic policies and the economy is thought to be growing quickly, this might mean that customers worry less about the future and may therefore be more willing to spend more.

  An increase in spending might also occur if taxes on households' incomes are reduced, increasing the amount of income consumers have left over after tax to spend (this is known as 'disposable income'), or if interest rates fall, making it cheaper to borrow.

- *An increase in investment* This might occur if businesses have become more optimistic about the future state of the economy. If managers believe that demand for their products is likely to increase in the future because of a strong economy, then they may be more likely to invest now in anticipation of higher rewards in the future. They will invest in equipment, machines, and transport to be able to produce more for the higher levels of demand anticipated.

  Investment might also increase if interest rates fall, because this reduces the cost of borrowing: with lower interest rates, it is cheaper to borrow and more investment projects become affordable now. The precise effect of a change in interest rates on investment depends on how interest elastic investment demand is.

Data analysis 10.2

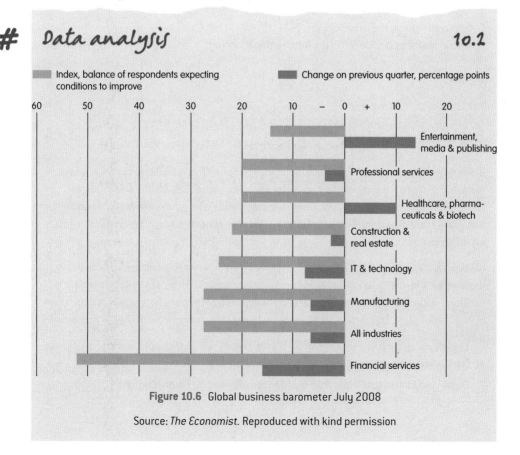

Figure 10.6 Global business barometer July 2008

Source: *The Economist*. Reproduced with kind permission

Figure 10.6 shows the balance of businesses expecting conditions in the economy to improve.

1. How might the data above affect business decision making and the future level of aggregate demand in the economy?

2. Is there anything that a government can do to change these expectations?

■ *An increase in government spending* An increase in spending by the government may occur if it adopts a more interventionist approach. Spending may be by the local or national government.

■ *An increase in exports* This might occur if a country's major trading partners begin to grow faster and spend some of this income on the country's products.

 Think about it ...   10.4

Which of the following are likely to increase aggregate demand?

A Lower interest rates.

B Higher taxes on company profits.

C A stronger value of the currency.

D Greater business confidence in the future of the economy.

 Business Analysis   10.4

Unlike many other developed countries, Germany still has a large manufacturing base, and is particularly strong in producing vehicles, machinery, and chemicals. It is the world's largest exporter of goods. In 2009, however, German output shrank by around 5 per cent, compared with a 4 per cent drop in the European Union (EU) overall. Most of the contraction was due to a fall in its exports.

Germany has been good at exporting because it has held down wage increases and has a fairly flexible labour market, making it relatively easy for businesses to increase or decrease their workforce according to demand. Between 2004 and 2007, net exports accounted for 60 per cent of its growth. But in 2009, exports fell by around 19 per cent, because the decline in economies worldwide affected sales.

1. Explain why Germany has been such a major exporter of goods.

2. Explain two factors that might have led to a fall in demand for German exports.

Figure 10.7 Abroad, not at home—German exports and consumer spending

Source: *The Economist*. Reproduced with kind permission

An increase in elements of aggregate demand, such as consumption, investment, government spending, and exports, will shift the aggregate demand outwards, showing more demand at any price level (see Figure 10.8).

? *Think about it ...*   *10.5*

What is the likely effect in aggregate demand of the following?

A A fall in interest rates.

B A new government spending programme on education.

C High income tax.

D An increase in the external value of your currency.

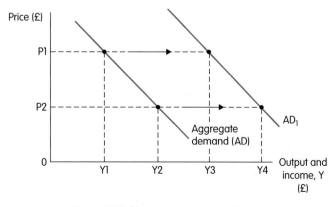

Figure 10.8 The aggregate demand curve

Can you now answer questions 1 and 4 from the opening case study?

Aggregate supply

The aggregate supply schedule shows the amount of final goods and services that an economy can produce at each and every price, all other things unchanged. The aggregate supply curve is generally upward-sloping: as the price level increases, firms can afford to produce more; a higher price is needed to cover higher costs. A change in price is shown as a movement along the aggregate supply curve.

The position of the aggregate supply curve depends on the availability and quality of resources in the economy—that is, the amount and productivity of land, labour, capital, and enterprise in an economy will determine what can be produced at any price. With more, or better quality, resources, aggregate supply should increase. For example, with more investment in capital equipment, better technology, or an increase in the supply of labour, more output could be produced. This would be shown by an outward shift of the aggregate supply curve. At each and every price, more can be produced.

? *Think about it ...* 10.6

1. What do you think determines how many people are willing and able to work at each wage level?

2. If one business produces more, what impact does this have on the aggregate supply in the economy?

3. What do you think influences the number of businesses that start up in an economy each year?

The price elasticity of aggregate supply

The price elasticity of aggregate supply shows how responsive the quantity supplied in the economy is to changes in the price level. It is shown by the slope of the aggregate supply curve (see Figure 10.9).

At low levels of output, for which there are many spare resources in the economy and the level of unemployment is high, aggregate supply is likely to be very sensitive to price. A relatively small increase in price may lead to significant increases in output, because managers are eager to start producing more and the extra costs of doing so are not high, because resources are readily available and have been sitting idle. For example, if there is office space available, and people ready and waiting to work, businesses can increase

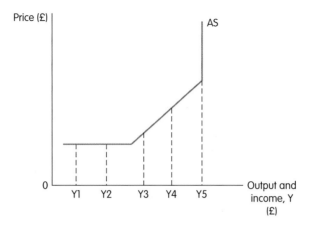

Figure 10.9 Aggregate supply

output without needing a large increase in price to cover the extra costs. Resources are underemployed, making supply relatively easy to increase.

This means that when the economy is operating well below capacity, aggregate supply is price elastic (for example, between Y1 and Y2). As the economy expands, however, it becomes increasingly difficult to produce more, because resources are in greater demand and the price of factors of production, such as labour and land, has to increase because of the higher demand. More firms are competing for limited resources. The aggregate supply therefore becomes steeper because bigger increases in price are needed to bring about a given increase in output.

At Y5, the economy is at full employment. This means that resources are fully employed and the economy is producing at its full capacity. Businesses cannot produce any more, given the existing level of resources. Supply in the economy at this point is totally price inelastic. Whatever happens to price, the quantity of products supplied cannot increase. Full employment means that, in the labour market, all of those willing and able to work are working; note, however, that this does not mean that unemployment is zero, because there will always be some people unwilling to or unable to work at a given wage.

? *Think about it...*   10.7

Do you think that aggregate supply in your economy is likely to be price elastic or inelastic at the moment? Explain your reasoning.

Data Analysis   10.3

1. If a 2 per cent price increase led to a 6 per cent increase in the quantity supplied, what is the price elasticity of supply? Is supply price elastic or inelastic? Explain your answer.

2. If the price elasticity of supply was +0.6, what would be the effect on the quantity supplied of a 3 per cent increase in prices?

3. Explain why aggregate supply might be price elastic or inelastic.

Macroeconomic equilibrium

In the macroeconomy, just as in the microeconomy, the price level should adjust to bring about equilibrium. If the general price level is at P1, for example, there is excess supply in the economy (see Figure 10.10). Producers are willing and able to produce more than is demanded. This would put downward pressure on prices; as prices fall, this reduces the quantity that businesses want to produce and increases the quantity demanded. This process continues until equilibrium is reached.

If the price were at P2, there would be excess demand in the economy and there would be upward pressure on prices. As prices increase, this leads to an increase in the quantity supplied, because producers can afford to produce more, and a decrease in the quantity demanded, because products are more expensive. This process continues until equilibrium is reached.

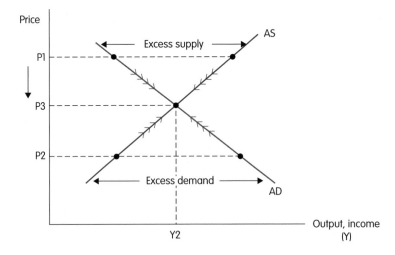

Figure 10.10 Equilibrium in the economy

Equilibrium in the economy is, therefore, determined by aggregate demand and supply conditions. Demand and supply in the economy can change due to factors out of the control of the government, and therefore governments often have to respond to such changes to try to achieve their desired price and output targets.

Managers will be interested in future changes in the equilibrium of economies because this might affect the income of their target export markets or the costs of items bought in from abroad.

Shifts in aggregate demand and aggregate supply

Imagine that an economy is at equilibrium at P1,Y1. If there is an increase in aggregate demand in the economy, the aggregate demand schedule would shift to the right: more would be demanded at each and every price. This shift could be because of increased government spending, more household expenditure, and/or more spending from abroad. The consequence of this shift is that, at the old price level, there is excess demand; prices will increase, thereby reducing the quantity demanded and increasing the quantity supplied. The new equilibrium occurs with a higher price and a higher quantity demanded, as can be seen from the movement from P1,Y1 to P2,Y2 in Figure 10.11.

An increase in aggregate demand is likely to lead to an increase in output in the economy and the price level. The relative impact of a shift on price and quantity will, however, depend on the extent of the shift and the price elasticity of the aggregate supply.

At low levels of output when aggregate supply is price elastic, an increase in aggregate demand leads to a significant increase in output relative to the price increase.

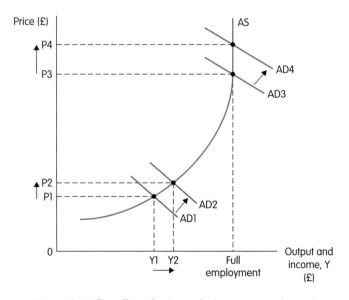

Figure 10.11 The effect of a change in the aggregate demand

As demand continues to increase, the demand for resources starts to bid up their costs more and, increasingly, the effect is on price rather than output (compare the effect on price and quantity of an increase in aggregate demand from AD3 to AD4 with that of an increase from AD1 to AD2). At full employment when the economy is at maximum capacity, an increase in aggregate demand increases prices and does not affect the amount produced.

The price elasticity of the aggregate supply schedule is therefore crucial in terms of the impact of an increase in aggregate demand. If the economy is in equilibrium below capacity, governments may well want an increase in aggregate demand to boost output and the impact on prices will not be significant. But as the economy approaches full employment, increases in demand simply make resources and products more expensive.

Economists often disagree about the price elasticity of aggregate supply in an economy, and therefore about the effects and desirability of an increase in demand. Keynesian economists believe that the economy is often below full employment and that a government should intervene in such circumstances to boost aggregate demand. Classical economists believe that the economy is nearer to full employment and so any increase in aggregate demand is likely mainly to affect prices.

? *Think about it ...* 10.8

What is the likely effect on the equilibrium price and quantity of the following? Explain your answers.

A Higher levels of productivity in the economy.
B Lower incomes in export markets.
C Cheaper borrowing for households.

Can you now answer question 6 from the opening case study?

Government intervention in the economy

All governments will have various macroeconomic objectives and will intervene in the economy to try to achieve these.

For example, the government may want to achieve:

- full employment in the economy, so that all those willing and able to work at the given wage are working;
- economic growth, so that the income of the economy is increasing each year;
- stable prices, so that any price increases are relatively low and are predictable;

■ an appropriate level of export spending relative to imports; for example a government may be worried if the country is spending too much on importing products and is not exporting enough, so it may aim to balance these inflows and outflows.

? *Think about it ...* 10.9

1. To what extent do you think your government is successful at managing the economy at the moment on the basis of the above objectives?

2. What other economic objectives do you think your government has?

>> *You Decide*

As a manager, which of the above objectives do you think should be the most important for present governments?

To achieve its aims, the government can use fiscal and monetary policies.

■ *Fiscal policies* involve changes in government spending, and the taxation and benefit system, to affect the aggregate supply and demand in the economy.

■ *Monetary policies* involve the use of interest rates and control over the amount of money in the economy.

A policy aimed at increasing the level of aggregate demand in an economy is known as an 'expansionist (or reflationary) policy'. A policy aimed at reducing the level of aggregate demand is known as a 'contractionary (or deflationary) policy'.

Demand-side policies

Demand-side policies are policies adopted by a government to influence aggregate demand in the economy. If, for example, the economy is below full employment, the government may want to boost demand to increase output. If, however, the economy is at full employment and demand is still growing, then the effect of this is likely to pull up prices. In this instance, to prevent further price increases, the government may want to reduce aggregate demand using deflationary policies. Whether or not it is appropriate to use demand-side policies depends, in part, on where the economy is at that instant.

To influence the level of aggregate demand in the economy, a government may take one of the following actions.

- *Change its own spending* For example, it may cut back its investment in transport or education. At any moment in time, however, the government will be committed to certain plans that it has already made and it will not be able to change these easily. Any changes in government spending are likely to take time to be approved; they may also take years to take full effect. A decision to invest in a new building programme, for example, may lead to spending that occurs over many years as the project is actually built.

- *Change the taxation and benefit system* There are numerous taxes in the economy that can be changed to influence demand. These include:

  - direct taxes, which are taxes such as income tax and corporation tax, which are taken directly from the income of individuals or organizations;

  - indirect taxes, which are taxes such as value added tax (VAT), which are paid when products are bought;

  - council taxes, which are taxes that depend on the value of your house and are paid to the local authorities.

The government can also change factors such as:

- the levels at which these taxes are paid—for example, it could increase the amount that you can be given without paying inheritance tax;

- on what you pay tax—for example, it could reduce the number of goods on which indirect taxes are charged. At the moment, in the UK, you do not pay VAT on most foods, but do pay it on crisps; the government could reduce this tax rate;

- the rate at which tax is paid—for example, to reduce spending by households, the government might increase the rate of income tax paid; this would leave households with less income after tax and so it is likely to reduce their spending.

? *Think about it ...*   10.10

1. How do you think changes in the direct tax system might affect the performance of a business?

2. What effect do you think an increase in demand due to government spending might have on output and prices in the economy? Illustrate your answer using an aggregate demand and supply diagram.

Data Analysis   10.4

A progressive tax system is one in which the average rate of tax increases with higher levels of income; in a regressive tax system, the average rate of tax actually falls with higher incomes. For example, VAT is regressive because everyone pays the same amount on an item regardless of his or her income level (see Figure 10.12).

Imagine a tax system in which income up to £50,000 is taxed at 20 per cent and income earned over £50,000 is taxed at 40 per cent.

1. If your income is £40,000, how much tax do you pay? What is the average tax paid per pound?
2. If your income is £80,000, how much tax do you pay? What is the average tax paid per pound?
3. Is this tax system progressive or regressive? Explain your answer.
4. Why might a government want to have a progressive tax system? What will determine how progressive it is?

A government could also change the benefits and subsidies system by:

■ increasing the number of benefits available to individuals—for example, there could be greater benefits for carers of sick relatives;

■ perhaps offering more benefits for people while they are ill or unemployed;

■ increasing the number of subsidies available to organizations;

■ offering more finance for businesses investing in research and development;

■ making it easier for individuals to qualify for benefits.

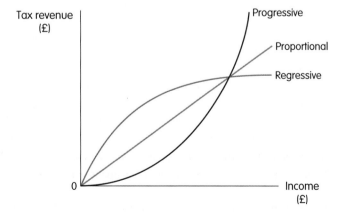

Figure 10.12 Progressive, proportional, and regressive taxation systems

You Decide ...

As a manager of a national bus company, would you prefer the government to cut taxes or increase its spending? Explain your answer.

Think about it ...   10.11

Which of the following changes in government policy will boost aggregate demand?

A Higher rates of income tax.

B Less spending on education.

C A lower tax threshold (that is, a lower level of income that can be earned before tax is paid).

D Higher interest rates.

The budget position

All governments intervene in an economy to some extent to provide various services; these can include defence, education, health care, and transport. The government is intervening in the market system in areas in which it feels there are market failures or imperfections.

To finance its spending, a government will have to raise revenue and/or borrow. Revenue is raised through a variety of taxes and charges, such as income tax and taxes on the sale of products. Borrowing can be undertaken by selling bonds, which are effectively IOUs. These bonds are mainly sold to financial institutions, such as banks. They have a final repayment date and pay interest annually.

The difference between a government's spending and income in any year is shown by its **budget position**. A budget deficit means that the spending is greater than the revenue raised and so the government has to borrow. A budget surplus means that the income is greater than the spending. In the recession of 2008, many governments had to spend more to try to boost demand in their economies because of less spending by households and businesses; at the same time, with fewer people working and paying taxes, and lower company profits being taxed, the income of the government was lower, leading to higher budget deficits.

The budget position in the UK is shown by the 'public sector net cash requirement' (PSNCR); this shows the deficit or surplus for a given year. The total amount owed at any moment is called the 'national debt'. In 2009, the UK national debt hit a record of £799,000 million—that is, 56.6 per cent of **gross domestic product (GDP)**—the highest since records began.

 Data Analysis 10.5

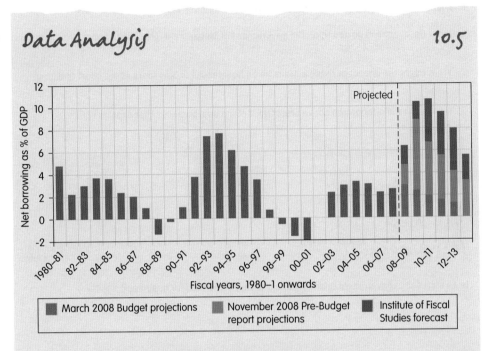

Figure 10.13 UK budget deficits

Source: HM Treasury/IFS. Reproduced with kind permission

Figure 10.13 shows forecasts for the UK budget position that were made in 2009.

1. What factors might influence the forecasted budget position for a country?

2. What problems do you think might be created for the UK economy by the increased budget deficit projected in Figure 10.13?

3. What might lead to changes in the actual budget position?

4. Why might managers be interested in the forecasted budget position of the economy?

 Business Analysis 10.5

Singapore's economy shrank by 19.7 per cent in the first quarter of 2009—its biggest quarterly fall on record. The country was hit by a reduction in exports during the economic downturn.

'With most of Singapore's key trading partners still in recession, the manufacturing sector will remain weak for the rest of the year,' said the Ministry of Trade and Industry.

Earlier in the year, Singapore announced a US$13,000 million (£8,600 million) stimulus fiscal policy package from the government to try to boost economic activity.

1. What fiscal actions do you think the government of Singapore might take to boost economic activity?

2. What might the impact of these actions be on businesses in Singapore in the short and long runs?

3. How might the information above affect your plans as a business that exports whisky to Singapore?

?   *Think about it ...*   10.12

Is an increase in government spending likely to be good or bad for business?

Automatic and discretionary changes in fiscal policy

When analysing the underlying **fiscal policy** of a government, it is important to distinguish between changes in the budget position that occur automatically, because of changes in the level of output and income, and those that change because of deliberate changes in policy, which are called 'discretionary changes'.

If an economy declines, and there is negative growth and more unemployment in an economy, this means that, automatically, the government will gain less tax revenue (because there are less earnings and less spending) and will have to spend more on benefits (for example, to the unemployed). This means that the budget position will automatically worsen without any deliberate change in fiscal policy. If, on top of this, the government increases its spending and cuts the rate of tax, this will further worsen the budget position, but this reflects deliberate discretionary changes to try to boost demand. The UK government intervened extensively in 2008 and 2009 to try to prevent a major recession; the automatic effects of recession plus the discretionary changes meant that, by July 2009, government borrowing for that year reached £175,000 million—that is, 12.4 per cent of GDP.

As national income grows, tax revenue automatically increases and benefit spending falls. This improves the net tax revenue position. An improvement in national income such as Y1 to Y2 therefore automatically improves the budget position; a decline in income such as Y2 to Y1 automatically worsens it (see Figure 10.14). But a government may make discretionary changes as well: a decision to pump more money into the economy would shift the spending line up; a decision to cut taxation would lower the slope of the net tax revenue line, because less would be earned at each level of income. Changes in the budget position due to changes in income alone are automatic; discretionary changes change the position of the spending or net tax revenue line.

In Figure 10.15, a discretionary increase in government spending (from B to C at income level Y2) and a cut in the rate of tax (which reduces the tax revenue from A to D) worsens

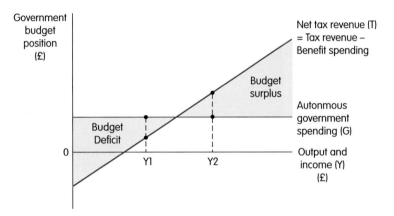

Figure 10.14 Budget deficits and budget surpluses

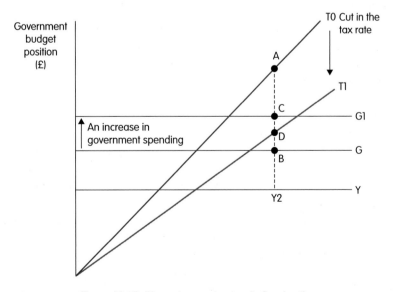

Figure 10.15 Discretionary changes in fiscal policy

the budget position because of changes in government policy. At Y2, the surplus position of 'AB' worsens to a deficit of 'cd'.

Business Analysis   10.6

The state of California (the largest state economy in the USA) is in a poor financial position. Legally unable to declare bankruptcy as a company would, the state has begun paying many of its bills with bonds instead of cash. One of the three big credit-rating agencies, Fitch, downgraded the state's bonds in 2009, already the lowest rated in the country, to BBB.

Government offices are closed on some days, as state workers take involuntary and unpaid leave. Taxpayers are still waiting for refunds. Poor people are afraid of losing their state-funded health insurance.

The largest part of the budget—and thus the biggest target for cuts—is education. The next largest part of the budget is the state's social safety net, including its healthcare programme for the poor. The Governor of California initially wanted to eliminate entire programmes, but now appears ready to settle for shrinking them. The argument, such as it is, is now about how many children will lose coverage, how many elderly patients will stop receiving visits from nurses, whether to treat young offenders and so forth.

The effects seem likely to be felt at the bottom of the social hierarchy. But all Californians will notice.

Sources: *The Economist*, 9 July 2009, *Business Week*, June 2009, CNN, July 2009

1. Explain the possible causes of the budget deficit of California.
2. Explain the possible consequences of such a deficit for businesses in California.

Monetary policy

As well as, or instead of, changing its spending and taxation and benefits (which are fiscal measures), a government can also try to influence the money supply in the economy and the interest rates. This is known as monetary policy.

Money supply

When thinking about the amount of money in an economy, we obviously have to define what we mean by 'money'. A good starting point is to think what functions money performs.

- *It acts as a medium of exchange.* This means that money is something that is accepted widely by people and can be used in transactions—that is, it can be used to buy items and will be accepted by the seller.

- *It acts a unit of account.* This means that we use money to measure the value of items.

- *It is a store of value.* This means that people are willing to hold on to money in the belief that it will retain its value and still be valuable in the future.

These features of 'money' can be demonstrated by many different items. Obviously, notes and coins perform these functions, but so do the funds that you have in your bank account; these funds may not physically exist (that is, the amount of 'money' shown on bank statements is far greater than the amount of cash that exists), but you can still use it via cheques and bank cards to buy things and to hold value.

There are, in fact, many definitions of money. Narrow definitions focus on very liquid assets, such as cash and accounts from which you can draw your money out quickly. Broader definitions include funds in accounts or investments, from which you have to give notice to withdraw. The key point is that the money supply depends a great deal on the banking system because many of the funds in there are part of what we now use as 'money'. The banking system, therefore, can affect the size of the money supply through its lending.

When money is placed in a bank, a proportion of it is kept to meet future requests for withdrawals and the rest is lent out. This is how banks make their profits: by lending out money at a higher rate of interest than the rate that they pay to depositors. The money lent by banks will be spent by the borrowers (for example, on new consumer electronics or an extension to the house) and then these funds are likely to be deposited again in the banking system by the person who received them. Imagine that you borrow £10,000 to build an extension to your house; this pays the builder and his or her suppliers, and this money is likely to be deposited by them in their banks. Of this money, a proportion is again kept back by the banks to meet requests for withdrawals and the rest is lent out to more borrowers, further increasing the amount of money in the economy. (Notice that, in this case, the same physical money may be passing from one group to another, increasing the money available in the economy because of the lending by the bank.)

The repeated lending by banks highlights the money multiplier. This shows that any initial deposit in a bank leads to a much bigger overall increase in the money supply. To control the money supply in an economy, a government might therefore:

- encourage or instruct banks to keep more funds in reserve, which restricts their lending and so slows up the growth of money in the economy;

- place restrictions on borrowing to reduce the demand for loans.

By comparison, to increase the money supply, the government could encourage more lending and reduce any restrictions on banks' holding reserves. It could also inject more money into the system, via **quantitative easing**. This was undertaken by the Bank of England in 2009, when it injected £125,000 million into the financial system. The aim of this was to increase the amount of money in the banking system, which it was hoped would then be lent to households and businesses to spend and increase aggregate demand. Quantitative easing occurs when the bank buys up assets—particularly

% Worked Example

Imagine that banks keep 0.1 of any deposit in reserve; this means that, if £1,000 is deposited, £100 is kept back and £900 is lent out.

When this £900 is spent and deposited back into the banking system, £90 will be kept back and £810 lent.

This again will end up in the banking system, and around £81 will be kept back and £729 lent out.

This process continues, meaning that an initial deposit of £1,000 leads to an increase in lending (and therefore the amount of money in the economy) of:

$$£1,000 + £900 + £810 + £729 + ...$$

This will add up to £10,000.

The size of the money multiplier is calculated using:

$$\frac{1}{\text{Reserve ratio}}$$

In this case, this is:

$$\frac{1}{0.1} = 10$$

The more that is held in reserve, the less is lent out at each stage and the lower the impact of a deposit on the money supply. A reserve ratio of 0.5 means that the money multiplier is:

$$\frac{1}{0.5} = 2$$

? Think about it ...   10.13

What is the money multiplier if the reserve ratio is 0.2?

government bonds—such as banks and pension funds. Usually, if the government were to want to buy up any assets, it would issue further bonds, borrowing money on the international money markets. This means that, although it has injected money into the system, it has also taken money out by selling bonds to balance this. With quantitative easing, it does not do this: it only pays for the bonds by creating funds electronically and transferring 'new' money across to the investors. A similar approach was used in Japan in the 1990s and reduced the effects of the recession. It is essentially simply 'creating' money.

Business Analysis 10.7

In 2009, the UK Chancellor outlined proposals to force banks to increase their capital to protect themselves against future crises and to give more powers to the Financial Services Authority (FSA), the regulator. Banks that would pose a significant threat to the financial system if they were to collapse would be subject to tough capital and liquidity standards, e.g. having to hold more funds in reserve.

Why might banks want to find ways of avoiding restrictions on their lending?

Interest rates

Rather than controlling the amount of money available via the banking system, monetary policy may focus on the cost of borrowing money (that is, the interest rate) to influence the **demand for money**. Interest rates in the UK are controlled by the Bank of England. The interest rate is the price of money—that is, it represents the cost of borrowing money and the reward for saving. By changing the interest rate, the Bank of England aims to control aggregate demand.

There are, in fact, many different interest rates. For example, there is a difference between the rate for borrowing and saving. Banks will charge borrowers more than they pay savers (see Figure 10.16), which is how they make their profits; the borrowing interest rate is generally higher than the saving rate.

The precise amount charged to borrowers will depend on factors such as:

- the amount being borrowed—the more that a bank is lending, the less it may charge, in that it will still make high levels of profit;
- the risk involved—for example, the track record of those who are asking to borrow money, because the higher the risk (for example, if there is little collateral to guarantee the loan), the more a bank will charge.

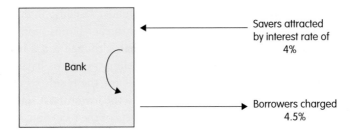

Figure 10.16   Banks and interest rates

The Bank of England

The Bank of England is the central bank of the UK. It was founded in 1694, nationalized in 1946, and made independent of government control in 1997. Its core purpose is to maintain monetary and financial stability in the economy. Interest rate decisions are taken by the Bank's Monetary Policy Committee (MPC).

The MPC has to judge what interest rate is necessary to meet a target for overall inflation in the economy. The inflation target is set each year by the Chancellor of the Exchequer. To reduce inflation, the MPC will increase interest rates to bring down the level of aggregate demand.

The interest rate and aggregate demand

The Bank of England is the final provider of cash to the banking system in the UK and it is able to choose the interest rate at which it will provide funds to the other banks each day. The interest rate at which the Bank supplies these funds is quickly passed throughout the financial system, influencing interest rates for the whole economy—that is, if the Bank of England increases the rate at which it lends to other banks, they will charge lenders more as well to cover their costs. Banks need to borrow from the Bank of England because, on any given day, there may be more requests from depositors for funds than they have readily available, having lent the money out.

To reduce inflation in the economy, the MPC will increase interest rates to dampen aggregate demand. An increase in interest rates will affect:

■ the rate at which financial institutions lend to businesses and households—higher interest rates will discourage borrowing and spending;

■ the price of financial assets, such as shares—higher interest rates mean that there are higher rewards from saving. This is likely to reduce demand for shares and other assets, and thereby lower their price. This reduces the wealth of companies and households, and will probably reduce their spending.

■ A high interest rate in the UK is also likely to attract funds from abroad to the UK as foreign investors seek high returns for their money. This increases demand for the UK currency, which increases the value of the pound. A stronger currency makes imports cheaper in pounds, which reduces the pressure from costs for higher prices;

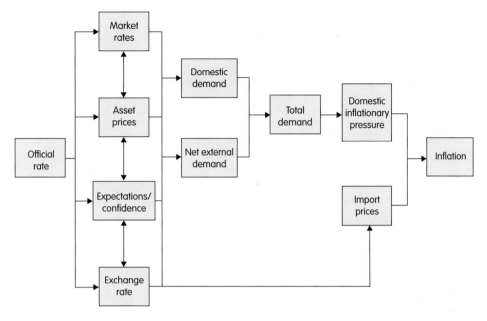

Figure 10.17 Interest rates and demand in the economy

it also makes exports more expensive, which dampens aggregate demand, reducing the pressure to pull up prices. Both of these effects should limit the rate at which prices increase.

The precise effects of changes in interest rates are difficult to determine. Some of the influences are likely to work through the economy more quickly than others, but there are certainly time lags for some of the effects. For example, higher rates may not immediately lead to a fall in household borrowing, but, gradually, consumers may reduce their overdrafts and loans, or at least not increase them further. According to the Bank of England, the maximum impact of a change in interest rates on consumer price inflation takes up to about two years. So interest rates have to be set based on judgements about what inflation might be—that is, the outlook over the coming few years—not what it is today.

>> *You Decide*

1. As a managing director of a hotel chain, would you prefer higher or lower interest rates?

2. How do you think changes in the interest rate would affect your marketing decisions?

Business Analysis   10.8

In March 2009, the MPC voted to reduce the official Bank Rate (that is, the interest rate charged to other banks) to 0.5 per cent. This was the lowest that it had ever been in the UK.

The world economy appeared to be undergoing an unusually sharp downturn. Measures of business and consumer confidence had fallen markedly. World trade growth was likely to be the weakest for a significant period of time.

1. Explain how a cut in the interest rate might help the UK economy in the circumstances described in the passage above.

2. Show the possible effects on prices and output in the economy of a cut in interest rates using aggregate supply and aggregate demand diagrams.

Fiscal versus monetary policies

Governments will vary in their view of whether fiscal or monetary policies are more effective. There will always be some elements of fiscal policy and monetary policy: for example, a government will always have some spending and some taxes. But the question is whether spending, tax, interest rates, or banking regulations are the best way in which to control aggregate demand. In the 1950s and 1960s, the general view was that fiscal policy could be used to 'fine tune' the economy. A boost to government spending or a change in tax rates could effectively change the level of demand to a desired level. This was known as a 'Keynesian approach' after the economist John Maynard Keynes. But fiscal policy does have problems—not least that changes cannot be made quickly, but rely on new policies being introduced in the annual budget. Even then, an increase in the spending programme may take years to actually come online.

In the mid to late 1970s, many countries were faced with high inflation and high unemployment, and fiscal policies did not seem to be working. The focus of government policy in many countries switched to monetary policy to influence the amount of money in the economy and the overall level of demand; in particular, in recent years, interest rates were used to try to achieve government objectives. Interest rate changes can be made regularly and have been left as the Bank of England's responsibility, in order to remove any political influence. There remains a time lag, however, and predicting the precise impact on the economy can be difficult.

In response to the global recession of 2008, most governments have had to use a combination of expansionist fiscal and monetary policy. Increased spending by the government, increases to the money supply, and low interest rates have been used to prevent a major decline in demand. The need for more stimuli to the economy has led to a greater role for fiscal policy through greater government spending,

Can you now answer question 5 from the opening case study?

Supply-side policies

Demand-side policies focus on influencing aggregate demand. They are most effective in terms of boosting national income when aggregate supply is elastic (for example, when aggregate demand shifts AD1 to AD2). At full employment (Y5), the effect of an increase in aggregate demand is simply inflationary.

By comparison, **supply-side policies** are government policies (mainly microeconomic) designed to help markets and industries work more efficiently. Supply-side policies aim to increase aggregate supply and economic growth.

Supply-side policies shift the aggregate supply to the right (see Figure 10.18). These are unlikely to be a priority when demand is very low (for example, at Y1); at full employment, demand-side policies are inflationary unless supply increases as well. Supply-side policies are likely to be regarded as more significant as the economy gets nearer to capacity. Increasing supply enables demand to rise without being inflationary: for example, if demand increases from AD3 to AD4, this is not inflationary if supply also increases from AS to AS1.

The majority of supply-side policies focus on product markets or the labour market.

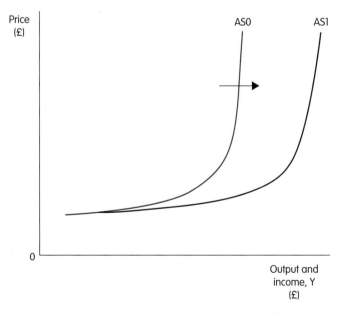

Figure 10.18 Supply-side policies shift the aggregate supply to the right

Product markets

The aim of supply-side policies in product markets is to make markets for goods and services more competitive, and to increase the pressure on firms to be efficient, productive, and innovative. With more competition, businesses will need to meet customer needs more effectively. This should lead to better quality products and a constant search for improvements.

These policies include the following.

- *Competition policy* This policy is used to regulate large firms and ensure that they do not abuse their market power—for example, ensuring that price fixing is not occurring, that monopolies do not exploit customers, and that smaller new businesses have the opportunity to compete;

- *Privatization* This involves the selling of assets from the public sector to the private sector. This should put pressure on managers by investors to improve the performance of their businesses compared to when they were in the government sector. In the last twenty-five years, many UK businesses have been privatized, including British Airways, British Steel, British Telecom, and British Gas. Privatization often breaks up government monopolies and allows more competition in a market, putting further pressure on organizations to be more efficient.

- *Deregulation* This occurs when regulations are removed to enable more firms to compete, thereby encouraging better customer service and innovation. Markets such as bus transport, telecommunications, and gas supply have been opened up to competition in the UK in the last thirty years by allowing more firms to provide the service and removing barriers to competition.

- *Encouraging free trade between countries* This provides more competition from abroad and puts pressure on businesses to be more efficient.

- *Encouraging business start-ups* Entrepreneurs can create competitive pressure and generate new ideas.

- *Providing incentives for innovation* For example, by subsidizing or providing tax breaks, businesses can be encouraged to undertake research and development into new products and processes.

? *Think about it ...*   10.14

1. What determines the impact of greater competition in a market on a particular business?

2. How might greater competition in an economy affect different stakeholders?

Labour markets

Supply-side policies in the labour market are aimed at increasing the supply of labour and making labour markets generally more flexible, so that they can respond to changes in demand more easily.

Policies in labour markets include the following.

■ *Reforming trade unions to restrict their power* Some economists argue that unions can push up the wage beyond equilibrium level by threatening industrial action, such as strikes. Less union power may increase the supply of labour, increasing the resources available in the economy and the aggregate supply.

■ *Spending more on training and education, so that workers are in a better position to accept jobs* This can be important, for example, when helping employees to move from one industry to another and to prevent structural unemployment by reducing occupational immobility.

■ *Changing the tax and benefits systems to ensure that working is an attractive option* For example, lower income taxes and lower benefits may provide a greater incentive to work rather than to stay at home. Cutting tax rates for lower paid workers may help to reduce the extent of the 'unemployment trap', which occurs when people calculate that they may be no better off from working than if they remain unemployed.

Supply-side policies should be linked to the expected levels of aggregate demand. After all, if supply-side policies lead to more products being produced, this is only valuable if the demand is there to buy what is being offered.

In Figure 10.19, the JA curve shows the number of people willing and able to accept a job at each real wage. LF shows the number of people in the labour force—that is, the

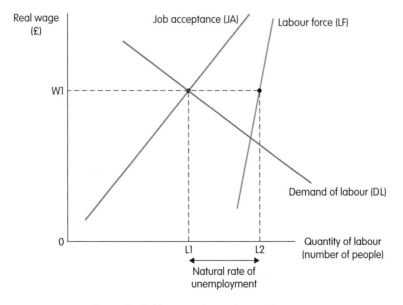

Figure 10.19 The natural rate of unemployment

number who could work at each real wage. The labour force slopes to the right slightly because, as the real wage increases, some people re-enter the labour market: for example, rather than be a homemaker, they decide that leisure is too expensive given a high real wage and decide that they want to work.

The JA also slopes to the right because more people will want to accept a job at higher real wages; the JA and LF converge (see Figure 10.20) because the number of people will-ing to wait in the labour force for a better offer will decrease as the real wage gets higher. At very high real wages, most of those in the labour force will accept a job. The demand for labour is downward-sloping because fewer people will be demanded at higher real wages.

Equilibrium in the labour market is originally at W1. At this wage rate, the number of people accepting jobs is L1; the number in the labour force is L2. This means that L1,L2 is the natural rate of unemployment (that is, that all those unemployed are voluntarily unemployed).

Supply-side policies in the labour market should shift the job acceptance to the right; at each and every real wage, more people can accept a job if they are better trained and aware of what vacancies exist, for example. The new equilibrium is at W2 with a lower natural rate of L3,L4. There are more people employed, increasing the capacity of the economy.

An increase in aggregate supply as a result of effective supply-side policies will be shown by an outward shift of the aggregate supply schedule. This should increase the quantity produced and put downward pressure on prices, because the quantity of products available has increased.

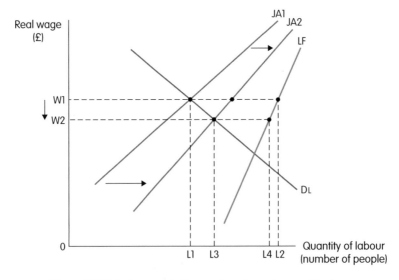

Figure 10.20 An increase in the number of people accepting jobs

Business Analysis 10.9

The 'tax wedge' is the difference between the cost of labour to employers and what employees receive as take-home pay. It is made up of income tax, and the contributions paid to social security funds by firms and workers. The bigger the tax wedge, the less incentive there may be to work, because employees take home less money. In the 2008 survey, the tax wedge went up in fifteen of the Organisation for Economic Co-operation and Development (OECD) member states and fell in the remaining fifteen. In Hungary and Germany, the wedge is over 50 per cent of total labour cost.

Sources: *The Economist*, 16 May 2009, www.oecd.org

What is the possible effect for businesses of an increase in the tax wedge?

An increase in aggregate supply represents an outward shift in the production possibility frontier (see Figure 10.21).

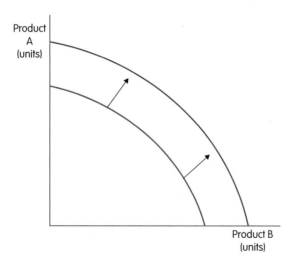

Figure 10.21 An outward shift in the production possibility frontier

Supply-side v. demand-side policies

The decision of whether you should focus on supply-side or demand-side policies depends mainly on your view of where the economy is at the moment. If you think that the economy is in equilibrium, but a long way below full employment, the emphasis will probably be on demand-side policies to get the economy to produce at its capacity. If you think that the economy is near or at full employment, then growth will only occur by increasing capacity, which occurs with supply-side policies; there is no point relying on boosting aggregate demand, because firms are already producing what they can.

?

Think about it...   10.15

1. Read the news and study economic information about your economy. Do you think that it is close to full employment or not at the moment? Justify your answer.

2. What are the key changes in government economic policies that have been made recently by your government? Why do you think it has made these changes?

Imperfect information and time lags

The main economic objectives of a government are likely to involve economic growth, full employment, stable prices, and a healthy level of exports relative to imports. But achieving these can be extremely difficult. In part, this is because information about the state of the economy is often weeks or months out of date: just think of the vast information-gathering exercise involved in trying to calculate how much is being earned in an economy. With imperfect information, it is easy to make the wrong decisions. This is made worse by the time lag between making a decision, it coming into effect, and it making an impact on the economy. For example, the government may decide that it wants to invest in the economy and put together a programme of greater spending on health care. This has to go into the budget, be voted on, and then put into action. The spending programme may take years to happen, and for this to feed through into more jobs and greater spending by the construction firms and employees may take even longer. By the time the effects work through, the position of the economy may have changed dramatically. Like managers, politicians and their economic advisers are dealing in a world of imperfect information, but their decisions affect millions of businesses, employees, and households—no simple task.

Summary

Macroeconomics involves the analysis of the economy as a whole, rather than one particular market. The total demand in the economy is known as 'aggregate demand'; the total supply in the economy is known as 'aggregate supply'. Equilibrium in the economy occurs when aggregate demand equals aggregate supply. The government can try to influence aggregate demand and supply using fiscal and monetary policies. Whether the focus is on aggregate demand or aggregate supply depends, in part, on the government's political stance and also the extent to which the economy is at or near full employment.

Changes in the state of the economy will have major implications for businesses. An increase in aggregate demand will affect sales and may also affect the ease of attracting resources if there are more firms competing for them. Changes in aggregate supply may affect price levels generally and the ease of recruitment. On both the demand and supply sides, macroeconomic changes can affect the success of every business. Macro factors are out of the control of managers, which makes it even more important to monitor their development and be prepared for them, if possible.

Checklist

Having read this chapter, you should now understand:

- [ ] the meaning of aggregate demand;
- [ ] the meaning of consumption and investment;
- [ ] the meaning of exports and imports;
- [ ] the meaning of aggregate supply;
- [ ] the meaning of full employment;
- [ ] the meaning of the tax wedge;
- [ ] government economic objectives;
- [ ] the meaning of fiscal policy and monetary policy;
- [ ] the meaning of demand-side and supply-side policies;
- [ ] the meaning of the government budget.

Case Study Review

Having read this chapter, you should now be able to answer the following questions.

1. Why do you think Japan may have experienced a fall in demand in its economy in the 1990s and in 2008–09?

2. How do you think the different functions of a business such as Toyota might be affected by a major fall in demand in the economy?

3. Why might managers in Japan have been slow to make redundancies in the past?

4. Why is the value of the currency important to the level of demand in an economy? Explain your answer.

5. What could the Japanese government do to try to increase aggregate demand?

6. Do you think that an increase in demand in the circumstances described above would be likely to increase output or prices? Illustrate your answer using an aggregate demand and supply diagram.

Short Answer Questions

1. What is meant by aggregate demand?

2. What is meant by aggregate supply?

3. Distinguish between consumption and investment.

4. Distinguish between exports and imports.

5. What is meant by fiscal policies?

6. What is meant by monetary policies?

7. Explain two demand-side policies that a government might use to increase aggregate demand.

8. Explain two supply-side policies that a government might use to increase aggregate supply.

9. Outline the main economic objectives of most governments.

10. What determines the relative impact of an increase in aggregate demand on the prices and output levels in the economy?

Essay Questions

1. Should the government focus on increasing aggregate demand or aggregate supply?

2. To what extent is a budget deficit a good indicator of an expansionist government fiscal policy?

3. Is fiscal policy a better way of controlling the economy than monetary policy?

 ## One Step Further

Visit our Online Resource Centre at **www.oxfordtextbooks.co.uk/orc/gillespiebusiness/** for test questions, podcasts, and further information on topics covered in this chapter.

Macroeconomic issues

11

Learning Objectives

In this chapter, we examine some of the key issues in macroeconomics.

By the end of this chapter, you should:

- ✓ understand the causes of economic growth and possible government actions to achieve this;

- ✓ understand the causes of inflation and possible government actions to reduce it;

- ✓ understand the causes of a balance of payments deficit and possible government actions to reduce it;

- ✓ understand the causes of unemployment and possible government actions to reduce it.

Case Study

Review the following table.

Table 11.1 Key economic data on selected economies

	GDP 2009 forecast (%)	Current account balance last 12 mths (% GDP)	Currency (units per US$) this year (last year)	Unemployment rates (%)	Inflation rate (%)
USA	−2.7	−3.0	n/a	9.5	−0.4
Japan	−6.1	+1.9	93.9 (105)	5.2	−1.1
UK	−3.7	−1.7	0.61 (0.5)	7.6	1.7
China	+7.2	+7.2	6.83 (6.81)	9	−0.5
Malaysia	−3.0	+0.9	10122 (9141)	4.0	−0.4
Singapore	−8.6	+14.9	1.45 (1.35)	3.3	−0.2
India	+5.5	−1.9	48.6 (43.1)	6.8	5.2
Russia	−5.0	+0.9	31.9 (23.3)	9.9	12.1

Questions

With reference to the countries above or others that you know, answer the following.

1. Explain the possible reasons why some countries have negative gross domestic product (GDP) growth, while others have positive. What do you think determines the rate of growth of an economy?

2. What might be the implications of negative economic growth for businesses in that country?

3. Explain the possible reasons for the differences in the current account position shown above.

4. What could the government of a country with a current account deficit do to improve this position?

5. Explain why some currencies might have got weaker against the dollar and some might have got stronger.

6. What are the possible effects on businesses of the changes in the exchange rates shown above?

7. Explain the possible reasons why the unemployment rates between countries vary so much.

8. What could governments do to reduce unemployment rates?

9. Explain the possible reasons why so many countries are experiencing deflation.

10. Compare and contrast two of the economies above in terms of their strengths and weaknesses. Discuss the implications for businesses in these economies in terms of their economic position.

Introduction

The macroeconomic environment can create opportunities and threats for businesses. In a booming economy, demand may be growing fast, creating more sales opportunities. In a declining economy, a business may have to consider redundancies. If prices are stable, planning will be easier than if they are changing rapidly. The state of the economy will therefore affect the ease of doing business and the likelihood of success. It will also affect the extent to which a country attracts investment from overseas. Not surprisingly, economic change often makes headline news because it has a direct effect on jobs, households' standard of living, and economic growth.

The most common indicators of the health of an economy are:

- the rate of economic growth;
- the rate of unemployment;
- the rate of change in the price level;
- the balance-of-payments position.

When managers are considering economic conditions domestically or, indeed, considering entering overseas markets, they should monitor these key macroeconomic indicators carefully. Managers will be interested in the present situation and also forecasts of these factors, because they will have a significant effect on the trading environment. They will affect a whole range of management decisions, such as:

- which markets to target;
- whether to invest in more capacity;
- whether to agree to a pay increase;
- whether to recruit or not.

? *Think about it ...*   11.1

What other indicators might you use to judge the performance of an economy?

Data Analysis   11.1

Table 11.2

	GDP (%)	2009 Prices change (%)	Unemployment rate (%)
China	+6.0	−0.8	9.0
UK	−3.5	+1.2	6.5
Eurozone	−3.4	+0.4	8.5
Germany	−4.3	+0.3	8.1

Source: Adapted from *The Economist*, April 2009

1. Which economy do you think is doing best based on the data above if the targets are economic growth, stable prices, low unemployment, and a healthy trade position? Explain your answer.
2. What other data might be useful to make a decision?

 ## Business Analysis   11.1

• Singapore has a highly developed and successful free-market economy. It has an open business environment, stable prices, and a GDP per person equal to that of the four largest west European countries. The economy depends heavily on exports—particularly in consumer electronics, IT products, and pharmaceuticals—and on a growing service sector. Real GDP growth averaged 7 per cent between 2004 and 2007, but dropped to 1.2 per cent in 2008 as a result of the global financial crisis. It has attracted major investments in pharmaceuticals and medical technology production, and aims to become South East Asia's financial and high-tech hub.

• Zimbabwe faces a wide variety of difficult economic problems as it struggles with an unsustainable budget deficit, an overvalued official exchange rate, rapidly increasing prices, and empty shelves in the stores. Its 1998–2002 involvement in the war in the Democratic Republic of the Congo drained hundreds of millions of dollars from the economy. The government's land reform programme has badly damaged the commercial farming sector, the traditional source of exports and foreign exchange, and the provider of 400,000 jobs, turning Zimbabwe into a net importer of food products. The Reserve Bank of Zimbabwe routinely prints money to fund the budget deficit, causing the official annual rate of inflation to go up from 32 per cent in 1998, to 133 per cent in 2004, 585 per cent in 2005, past 1,000 per cent in 2006, to 26,000 per cent in November 2007, and reaching 11.2 million per cent in 2008.

Source: Adapted from CIA Factbook, April 2009.
Reproduced with kind permission

1. These two economies are very different in terms of economic success. Why do you think this might be?

2. What type of business might have an export market in Singapore?

3. What problems might you have trading in Zimbabwe?

4. How might the success of Singapore and the problems in Zimbabwe affect businesses in your economy?

National income—gross domestic product versus gross national product

There are several different measures of the income of an economy. **Gross domestic product (GDP)** measures the value of the income produced within an economy regardless of who owns the factors of production. The GDP of the UK, for example, measures the income produced within this country, including the earnings of overseas companies and citizens based here.

Gross national product (GNP), by comparison, measures the income of a country's citizens regardless of where they are based in the world. It is calculated by taking GDP, adding on the income earned by UK citizens abroad, and deducting earnings within the UK by non-UK citizens.

The GDP and GNP figures show the total earnings of an economy or of a country's citizens, respectively. Economists and managers will also be interested in the income per

Data Analysis   11.2

1. China's GDP per person is growing at around 10 per cent a year. If someone were to be earning £10,000 a year now, how much would they earn in five years' time at this growth rate?

2. In the USA, the growth rate is nearer 2 per cent a year. If someone were to earn £10,000 a year now, how much would they earn in five years' time at this growth rate?

3. If GDP growth is 5 per cent and population growth is 7 per cent, is GDP per person rising or falling?

person (that is, GDP per capita or GNP per capita) and in the rate of growth of income. This will be likely to influence factors such as spending patterns and wage rates.

Economic growth

The growth of an economy is usually measured by changes in GDP. The average growth rate in GDP in the UK historically is between 2 per cent and 3 per cent a year. This means that managers can expect the income of the UK to increase in size by approximately this proportion a year over time; this has implications for likely levels of demand, and therefore the desired levels of capacity and production for businesses.

To achieve economic growth, a government may attempt to increase the level of aggregate demand and/or aggregate supply. Increasing aggregate demand will take the economy nearer to full employment and is shown in Figure 11.1 as a movement from W to Z; it is taking the economy from a position of underemployment of resources to one of full employment.

An increase in aggregate demand can be seen by a movement from X on the production possibility frontier (PPF) to a point such as Y. An increase in aggregate supply can be seen as an outward shift in the frontier.

To boost aggregate demand, a government might undertake policies such as:

- increasing its spending;
- cutting direct taxes to give households or firms more income, which should encourage spending;
- lowering interest rates to encourage borrowing;
- selling currency to lower the exchange rate, in the hope that doing so might boost export sales and lower imports.

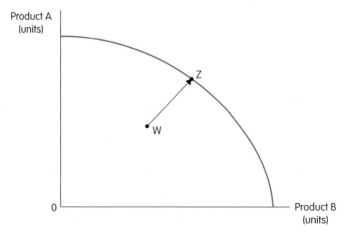

Figure 11.1 Economic growth and the production possibility frontier

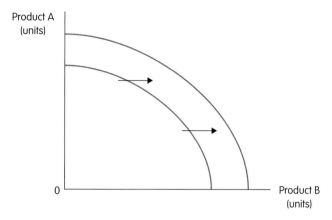

Figure 11.2 Supply-side policies leading to an outward shift of the production possibility frontier

? *Think about it ...* 11.1

Which of the following are examples of fiscal policy to boost aggregate demand?

A An increase in the threshold before income tax is charged.

B Quantitative easing.

C An increase in government provision of transport services.

D An instruction to banks to lend more.

Increasing aggregate supply will increase the capacity of the economy, which is shown by an outward shift of the PPF (see Figure 11.2).

The economic cycle

Although there may be an underlying trend in the growth rate of an economy, the actual growth year on year may not be this stable. In fact, economies tend to follow a cyclical pattern, which is known as the 'economic (or business) cycle'. While the trend rate of the UK economy may be a growth of between 2 per cent and 3 per cent, in any given year, it can be significantly higher or lower than this. Around the overall trend, there will often be periods of boom, recession, slump, and recovery (see Figure 11.3).

■ A *boom* occurs when an economy is growing at a fast rate. This tends to be associated with low levels of unemployment, because there are plenty of jobs around, and

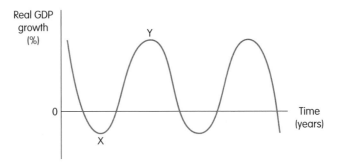

Figure 11.3 Boom, recession, slump, and recovery

a shortage of land and office accommodation, because of the demand to produce more. A boom involves faster growth in aggregate demand and demand for most products tends to be high (although inferior products may suffer); this leads to an increased demand for factors of production. Given higher levels of demand, a manager will want to consider whether to expand and increase capacity. Order books should be full and businesses, in general, should be growing. Given the high levels of demand, it may be possible to increase prices.

■ A *recession* occurs when an economy is shrinking. This means that GDP growth is actually negative. The official definition of a recession in the UK is two quarters of negative economic growth. A recession tends to be associated with high levels of unemployment because of a lack of aggregate demand and spare capacity in the UK. With falling levels of demand, a business may consider laying off staff temporarily or even making redundancies if the fall in demand is believed to be long term. The business may also reduce capacity either by selling off land or capital, or by mothballing facilities until they are needed again. A recession began in the UK in January 2009; by August 2009, unemployment had risen by over 800,000, the average value of a house had fallen by nearly £20,000, nearly 56,000 homes had been repossessed, nearly 35,000 businesses had closed, and over 176,000 people had become insolvent.

■ A *slump* occurs when the recession is severe and prolonged, leading to very high levels of unemployment. In this situation, confidence in the economy is low and there are high levels of spare capacity in the economy.

■ A *recovery* occurs when the economy begins to pick up and starts to grow after a slump. As it recovers, businesses begin to invest, consumers begin to gain confidence, and unemployment levels begin to fall.

In Figure 11.3, real GDP growth is negative at X and the economy is shrinking. The economy is in a slump. After this the economy begins to recover. At Y the economy is growing fast and in a boom.

Business Analysis 11.2

In May 2009, Robert Shiller, Professor of Economics at Yale University, warned that recent improvements in share prices should not be seen as evidence of a bounce in the economy: 'You don't know whether the argument with your wife is really over or not. Is the problem something that your spouse will bring up again and again.' Similarly, in the 1930s and 1980s, economies seemed to recover before dipping again, causing a 'W' shape recession.

Other shapes of recessions are:

- V-shaped, as occurred in the UK in the early 1990s—the recession was short-lived and then the economy accelerated quickly;
- U-shaped, as occurred in the UK in 1980–81—this is similar to the V shape, but the decline and recovery are more prolonged;
- L-shaped, as experienced by Japan in the 1990s—this occurs when an economy stays stuck in a recession for a long time.

Why does it matter whether the recession is V-shaped, U-shaped, or L-shaped?

Managers need to be aware of the present level of income in the economy and the expected rate of growth in the future, because this is likely to affect:

- the levels of demand for the business;
- the ease of recruiting staff;
- the likely demand for pay by staff;
- the ability to increase prices.

For example, if the economy moves into a recession, it would be easier for managers to recruit staff and there is likely to be less pressure from staff to increase their wages, because they will be worried about their jobs. But managers will worry whether there is sufficient demand for their product and this will depend, in part, on the nature of the product, the sensitivity of demand to income changes, and their marketing actions.

Some businesses are cyclical. The demand for their product follows the level of income in the economy and therefore the economy cycle very closely. For example, the construction industry will suffer heavily in a recession and do well in a boom. But some industries are counter-cyclical—that is, they do better in a recession: for example, company administrators that take over failing businesses will be busier in a poor economic climate. In the UK recession of 2008, discount stores such as Aldi and Primark found that their sales grew relatively quickly as customers traded down.

Business Analysis   11.3

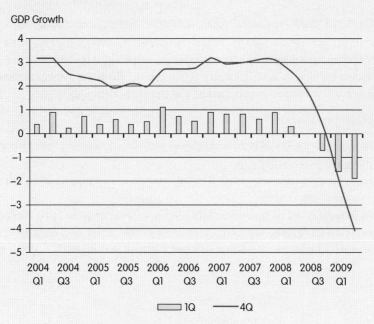

Figure 11.4 Economic growth in the UK

Source: ONS Reproduced with kind permission

Discuss the possible implications for UK businesses of the growth in the first quarter of 2009.

>> You Decide ...

Is a recession a good time for a business to invest?

? Think about it ...   11.3

1. How might the economic cycle affect business planning?

2. Which other businesses can you think of that might benefit in a recession?

3. Find the growth figures for your own economy. At what stage of the economic cycle do you think this is?

The benefits and cost of economic growth

Economic growth occurs when there is an increase in the income in the economy. If an economy grows faster than its population, this will result in a higher income per person. This, in turn, should mean a higher standard of living for a country's citizens. Many people measure their own success and the success of an economy in terms of their income and possessions, so a growth in GDP per person is often a government target. With higher incomes, people may spend more, which creates opportunities for business. In particular, there will be changes in consumption patterns as households trade up: for example, from a bicycle to a moped, or from a moped to car. Many businesses operating in the more mature economies, including the USA and the UK, are seeing new markets being created in emerging economies, such as Brazil and China, in which fast growth opens up much bigger sales possibilities.

Economic growth also means that tax revenues of governments should automatically increase (because more people are earning and firms are making more profits) and there is less spending on benefits as unemployment is lower. These changes should improve the government's financial position, potentially allowing more spending on merit and public goods.

Economic growth can, however, also bring problems to a country, such as:

- faster economic growth may create negative externalities—for example, there may be pollution and damage to the environment because of more deliveries and more output;

- if demand grows too quickly relative to supply, it may create upward pressure on prices and lead to what is known as **demand pull inflation** (see later in this chapter).

Also, while growth may improve the average income per person, this does not mean that everyone is better off: the income and wealth inequalities in an economy may increase; there may also be significant regional differences. Income inequality can be analysed using the Gini coefficient (see Chapter 7).

Another problem of economic growth is that it may not be sustainable. Growth may use up resources that are non-renewable, such as oil, and overexploit natural resources, such as fish and trees, by using them up faster than they are being replaced. Sustainable development was defined in 1987 by the Brundtland Commission on Environment and Development as 'development that meets the needs of the present without compromising the ability of future generations to meet their own needs'. Fast growth now may be at the expense of the future welfare of society. Some economists argue that when the external costs of growth are considered, increasing GDP is not necessarily desirable.

 Business Analysis 11.4

In 1972, concerned about the problems afflicting other developing countries that focused only on economic growth, Bhutan's newly crowned leader, King Jigme Singye Wangchuck, decided to make his nation's priority not its GDP, but its gross national happiness (GNH). Bhutan, the king said, needed to ensure that prosperity was shared across society and that it was balanced against preserving cultural traditions, protecting the environment, and maintaining a responsive government.

While household incomes in Bhutan remain among the world's lowest, life expectancy increased by nineteen years between 1984 and 1998, jumping to 66 years. The country, which is preparing to shift to a constitution and an elected government, requires that at least 60 per cent of its lands remain forested, welcomes a limited stream of wealthy tourists, and exports hydropower to India.

1. What factors do you think are likely to contribute most towards a country's happiness?
2. What could a government do to promote happiness?
3. What can businesses do to promote more happiness in an economy?

Business Analysis   11.5

Tourism has been common in the Galapagos Islands for many years. In fact, visitors are now crucial to the future of the archipelago. Tourist income is needed to improve the standard of living. Between 1999 and 2005, GDP increased by an estimated 78 per cent, from a base of US$41 million, giving the archipelago an annual growth rate of around 10 per cent and making it one of the world's fastest growing economies. Tourism provided 68 per cent of this growth. Despite this, the average income per head rose by only 1.8 per cent annually. This is because Ecuador's economy collapsed in 1999 and large numbers of migrants came to the islands in search of a better standard of living. The islands' population rose by 60 per cent. The consequence was greater strain on the islands' water supply, sewerage, and waste disposal, as well as its wildlife.

Sources: The Central Intelligence Agency, *The Economist*, 27 March 2008

1. Do you think that slowing the population growth would affect the economic growth of the islands?
2. Do you think that the Galapagos Islands should aim to grow more slowly?

Think about it ...   11.4

Do you think that your country should aim to grow more quickly? Justify your answer.

Can you now answer question 1 and 2 from the opening case study?

Unemployment

Unemployment represents a wasted resource in an economy because it means that there are people who are not working who could be adding to production. They also receive benefits, which takes money away from other areas of the economy, such as education. Not surprisingly, then, governments are eager to find ways of reducing the level of unemployment in the economy. From a business perspective, if fewer people are working, this is likely to reduce incomes in the economy and therefore, for many businesses, this is likely to reduce sales opportunities.

Measuring unemployment

The two main ways of measuring unemployment are the Labour Force Survey (LFS) and the claimant count. The LFS is based on a random sample throughout the country. This is conducted every three months using around 53,000 households. The survey collects information about the personal circumstances and work of everyone living in these households.

Under the LFS guidelines, all people aged 16 years and over can be classified into one of three states: 'in employment'; 'unemployed'; or 'economically inactive'.

■ Unemployed people have no job, want a job, have actively sought work in the last four weeks, and are available to start work in the next two weeks, or are out of work, have found a job, and are waiting to start it in the next two weeks.

■ In general, anybody who carries out at least one hour's paid work in a week, or who is temporarily away from a job (for example, on holiday) is in employment.

■ Those who are out of work, but do not meet the criteria of unemployment, are economically inactive.

The claimant count measures the number of people eligible for unemployment benefits. By changing the rules rewarding who can and who cannot claim benefits, this figure can change quite significantly, leading to major differences between the claimant count and the findings of the LFS.

? *Think about it...* 11.5

1. Do you think that someone who works only one hour a week should be regarded as in employment? Why might this suggest that underlying unemployment is actually much higher than reported figures?

2. Do you think that the Labour Force Survey or the claimant count is a better way of measuring unemployment? Explain your answer.

Causes of unemployment

Unemployment may be caused by a number of reasons, including the following.

- *A lack of demand in the economy due to low levels of aggregate demand* This is known as **cyclical unemployment**. In this instance, a government might intervene to try to boost the level of aggregate demand. This would aim to increase demand for goods and services, and encourage businesses to expand and employ more people.

- *A change in the structure of the economy, so that some people lack the skills that they need to move from the declining sectors into the growth areas* This is called 'structural unemployment' and would require supply-side policies by a government to help to retrain employees.

- *Seasonal changes reducing demand for staff in some sectors, such as fruit picking or the hotel industry* This is unlikely to affect huge numbers of employees, and these people are likely to find work again next season and so are not a major concern.

- *People not willing to accept a job at the given wage* This could be because of the unemployment trap, whereby people end up worse off by working because they start incurring taxes and lose their benefits, and so may earn less than they do by remaining unemployed. In this situation, the government may use supply-side policies, by reducing the benefits that are given to those who are unemployed and having lower taxes at low incomes.

- *A restriction in supply due to employees wanting to push up wages, perhaps via a trade union* By restricting supply, those in work do earn more, but fewer people are employed than would be the case in a free market. In this case, the government may try to reduce power of unions, perhaps through legislation.

Data Analysis   11.3

Unemployment in the UK in 2009 reached 2.261 million, its highest rate since November 1996. This represented 7.2 per cent of the working population.

Young people have been particularly susceptible to the recession, with the unemployment rate in the 18–24 age group reaching 16.6 per cent, its highest point since 1993.

1. Explain why unemployment rates may have differed so much over the last sixteen years.

2. Explain why the claimant count is less than the unemployment figure in Figure 11.5.

3. Should the government worry about young people's unemployment more than that of older age groups? Justify your answer.

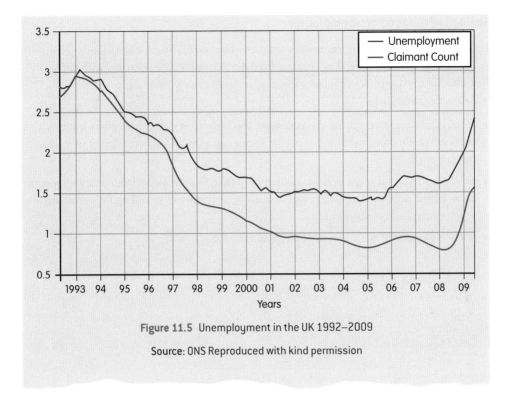

Figure 11.5 Unemployment in the UK 1992–2009

Source: ONS Reproduced with kind permission

Voluntary and involuntary unemployment

An important distinction to make when analysing unemployment is between 'voluntary' and 'involuntary' unemployment. **Voluntary unemployment** occurs when all of those willing and able to accept a job at the given real wage are working; there will still be some people unemployed if they lack the desire to work or the necessary skills. **Involuntary unemployment** occurs when people are willing and able to work, but there is not enough demand; this occurs when the economy is in a slump, for example.

The natural rate of unemployment

The natural rate of unemployment is the equilibrium rate of unemployment—that is, the rate of unemployment for which the aggregate supply of labour equals the aggregate demand for labour. At the natural rate of unemployment, all of those willing and able to work at the given real wage rate are employed. This means that all unemployment is 'voluntary' (that is, employees are not willing or not able to work) and there is no involuntary unemployment.

To reduce the natural rate of unemployment, the government may focus on supply-side policies to make the labour market work more efficiently and bring about market equilibrium.

The consequences of unemployment

Involuntary unemployment represents a waste of resources and means that the economy is below full employment. This means that the economy is operating within the PPF (for example, at point X in Figure 11.6) and is productively inefficient.

Unemployment also:

- reduces the tax income for the economy, because fewer people are working, which reduces the finance available for public sector projects and automatically worsens the budget position;
- involves a higher level of benefits, which may take finance away from other important areas of the economy, and therefore has an opportunity cost and again automatically worsens the budget position;
- is often associated with social costs, such as crime.

? **Think about it ...**   11.6

1. What is the level of unemployment in your economy at the moment?
2. What do you think are the main causes of unemployment in your economy?
3. If you were in government, what would you do to reduce unemployment?

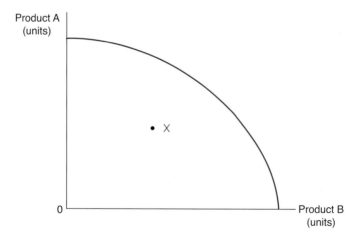

Figure 11.6 Productive inefficiency

You Decide ...

How might a significant increase in unemployment affect the marketing and human resource (HR) decisions of a large insurance business?

Hysteresis

The 'hysteresis' effect occurs if there is long-term unemployment. If people are out of work for a long time, they tend to lose their skills and become less attractive to employers, because they have not been employed for a while. This may increase the natural rate of unemployment by, in effect, making more people less able to work.

Analysing unemployment within labour markets

Understanding unemployment levels and patterns is important to managers because it affects their ability to recruit, as well as reflects the state of the economy as a whole. High levels of unemployment put less upward pressure on wages and make it easier to recruit.

But simply looking at the overall figure of unemployment does not necessarily reflect the state of the labour markets in which a specific manager is most interested. For example, a particular business may be recruiting skilled engineers or surgeons and therefore the trends in the overall unemployment rates in the UK might not reflect what is happening in these particular labour markets.

There may also be significant differences between the unemployment rates in different regions that need to be taken into account. For a business that recruits locally, it is the local unemployment rate that matters more than the national figure.

You Decide ...

1. Should the government remove all unemployment benefits?

2. Are high levels of unemployment good or bad for businesses?

Think about it ...   11.7

1. Find out the unemployment levels in your country. How much do these levels vary between skills and regions? How much have they changed over time?

2. Is unemployment a major economic issue in your country?

£ **Business Analysis**   11.6

In 2009, the world economy experienced the biggest increase in unemployment for many years. The US unemployment rate rose to over 8 per cent, its highest for twenty-five years. In China, 20 million migrant workers (around 3 per cent of the labour force) were laid off. In Cambodia, the textile industry, its main source of exports, cut one worker in ten. In Spain, the collapse in the construction industry increased unemployment to 14.8 per cent.

And these official unemployment rates almost certainly understate the amount of slack in the economy. This is because many companies were cutting hours to reduce costs, so people were still employed but working less. At 33.3 hours, the average working week was the shortest since at least 1964 and unpaid leave became more common.

What is the likely impact of a significant increase in unemployment on the different functional areas of business?

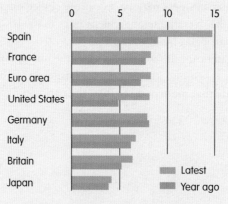

Figure 11.7 Unemployment rates

Source: National statistics; eurostat

Can you now answer question 7 and 8 from the opening case study?

Inflation

Inflation occurs when there is a sustained increase in the general price level. With inflation of 2 per cent, for example, prices in general are increasing by 2 per cent over the year. This does not mean that all prices are increasing at this rate: some may increase by more, some by less, but, on average, prices are increasing by 2 per cent.

How to measure inflation

In the UK, the Retail Prices Index (RPI) measures what is happening to prices in a typical basket of goods and services for a household in the UK. It takes account of the relative importance of difference items in terms of spending and calculates overall how much prices increase. The Consumer Prices Index (CPI) is similar, but does not include mortgage repayments when calculated; this means that the two measures can give different results (for example, if mortgage rates are cut, the RPI will be lower than the CPI).

Business Analysis   11.7

Inflation is measured by looking at the prices in a typical shopping 'basket'. The government's Office for National Statistics (ONS) collects about 120,000 prices every month for a 'basket' of about 650 goods and services. As our spending patterns change, this means that the items included in the basket must be changed as well. In recent years, for example, digital technology products have featured much more. Also our growing interest in our health has increased the significance of products such as smoothies, fresh groceries, and small types of orange (for example, satsumas and clementines).

The way in which we buy music has also changed, with consumers preferring to download individual tracks rather than purchase 'Top 40' CD singles, which are now completely removed from the basket. Audio CDs are still represented and a new item covering the nostalgic consumption of non-chart 'classic' albums by artists such as U2, Pink Floyd, and Madonna has been introduced alongside the existing 'Top 40' CD album.

Camera film has been altogether replaced by universal digital storage devices (such as USB sticks), which provide memory capacity for cameras, mp3 players, mobile phones, and computers.

Source: Adapted from ONS

What other differences do you think there are between a typical shopping basket now and that of ten years ago?

The causes of inflation include the following.

- *Demand pull inflation* At any moment in an economy, aggregate demand may be growing faster than aggregate supply. In this situation, businesses are likely to increase their prices given the ever higher levels of demand. High demand pulls up prices.

As illustrated in Figure 11.8, an increase in aggregate demand usually leads to a higher price and quantity. As supply becomes more price inelastic, the effect is on price more than output (for example, when aggregate demand increases from AD3 to AD4, compared to from AD1 to AD2, there is more impact on inflation).

In this situation, a government will want to reduce aggregate demand (or at least restrict its growth in line with supply) to control inflation. In the UK, the Bank of England's Monetary Policy Committee (MPC) uses interest rates to influence spending to control demand and therefore prices. Higher interest rates would deter spending and are likely to lead to a fall in aggregate demand; this should prevent prices from increasing.

- **Cost push inflation** The price level in an economy is inevitably sensitive to the level of costs: if costs increase, perhaps because of wage demands or higher imported prices of inputs such as oil, businesses may be forced to push up their prices to maintain their profits. Higher costs shift the aggregate supply curve upwards because a higher price is needed for any given level of output. This leads to higher prices in the economy.

As illustrated in Figure 11.9, an increase in costs means that a higher price is required to produce any level of output. This leads to an upward shift of the aggregate supply curve. The effect of an increase in costs will usually be lower output and a higher price.

In this situation, the government will aim to reduce costs, perhaps by intervening with the exchange rate to reduce import costs, or by introducing limits on wage and price increases.

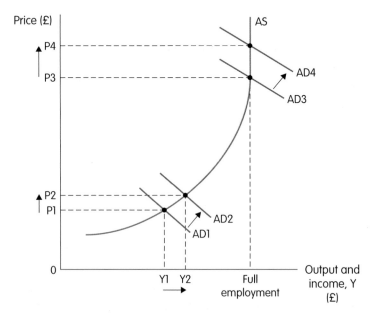

Figure 11.8 The effect of a change in the aggregate demand

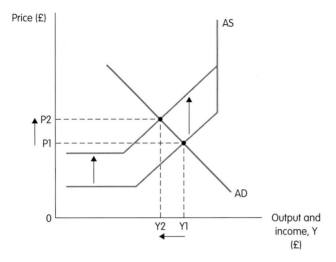

Figure 11.9 The effect of a change in the aggregate supply

If prices are falling, this is known as 'deflation'; this can happen if aggregate demand is falling. Falling prices mean that profit margins of businesses may be squeezed and this leaves less funds for the owners and for investment. Managers may seek to reduce costs to cope with falling prices. This may be through policies aimed at reducing waste, getting better prices from suppliers and seeking productivity improvements (perhaps by employing less staff).

? **Think about it...**   **11.8**

1. Explain two reasons why aggregate demand might be falling.

2. An increase in which of the following is most likely to lead to an increase in inflationary pressure?

   A Savings.
   B Imports.
   C Exports.
   D The exchange rate.

  Business Analysis   **11.8**

In 2009, the pound was weak against many currencies due to concerns about the state of the UK economy. This made imports of food expensive and also increased the price of UK-produced food, because the low pound led to more demand from overseas, pulling up prices. These combined effects pushed up UK shop prices of food.

What would the likely effect on inflation be if the pound were to rise against other currencies? Explain your answer.

>> *You Decide ...*

1. Your costs have increased 5 per cent this year. Do you pass this cost increase on to your customers? On what does your answer depend?

2. What would you do if prices in your market were falling by 5 per cent?

? *Think about it ...*   11.9

Explain, using supply and demand analysis, what might have caused the following.

A The fall in gas bills.
B The increase in computer game prices.

The problems of inflation

Inflation is significant because it can have the following effects.

■ *Making planning more difficult* If inflation is unpredictable, for example, it means that, when managers are setting budgets, they will be unsure of what their costs will be and this makes it difficult to forecast profits or cash flow. Unanticipated inflation is likely to deter investment because of the uncertainty that it brings. Less investment may damage the long-term growth of the economy.

■ *Reducing consumers' real incomes* If prices are increasing faster than individuals' incomes, then, in real terms, they are worse off: they cannot buy as many products, which can affect future sales of many businesses. The impact of inflation on real incomes will depend on employees' bargaining power: some groups will suffer more than others. Pensioners, for example, often have relatively little power compared to some trade unions and therefore tend to suffer from falling real incomes.

- *Influencing wage demands* If inflation is predicted to be 3 per cent, for example, employees are likely to demand at least this increase in wages to ensure the purchasing power of their earnings. If you had intended to offer your employees only a 2 per cent pay increase, then they will be worse off in real terms and this might affect your relations with them as they bargain for more. It might even lead to industrial action if employees continue to want more money than you are prepared to offer. If you do increase their pay, this will lead to even higher costs, which might lead to higher prices, which then leads to higher demand for pay—a phenomenon known as the 'wage–price spiral'.

- *Squeezing profit margins* If inflation occurs, a business may find that its costs are rising to a greater extent than it feels it can increase the prices of its products. This means that its profit margins may be squeezed, reducing funds for investors and further investment.

- *Reducing the international competitiveness of an economy* If inflation is higher in one country than it is in others, this will mean that its products are relatively more expensive, which could reduce its exports.

The effects of inflation on individuals and on businesses depend partly on whether it is anticipated or unanticipated.

- *Anticipated inflation* If individuals and businesses know that inflation is occurring, they can try to take suitable steps to prepare. For example, employees may bargain for pay increases to maintain their real wages. Individuals may look for savings accounts that offer interest rates that match or exceed the expected inflation rate. Businesses can adjust their prices and try to negotiate with suppliers to keep prices fixed. If interest rates and wages are growing with inflation, then, in real terms, they are staying constant.

- *Unanticipated inflation* This is inflation that is not expected and for which it has not been planned. This may have more damaging effects than anticipated inflation because it causes uncertainty, which reduces spending decisions; it also means that some people will be caught out by higher-than-expected inflation, making them worse off.

? **Think about it ...** **11.10**

1. What is inflation in your country at the moment?

2. Is it perceived as a major economic problem?

3. What actions do you think the government could take to reduce it?

Analysing inflation

While the CPI and RPI give some idea of what is happening to prices generally in the shops, managers will tend to be more interested in what is happening to prices within their own businesses and sector, and therefore the general measure of inflation may not be appropriate. This is because the headline inflation figure is calculated by measuring the changes in prices in a 'typical basket of goods' bought by a household. Given that the types of purchase of most business are not in a typical basket of goods, this means that the relative inflation rates for your business can be significantly different from the general rate.

Can you now answer question 9 from the opening case study?

Balance of payments

Economic growth, unemployment rates, and inflation rates are all important indicators of success. But businesses and governments will also be interested in how well the country is competing internationally. All countries trade with each other. Individuals and organizations within one country buy products from abroad—that is, imports. At the same time, businesses within a particular country will sell their products abroad—that is, exports. The difference between the revenue earned from exports and the spending on imports is called the 'balance of payments'; this is often used as an indicator of the competitive position of a country. Some economies, such as the UK, are very 'open', which means that international trade is a very significant part of business activity and therefore what happens in international trade is particularly important. Other economies, such as North Korea, are more 'closed', meaning that they are more self-reliant.

The elements of the balance of payments

Governments will not only worry about the overall balance-of-payments position, but they will also be concerned about its composition.

Economic transactions that make up the balance of payments include:

- exports and imports of goods such as oil, agricultural products, other raw materials, machinery and transport equipment, computers, and clothing—for example, the UK has tended to import more goods than it exports;
- exports and imports of services such as international transport, travel, financial, and business services—for example, the UK exports more services than it imports;
- income flows, such as dividends and interest earned by non-residents on investments in the UK and by UK residents investing abroad;
- financial flows, such as investment in shares and loans;
- transfers, such as foreign aid and funds brought by migrants to the UK.

A government will analyse the trends within the overall balance of payments. It may, for example, be concerned if there is a big deficit in relation to goods or services if this suggests that the country's businesses are uncompetitive in these areas. The **balance of trade** specifically measures the difference between a country's exports of goods and services, and its imports of goods and services, if all financial transfers, investments, and the like are ignored. A nation is said to have a 'trade deficit' if it is importing more than it exports. It has a 'trade surplus' if the export revenue is greater than the spending on imports. The UK has had a major deficit in goods for over twenty years, but a surplus in services, reflecting that it is relatively efficient at producing services, such as banking and insurance, and relatively inefficient at producing manufactured goods.

The current account of the balance of payments comprises the balance of trade in goods and services plus the net investment incomes from overseas assets (for example, interest payments, profits, and dividends from assets), and net balance of private transfers between countries and government transfers (for example, UK government payments to help to fund the various spending programmes of the European Union).

For the UK, the net investment income is positive, reflecting major investments overseas by British businesses and individuals. The transfer balance is negative; one reason is that the UK government is a net contributor to the European Union (EU) budget.

Causes of a current account deficit

A deficit on the current account of the balance of payments could be caused by:

- fast economic growth, sucking in imports;
- a high propensity to import, rather than buy domestic products;
- a strong currency, making your products more expensive abroad;
- domestic inflation being higher than inflation overseas, making your products uncompetitive;
- a lack of investment and innovation, reducing the quality of your products;

Business Analysis   11.9

The 'Asian model' of export-led growth explains how economies such as Japan, South Korea, Hong Kong, and Taiwan have grown through trade. The governments in these countries used exports as a method of encouraging economic growth. China also boomed after opening its economy in 1978, using 'special economic zones' designed to attract foreign capital which would allow them to build factories for export production. Countries such as Malaysia, Indonesia and Thailand also relied heavily on exports for growth. Much of Asia has come out of poverty through globalization.

In the last ten years Asia's exports as a share of its GDP have grown from 37 per cent to 47 per cent. Whereas countries such as North Korea which have not focused on exports have remained relatively poor. Whilst some argue against the existence of an 'Asian model', because the region's growth is diverse, for example Hong Kong enjoyed a free economy and Singapore, a controlled one, all have required exports for growth.

Sources: International Monetary Fund, December 2009,
The Economist, March 2009, Bloomberg, July 2009

What do you think might have enabled these countries to succeed at exporting?

 Data Analysis   11.4

The five biggest exporters in 2008 were as follows.

1. Germany (US$1,530,000 million)
2. China (US$1,465,000 million)
3. USA (US$1,377,000 million)
4. Japan (US$766,000 million)
5. France (US$761,000 million)

Source: The World Factbook. Reproduced with kind permission.

Why does the data above not show the balance-of-trade position for these economies?

Reducing a current account deficit

If a government is worried about a current account deficit, it may adopt the following types of policy.

- *Expenditure-reducing policies* These are policies that aim to reduce the total spending in the country. For example, a government may try to reduce aggregate demand by increasing direct taxes, reducing government spending, or increasing interest rates. With less spending overall in an economy, there should be less money spent on imports, which should reduce the deficit. But the consequence is also less spending throughout the economy, which may lead to slower growth and higher unemployment.

- *Expenditure-switching policies* These are policies aimed at reducing the spending on imports specifically. These could include protectionist measures that protect domestic businesses against foreign competitors. For example, a tax on foreign products makes them relatively more expensive, making customers switch away, or a quota limiting the total number of foreign products sold in a country. But the consequence of these policies is less choice and more expensive products for customers.

? **Think about it ...** 11.11

What determines the effectiveness of a tax on foreign producers in terms of reducing spending on imports?

>> **You Decide ...**

As a manager, do you think that the amount of imports into a country should be limited?

A government might also try to stimulate exports and reduce import spending by reducing the value of its currency. It can do this by cutting interest rates and/or selling its own currency. When a currency falls in value, this will make its products cheaper in terms of foreign currency, making the country more competitive. This should lead to an increase in the quantity demanded of exports and an increase in spending on exports. The extent of the increase in export earnings will depend on the price elasticity of demand for exports: the more price elastic demand is, the greater the increase in export sales and earnings.

But the decrease in the value of the currency also increases the price of imports in the domestic currency. As we have seen in Chapter 6, the effect on spending on imports depends on the price elasticity of demand for imports. If demand for imports is price elastic, sales will fall by more than the price increase (in percentages) and spending on imports will fall.

This means that if demand for exports is sensitive to price, then a fall in the value of the currency will boost export earnings significantly; if demand for imports is price elastic, import spending will fall and so, overall, the balance of trade has improved. The importance of the price elasticity of demand for exports and imports is highlighted by the 'Marshall-Lerner condition', which states that if the price elasticity of demand for exports (PED exports) plus the price elasticity of demand for imports (PED imports) is greater than one, then a fall in the value of a currency will improve the balance of trade—that is:

PED exports + PED imports must be greater or equal to 1

Think about it ...   **11.12**

If the Marshall-Lerner condition is not met, what do you think happens to a country's current account position on the balance of payments if its currency falls? Explain your answer.

 # Data Analysis   **11.5**

A 10 per cent increase in the value of a currency leads to a 5 per cent fall in export sales and a 2 per cent increase in import sales.

1. What are the price elasticities for exports and imports?
2. Is the Marshall-Lerner condition met?

Can you now answer questions 3 and 4 from the opening case study?

Conflicting objectives

While the action required to improve a country's economic position may seem clear in some areas, the difficulty often comes in trying to achieve all economic objectives simultaneously. An increase in demand may, for example, lead to upward pressure on prices and create demand pull inflation. Faster economic growth may lead to more spending on imports, worsening the current account position. Juggling different demands may therefore cause problems for economic policymakers.

Forecasting economic change

Managers clearly want to try to know what is likely to happen in their key markets to economic variables such as national income, unemployment, inflation, and the levels of exports and imports. This means not only examining past trends, but also forecasting what will happen to these variables in the future. Managers' strategies will want to take account of emerging opportunities and threats, some of which will be created by economic change. Forecasting the economy is therefore an important part of business planning and environmental analysis.

Forecasts may be produced based on past trends and models that have been developed. But an economy is made up of millions of markets, millions of households, and millions of businesses making decisions that can affect each other through a series of complex relationships. Not surprisingly, accurately predicting the economy is far from easy.

>> You Decide ...

If the economy is predicted to enter a recession in two years' time, what might you do now to prepare for it?

 ## Business Analysis 11.10

According to Hal Varian, Professor of Economics at the University of California, who is also Google's chief economist, data on Internet searches can predict some economic statistics before they become available.

Fluctuations in the frequency with which people search for terms and phrases online can help to predict data, such as retail sales and house sales. Search data is captured every day, and so may capture shifts in economic patterns before data is officially recorded and released.

To what extent do you think data on Google searches could be of use to economists and managers?

 ## Data Analysis 11.6

Figure 11.10 shows the UK government's estimates of the economy's growth and highlights that it cannot predict exactly. The darker the shading, the more likely it is that this will be the actual figure. Notice how the further ahead the projection is, the greater the uncertainty that exists.

How useful do you think the data in Figure 11.10 is to managers operating in the UK?

Can you now answer question 10 from the opening case study?

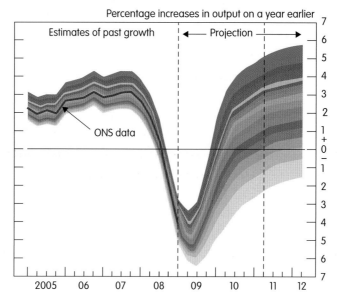

Figure 11.10 Estimates of economic growth

Source: Bank of England

Summary

The main economic indicators that a manager may examine to analyse an economy include GDP, inflation, the balance of payments, and unemployment. Changes in these can indicate shifts in aggregate demand and supply. Managers need to understand the causes and possible consequences of such changes—but forecasting future economic changes is far from easy.

Checklist

Having read this chapter, you should now understand:

- gross domestic product;
- gross national product;
- economic growth;
- the economic cycle;
- a boom and a recession;
- inflation and possible causes of inflation;
- deflation;
- unemployment and possible causes of unemployment;
- voluntary and involuntary unemployment;
- the natural rate of unemployment;
- balance of payments and the current account deficit;
- government actions to achieve its objectives.

Case Study Review

Having read this chapter, you should now be able to answer the following questions.

1. Explain the possible reasons why some countries have negative gross domestic product (GDP) growth, while others have positive. What do you think determines the rate of growth of an economy?

2. What might be the implications of negative economic growth for businesses in that country?

3. Explain the possible reasons for the differences in the current account position shown above.

4. What could the government of a country with a current account deficit do to improve this position?

5. Explain why some currencies might have got weaker against the dollar and some might have got stronger.

6. What are the possible effects on businesses of the changes in the exchange rates shown above?

7. Explain the possible reasons why the unemployment rates between countries vary so much.

8. What could governments do to reduce unemployment rates?

9. Explain the possible reasons why so many countries are experiencing deflation.

10. Compare and contrast two of the economies above in terms of their strengths and weaknesses. Discuss the implications for businesses in these economies in terms of their economic position.

Short Answer Questions

1. What is meant by GDP?

2. Explain the possible implications of a recession for a business.

3. Explain the possible implications of a boom for a business.

4. If inflation falls from 3 per cent to 2 per cent, what is happening to prices?

5. How is inflation measured?

6. What is meant by a balance-of-payments surplus?

7. Explain the possible consequences of high unemployment levels for a business.

8. Explain how the government might attempt to reduce unemployment.

9. Explain how the government might attempt to reduce inflation.

10. Explain the difference between expenditure-switching and expenditure-reducing policies.

Essay Questions

1. What is the best way in which a government can reduce unemployment? Justify your answer.

2. To what extent will a fall in the value of a currency improve a country's current account position?

3. What is the best way in which a government can reduce inflation? Justify your answer.

 One Step Further

Visit our Online Resource Centre at **www.oxfordtextbooks.co.uk/orc/gillespiebusiness/** for test questions, podcasts, and further information on topics covered in this chapter.

International business and trade

12

Learning Objectives

By the end of this chapter, you should:

- ✓ understand the reasons for trade;
- ✓ understand the benefits of trade;
- ✓ be able to explain protectionism;
- ✓ be able to analyse the reasons for and arguments against protectionism.

ⓒ Case Study

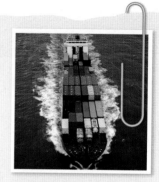

In 2009, the leaders of the major twenty economies in the world (known as the G20) met in London to co-ordinate policies to ensure as fast a recovery as possible from the global recession.

Lord Mandelson, the UK Secretary for Business, gave an informative speech reflecting on the recession and suggestions for how to recover from the credit crunch.

He noted that open trade had significantly contributed to the growing levels of global prosperity and that the rapid growth in developing countries' economies had created huge demand for products from the developed world. He argued that it was this demand which fuelled the economic growth of the past decades and that open trading was necessary to kick-start demand following the impact of the credit crunch.

Whilst praising open trade, he also stressed the importance of ensuring the implementation of suitable policies to protect and help workers, and to enable poorer countries to compete with developed and more advanced countries. Importantly, he emphasized the necessity of ensuring future growth was maintainable and properly governed.

Questions

1. Why do you think open (or free) trade has created rising levels of global prosperity?

2. Why do you think free trade has its critics?

3. Why do you think open trade must be flanked by policies that help workers to adapt to change?

4. Given that free trade 'does not come without costs for industries exposed to greater competition', should governments adopt more protectionist measures?

Introduction

All countries are open economies. This means that businesses and households within an economy are involved in trade with other countries. As a manager, you may source some of your components from abroad; you may even produce abroad. You are also likely to sell some of your products overseas. Understanding overseas markets both from a production and marketing perspective is therefore an important element of business. It has become increasingly important as economies become more inextricably linked to each other via trade and so the success of any one economy depends on others. For example, world trade in manufactured goods and in services has grown far faster than national incomes in the last fifty years, highlighting an increased global dependency on trade. The UK is particularly dependent on trade, with sectors such as communications, finance, and entertainment generating high levels of export revenues.

? *Think about it ...*   12.1

1. What are the main exports of your country?

2. Have these changed over time? If so, why do you think this is?

3. What are the main imports?

Why do countries trade?

International trade occurs when a business, household, or government in one country buys or sells a product from a business, household, or government in another country. An export occurs when a country earns revenue from a sale abroad; an import occurs when money leaves an economy to buy from overseas (see Figure 12.1).

International trade occurs when you can get better value buying a product from abroad than producing it yourself domestically. This occurs when businesses in one country have a **comparative advantage** over businesses in other countries. Comparative advantage occurs when the opportunity cost of producing an item of the same quality is less than it is elsewhere; this means that businesses sacrifice fewer resources to produce an item than other organizations would do. When businesses have a comparative advantage, they are more efficient than their overseas rivals.

Imagine that farmers in the UK wanted to grow bananas: it could be done, but the resources involved to create conditions favourable to banana growing would be so enormous that it would be very inefficient compared to buying these products from a country

Figure 12.1 International trade

that naturally had the climate to grow this type of fruit. Similarly, if a country such as China has enormous resources of relatively cheap unskilled labour, it makes sense for this economy to focus on producing products that use a lot of this resource, while another country focuses on sectors that build on its own resources and skills. The UK, for example, focuses more on finance and the creative industries, in which it has specialist skills. But it is not only 'whole products' that are traded: take apart any laptop and you will find, for example, that the screen is made in one country, the DVD slot in another, the keyboard somewhere else, the hard drive somewhere else, and that all of these are assembled somewhere completely different, as managers seek the best and cheapest place to produce particular elements of their products.

Of course, some products are easier to trade than others. Products such as razors, cigarettes, and perfumes are fairly global because they are essentially the same anywhere in the world. UK football has also become a global product, with a huge number of players and managers in the UK coming from overseas, and many clubs being owned by foreign owners. Other products, such as foods and books, can become global successes, but need to be adapted to meet the tastes, culture, and interests of different regions. Services such as a bus journey, a haircut, and dental treatment cannot be exported because they are not physical items that can be moved globally. (Although the Sultan of Brunei is said to fly his favourite barber from Harrods in the UK to Brunei to cut his hair every few weeks!)

 ## Business Analysis 12.1

Malaysia consists of two regions separated by some 640 miles of the South China Sea. It is one of the region's key tourist destinations, offering excellent beaches and brilliant scenery. The country is among the world's biggest producers of computer disk drives, palm oil, rubber, and timber. It has a state-controlled car maker, Proton.

The country's economic prospects have, however, been hit by the global economic downturn, which has affected its export markets badly. In March 2009, the government unveiled a US$16,000 million economic stimulus plan as it sought to prevent a deep recession.

1. How does Malaysia benefit from trade?
2. Why do you think it is among the world's biggest producers of computer disk drives and timber?
3. What actions might the government take to help the economy in the economic downturn?
4. How might conditions in Malaysia affect UK firms?

Free trade

Free trade occurs when there are no barriers to trade; this means that businesses can easily export or import products, without limits being placed on the nature or level of trade between countries. Free trade would occur if governments were not to intervene and limit trade between countries.

The benefits of free trade are that countries and businesses can specialize in products in relation to which they have relatively low opportunity costs, and buy in other products or resources from abroad.

Free trade means that domestic businesses should produce products for which the cost per unit, given the nature of the product and the level of quality provided, is relatively low compared to businesses in other countries; this should mean that they are competitive and can export abroad.

By specializing and selling abroad, businesses can:

■ grow much faster than they could if they were only to sell domestically, because markets are much bigger; this may enable them to benefit from economies of scale, thereby reducing unit costs even further. The domestic market may be saturated or there may be restrictions on further growth domestically; international trade enables continued sales growth;

■ buy other products from abroad where companies are specializing in areas of expertise at a lower price than the business could produce itself.

? Think about it ... 12.2

1. Can you think of three types of economy of scale from which a business might gain if it were to expand abroad?

2. A business sells its products for £20 and the unit cost is £15. If, through expansion overseas, the unit cost falls to £14, what has happened to its profit margin?

>> You Decide ...

You produce kettles in the UK. Do you think that this is a global product? Will there be many possible export markets?

Trade also means that there will be greater competition within markets, which should encourage innovation and greater efficiency. Businesses have to get better to survive. This should lead to more choice and better products for consumers. Given that businesses are consumers themselves, as they buy inputs, they will also gain from cheaper, better quality supplies. The growth of the Internet has made it easier to find suppliers anywhere in the world; free trade would enable you to buy these supplies unhindered.

Trade can therefore offer enormous benefits to businesses and households. But success abroad cannot be guaranteed over time in any specific market. The ability to compete well in particular products can shift from one company to another when the market changes, or when new technologies make cheaper and better substitute products possible. Producers need to be ready to change and develop in response to new conditions and new opportunities. In 2009, Toshiba produced the last television in the UK. John Logie Baird invented the television in 1926 and, for many years, UK producers, such as Decca, dominated the worldwide industry. In the 1960s, however, Japanese producers, such as Sony and Toshiba, entered the market and were able to produce better quality products at a lower price; over time, they took market share away from UK and US producers. But they continued to produce in the UK, because this was within the European Union (EU) and meant that they had easy access to European markets, until the costs of producing elsewhere become so much more attractive. At that point, Toshiba shifted production to Poland, where costs were lower.

Although the possibility of the export market generates opportunities, international trade also brings threats to individual businesses. While free trade may be in the interest of businesses and households generally, individual firms or industries may suffer due to more efficient production overseas in their sector, which attacks their market share. Open markets also mean that UK companies are vulnerable to being taken over by, or losing market share to, foreign companies.

? *Think about it ...* 12.3

Which of the following are possible benefits of trade to your business?

A Greater export opportunities.

B Greater competition from abroad from low-cost producers.

C Cheaper imported components.

D Economies of scale.

 Business Analysis 12.2

The luxury car company Jaguar announced in 2009 that it would target India as a new market. It will sell the Jaguar XF and XK, as well as Land Rover's Freelander, Discovery, and Range Rover models. Jaguar Land Rover confirmed that it was a strategic move to capitalize on India's 'rapidly expanding market'.

Domestic sales of all passenger vehicles grew 12 per cent in India in 2008, according to the Society of Indian Automobile Manufacturers. BMWs are already being produced in India and Jaguars could be a popular option for the country's expanding middle classes.

Source: Adapted from BBC News, 'Jaguar to target Indian motorists', available online at http://news.bbc.co.uk/1/hi/business/8029092.stm

1. What do you think are the main factors that will determine the success of Jaguar in India?

2. Where else do you think Jaguar cars might sell well? Justify your choice.

The benefits of trade

Imagine, for simplicity, that there are two economies A and B; the table below shows the output of product X or product Y that could be achieved if the resources in the economy were split equally between the two industries X and Y.

Table 12.1

	Product X	Product Y
Country A	40	10
Country B	30	20

The opportunity cost of product X in country A is 0.25 of a unit of Y, because this is how much would be sacrificed for each extra X if resources were moved out of industry Y. If resources were moved out of X and into Y, the country would lose forty units of X and gain ten units of Y, so one unit of X equals 0.25 units of Y.

By comparison, the opportunity cost of one unit of Y is four units of X. If the resources were moved out of Y and into X, the country would lose ten Ys and gain forty Xs, so one Y is equal to four Xs.

By comparison, for country B, the opportunity cost of one unit of X is two-thirds of a unit of Y; the opportunity costs of one unit of Y is 1.5 units of X.

Table 12.2

	Product X	Product Y
Country A	0.25Y	4X
Country B	0.67Y	1.5X

Opportunity cost ratios

There are, therefore, clear differences in the opportunity cost ratios for these two countries. To produce a unit of X, for example, costs 0.25 a unit of Y in country A, but 0.67 units of Y in country B. Country A is therefore more efficient at producing X than country B, because it has the lower opportunity cost. If there is free trade, country B could buy these units from A for less than it could produce them itself.

The possible terms at which both countries could trade and benefit are given by the opportunity cost ratios, calculated as:

$$0.25Y < 1X < 0.67Y$$

If the rate of exchange of Xs for Ys when the two countries traded lies in this range, they could both benefit. Provided that country A sells each unit of X for more than 0.5 Ys, it will make a profit (that is, it will more than cover its opportunity cost); provided that country B can buy an X for less than 1.67 Ys, it will be cheaper than producing them itself. There are, therefore, **terms of trade** that are mutually beneficial for both countries. A rate can be found that makes the seller a profit and saves the buyer money. This rate is known as the 'terms of trade'. For example, if the terms of trade were to be that one X is equal to 0.5 Ys, then country A could sell and make a profit of 0.25 Ys per sale; country B could buy and save 0.17 Ys per purchase.

If the resources were allocated to the industry in which each country has a comparative advantage (a lower opportunity cost), then the overall outcome would be as follows.

Table 12.3

	Product X	Product Y
Country A	80	0
Country B	0	40
Total	80	40

Output has doubled in the industry to which all of the resources have been transferred. Total world output is eighty Xs and forty Ys thanks to specialization. Before specialization occurred and resources were split in both countries between both industries, the total output was seventy Xs and thirty Ys. With each country concentrating on an industry in which its skills lie, the world output increases by ten Xs and ten Ys; by trading at suitable terms of trade with A selling Xs and B selling Ys, both countries can gain.

 # Data Analysis   12.1

Table 12.4

	Product X	Product Y
Country A	30	10
Country B	40	20

1. Calculate the opportunity cost ratios for each product for each country.
2. What terms of trade might be mutually beneficial?

Trade therefore enables businesses to find cheaper resources and to find export markets that boost its sales. For the economy as a whole, it enables businesses, governments, and households to consume combinations of products outside of its production possibility frontier (PPF).

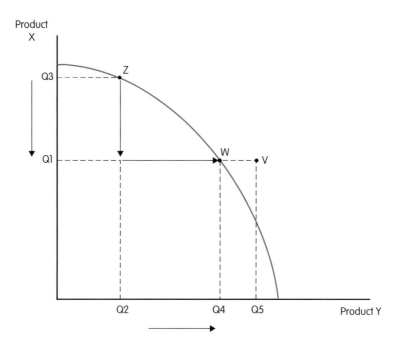

Figure 12.2 International trade and the production possibility frontier

Imagine that an economy was originally producing and consuming at Z, where it has Q3 units of X and Q2 units of Y (see Figure 12.2). If it were to reallocate resources domestically from X to Y, it could move from Z to W on the PPF. Reallocation of resources leads to a loss of output of Q1,Q3 of X and an increase in output from Q2,Q4 of Y. But if these units (Q1,Q3) can be sold abroad at a profit, it may be able to gain, say, Q2,Q5. This means that, by trading, the economy can end up consuming at V, which is outside the PPF.

The case for free trade seems to be proved by the experience of world trade and economic growth since the Second World War. Tariffs on industrial products have fallen steeply since the late 1940s and now average less than 5 per cent in industrial countries. During the first twenty-five years after the war, world economic growth averaged about 5 per cent per year—a high rate that was partly the result of these lower trade barriers. World trade grew even faster, averaging about 8 per cent during the period. The data therefore seems to show a definite statistical link between freer trade and economic growth.

In other words, trade policies that allow the unrestricted flow of goods and services make markets more competitive, and should lead to the best products being available at the best price.

Business Analysis   12.3

Uganda is aiming to focus on commercial agriculture as a way of boosting its economic growth, but it remains very dependent on financing by overseas governments. The Ugandan government believes that the country's comparative advantage in food production is the best immediate opportunity for achieving economic growth. The government wants Uganda to become the region's 'food basket' and to use its location to develop as a regional trading hub. Economic policy initiatives will aim to increase agricultural production and productivity, increase agro-processing and value added, and make the investments in infrastructure and human resources to bring this about.

- Pests and diseases, lack of inputs and technology, and the weather have been identified as the biggest constraints to the intended strategy. To address these problems, the government will provide various vaccinations for cattle and poultry; twenty-five new crop varieties will be introduced; and 20 million disease-resistant coffee seedlings and 4,000 tonnes of cotton seeds will be made available. Drought is to be tackled by the construction of dams and piped storage facilities.

- In the area of transport and communications, the roads sector will receive the largest budget and the work will create more than 100,000 jobs. The emphasis on the maintenance and building of roads will be continued, including the upgrading to tarmac of more than 1,000 km of national network.

- In the area of energy infrastructure, the first generating units of the Bujagali power project will come on stream in December 2010. Mini-projects will continue to be used to mitigate short-term power shortage problems.

What factors do you think are likely to determine the success of the strategy outlined above?

 You Decide ...

You have decided to expand your coffee retail business overseas. What should you consider when deciding which country to target?

Data Analysis   12.2

Table 12.5   Shares of regional trade flows in world merchandise exports, 2007

| | | | Destination (% share) | | | | | |
Origin	World	North America	South and Central America	Europe	CIS	Africa	Middle East	Asia
World	100.0	100.0	100.0	100.0	100.0	100.0	100.0	100.0
North America	13.6	37.8	29.0	5.5	3.1	7.7	10.4	10.7
South and Central America	3.7	6.0	27.1	1.8	1.6	3.9	1.9	2.4
Europe	42.4	18.2	17.8	71.2	47.7	41.6	31.7	13.2
CIS	3.7	0.9	1.4	4.8	26.0	1.9	3.4	1.8
Africa	3.1	3.7	3.2	2.8	0.2	11.4	2.2	2.5
Middle East	5.6	3.3	1.0	1.8	1.2	7.8	19.3	12.1
Asia	27.9	30.1	20.5	12.0	20.1	25.7	31.2	57.4

Source: WTO

Look at the table above, which shows the shares of regional trade flows in world merchandise exports during 2007.

Choose one region and summarize its pattern of exports. What factors do you think determine the regions to which exports are made?

The importance of clusters

Michael Porter, a well-known business analyst, highlighted the importance of business clusters in determining the comparative advantage of a region or country in *The Competitive Advantage of Nations* (1990). A 'business cluster' is a geographic concentration of interlinked businesses, suppliers, and associated organizations in a particular sector. These organizations can share expertise and resources, and can collaborate and benefit from synergy. Clusters, claims Porter, improve innovation and productivity. Successful clusters include Silicon Valley in the USA, the City of London as a financial centre, and Northern California and Bordeaux in France as wine regions.

The benefits of clusters can change over time. Near Birmingham in the UK, for example, the cluster of car-industry service firms that developed when the city was a big car producer has now become an important element in the development of Formula One and other specialist vehicle businesses.

According to Porter:

'The UK needs to mount a sustained programme of cluster development to create a more conducive environment for productivity growth and innovation through the collective action of companies and other institutions ... It will be essential to mobilise businesses and business institutions that are willing and able to engage in the upgrading of their clusters.'

>> *You Decide ...*

You are an advertising agency. Should you aim to locate near other advertising agencies or not?

? *Think about it ...*   12.4

How do you think the government could encourage clusters?

What determines what and how much a country exports?

Exports are a key part of aggregate demand for many countries such as the UK. Export markets provide enormous opportunities for businesses to boost their sales. This is because doing so:

■ provides access to bigger markets;

■ provides access to faster growing markets;

■ enables a business to grow even if the domestic market is saturated, or of they are not allowed to grow further domestically due to competition policy.

The exports from a country will depend on:

■ the sectors in which it has comparative advantage—that is, the products in relation to which businesses are relatively efficient and which they should be able to sell abroad more cheaply than other companies can produce for themselves;

■ the exchange rate—that is, the value of the currency will affect the price of a country's products abroad (a strong currency makes a country's exports expensive in terms of foreign currencies);

■ the competitiveness of a country's businesses—for example, in terms of design and costs (high labour costs or raw material costs will push up prices, which could dampen competitiveness);

- incomes abroad—that is, the success of one economy is very dependent on the growth of others;
- whether barriers to trade exist—some governments may limit imports into their country.

 Business Analysis   **12.4**

In 2009, China's exports started to fall due to the recessions in many of its trading partners. But the Chinese government lent heavily to businesses to help them to invest and improve their factories and plants. This investment stimulated the economy, making recovery faster than it would otherwise have been.

1. Is it fair for a government to subsidize its businesses? Should your government do the same?
2. How might UK businesses benefit from Chinese growth?

Can you now answer question 1 from the opening case study?

 Data Analysis   **12.3**

The table below shows the leading exporters and importers in world merchandise trade during 2007.

Table 12.6

Rank	Exporter
1	Germany
2	China
3	USA
4	Japan
5	France

Rank	Importer
1	USA
2	Germany
3	China
4	Japan
5	UK

Source: World Trade Organisation.

1. Why do you think Germany is the biggest exporter of goods?

2. Why do you think the USA is the largest importer of goods?

Protectionism

Although there are many potential benefits of free trade, in reality, many barriers to trade between countries do exist—known as **protectionism**.

Protectionism occurs when a government prevents or limits the flow of products from one country to another, for the following reasons.

■ *To protect jobs in a particular industry that is suffering* Over time, the competitive advantage of one country in one industry may fall as new competitors come along; this means that resources have to be shifted into others sectors in which a new comparative advantage may be emerging. This reallocation can take time and can involve unemployment as resources try to shift (for example, employees may lack the necessary skills to move from one sector to another easily). During this period, a government may decide to protect the declining sector to ease, or even halt, the transition process.

■ *To retaliate against actions taken by the other government to limit trade* If, for example, the US government were to place restrictions on European wheat being sold into the USA, then the European governments might place similar restrictions on US wheat being sold into Europe. This is done for political reasons, rather than economic ones. Over the years, there have numerous trade wars over products such as steel, bananas, and T-shirts.

■ *To protect strategic industries that may be thought of as essential to the safety of the economy* For example, the weapons sector may be protected and the government may want to protect some of the food sector to ensure supplies in times of war. Once again, this is a political, rather than an economic, reason for protectionism.

■ *To protect infant industries* When new industries are developing in an economy (perhaps a new technology-based industry), then it will lack the expertise and economies of scale of countries that have been building in this area for a while. Some governments argue that they need to protect their 'infant industries' to help them to grow and be able to compete on equal terms. The danger, however, is that the protectionist measures are never removed, enabling inefficient domestic producers to continue in production. Also, if these industries are viable in the long term, they should be able to raise finance from the private sector. If the government needs to intervene, it suggests either that there are problems in the private-sector financial markets or that the government may be financing industries that are not viable. Providing financial assistance can encourage inefficiency if firms come to rely on such aid, and do not make the changes and improvements necessary to compete in global markets.

Whilst protectionism might appeal to a government in that it enables it to be seen to be acting and doing something—and this may win votes from electors—it does not necessarily benefit their economies. In many cases, the arguments for protectionism are political, not economic, and, in fact, the long-term effect is often damaging to the economy. This is because households and firms end up having less choice of products (because they must rely more on domestic production), and because they will pay more for these products than they could buy them for abroad. By protecting domestic firms, governments are, in effect, subsidizing these businesses and enabling them to be inefficient. But big businesses in some industries are often well organized and can place a great deal of pressure on the government to protect them. Consumers, by contrast, tend not to be well organized and do not group together to give themselves bargaining power, and therefore their interests can be easily overlooked by governments.

Can you now answer question 4 from the opening case study?

Forms of protectionism

There are many different barriers to trade that can be adopted, including the following measures.

- *Tariffs* These occur when a government places a tax on foreign products; this increases their price and therefore domestic customers will tend to switch away towards domestic products. The extent to which customers switch away will depend on the price elasticity of demand.

- Quotas These limit the number of foreign products allowed into an economy. This means that domestic customers have to use domestic businesses if they want to consume more than a given quantity. The lack of competition allows inefficient domestic producers to survive.

- *Administrative regulations* A country can introduce administrative regulations, such as different safety standards, or rules about which ports or airports can be used to import products (which, in effect, limits the quantity that can enter a country in a given time). Indonesia, for example, has specified that certain categories of good, such as clothes, shoes, and toys, can only be imported through five ports, thereby restricting quantities coming in. Argentina recently imposed discretionary licensing requirements on car parts, textiles, televisions, toys, shoes, and leather goods; licences for all of these used to be granted automatically. Some countries have imposed outright import bans, often justified by a tightening of safety rules or by environmental concerns. For example, China has stopped imports of a wide range of European food and drink, including Irish pork, Italian brandy, and Spanish dairy products. The Indian government has banned Chinese toys.

- *Subsidies* A government can subsidize its own businesses, which reduces their costs and enables them to undercut some foreign producers. This, again, is subsidizing inefficient local producers who could not otherwise compete against foreign businesses. The funds for these subsidies have to be raised from somewhere and the consequences of this (for example, in the form of higher taxes) have to be considered when looking at the overall effects of subsidizing. From a consumer's point of view, however, a subsidy does have the advantage of not directly increasing the price of the products (unlike a tariff). Protectionist subsidies that governments have used include funding for peanut farmers in the USA and subsidies for sugar beet farmers in the EU.

One issue that has arisen in recent years is the protectionism that it is claimed developed countries use in relation to developing countries. Many poorer nations claim that richer nations demand access to their resources, but make it difficult for developing countries to sell their products in the richer economies.

 Data Analysis   12.4

The effect of a tariff on demand depends on the price elasticity of demand. If a 5 per cent increase in price reduces the quantity demanded by 8 per cent, what is the price elasticity of demand? Is demand price elastic or inelastic?

 Business Analysis   12.5

In 2009, trade unions that were fighting to save the last steelworks in the Teeside region of the UK asked the UK government to consider subsidizing the business. The plant's owner, Corus, said that it wanted to mothball the facility, because of a drop in demand for steel. Analysts forecasted that the steel market would recover in due course. Unions representing workers on Teeside were worried that the blast furnace would be too expensive to reactivate if a temporary shutdown were to go ahead. The union believed that the government should intervene to save the industry.

Do you think that the government should intervene and subsidize this business?

 You Decide ...

You are the manager of a business suffering from losing sales to foreign producers. What is the best way of getting government support do you think? What could you argue to the government to gain its protection?

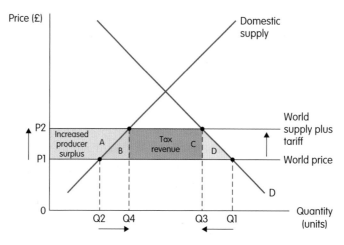

Figure 12.3 The effect of a tariff

The effect of a tariff

A tax placed on foreign products will increase the costs of overseas producers. Imagine that there is a world price for a product of P1 and then a tariff is added on: this would shift the supply upwards, meaning that a higher price needs to be paid for the product on the world market (P2 in Figure 12.3). The effect of this is to lower the quantity of products demanded, but increase the quantity supplied by domestic producers.

The effect of the tariff is to:

- raise the price in the market from P1 to P2 (so that domestic businesses and households pay more for products), which reduces the consumer surplus by ABCD.

- allow inefficient domestic producers to produce when they could not have done without the tariff (because the higher price enables them to cover their higher costs), meaning that the domestic producer surplus increases by area A and B represents the payment for inefficiency;

- transfer money from consumers to the government, because of the tax paid on the foreign goods (area C).

When analysing the overall effect of a tariff, it is also important to consider what happens to this tax revenue and how it is used elsewhere in the economy.

 Business Analysis   12.6

In April 2009, the World Bank accused the USA and EU of carrying out or planning protectionist measures, despite a recent pledge not to do so. These measures included new taxes on Chinese candles, and iron and steel pipes. The USA had already introduced limits on Canadian wood and citric acid from China.

1. Why do you think these protectionist measures might have been introduced by the USA and the EU?

2. Do you think that they are a good idea?

The effects of introducing a quota

In the free market, the world price is P1 and the quantity consumed is Q2. A quota limits the amount of imports to Q3,Q4 and, as a result, with less quantity available, the world price increases to P2 (see Figure 12.4). This increases the amount produced domestically to Q3. As with a tariff, a quota allows inefficient domestic producers to survive.

>> You Decide ...

You are a producer of consumer electronics. You are losing a significant amount of market share to foreign producers.

Would it be right for you and other domestic companies in this industry to lobby government to introduce a quota on foreign producers?

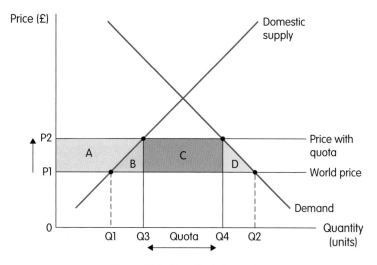

Figure 12.4 The effect of a quota

Trading blocs—free trade areas and customs unions

To promote more free trade among themselves, some countries have joined together to create areas in which any barriers to trade are removed (or are to be removed over time); these are called 'trading blocs'.

If there is an agreement between countries simply to remove barriers between them, but to allow members to adopt whatever policies they want with other non-member countries, this is known as a 'free trade area'. If the member countries have free trade between them and also agree to have a common policy, such as a tariff, against all non-member countries, this is known as a 'customs union'.

 Business Analysis   12.7

In 2008, China and Singapore signed a bilateral (two-way) free trade agreement (FTA) after two years of negotiation. This agreement covered trade in goods, rules of origin, trade in services, the movement of people, investment, customs procedures, technical barriers to trade, and economic cooperation. Trade between the two countries had reached US$47,150 million the year before.

Singapore is China's eighth largest trade partner and the seventh largest investor. 'It is important for Asian countries to work together, exchange wills, and maintain the dynamic and stamina which characterize the past decades of Asia development,' said the Prime Minister of Singapore.

What do you think are the benefits for businesses in Singapore of an FTA?

The EU, for example, is a customs union made up of twenty-seven countries with freedom of movement of goods, services, people, and capital between them (see Figure 12.5). The EU has a population of nearly half a billion, providing a large market for UK producers, as well as a good source of supplies. The lack of trade barriers means that the EU represents a huge potential market for UK producers that is relatively easy to enter. It provides a market for over 50 per cent of UK exports.

Other examples of free trade areas include:

- the North American Free Trade Agreement (NAFTA), which was negotiated in 1994 involving the governments of Canada, Mexico, and the USA, and which covers environmental and labour issues, as well as trade and investment;
- the Central American Free Trade Area (CAFTA), which includes Guatemala, Honduras, Nicaragua, El Salvador, Costa Rica, and the Dominican Republic;
- Mercado Común del Sur, or the Southern Common Market (Mercosur), which is an FTA between Brazil, Argentina, Uruguay, Venezuela, and Paraguay;

Figure 12.5 Current and prospective EU member states

■ the Association of South-East Asian Nations (ASEAN), which aims to bolster economic growth among its ten members—that is, Thailand, Indonesia, Malaysia, the Philippines, Singapore, Brunei, Vietnam, Laos, Burma, and Cambodia—and to promote peace and stability across the region. ASEAN aims to create a single market by scrapping tariffs and removing barriers to trade.

? *Think about it...*   *12.5*

1. Is your country a member of a trading bloc?

2. What do you think determines whether a country is willing to join a trading bloc or not?

Trade creation and trade diversion

Within a customs union, member countries usually trade more among themselves due to the reduced barriers to trade. 'Trade creation' occurs when, having joined a free trade area with trade barriers removed, producers can buy products more cheaply from suppliers in member countries compared to domestic suppliers. The removal of tariffs, for example, may make supplies available more cheaply from member states than local suppliers.

Trade diversion may also occur when a country joins a customs union. This is when trade is switched from other lower cost countries towards more expensive members of the agreement; products may be cheaper from outside the customs union, but the tariff makes them more expensive, so producers switch to member-country producers. The result is that producers may now pay more than they would have done before the country joined the customs union.

Imagine that a product from a member country costs £10, but would cost £9 from a non-member without a tariff. If the tariff increases the non-member's price to £12, you will switch to the £10 option, even though the product is more expensive than you could have bought it for before joining the union; this is 'trade diversion'.

>> **You Decide ...**

Should your business focus on trading with other member countries in your trading bloc?

Organizations affecting world trade

The importance of world trade to the growth of the world economy and the increasing trade links that exist between countries mean that trade is a key economic issue. As a result, governments often belong to various trade agreements, or join customs unions to enable their countries to benefit from importing and exporting. There are also various international organizations that exist to facilitate trade, and to try to ensure that it continues to grow and that economies remain relatively stable.

? **Think about it ...**   12.6

Why do you think industries such as steel and agriculture are often protected?

The World Trade Organization

The World Trade Organization (WTO) was established on 1 January 1995, but grew out of the General Agreement on Tariffs and Trade (GATT), which was started in 1948. The aim of the WTO is to reduce barriers to trade worldwide. Whereas GATT had mainly dealt with trade in goods, the WTO and its agreements now cover trade in services and in traded inventions, creations, and designs (that is, intellectual property).

Since GATT was created, there have been nine rounds of trade negotiations between member countries. At first, these focused on lowering tariffs (customs duties) on imported goods. As a result of these negotiations, by the mid-1990s, industrial countries' tariff rates on industrial goods had fallen steadily to less than 4 per cent.

The WTO provides:

- a forum in which governments can negotiate trade agreements;
- a place in which to settle trade disputes;
- enforcement of agreed trade rules.

The principles of WTO include the following.

- *Most-favoured nation* (MFN) Under the WTO agreements, countries cannot usually discriminate between their trading partners. If a member country grants another country a special favour (such as a lower customs rate for one of their products), it has to do the same for all other WTO members.
- *National treatment* Treating foreigners and locals equally means that imported and locally produced goods should be treated equally. The same should apply to foreign and domestic services, and to foreign and local trademarks, copyrights, and patents.

In the WTO, when countries agree to open their markets for goods or services, they 'bind' their commitments. For goods, these bindings amount to ceilings on customs tariff rates. One of the achievements of the Uruguay Round of multilateral trade talks was to increase the amount of trade under binding commitments. In agriculture, 100 per cent of products now have bound tariffs. The result of all of this is a substantially higher degree of market security for traders and investors.

The International Monetary Fund

The International Monetary Fund (IMF) is an organization of 186 countries, working to:

- bring about greater global monetary cooperation;
- secure financial stability;
- facilitate international trade;
- promote high employment and sustainable economic growth;
- reduce poverty around the world.

The IMF monitors the economic position of countries and provides economic policy advice. It also lends to countries that are in difficulty, and provides technical assistance and training to help countries to improve their economic management.

Assessing overseas markets

Selling abroad can be a means of growing your business. Many multinationals, such as Sony and Unilever, have been targeting the emerging economies, such as China and

Business Analysis   12.8

In 2009, the IMF announced that Ghana was to get a US$600 million three-year loan, amid concerns about the impact of the recession on poorer countries. It will also be able to draw up to US$450 million from the IMF through a special facility.

Ghana needs funds to reduce its budget deficit and support its currency. It has been hit by high food and fuel prices, an energy crisis, and heavy spending before last year's elections. But the Ghanaian economy has proved 'relatively resilient', the IMF said, supported by the high prices of cocoa and gold. The extra US$450 million will come from the money that Ghana and others have deposited in the fund. These are held as 'special drawing rights'—that is, a basket of currencies composed of the dollar, euro, yen, and pound, from which members can borrow.

Ghana is the world's second biggest cocoa producer, Africa's second-biggest gold exporter, and is also set to become the continent's newest oil producer.

Sources: BBC News, 'Ghana secures $600m loan from IMF', available online at http://news. bbc.co.uk/go/pr/fr/-/1/hi/business/8155374.stm, www.imf.org, Reuters, July 2009

1. Why do you think the IMF is willing to lend to Ghana? What restrictions might it place on the lending?

2. How might the health of the Ghanaian economy affect producers in your economy?

India, as a critical part of their long-term strategy, because this is where they see fast sales growth coming from rather than the more mature markets of Europe or the USA.

As with any market, assessing an international market will involve forecasting its size and growth, and calculating the likely costs of entry. Managers need to estimate the likely return on the investment to determine whether investment is desirable. Factors such as the market share and power of existing firms, their likely reaction to a new entrant, and the risk involved in competing will all be worth considering. In international markets, understanding the cultural issues of a market may prove particularly difficult because of greater differences in buying habits, management styles, and ways of doing business. International business may also involve exchange rate issues, which can make planning more difficult: an increase in the value of your currency may make your products more expensive in foreign currencies and this may reduce sales; it would also make imports from overseas competitors cheaper in pounds, which might make domestic customers switch to them. Given the instability of some currencies and the significant changes in value there can be in relatively short periods of time, this can make business planning very difficult and means that a significant influence on business success can be out of managers' direct control.

>> *You Decide ...*

Imagine that you are a major UK-based clothes retailer. You are considering expanding retail operations overseas. What would be the key factors to consider when choosing which markets to target?

Entering overseas markets

Initially, many businesses first sell abroad by exporting some of their products. They may, for example, receive some enquiries from abroad and send their products in response to these requests. At this stage, there is no risk involved in selling abroad. But if interest in selling abroad continues, managers might consider the following options.

- *Using an agent to represent the business abroad* This would mean hiring someone who understands the market well and who may be able to generate more business for you. The agent will usually take a percentage of the sales.
- *Forming a partnership or venture with a local business* For example, the overseas business might help you to distribute, or you might share product development. The advantage, again, is using a business that knows the market well, which reduces the risk of operating in unfamiliar markets.
- *Taking over an existing business in that country* This can be a fast way of entering a market, but, inevitably, it is quite risky, because of the cost and expense of buying an existing business, and the possible operational and cultural issues involved in acquiring and running a new company.
- *Setting up your own operations abroad* This is the most risky option, because it involves major investment and relies on your understanding of local conditions.

The method of entering a market that is chosen by a manager will depend on factors such as the likely level of sales and return, the extent to which the market is unfamiliar, and the degree of risk that a manager is willing to take.

>> *You Decide ...*

You are the manager of a soft drinks business wanting to expand abroad. What do you think is the best method of entering an overseas market?

Business Analysis   12.9

In 2008, Coca Cola made a US$2,500 million bid for the Chinese juice company Huiyan. China is the world's fastest growing drinks market. The bid was three times the existing share price just before the offer was made. Huiyan had a 44 per cent market share by sales value in China's pure juice sector and 42 per cent of the nectar sector in the first half of 2008, according to data from research firm AC Nielsen. The deal was eventually prevented by the Chinese government, which wanted to protect its own firms.

1. Why would Coca Cola want to buy Huiyan and be willing to pay so much for it?
2. Why would the Chinese government not want to allow a bid such as this?

 ## Business Analysis   12.10

'In 2003, 24 per cent of our Group sales, or $2.5 billion, was outside India, and most of that was exports. Five years on, more than 60 per cent of our Group sales is outside India, and that is $38 billion (an increase of 1,400 per cent). Not only has the size of the international business grown, but so has the nature of that business changed, as more senior management, research and development and manufacturing are located offshore, rather than a simple export model. Five years ago, Tata Steel had a capacity of 3.5 million tonnes per annum (mtpa) in one plant in India, and 100 per cent of its board, management and employees were Indian. Today Tata Steel has a capacity of 26.5mtpa (making it No 6 globally); its primary production is in India, the UK, the Netherlands and Singapore; 55 per cent of the staff are non-Indian and 35 per cent of the Board are non-Indian.

Five years ago, Tata Chemicals was a $300m business, 98 per cent of which was domestic India. Today Tata Chemicals is a $1.7 billion business, 30 per cent of which is overseas. It is the world's number two soda ash player with production in the US, UK, the Netherlands, Kenya and India.

The development of new products like the Nano and the World Truck, together with overseas assembly in key markets, and the acquisition of JLR and Daewoo Commercial Vehicles has transformed Tata Motors into a major integrated automotive company.

Tata Steel has major R&D capability in the UK as well as India, while Tata Motors has product technology and design facilities in the UK and Korea as well as India.'

Over the past five years, the Tata Group has been transformed a second time under Mr Tata's leadership. The first transformation was a domestic one, earning the right to survive global competition; the second transformation has been international, making it India's first true multinational.

Source: Adapted from Tata Annual Report 2008

1. Why do you think Tata wanted to become global?

2. What problems is it likely to have encountered?

The business implications of trade

Trade opens up new markets and therefore new opportunities for business. The EU, for example is a customs union, which means that there is free movement of goods, services, people, and money among member countries. This makes trade easier because there are no barriers within it: if you can sell a product in Liverpool, you can also export it and sell it in Berlin, Barcelona, and Toulouse.

Trade also creates opportunities in the form of cheaper production bases and cheaper materials. By producing in China, for example, a UK manufacturer pays far lower wages on average, and this brings down the costs and increases profits. This is why companies such as Hornby and Dyson have switched production overseas, and why other companies outsource aspects of their production, such as their call centres, abroad. The fixed costs of production will be lower if rents and overheads are lower.

But trade also brings threats to individual businesses. While free trade may be in the interest of businesses and households generally, individual firms or industries may suffer due to more efficient production overseas in their sector, which attacks their market share. Open markets also mean that UK companies are vulnerable to being taken over by foreign companies. Many 'UK' businesses are actually foreign-owned (such as Jaguar being owned by the Indian business Tata, BAA and O_2 by Spanish business Ferrovial, P&O by Dubai Ports, and Manchester United by Canadian Malcolm Glazer).

Trade and the recession

In the recent global recession, world trade slowed down. With lower incomes, households, firms, and governments bought fewer products from abroad. This then contributed to slower growth in these countries, which reduced their ability to import. The recession highlighted how interconnected countries are, with a decline in one having a major knock-on effect on its trading partners (see Figure 12.6).

The recession led to high levels of unemployment in many countries, and demand from producers for subsidies and protectionist measures. (For more on the recession, see Chapter 13.) While there may be some economic arguments for protectionism, the pressure was mainly political, as businesses demanded they be helped and that jobs not be lost.

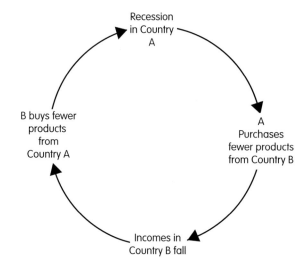

Figure 12.6 The growth of economies is increasingly interrelated

Business Analysis   12.11

In 2008, 11 percent of global capacity—453 container ships were waiting outside the harbours of Hong Kong and other South-East Asian ports. Neither their customers or their hosts needed or wanted them.

Yet just five years ago China's demand meant that even extra ships were needed. Of course this had a huge impact on supply and shipping rates. In fact shipyards were receiving sufficient commissions to actually double the world's fleet. However, all of these ships set sail just as the demand faltered.

After witnessing dramatic increases in the period 2003–2008, charter rates and prices are now back to where they were in 2003. The orders for new ships have disappeared and customers now focus on what can be cancelled rather then what can be bought. Importantly for the shipyard workers, the shipyards have learnt from previous busts and in South Korea demand 20 per cent up front followed by 60 per cent during construction.

Sources: *China Economic Review*, March 2009, *The Economist*, 26 March 2009

1. What other industries do you think would see a major decline due to the global recession?

2. How will the decline in demand affect businesses in these industries?

Summary

Trade between countries is based on the principle of comparative advantage. This means that countries' trade will relate to the sectors in which they have a comparative advantage—that is, a lower opportunity cost. Protectionism occurs when a government tries to protect its own businesses. In a free trade area, barriers to trade are removed. Trade creates opportunities and threats for managers. Trade is hugely important to businesses, both on the supply side and the demand side. Inputs are bought in from abroad, production is outsourced to overseas companies, and products are sold in foreign markets. Understanding what drives trade is therefore vitally important to managers.

Checklist

Having read this chapter, you should now understand:

- free trade;
- comparative advantage;
- opportunity cost;
- the meaning of clusters;
- the meaning of terms of trade;
- the meaning of protectionism;
- the meaning of a quota;
- the meaning of a tariff.

Case Study Review

Having read this chapter, you should now be able to answer the following questions.

1. Why do you think open (or free) trade has created rising levels of global prosperity?
2. Why do you think free trade has its critics?
3. Why do you think open trade must be flanked by policies that help workers to adapt to change?
4. Given that free trade 'does not come without costs for industries exposed to greater competition', should governments adopt more protectionist measures?

Short Answer Questions

1. Explain the link between comparative advantage and opportunity cost.
2. If the opportunity cost ratios for one unit of X are two units of Y in country A and three units of Y in country X, what are possible terms of trade? Explain your answer.
3. Does a high or low exchange rate encourage exports? Explain your answer.
4. Distinguish between a tariff and a quota.

5. Explain how a tariff affects consumers.

6. Explain two reasons why governments introduce protectionist measures.

7. What is the difference between a free trade area and a customs union?

8. Explain two benefits of free trade to businesses.

9. Explain two threats of free trade to businesses.

10. Explain the possible benefits of clusters of businesses in the same industry within a country.

Essay Questions

1. Discuss the benefits of free trade to a country and the businesses within it.

2. Should governments introduce protectionist measures to save jobs within a country?

3. Discuss the effects on different stakeholders of introducing a tariff.

 One Step Further

Visit our Online Resource Centre at **www.oxfordtextbooks.co.uk/orc/gillespiebusiness/** for test questions, podcasts, and further information on topics covered in this chapter.

Current economic issues

13

Learning Objectives

In this chapter, we examine some of the key issues facing businesses and economies at the moment.

By the end of the chapter, you should:

- ✓ understand the causes of an ageing population;
- ✓ understand the possible effects on business of an ageing population;
- ✓ be aware of the causes of the recent economic recession;
- ✓ understand the impact of the recent recession;
- ✓ be able to define corporate social responsibility (CSR);
- ✓ understand the reasons for the increased pressure on businesses to behave in a socially responsible manner.

© Case Study

Officials in Shanghai are urging parents to have a second child—the first time in decades that the government has pushed for more babies. Couples who were both only children, which includes most of the city's newly-weds, are allowed a second child. The move comes as China's most populous city becomes richer and older, with the number of retired residents soaring.

'Shanghai's over-60 population already exceeds three million, or 21.6 per cent of registered residents,' said a spokesman for the city's Municipal Population and Family Planning Commission. The current average number of children born to a woman over her lifetime is less than one.

If the country continues as it is, the proportion of elderly people in society will continue to increase. But central government officials have consistently ruled out changing the national family planning policy. They still believe that China has too many people—an opinion shared by almost everyone in the country.

That has left individual cities, such as Shanghai, to think up ways of coping with their own ageing communities.

Decades of a strictly enforced one-child policy has produced new strains across the population and prompted exceptions in some family categories. Rural parents are also allowed to have a second child, if the first-born is a girl.

By 2020, Shanghai is expected to have more than a third of residents aged 60 or over. According to the US-based Center for Strategic and International Studies, by 2050, the country will have only 1.6 working-age adults to support each retired person, compared to 7.7 in 1975.

Couples who ignore China's birth control policies usually pay fines and may face discrimination at work.

Sources: BBC News, 'Shanghai urges 'two-child' policy', available online at http://news.bbc.co.uk/go/pr/fr/-/1/hi/world/asia-pacific/8166413.stm, *Guardian*, July 2009, *Business Week*, July 2009

Questions

1. Why do you think the population in China is ageing?

2. What problems do you think an ageing population in Shanghai might cause for the local government?

3. What opportunities and threats might be created for businesses in Shanghai as a result of an ageing population?

4. What economic policies has the Chinese government used to limit the number of births in the country? What might determine the effectiveness of these policies?

5. What demographic changes are forecasted to occur in your country over the next twenty years? How might this affect your government and businesses in your country?

Introduction

We began this book by highlighting the importance of the external factors and their impact on business decision making. There have been many significant changes in the external business environment in recent years, such as the rise of the Chinese economy, the growth in the use of IT and e-commerce, and concern over the imbalance of wealth between developing and developed economies.

In this chapter, we focus on three of these important changes in the business environment: the ageing of the world population; the recent global economic downturn; and greater interest in corporate social responsibility (CSR).

Ageing population

A major problem facing many governments now and in the future is the ageing of their populations. At the moment, just under 11 per cent of the world's 6.9 billion population are aged over 60. According to a forecast by the United Nations (UN), by 2050, the proportion of people aged over 60 is likely to rise to 22 per cent of the population, which, by then, will be more than 9 billion people. In developed countries, this proportion will be nearer 33 per cent—that is, one person in three will be a pensioner; nearly one in ten will be over the age of 80. In the next thirty years, for the first time ever, there will be more people in the world aged over 60 than those under the age of 15. These statistics show that a major change is occurring in world demographics.

This ageing of the population has major economic implications for which managers should be prepared. Unlike some changes, this is a long-term one that should, therefore, have been anticipated. Like any change, it creates opportunities and threats.

 Data Analysis 13.1

1. Summarize the key changes in the UK population in Figure 13.1.

2. Which age group is forecast to increase the most between 1983 and 2003?

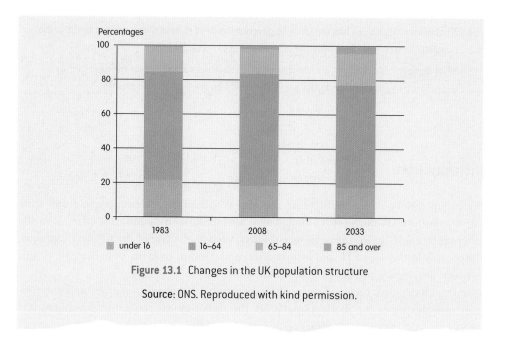

Figure 13.1 Changes in the UK population structure

Source: ONS. Reproduced with kind permission.

Causes of the ageing population

The two main reasons for the long-term increase in the age of the world population are as follows.

■ *An increase in life expectancy* In 1900, the average life expectancy in the world at birth was around 30 years; in developed economies it was nearer to 50 years. Now, the relevant numbers are around 67 and 78 years. Thanks to changes, such as better diets, better sanitation, and improvements in medical care, people are fitter and healthier, and living longer.

■ *A decline in fertility rates* People are having fewer children. In the early 1970s, women, on average, had 4.3 children; now, the average is 2.6. In developed economies, it is only 1.6. This is caused by women pursuing their own careers and having children later, and by greater usage of birth control.

The effect of these two long-term trends has been exaggerated by a short-term impact of the 'baby boom' that occurred in many developed economies after the Second World War. The first of the children born in 1945 are now coming up to their retirement. Over the next ten to twenty years, these baby boomers will be increasing the numbers of pensioners, which provides a short-term surge to the ageing figures.

Obviously, within this general picture of an ageing population, there are major differences between regions and countries. For example:

■ in the more developed parts of Asia, the populations of Japan and South Korea are already facing the challenges of a much older age population;

■ in Europe, some countries, such as Germany, Italy, and Spain, have very low birth rates and so are ageing quickly; others, such as France and the UK, have more children, which keeps them younger;

- in Eastern Europe, birth rates tend to be low (whereas, in the USA, the birth rate is relatively high);

- in most developing economies, the populations are still fairly young, although the decline in birth rates means that, in the future, they will also face problems of an ageing population. One of the few developing countries in which the population is already ageing quickly is China; this is because of government taxes on families having more than one child.

While economies may be at different stages in the process, the effects of an older population are having an impact on most of them and this raises important issues for the government, as well as business.

Can you now answer question 1 from the opening case study?

The economic impact of ageing populations

As people get older and there are fewer young people to take their place in the workforce, economies are likely to grow much more slowly. The size of the working population will shrink, providing fewer resources for the economy. The ratio of people of working age to those of retirement age is expected to deteriorate dramatically over the next few decades. Japan, for example, currently has about three workers to every pensioner, but this number is expected to halve by 2050. Unless developments in other resources, perhaps through technological innovation, can offset the decline in the size of the workforce, economies will inevitably grow at a slower rate. The Organisation for Economic Co-operation and Development (OECD) has forecasted that the decline in growth for its members' countries will fall over the next three decades by a third compared with the previous thirty years, due to ageing populations.

? *Think about it ...*   13.1

1. How is economic growth shown on a production possibility frontier (PPF) diagram?

2. What do you think are the economic consequences of slower economic growth?

3. How might a country allowing greater immigration help to offset the ageing of its population?

An ageing population will have a major impact on a government's financial position. With fewer people working, and greater demands on the pension funds and medical care, a government will be spending more and, at the same time, earning less through income tax. At the moment, state pensions in developed economies are around 7 per cent of gross domestic product (GDP); if the present levels of provision were to continue, this would rise to around 15 per cent by 2050. Add in health care and this would account for around 25 per cent of GDP. These levels of spending are not sustainable, which means that pensions will be lowered and the retirement age will increase, so that individuals have more time to save for themselves. Early retirement may have been possible when, in developed economies, there were only about twenty people of retirement age for every hundred in work, but will be far less possible in the world of 2050, when this is going to be 45 per cent, meaning that there will only be around two employees for every pensioner.

People wanting to maintain a good standard of living in their retirement must now try to save more when they earn and will have to work for longer.

From a firm's perspective, the ageing population therefore means that there are likely to be:

- more taxes imposed by the government to fund increasing levels of health care, which may affect levels of profits and investment;

- demands for better pension provision by companies as the government reduces the funds that it provides; at the same time, companies will struggle to fund generous schemes given the numbers of older ex-employees. Already, many companies are having to reduce their pension schemes because, otherwise, they would not be able to meet their existing obligations;

- a smaller supply of younger workers, meaning that managers must be prepared to widen their 'labour pool' when recruiting and look for older employees;

- changes in demand patterns—that is, shifts in the demographic structure of a population create marketing opportunities for businesses, provided that they react effectively. Some businesses, such as Saga, clearly target older buyers already; other firms have started to adjust their product range to tap into this increasingly important market segment. The Volkswagen Golf Plus, for example, has higher seats, making it easier for older people to get into the car. An ageing population will create growth in some markets, such as health care, while reducing demand for other products, such as children's toys. Managers will need to be aware of such changes, and consider their product mix and marketing strategies accordingly.

Can you now answer questions 2 and 3 from the opening case study?

?   Think about it ...   13.2

1. How might the marketing mix of a health club have to change, given an ageing population?
2. Illustrate the effect in the labour market of a fall in the supply of labour.

Business Analysis   13.1

According to Eurostat, which collects data across the European Union's twenty-seven member states, there are now four people of working age (that is, aged 15–64) in the EU for every person aged 65 or older. By 2060, the ratio is expected to fall to two to one.

The good news is that this provides an opportunity for investors who can find sound companies that provide goods and services catering to the needs of an ageing population.

Sectors that should benefit from this trend should include the following.

- *Health care* With a rapidly ageing population and lengthening lifespans, the demand for medical intervention and care is going to increase. There will more demand for drugs to treat diseases and procedures to cure problems to which the old are particularly prone (that is, operations such as hip replacements).
- *Personal security (physical and financial)* An older population is going to be more concerned with issues of personal security, whether that is related to fear of crime or personal injury due to falling. They will also be greatly concerned about living in poverty due to inadequate pension provision.
- *Retailers offering goods and services to senior citizens* This will include everyone from publishers of books and cruise operators, to funeral directors. For example, with more old people, there is obviously set to be an increase in the number of infirm and they will eventually die. Hence, there will be an increase in provision of care homes and funerals.

Source: Adapted from The Motley Fool, 'Profit from an aging population', available online at http://www.fool.co.uk/news/investing/company-comment/2009/06/11/ profit-from-an-ageing-population.aspx

Can you think of any other industries that will gain and any that are likely to shrink as the population gets older?

 Data Analysis   13.2

Show, using supply and demand analysis, the effect on a market of the following.

A A decline in demand due to an ageing population.

B An increase in demand due to an ageing population.

>> **You Decide ...**

1. Is an older workforce better than a younger workforce?
2. What do you think is the best way in which to reward and motivate an older workforce?

Corporate social responsibility

One aspect of business that has been the focus of an increasing amount of media and pressure group attention is Corporate Social Responsibility (CSR). This refers to an approach to business in which managers try to meet the needs of their stakeholders rather than focus only on their shareholders. For example, CSR may include more attention to the quality of working life of employees, better treatment of suppliers, investment in the community, and thinking about the role of your business as an important contributor to the welfare and wealth of society. Marks and Spencer plc, for example, has developed what it calls 'Plan A' (because, it says, 'there is no plan B'), setting out a series of targets relating to social and environmental targets. These include sponsoring the education of underprivileged children, reducing CO_2 emissions, recycling clothes hangers, increasing sales of organic food, and using Fairtrade cotton. According to the UK government, CSR:

> is about how business takes account of its economic, social and environmental impacts in the way it operates – maximising the benefits and minimising the downsides. Specifically, we see CSR as the voluntary actions that business can take, over and above compliance with minimum legal requirements, to address both its own competitive interests and the interests of wider society.

An important point here is that CSR involves actions that go beyond the legal requirements; it involves accepting obligations over and above what the law says a business has to do.

 Business Analysis 13.2

United Utilities is the UK's largest water company. It owns, operates, and maintains utility assets such as water, waste water, electricity, and gas. The business is committed to leading the way in projects that are environmentally friendly. This has been shown by its conversion of sewage treatment into fuel for vehicles and exporting it to the National Grid. Its heat-and-power engines harvest methane from sewage sludge, and, from this, provide electricity and heat for the sewage works, saving nearly £7 million and earning an income of £4.5 million when the excess energy generated is sold.

In the community, United Utilities' employees give more than 20,000 hours to volunteering projects. The company provides climate education programmes to over 18,000 pupils, has raised more than £11 million for Water Aid, and works closely with vulnerable customers on debt issues to help them to sort out their repayments.

The company also works on sustainability projects, including a pioneering £10 million programme to improve the condition of the Peak District and Trough of Bowland water catchment estates. It has also invested heavily in full-time staff at its call centres in place of temporary staff; this has seen the proportion of full-timers increase from 40 per cent to 80 per cent, with a customer satisfaction rating of 80 per cent.

Source: Adapted from Business in the Community

Why might United Utilities have adopted socially responsible policies such as those outlined above?

Given the high levels of interest in the ways in which companies are treating their stakeholders, managers are finding it more difficult to ignore CSR (if they want to do so). Issues such as a company's approach to recycling, its treatment of suppliers, and its investment in the local community are firmly on the agenda of most big companies.

Growing interest in corporate social responsibility

There have always been companies that cared about their role in society. Cadbury's and Unilever both were well known in their early years for the attention that they paid to the treatment of staff. Both companies built small towns that provided accommodation and welfare services for employees, because they believed that business went beyond only profits. But such cases were rare and the general view of businesses has been that they exist for their owners. In recent years, there has been growing interest in the behaviour of companies and CSR has moved much higher up the agenda for managers.

This greater interest is due to:

■ greater awareness by managers, investors, and employees of social issues, such as global warming;

■ greater expectations of business as standards of living rise and customers have more choice, meaning that buyers are increasingly expecting more from a business apart from a 'good' product at a reasonable price; they also want to know where it was made, how it was made, what was used to make it, who made it, and who was affected during the process. Just look in your supermarket at the labels stating 'free range', 'made in Britain', 'no additives', 'local produce', or 'organic', and you can tell how curious and demanding customers are becoming;

■ greater media attention—for example, a story about using child labour can be seen around the world within hours. Companies are generally afraid of being seen to act in an unethical way. Stories about using 'sweat shop' labour, oil spills ruining beaches, or the use of bribes to win contracts can seriously damage a firm's reputation.

This does not mean that CSR is free from criticism, however. Writers such as Milton Friedman believe that CSR distracts managers from their primary purpose. Some argue that it diverts managers' attention away from what they should be focused on, which is the objectives of their investors. These writers believe that investors own the business and therefore managers should not try to second-guess how the funds they generate should be used; they should generate the highest returns possible for investors and let them decide how they want to use the money. Managers should not pursue what they think is socially responsible, because this may not match what investors want to do with the money.

Corporate social responsibility and externalities

In economic terms, CSR involves managers thinking more about the negative external effects and the external benefits of their actions. For example, rather than wait for governments to tax them or for legislation to change to force them to act in a more socially responsible way, more managers are looking to identify the negative impact of their actions and reduce these voluntarily. Over 80 per cent of the biggest 100 companies in the UK refer to CSR in their annual reports. Many businesses, such as BT, BP, and Shell, now conduct social and environmental audits to assess the impact of their actions on society, and measure their progress in these areas.

Data Analysis
13.3

1. Draw a diagram showing a negative externality.

2. Draw a diagram showing a positive externality.

3. What is the effect on the equilibrium price and output relative to the socially optimal level of the following?

   A A negative externality.

   B A positive externality.

The benefits of corporate social responsibility

The benefits to a business of being more socially responsible may include the following.

■ *Attracting more staff* More employees are now concerned about the values of an organization and may be attracted by a socially responsible attitude. Businesses nowadays depend a great deal on their employees and some managers talk of a 'battle for talent' to get the best staff. Companies such as Microsoft, Google, Sony, and Coca Cola want the most able employees, and a reputation for socially responsible behaviour may prove an important factor in employees' decisions.

- *Attracting more investors* As investors become more concerned about the behaviour of organizations adopting a CSR approach, doing so will be likely to attract more funds.

- *Attracting more customers* Greater interest in the behaviour of firms can lead customers to switch from one supplier to another.

- *Reducing costs* A CSR approach can lead to greater efficiency and less waste. This can reduce costs and boost the possible profits.

There are, however, possible disadvantages as well, in that more responsible behaviour can involve the following.

- *Rejecting some potential orders* For example, to win an order may require unethical behaviour (buyers may ask for a bribe) or may involve the sale of products regarded as undesirable (such as weapons sales); an ethical business may refuse to do business in this way or trade these types of products.

- *Higher costs* For example, it may be possible to relocate production from the UK to China to reduce costs, but this may be regarded as undesirable because of the impact on the local community. Some companies have very strong links with the communities in which they started. Ben and Jerry's ice cream, for example, uses milk from Vermont farmers because this is the state in which the company started up.

Clearly, the effect of CSR on profits is not clear-cut: there may well be a business case for it, but this is not guaranteed. It should be remembered, however, that the primary motive for CSR is meant to be ensuring that a business does the 'right' thing regardless of the effect on profits.

Data Analysis 13.4

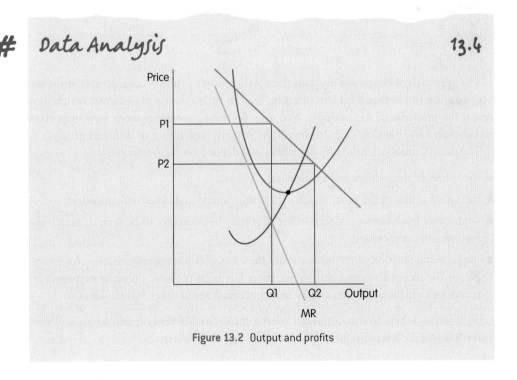

Figure 13.2 Output and profits

Imagine a business produced at Q2, not the profit-maximizing output of Q1, because it wanted to maintain output and jobs in the area. Show the profit being made at this level of output.

Business Analysis   13.3

Research released by the Business in the Community (BITC) organization reveals a statistically significant link between effective management and governance of environmental and social issues and financial performance.

The research clearly shows that companies listed in the Financial Times Stock Exchange (FTSE) that actively managed and measured corporate responsibility issues outperformed other FTSE companies in terms of the total return to shareholders by between 3.3 per cent and 7.7 per cent throughout the period 2002–07.

The chief executive of Business in the Community, said:

Now more than ever, businesses need to demonstrate that corporate responsibility isn't an overhead but a value creator. This research clearly shows that sustained environmental and social performance does pay dividends – literally.

Source: Adapted from Business in the Community

What do you think determines whether CSR is a value creator or an overhead?

The approach of businesses towards their stakeholders will vary considerably from one organization to another. This can often be seen in their mission statements, which may reveal the priorities of the business. Not only do these statements show how important stakeholders are, but they can also reveal the relative importance of different groups.

The overall approach taken by managers will depend on factors such as:

- the values of the owners and employees;
- the social values of the time, which affects customers' and investors' attitudes;
- what other businesses are doing—that is, it may be necessary to be seen to match the activities of competitors;
- the financial position of the business and the costs of behaving responsibly—for example, in the recent economic downturn, there has been pressure on some managers by investors to focus on profits and be less concerned about other stakeholders.

CSR, it seems, is here to stay, although what it means to different organizations will vary and what specific issues are prioritized may change over time.

The global downturn

The macroeconomic environment is a dynamic one, with changes in economic variables such as government spending, tax rates, interest rates, or the exchange rate happening regularly. As we have seen throughout this book, managers need to understand these economic variables and prepare for, and respond to, economic change. But the global downturn of 2008 and 2009 was on such a scale and occurred so swiftly that few managers (or indeed governments) were ready for it. Whereas the ageing population is a fairly slow shift over many years, the recent recession arrived dramatically, with devastating effects that will be felt for many years to come.

The origins of the crash began in the USA in what is known as the 'sub-prime market'. US banks had been providing loans and mortgages to high-risk individuals; these were potentially very profitable, but the risk of non-payment was high, making these loans 'less than prime' (that is, sub-prime). An increase in loan incentives, such as easy initial payment terms, combined with a long-term trend of rising housing prices, encouraged borrowers to apply for large mortgages, believing that they could meet the repayments and end up with property worth far more than they paid for it. Banks were willing to lend, thinking that an increase in house prices would ensure that they had sufficient collateral.

Problems occurred when US interest rates increased from 1 per cent to 5.35 per cent between 2004 and 2006. This increased repayment costs and led to many borrowers defaulting on their loans. This meant that banks had lost the money that they lent. In the past, this might have been simply a US problem, but given the global nature of business nowadays, it affected banks all over the world. US banks had bundled together millions of mortgages and sold them on to other banks in other countries; this had reduced their own exposure to some extent, but had extended the risk to banks worldwide. The defaults therefore affected financial institutions globally. Warning signs began in July 2007, when the investment bank Bear Stearns announced that many of its investors had lost their money. It gradually became clear quite how many banks all over the word were affected. This, in turn, contributed to an unwillingness to lend, which became known as the 'credit crunch'. Banks were reluctant to lend to businesses and households because they were afraid of the borrowers defaulting; they were also reluctant to lend to each other. Typically, banks lend to each other whenever one needs support; every bank will have times at which the repayments that it receives on its loans do not come at the right time relative to requests from their customers to withdraw their funds. In these instances, banks borrow off each other. At a time when some banks began declaring huge losses, organizations within the financial system became wary of lending to each other. In September 2008, for example, Lehman Brothers announced a loss of US$3,900 million for the three months to August; it collapsed soon after this, sending shockwaves all over the world and throughout the global financial system.

The lack of lending throughout the financial system led to severe reductions in aggregate demand. Households and firms were unable to borrow as much as they wanted, which significantly reduced their spending and investment. In the UK, the recession became official in January 2009, following two quarters of negative growth. The global downturn affected many aspects of economies, including:

- share prices tumbled, reducing the value of individuals' savings and pensions;
- house prices fell, reducing the value of the largest asset of most households;
- many businesses closed or cut back, leading to millions of people worldwide looking for jobs. In the UK, for example, unemployment reached 2.47 million in September 2009, representing 7.9 per cent of the workforce.

The impact of such changes led to great concerns as individuals worried about their jobs, their savings, and their future when they retired. The value of millions of assets was reduced within months.

Data Analysis   13.5

Illustrate the effect of a fall in aggregate demand on prices and output in an economy.

? Think about it...   13.3

Which of the following statements are true and which are false?

A The type of unemployment created by the recession is known as 'structural unemployment'.
B A cut in interest rates is known as 'expansionist fiscal policy'.
C Reducing value-added tax (VAT) means a cut in an indirect tax.
D A recession automatically worsens a government's budget position.
E If banks hold onto a greater percentage of money saved with them, the money multiplier reduces in value.

The economic crisis was so bad that, all over the world, governments decided that they had to step in to encourage banks to lend by helping to provide funds for borrowing. In some cases, governments took a controlling interest in banks to ensure their survival; in many cases, they guaranteed funds or provided financial support. Keeping the financial system liquid and trying to get it lending again was seen as a priority. In the UK, for example, the UK government took a majority stake in the Royal Bank of Scotland (RBS).

In addition, several governments were forced to subsidize some of their domestic industries to keep them in existence and pump money or cut taxes into their economies to encourage spending. In the UK, for example, VAT was cut from 17.5 per cent to 15 per cent to help to stimulate spending and the Bank of England introduced quantitative easing to provide greater liquidity in the economy (see Chapter 10). In the USA, the government agreed to spend US$787,000 million (£548,000 million) to help to boost aggregate demand; President Obama called this 'the most sweeping recovery package in our history'. In China, the government set out a two-year US$586,000 million economic stimulus package, which involved investing in infrastructure and social projects, and cutting corporate taxes.

£ Business Analysis   13.4

The recession in Iceland was deeper than in most developed countries, with a major shrinking of domestic demand. The Organisation for Economic Cooperation and Development (OECD) stressed the need to get the banking system working effectively again for the economy to recover. The Icelandic government had had to rescue the country's three main banks (Kaupthing, Landsbanki, and Glitnir) in 2008, but the OECD recommended that they did not stay in state ownership forever.

After the banks had been privatized in 2003, they had been allowed to grow aggressively without sufficient regulation, increasing their combined assets to around 880 per cent of Iceland's GDP by 2007. The Icelandic economy had traditionally been dependent on fishing, but the banks came to dominate it, until they crashed in 2008. Several UK businesses and councils were affected because they had their savings in these Icelandic banks.

Why do you think that banks all over the world, including Iceland, had made too many high-risk loans?

>> You Decide ...

Do you think that banks should be run by governments rather than being private organizations?

Governments across the world were forced to become far more interventionist than they had been before in a desperate attempt to push up aggregate demand.

Interest rates were also cut to stimulate borrowing. In the UK, the Bank of England's Monetary Policy Committee (MPC) cut interest rates to 1 per cent in February 2009—their lowest ever in the Bank of England's 315-year history.

The seriousness of the problem can be seen by the fact that the governments of the largest twenty economies in the world (known as the G20) met specifically to deal with the problems created by the recession and to try to coordinate their policies to stabilize the global economy.

? Think about it ...   13.4

Explain how a cut in interest rates might stimulate aggregate demand.

 ## Business Analysis   13.5

The recession had dramatic effects in a range of countries and industries. Famous business names teetered in the edge of collapse or did actually fail and governments had to take strong action quickly. Examples of some of the notable occurrences in the recession include the following.

In the USA

- In March 2008, the fifth largest US bank, Bear Stearns, had financial problems and was acquired by rival JP Morgan Chase for US$240 million in a deal backed by US$30,000 million of loans from the Federal Reserve (the US central bank).
- In September 2008, the huge mortgage lenders Fannie Mae and Freddie Mac, which accounted for nearly half of the outstanding mortgages in the USA, had to be rescued by the US government. These organizations had US$5 million million of home loans and could not be allowed to fail. The US Treasury Secretary said that the two firms' debt levels posed a 'systemic risk' to financial stability and that, without action, the situation would get worse. In the same month, the US bank Lehman Brothers had to close after failing to find a buyer. Another US bank Merrill Lynch agreed to be bought by the Bank of America for US$50,000 million.
- In September 2008, the Federal Reserve had to produce a US$85,000 million rescue package for AIG, the country's biggest insurance company, to save it from bankruptcy. AIG got the loan in return for an 80 per cent stake in the firm. Within days, Washington Mutual, a giant mortgage lender in the USA, which had assets supposedly valued at US$307,000 million was closed down by regulators because of its dangerous financial position; it was then sold to JP Morgan Chase.
- In October 2008, US bank Wachovia was taken over by Wells Fargo.
- In January 2009, the giant US banking group Citigroup decided to split into two parts after it reported a quarterly loss of US$8,290 million (£5,600 million).

In the UK

- The Northern Rock bank was first bailed out by the government and then nationalized in February 2008. The bank relied heavily on markets rather than savers for funds and so was hit particularly badly by the credit crunch. When concerns over its financial position became public, this led to a run on the bank as savers withdrew £1,000 million funds in September 2007. The government intervened at this stage to guarantee the savings and later had to take control of the bank.

- Lloyds TSB was allowed to take over the UK's biggest mortgage lender HBOS, which was in financial difficulty in September 2008. The £12,000 million deal was given the go-ahead by the government very rapidly even though it posed competition issues because it created a business that had over one third of the country's savings and mortgages. In the same month, the mortgage lender Bradford and Bingley was nationalized; the government took control of its mortgages, while selling its operations and branches to Santander.

1. Why were the UK and US governments so eager to intervene to help banks?

2. What was the opportunity cost of this intervention?

The recession and the budget position

The recession automatically worsened a government's financial position due to falling levels of tax income and greater spending on benefits. When many governments then took expansionist fiscal actions, this further worsened their budget deficit. This has left a financial legacy in many countries for many years to come. In the USA, the budget deficit in 2009 reached over US$1.8 million million (£1.1 million million)—that is, 12 per cent of gross national product (GNP)—per year. In the UK, the government's overall debt by September 2009 stood at £804,800 million, or 57.5 per cent of GDP; this represented an increase of £172,000 million in the past year, more than £140,000 million of which was due to money spent on helping the banking sector.

The need for governments to spend heavily was regarded as a priority because demand levels were so low. But it does mean that debt levels are extraordinarily high in some countries and, in order to borrow the money needed, governments may have to offer high interest rates increasing the amount that has to be repaid. As a result, in the UK, for example, there is no question that future governments will have to cut back on spending and almost certainly increase taxes in the future. This will undoubtedly affect the quantity and range of public sector services that are provided, and some difficult decisions will have to be made about which services have to be cut or which projects will have to be abandoned. Economists and politicians are, however, still debating when the cuts should occur: cut back on spending too early and economies may not pull out for years to come; keep spending and the consequences, in terms of cutbacks in the future, could be extremely unwelcome and unpopular.

 Business Analysis   13.6

Business, finance, news, and current affairs magazines sold well during the global slowdown, with titles such as *Moneyweek*, *The Economist*, and *The Spectator* all growing in terms of their year-on-year circulation figures. In the final six months of 2008, business and finance magazines increased their collective circulation by over 70 per cent compared to the year before (although this included the entrance of a new title called *Sense* into the market during this period). *Moneyweek* was the best performer in this sector of the magazine market, with sales up over 16 per cent. *The Economist*'s global growth was over 6 per cent, increasing total worldwide circulation to 1,390,780.

Business magazines are not the only products to do well in a recession. Google continued to go from strength to strength and, according to Interbrand, it has become one of the most valuable brands in the world. Google now dominates the global search market and has expanded into software, video, email, mapping, and web browsing. Interbrand values its brand at US$31,980 million.

Clothing retailers Zara and H&M also saw sales rise despite the recession, and even luxury brands such as Ferarri have done well.

1. Why do you think business magazines have done well in a recession?
2. What other products do you think might have sold well in a recession?

? Think about it ...   13.5

Which of the following products will experience the greatest fall in demand in a recession? Explain your answer.

Table 13.1

Product	Income elasticity
A	+2
B	+0.2
C	−1.2

Regulation and intervention

The economic crisis has raised important issues regarding the extent to which financial markets should be left to themselves and how much the government should intervene. In the UK, for example, the role of the Financial Services Authority (FSA) has been closely scrutinized, with concerns raised over the way in which it allowed banks to end up making such risky lending decisions. What questions should have been asked? How much should it, or perhaps the Bank of England, have investigated the nature of the lending occurring and what powers should it have to intervene?

The downturn has also called into question the role of governments in the economy and, in particular, the extent to which banks, which are a central driving force of any economy, can be left without extensive government regulation and intervention.

>> You Decide ...

In 2009, there was a great deal of debate over whether bankers should be allowed bonuses or not after the role of banks in causing the recession. Some governments debated introducing legislation to prevent bonuses being paid.

Should bonuses be made illegal?

 Data Analysis 13.6

Table 13.2

	GDP forecast 2009 (%)	Consumer prices forecast 2009 (%)	Unemployment rates (%)
USA	− 2.6	− 0.4	9.7 (Aug)
Japan	− 5.5	− 1.1	5.7 (July)
China	+8.1	− 0.8	9.0 (2008)
UK	+1.1	+1.7	7.9 (July)

1. At what stage of the economic cycle are the USA, Japan, and the UK? Explain why this might have occurred.

2. Does China's growth rate of 8.1 per cent mean that the global downturn did not affect it?

3. What is forecasted to happen to prices in the USA, Japan, and China? Explain your answer.

4. Explain why unemployment rates might be relatively high in the economies above.

Summary

The business environment is continually changing and managers must be alert to such change. Changes that have important economic effects include the ageing population in the UK, the recent recession, and the increased interest in CSR. If managers fail to take account of such developments, their strategies will be inappropriate and they are likely to see a fall in their performance relative to that of competitors who have adjusted what they do. The ageing population, for example, may mean that managers need to adapt their marketing, while also being more willing to recruit older members of staff. The recession certainly creates threats for many, but by changing their strategies (for example, by focusing on budget lines), managers may ensure their survival. The growing interest in CSR means that managers may need to think more carefully about the impact of their actions and how their decisions might be perceived by stakeholders.

Checklist

Having read this chapter, you should now understand:

- [ ] why the world population is ageing;
- [ ] the effects of an ageing population;
- [ ] the meaning of corporate social responsibility;
- [ ] the benefits and costs of corporate social responsibility;
- [ ] the causes of the recent recession;
- [ ] the credit crunch;
- [ ] the sub-prime market;
- [ ] the effects of the recession.

Case Study Review

Having read this chapter, you should now be able to answer the following questions.

1. Why do you think the population in China is ageing?

2. What problems do you think an ageing population in Shanghai might cause for the local government?

3. What opportunities and threats might be created for businesses in Shanghai as a result of an ageing population?

4. What economic policies has the Chinese government used to limit the number of births in the country? What might determine the effectiveness of these policies?

5. What demographic changes are forecasted to occur in your country over the next twenty years? How might this affect your government and businesses in your country?

Short Answer Questions

1. Explain one reason why populations across the world are ageing.

2. Explain two possible consequences of an ageing population for a government.

3. Explain two possible consequences of an ageing population for a business.

4. Explain what is meant by corporate social responsibility.

5. Explain two possible benefits for a business of being more socially responsible.

6. Explain one argument against managers being more socially responsible.

7. Explain two actions that governments might take to try and get its economy out of a recession.

8. Explain the likely effect of the global recession on prices.

9. Explain the likely effect of the global recession on unemployment rates.

10. Explain the likely effect of the global recession on a government's budget position.

Essay Questions

1. Should governments always increase their spending if an economy is in a recession?

2. To what extent does an ageing population create opportunities for business?

3. Is corporate social responsibility a good thing?

 One Step Further

Visit our Online Resource Centre at **www.oxfordtextbooks.co.uk/orc/gillespiebusiness/** for test questions, podcasts, and further information on topics covered in this chapter.

Glossary

abnormal profit occurs when the total revenue is greater than the total costs

adding value occurs when the output created by the transformation process is worth more than the inputs used in this process

aggregate demand the total planned demand for final goods and services in an economy

allocative efficiency occurs when the price paid by the customer equals the social marginal cost of producing the good

average cost (or the average total cost) the cost per unit

asymmetric information occurs when there is a difference in the information available to each of the two parties involved in a transaction

balance of trade measures the value of the difference between a country's exports, and its imports in goods and services

budget position measures the difference between government revenue and spending

community surplus measures the sum of consumer surplus and producer surplus

comparative advantage advantage held by a country in the production of a product if it has a lower opportunity cost than other countries

complements products with negative cross-price elasticity—that is, an increase in the price of one reduces the quantity demanded of the other

concentration ratio the 'n' firm concentration ratio measures the market share of the largest 'n' firms

consumer surplus the difference between the price charged for a product and the utility that consumers derive from it

consumption the level of planned spending by households on final goods and services

copyright copyrights protect literary works, dramatic works, musical works, artistic works, recordings, and broadcasts

Corporate Social Responsibility refers to behaviour that occurs if a business accepts responsibilities to society over and above its legal obligations

cost–benefit analysis used by governments to assess investments by considering private and social costs and benefits

cost push inflation occurs when higher costs force producers to put up their prices

cross-price elasticity of demand measures the responsiveness of demand for one product in relation to changes in the price of another

cyclical unemployment occurs when people are unemployed due to a lack of demand in the economy

demand curve shows the quantity demanded at each and every price, all other factors unchanged

demand pull inflation occurs when the aggregate demand is greater than the aggregate supply, thereby pulling up prices

demand-side policies policies focusing on increasing aggregate demand

diseconomies of scale (internal) occur when there are increases in the long-run average costs as the scale of production increases

dividend this is the payment made to shareholders out of profits

economies of scale (internal) occur when there are reductions in the long-run average costs as the scale of production increases

European Union a customs union of twenty-seven European countries in which there is free trade between members and a common tariff against non-members

exchange rate the price of one currency in terms of another

externality occurs when there is a difference between private and social costs and benefits; may be positive or negative

fiscal policy policy using government spending, taxation, and benefit rates to influence the economy

fixed costs costs that do not change with the amount of products produced

free goods goods for which provision involves no opportunity cost

free market allocates resources by letting market forces of supply and demand operate without any intervention

free trade occurs between countries when there are no barriers to trade

game theory an approach to oligopoly in which each firm's strategy depends on its expectations of how the others in the market will behave

Gini coefficient measures the extent of income inequality in an economy

gross domestic product (GDP) measures the value of final goods and services produced in an economy

income elasticity of demand measures the responsiveness of the demand for a product in relation to changes in income

index numbers show the percentage change in a variable relative to a base number

inferior good good for which demand falls when income increases

inflation occurs when there is a persistent increase in the general price level

involuntary unemployment measures the number of people who are willing and able to work at the given real wage, but who are not in employment

law of diminishing returns states that as additional units of a variable factor are added to a fixed factor, the marginal output will fall

lean production aims to reduce all forms of waste in the production process

long run the period of time during which all of the factors of production are variable

Lorenz curve illustrates the income distribution of an economy

marginal cost the extra cost of producing an extra unit

marginal efficiency of capital (MEC) shows the expected rate of return on investment projects

marginal revenue the extra revenue earned by selling another unit

marginal revenue product (MRP) measures the value of the output produced by employing an extra worker

market capitalization the market value of a company's shares

market segment this is a group of similar needs within an overall market

merit good good that the government believes has a higher benefit than individuals believe

minimum efficient scale (MES) the first level of output at which average costs stop falling with expansion

mixed economy allocates resources using a combination of market forces and government intervention

monopolistic competition a market structure in which there are many firms, but each offers a differentiated product

monopoly occurs when a single firm dominates a market; in the UK, a monopoly is defined as a business with more than 25 per cent of market share

nominal (data) actual amounts received at a given time; (compared to real data:)

normal profit occurs when the total revenue equals the total costs

normative economics focuses on economics decisions based on values; cf positive economics

oligopoly a market structure in which a few firms dominate the market

opportunity cost the benefit foregone in the next best alternative

output gap measures the difference between the amount that an economy is able to produce if its resources are fully employed and the level of demand at present

patent a patent protects new inventions and covers how things work, what they do, how they do it, what they are made of, and how they are made

PESTEL analysis provides a framework for managers when examining the external environment in terms of the political, economic, social, technological, environmental, and legal factors

planned (or command) economy occurs when the government allocates resources

positive economics focuses on economics decisions based on testable hypotheses; cf normative economics

price discrimination occurs when different prices are charged to different customers for the same product

price elasticity of demand measures the responsiveness of the demand for a product in relation to changes in its price

price elasticity of supply measures changes in the quantity supplied relative to changes in prices

producer surplus the difference between the price paid to producers for products and the cost of producing the items

production possibility frontier (PPF) shows the maximum combination of products that an economy can produce, given its resources

productive efficiency occurs when more of one product can only be produced if less of another product is produced; it also occurs when a firm produces at the minimum of the average cost curve—that is, at the lowest cost per unit possible

productivity measures outputs relative to inputs: for example, output per worker

protectionism occurs when a government protects its domestic firms against foreign competition

public goods products that are non-diminishable and non-excludable

public sector sector in which organizations are owned by the government

quantitative easing involves using monetary policy techniques to increase the money supply

quotas limits on the number of foreign products allowed into a market; limits on the amount that a firm can produce

real (data) amounts that are adjusted for inflation

recession occurs when there is negative growth in an economy for two successive quarters

resources inputs into the business used to produce outputs: for example, land, labour, capital, and entrepreneurship

short run period of time during which at least one factor of production is fixed

shortages occur when there is excess demand

shutdown point the price that just covers the average variable cost; if the price falls below this in the short run, the business will shut down

stakeholders individuals and organizations affected by a firm's activities

substitutes products that have positive cross-price elasticity—that is, an increase in the price of one increases the quantity demanded of the other

supply curve shows the quantity that producers are willing and able to produce at each and every price, all other factors unchanged

supply-side policies policies focusing on increasing the supply in the economy by improving the way in which markets work

surplus occurs when there is excess supply

tariffs taxes placed on foreign products

terms of trade measure the prices of exports from a country compared to the prices of imports into the country

total cost the fixed costs plus the variable costs

total revenue the value of sales (calculated as the price of a product multiplied by the quantity sold)

trade union an organization that represents employees

trademarks a trademark is a sign that can distinguish your goods and services from those of your competitors. It can be, for example, words, logos, or a combination of both

utility refers to the satisfaction that a consumer would receive from consuming a product

voluntary unemployment occurs when people who are looking for work are not yet willing to accept work at the given real wage rate

World Trade Organization (WTO) an international organization aimed at reducing barriers to trade worldwide

Index

Numbers in **bold** and *italic* indicate figures and boxed texts respectively.